For England and St George

Dedication

Jenny and Ysobel

For England and St George

A HISTORY OF THE ROYAL REGIMENT OF FUSILIERS

Simon Dunstan

Published in Great Britain by
The Royal Regiment of Fusiliers
HM Tower of London
EC3N 4AB.
www.thefusiliers.org

Design Concept	Simon Dunstan
Design	b1 creative
Art Direction	André Balkham
Design & production	Alex Bamford, Mantat Fung, Jason Merry
www.b1creative.com	

Printed by Craft Print International Ltd, Singapore
www.craftprint.com

ISBN 0 9540067 0 4

Contents

Foreword

YORK HOUSE
ST. JAMES'S PALACE
LONDON S.W.1

My family's long association with the Fusiliers goes back to 1789 when my great-great-great-grandfather commanded the Seventh of Foot, The Royal Fusiliers in Gibraltar and Canada. He was created the 1st Duke of Kent on St George's Day 1799 and was Colonel of the Seventh until 1801. My grandfather, later King George V, was appointed their Colonel-in-Chief in 1900 and my father also had this honour in 1937 . I was therefore delighted and very privileged in April 1969 to be appointed by Her Majesty The Queen as the first Colonel-in-Chief of The Royal Regiment of Fusiliers. I am, thus, particularly proud of the rich history of the Regiment and its forebears that shines through more than 328 years of military inheritance.

Over these thirty years I have witnessed at firsthand how the Regiment has matured and prospered. Despite the reductions and contractions wrought by successive Defence Reviews, which have meant that our four Regular battalions and two Territorial Army battalions are now reduced to only two Regular and the equivalent of one Territorial Army battalion, the morale and stature of the Fusiliers grows year by year.

During my visits to Battalions I am always impressed by the Fusiliers' openness and willingness to voice their opinions to me. This same individuality and self-confidence is apparent in this book in which are recorded in graphic detail many of the exploits of the Fusiliers since 1968. Mr Simon Dunstan's exhaustive research, which includes many interviews with serving and retired members of the Regiment who have given him their first-hand accounts of specific events, results in a most lively and readable history.

I am very proud of my Regiment and of their families. Wherever they have served, in Northern Ireland, in the Balkans, or with NATO forces in Europe, the Fusiliers have maintained and enhanced their splendid traditions of professionalism and service. In all their undertakings they have been wonderfully supported and sustained by their wives and families, to whom the Regiment owes a debt of gratitude.

I wish the Royal Regiment of Fusiliers every success in the future.

Edward

HRH The Duke of Kent, KG
Colonel-in-Chief
Royal Regiment of Fusiliers

Introduction

I see you standing like greyhounds in the slips,
Straining upon the start. The game's afoot:
Follow your spirit; and, upon this charge
Cry 'God for Harry! England and St George!'

King Henry V Shakespeare

'For England and St George' tells the story of a single infantry regiment in the modern British Army, concentrating on its operational service since its inception in 1968. However, a regiment is in many senses a family - a family that has been formed by, and cherishes, its historical heritage. The story can only be understood against the background of more than three centuries of service by the antecedent regiments which have evolved into The Royal Regiment of Fusiliers.

The British Army's regimental system is without parallel among the armed forces of today. Like so many things British, it is illogical and impossible to analyse in purely rational terms. It apparently flies in the face of all administrative convenience and efficiency. Yet it works and works superbly well - and the proof of that has been demonstrated on hundreds of battlefields all over the globe through three centuries of service to the Crown. The soldiers it has forged have been acknowledged by friend and foe alike to be arguably the finest infantry on earth - and still are. In The Royal Regiment of Fusiliers, it has produced an extraordinary amalgam of the English character. Drawn from major cities of the north and south of England, the Fusiliers retain all the attributes of their forebears - dogged in defence and determined in the attack, in the best traditions of British infantry from Minden to the Wadi al Batin.

The regimental system rests on a continuity of tradition and on the creation of a fierce pride in the unique character of each unit. The personal identification of every officer and man with the history and traditions of his Regiment breeds a loyalty and esprit de corps second to none in the world. Regiments delight in the outward signs of their particular tribal identity - those small differences of uniform and ceremonial that they can trace back to bloody fields and fallen heroes that the rest of the world has long forgotten. For this reason, the story of the Fusiliers is, by definition, both typical of that of the whole British Army and, at the same time, unique to those who wear 'the hackle'. But the Regiment is more, much more, than any of its accoutrements. Any attempt to define the meaning of the Regiment is invidious and its members are the last to try, because they do not need to do so. It is a sense of belonging, of service before self, of being part of a team with an ethos of support to others, of camaraderie and 'mateship' and, above all, of not letting the Regiment down by word or deed. Furthermore, it provides much of the spiritual sustenance lacking in today's materialistic society. Indeed, the Regiment maintains and cherishes those traditional values that many aspire to in their lives. For these reasons, the British Army is one of the few institutions still held in high esteem by the general public.

Since the 1680s, the antecedent regiments that have evolved and merged into The Royal Regiment of Fusiliers have distinguished themselves in battle in Britain itself, across Europe, in America, Africa, India and in Asia. They fought at Minden in 1759, Albuhera in 1811, the Alma in 1854, Lucknow in 1857, and Spion Kop in 1900. In 1914, the Royal Fusiliers were awarded the first two Victoria Crosses of the Great War and a year later the Lancashire Fusiliers famously won 'six VCs before breakfast' in the murderous Gallipoli landings; these among the 55 VCs to be gained by the antecedent regiments since the Crimean War. They raised no less than 196 battalions for service during the Great War – over five times the size of all the infantry in the present British Army. In the Second World War, they fought from Dunkirk to Tobruk and from Tunis to the Gothic Line; from the D-Day beaches to the Baltic, and as Chindits in the jungles of Burma. The post-war years brought operational service in the Korean War and in almost every overseas campaign during Britain's protracted withdrawal from Empire. There followed fierce committee-room battles to protect the identity and character of the Fusiliers from the machinations of bureaucrats during the inevitable process of unit amalgamation as the Army contracted to its latter-day NATO role.

However, this is not a history of the antecedent regiments. It is a record for today's Fusiliers and for those to come; those to whom, at 18 years of age, a hackle will mean little. Accordingly, only those episodes from the previous 300 years that relate specifically to today's Royal Regiment of Fusiliers are chronicled; such as the battles that are celebrated as Regimental Days or events that have shaped Regimental traditions. As to the story of The Royal Regiment of Fusiliers from 1968-2000, space allows only a cross-section of the most important operational tours of those 32 years, with the emphasis on the later overseas deployments of the Gulf War and the Balkans. The Regimental Council gave the present author carte blanche to record this history as he deemed fit without heed or hindrance. Any omissions or factual errors are therefore the author's alone and he craves the forbearance of those Fusiliers who have not been given due recognition in these pages.

The history of the Fusiliers is rich in examples of victory and sacrifices on the battlefield. However, in the dark and complex world of the late 20th Century, British infantrymen have had to be more than simply battle-winners. Since 1970, the Fusiliers have served many tours in the troubled Province of Northern Ireland, where the British soldier's discipline and professionalism despite the ugliest provocation have astonished all fair-minded observers. This experience of internal security operations among a hate-riven populace has stood the Regiment in good stead in recent years, when the two regular Fusilier Battalions played their part in protecting vulnerable communities in the former Republic of Yugoslavia. On such unhappy deployments, the British Army has set the standard on peace support operations to which other armies can only aspire. In all probability, these will become increasingly commonplace in the 21st Century. On the other hand, the Fusiliers have also fought a modern mechanised war in the Gulf as part of an armoured battlegroup within a United Nations coalition. Such broad military expertise and achievement are the hallmarks of true professionalism. This extraordinary versatility is unequalled among today's armies, and is one legacy, among many, of the British regimental system of which the Fusiliers stand as a proud exemplar. Long may they thrive.

Simon Dunstan London 2000

GR
TOWER

The Struggle for Empire

'Military action is important to the nation - it is the ground of life and death, the path of survival and destruction, so it is important to examine it'

Sun Tsu *The Art of War* 4th Century BC

THE FOUNDING OF THE REGIMENTS

The Royal Regiment of Fusiliers was raised by order of King James II in June 1685. In the same month, two regiments of infantry returned from service in Holland to bolster the army in response to a rebellion in the West Country fomented by the Duke of Monmouth, the eldest illegitimate son of King Charles II. These two regiments were among several that were raised in the Low Countries in 1674 from English, Irish and Scottish volunteers for service with the Protestant forces of Holland against the expansionist ambitions of Catholic France. As was customary at the time, these formations were known by the name of their Colonel but they subsequently became the 5th and 6th Regiments of Foot. After the failure of the Monmouth Rebellion, they returned to Holland in the service of Prince William of Orange. The Royal Regiment of Fusiliers was formed as an Ordnance Regiment to guard the royal arsenal at the Tower of London and to protect the army's artillery in time of war. To this end, it was equipped with French designed snaphaunce muskets or 'fusils'. These incorporated a flintlock firing mechanism and covered flash pan rather than the slow-burning matchlock of existing muskets, which were highly dangerous in the vicinity of the open barrels of gunpowder used by the artillery train. The Royal Regiment of Fusiliers became a standard infantry regiment in 1688 and was subsequently known as the 7th Regiment of Foot.

In November 1688, Prince William of Orange landed at Torbay in Devon to restore the primacy of the Protestant religion in England over the Catholic aspirations of King James II. With him was a professional army of some 12,000 troops drawn from several Protestant powers. It included the 5th and 6th Regiments of Foot (then known as Tollemache's and Babbington's Regiments), whose precedence within the English establishment was reaffirmed by the order in which they had disembarked. Following his successful landing in Torbay, William of Orange marched on the nearest city, Exeter, where he was met by a number of noblemen and gentry to whom he granted commissions to raise regiments of horse and foot for service with his expedition. One of them was issued to a soldier of fortune, Sir Robert Peyton, who was required to form six companies of picked recruits rather than labourers fresh from the plough. Colonel Peyton died seven months later but was succeeded by Gustavus Hamilton, Viscount Boyne, as Colonel of the formation which subsequently became the 20th Regiment of Foot. Together with the 5th and 7th, it was among the first six

In June 1685, alarmed by the initial success of Monmouth's insurrection, King James II expanded the size of the standing army. The first of nine new regiments to be raised was an 'Ordnance Regiment' which was referred to by the King as 'Our Royal Regiment of Fuzileers'. Its principal task was the protection of the King's Ordnance or artillery train. As Fusiliers, its troops were armed with a superior type of musket called fusils or 'snaphance musquets, strapt, with bright barrels of three feet eight inches long, and good swords, cartouch-boxes and bionetts'. The first Colonel of the regiment was Lord Dartmouth who, among other titles, was Master-General of the Ordnance and commander of two independent companies of Foot, which had been garrisoned for many years in the Tower of London where the KIng's Ordnance was stored. On 20 June 1685, he was ordered to raise, by beat of drum, Trained Bands of the City of London. This was achieved within weeks and the regiment was fully constituted with 12 companies of Fusiliers and one of Miners, following the French example. Later to be known as the Royal Fusiliers, the regiment was the only one within the British Army to be given the title Royal from the outset. As its regimental emblem, it adopted the Tudor rose within the garter, all under the crown - the same device as was cast on the cannon that the regiment had been formed to protect.

regiments of the English Army to be armed with the flintlock fusil from which the word Fusilier derives. Thus were born the four antecedent regiments that 300 years hence were to combine and become today's Royal Regiment of Fusiliers.

BAPTISM OF FIRE

With the success of the 'Glorious Revolution', King James fled to France and the Prince of Orange ascended the throne as King William III. He immediately faced insurrection in Scotland and Ireland. Following the defeat of government troops at the battle of Killiecrankie in the Scottish Highlands in July 1689, William's forces swiftly exacted revenge, crushing the Scottish Jacobites in the awful winter of that year when the last vestige of resistance was snuffed out at Glencoe with the massacre of the MacDonalds. Simultaneously, a new threat arose when James II landed in Ireland with a small but effective French army. With Catholic rebels holding much of the country, James besieged the last remaining Protestant enclaves of Derry and Enneskillen. His forces leavened by experienced Dutch, German and Danish troops, William sent numerous English regiments of foot to Ireland, including the 5th, 6th and 20th, which fought together for the first time at the battle of the Boyne on 1 July 1690. After this defeat, the disheartened James returned to France. In the campaign that followed, the 20th won distinction in June 1691 at the capture of Athlone in which the 5th and 6th also took part. All three regiments fought together in the decisive victory at Aughrim on 12 July and at the siege of Limerick, whose surrender in October effectively ended hostilities in Ireland, thus allowing William to withdraw large forces for the continuing campaign on the continent against the principal enemy, France. The 7th also served in Ireland in the last months of the campaign, having arrived from Flanders in a force commanded by John Churchill, later 1st Duke of Marlborough and Colonel of the 7th Regiment of Foot.

The drum of the 6th Regiment of Foot captured by Highlanders at the battle of Prestonpans during The 45 Rebellion is one of many fine artefacts at The Royal Regiment of Fusiliers Museum (Royal Warwickshire) at Warwick. The drum was discovered in a crofter's cottage in the Highlands in 1905 whereupon it was returned to the regiment. The Antelope is an ancient Royal badge, having been one of the supporters of the Royal Arms in the reign of Henry VI. By the Clothing Warrants of 1743, 1751 and 1768, it became the 'ancient badge' of the 6th Regiment of Foot, one of the 'Six Old Corps' which were permitted special devices. During the battle of Saragossa, several Spanish regimental standards were captured including one depicting an antelope to mark the African origins of the formation. After the battle, Colonel Harrison of the 6th Foot laid the standards at the feet of the sovereign, Queen Anne. As a reward from a grateful monarch, the antelope became the badge of the regiment. Contemporary sources, including the painting 'The Colours of the 6th Foot 1843' by Daniel Cunliffe in the possession of the museum, suggest that the 6th adopted the antelope as its regimental mascot before its return to England from India where it was stationed 1827-42. SD

THE MARK OF THE ANTELOPE

In the closing years of the 17th Century, the four antecedent regiments continued to serve in Ireland as garrison troops or in Flanders in the defence of Holland. The 6th and 7th Regiments gained their first Battle Honours for the storming of the great fortress at Namur in 1695. Two years later, peace was declared and the army was greatly reduced in numbers. Conflict with France resumed in 1702 with the outbreak of the War of the Spanish Succession. In one of the most glorious episodes of British military history, the Duke of Marlborough, in command of the allied armies of England, Holland, Prussia and the Hapsburg Empire against France, Spain and Bavaria, won immortal fame at Blenheim in 1704 and other victories that thwarted French designs to dominate the continent. As the fates would have it, none of the antecedent regiments took part in Marlborough's campaigns but all served in the Iberian peninsula between 1702 and 1713, to preserve the alliance with Portugal and provide a presence in the Mediterranean. Although various important gains were made, such as the capture of Gibraltar and Minorca, the war in Spain did not meet with the same degree of success as that on the Danube and in Flanders.

There were several notable victories including that of the 6th in the successful assault on the fortress of St Philip in Minorca, despite being heavily outnumbered by the entrenched enemy, which resulted in the capture of the island and its strategic harbour for the Royal Navy. The 6th also found fame at the battle of Saragossa - a brilliant victory over a combined French and Spanish army in 1710 when the regiment captured several enemy standards bearing the depiction of an antelope. As this was also an ancient royal badge of the English crown, Queen Anne bestowed the insignia of the antelope on the 6th Regiment of Foot as a mark of her appreciation for its gallantry: a device that The Royal Regiment of Fusiliers commemorates to this day upon their uniform buttons and in the form of their regimental mascot, Bobby.

After the end of the war in 1713, both the 5th and 20th were stationed in Gibraltar for the next 15 years where they served through the siege of 1727-28. At the height of the seven-month siege, 700 shots an hour from 92 guns and 72 mortars rained down on the defenders, with one officer of the 5th observing - 'For some time we seemed to live in flames'. As long as the Royal Navy delivered regular supplies Gibraltar was impregnable, and so it proved; in June the Spanish abandoned the siege though not their aspirations to regain the Rock. After service in Naples, Minorca, Ireland and England, the 7th also served in Gibraltar from 1732 to 1748 where it undertook tedious garrison duties. Of the years 1741-48, the historical record of the 7th laconically records - 'The regiment remained on the Rock during these years without any more material incident in its career'. However, these lengthy tours of duty on the Rock have fostered a lasting association between Gibraltar and the Fusiliers that survived until after the formation of The Royal Regiment of Fusiliers.

By now, England was once more in conflict with the French in the War of the Austrian Succession of 1741-45. Of the antecedent regiments, only the 20th saw action in the decisive battles fought in the Austrian Netherlands, gaining its first Battle Honour at the battle of Dettingen in 1743 where defeat was turned to victory through the courage and fortitude of the British soldier. Such virtues were displayed to even greater effect during the battle of Fontenoy in 1745, but on this occasion victory was elusive and thus it did not rank as a Battle Honour. Nevertheless, the 20th fought with great distinction and in the words of Sir John Fortescue, the noted historian of the British Army - 'As an example of the prowess of British infantry, Fontenoy stands almost without parallel in its history'.

THE '45 REBELLION

To England, the campaigns on the continent were always to be secondary to the vital need for supremacy at sea to secure the trade routes with her colonies that were the source of her wealth. Arguments as to the division of resources between the armies on the continent and the Royal Navy and the defence of these far-flung commitments were to continue throughout the 18th and 19th Centuries. Invariably, the maritime strategy prevailed, and the commitment of a few dozen battalions to the continent to bolster any alliance against France was deemed a small price to pay should they perish on a foreign field, the defence of the realm was unlikely to be imperilled. The Royal Navy remained the bulwark against invasion and only rarely did it falter. One occasion occurred shortly after Fontenoy on 25 July 1745 when a single brig escorted by a French man-of-war landed Prince Charles Edward Stuart and a few companions in Scotland. Raising his father's standard in the Highlands, the Young Pretender was joined by several clans and marched on Edinburgh, gaining wide support the while.

To guard against a Stuart invasion, the 6th Regiment of Foot had been ordered north in the summer of 1744. As one of the few regular formations in a motley array of militia and raw recruits, its companies were spread far and wide defending the Scottish forts. On 21 September 1745, battle was joined at Prestonpans south of Edinburgh. The government forces, including two companies of the 6th, were crushed under the ferocious charges of the Highlanders. The road south was open. Bonnie Prince Charlie and his band of 6,000 followers, (though rumour increased their number greatly) marched down the west coast, reaching Derby on 4 December. England was plunged into panic. Fears of a French invasion grew and forces were withdrawn from Flanders, denuding the continental army.

After a further government defeat at Falkirk, the Duke of Cumberland, the second son of King George II, was recalled from organising the defence of England against invasion to command the northern armies. Biding his time, he concentrated his veterans of Dettingen and Fontenoy, including the 20th Regiment of Foot, and then pursued the ill-equipped and exhausted Jacobites to a place and a time of his own choosing. On 16 April 1746, he brought them to battle on an open, barren moor at Culloden. Provoked by artillery and shattered by musket fire, the Highlanders were defeated in the last major battle to be fought on British soil. Among those present at Culloden was a young staff officer, James Wolfe, who joined the 20th in Scotland as a brevet major in 1749. He was promoted Lieutenant Colonel in the following year and assumed command of the regiment. Unusually for the time, his was a regime that combined military efficiency with firm but fair discipline and concerned welfare for his men. In 1758, he left the regiment to take command of an expeditionary force against the French in Canada. On 13 September 1759, he was to fall while gaining immortal fame on the Plains of Abraham outside Quebec in a short but decisive battle that won North America for Britain.

MINDEN - AN IMPROBABLE VICTORY

The 'Annus Mirabilis' 1759 was the year of victories in the struggle for Empire. War with France had resumed in 1756 when Britain became allied with Prussia on the basis that 'my enemy's enemy is my friend'. With France fixated on its continental armies, the Royal Navy won important victories at Cape Lagos off Portugal and Quiberon Bay off Brittany that defeated the French Mediterranean and Channel fleets and thwarted the planned invasion of England. Further victories in West Africa, the West Indies and India created an Empire 'on which the sun never set'. Nevertheless, it was at the small German town of Minden that a

In his monumental 13-volume work 'A History of the British Army', Sir John Fortescue gives a graphic account of the initial advance of the British infantry regiments at the battle of Minden following the order of the Prince of Brunswick to advance with drums beating - 'The order was either misdelivered or misunderstood, for to his surprise the leading brigade shook itself up and began to advance forthwith. A flight of aides-de-camp galloped to stop them; and the line of scarlet halted behind a belt of fir-wood to await the formation of the rest of the army.

'There they stood for a few minutes, while the second line, which was only partially deployed, hastened to complete the evolution; when suddenly, to the general amazement, the drums again began to roll, and the line stepped off once more, advancing rapidly but in perfect order, straight upon the French horse. The second line, though its formation was still incomplete, stepped off likewise in rear of its comrades, deploying as it moved, and therefore of necessity dropping somewhat in rear. And so the nine battalions, with the leading brigade far in advance, swung proudly forward into a crossfire of more than sixty cannon, alone and unsupported from the rest of the line. For nearly two hundred yards of the advance the French guns tore great gaps in their ranks; but they passed through the tempest of shot unbroken and untamed, and pressed on with the same majestic steadiness against the huge motionless bank of French horse.' The first charge was then launched. 'The scarlet battalions stood firm until the enemy were within ten yards of them; then pouring in one volley which strewed the ground with men and horses, they hurled the squadrons back in confused fragments upon their comrades, and continued their advance'. In such a situation, a formation of infantry in line is highly vulnerable to cavalry attack. To resist one charge was fortunate but three was extraordinary.

stunning victory was gained which will always be associated with the Fusiliers and a select band of other British regiments.

A French army of 54,000 men and 170 cannon under the command of the Marshal Duke Louis de Contades crossed the Rhine and occupied Bergen. It then advanced on Hanover, a possession of the King of England. On the night of 31 July, the army took up battle positions on the plain of Minden with its formidable force of cavalry in the centre flanked by the infantry. Facing it was an army of 45,000 British, Bavarian and Hanoverian troops under the command of Prince Ferdinand, Duke of Brunswick. The British contingent included six regiments of infantry divided into two brigades and 15 squadrons of British cavalry under the command of Lord George Sackville. The 20th Regiment of Foot was in the second brigade under the command of Major General William Kingsley, formerly Colonel of the 20th. As the two infantry brigades deployed into battle formation, Prince Ferdinand sent an order stating that 'its advance, when the time should come, should be made on sound of drum' - the drum then being one of the principal means to signal various movements on the battlefield.

By some misunderstanding, the long lines of scarlet immediately began to advance with drums beating towards the massed formations of the French cavalry, some 10,000 strong. Such a manoeuvre ran counter to all the rules of war. Joined by three Hanoverian battalions, the advance was subjected to the devastating crossfire of over 60 enemy guns. Their cannon balls cut great swathes through the lines of infantry, but each time the gaps were closed up and the advance continued in immaculate order. Lieutenant Thomas of the 20th later wrote - 'I saw heads, legs and arms taken off. My right-hand file of men were by one ball dashed to pieces and their blood flying over...'. Suddenly, 11 squadrons of cavalry charged down upon the oncoming infantry. In the first line, the 12th, 23rd and 37th Regiments of Foot stood firm, with the 20th overlapping on their right. Waiting until the enemy was within 20 yards, they let loose a murderous fusillade of musket fire. The attack crumpled at their feet. Three times the cavalry charged, and three times the horses and their riders were cut down by accurate volleys. Between the second and third charges, four brigades of Saxon infantry attacked the right flank of the 20th and the British lines. They too were thrown back in confusion. This was the moment for the Allied cavalry to attack. Five times Prince Ferdinand ordered Lord Sackville to advance, and five times he demurred. A final French charge of fresh cavalry broke through the right of the first line but foundered before the muskets of the 20th Regiment of Foot.

This was the turning point of the battle and, but for the failure of the cavalry under Lord George Sackville to exploit this famous victory, the French army would have been annihilated. The French commander, Marshal de Contades ruefully recorded - 'I have seen what I never thought possible - a single line of infantry break through three lines of cavalry ranked in order of battle and tumble them to ruin'. The price of victory was high: of the 4,434 British infantry

The Fusiliers Museum Lancashire at Bury has a fine collection devoted to the 20th Regiment of Foot and its successors including this Minden memorabilia of the original war diary for the period - *Records of the XXth or East Devonshire Regiment of Foot* - shown here open at the page describing the battle of Minden, together with the sword and water bottle carried by a young officer, Lt Maclachan, during the battle. SD

in the battle, 1,330 were killed. The 20th Regiment of Foot lost 17 officers and 304 men. As a result, Prince Ferdinand issued an order on the day after the battle - 'Kingsley's Regiment of the British Line, from its severe loss, will cease to do duty', only to issue another shortly thereafter to the effect that - 'Kingsley's Regiment, at its own request, will resume its portion of duty in the line'.

COLOURS AND CLOTHING

Over the years the British Army (as it had now become following the Act of Union with Scotland in 1707) had developed on an *ad hoc* basis with the minimum of central control. Thus, regiments were still known by the name of their Commanding Officer, although orders of precedence in a notional numerical sequence had been introduced by Royal Warrant of King James II on 3 August 1686 and amended by King William III on 10 June 1694. Over the years the army had waxed and waned with the wars it fought, gaining and losing regiments at parliamentary whim, until a definitive order of precedence depending on when the regiment first entered the permanent establishment, was decided on 24 May 1718 (excluding the Royal Regiment of Artillery). By Royal command in 1751, infantry regiments were to be known by their numerical titles, although it took some years before all of their Colonels fully complied. Indeed, the Army List continued to use their names until 1754. The positions of the 5th, 6th, 7th and 20th were confirmed within the hierarchy.

The regimental Colonels were further circumscribed by the Royal Warrant of 1 July 1751 concerning Colours and clothing which had previously been largely at their own fancy. Henceforth - 'No Colonel to put his Arms, Crest, Device or Livery on any part of the Appointments of the Regiment under his Command. No part of the Cloathing or Ornaments of the Regiments to be Allowed after the following Regulations are put into Execution, but by Us, or our Captain General's Permission'. In essence, this achieved a level of uniformity of dress while allowing the regiments and corps to express their individuality through particular forms of facing, head-dress or heraldic badges which had to be officially sanctioned. Similarly, regimental Colours - that essential rallying point in battle - were now to reflect allegiance to the Crown rather than to individuals within the regiment. The carrying of a Colour by each individual company had been abolished in 1707 and with it the role of the Ensign. In some older regiments the carriage of Lieutenant Colonels' standards as a third 'Colour' persisted through the second quarter of the century. However, from 1751 each Regiment of Infantry of the Line was to have only two Colours: the King's Colour, the Great Union, in place of the Lieutenant Colonel's standard and a regimental Colour to replace that of the Colonel - 'The Second Colour to be the Colour of the Faceing of the Regiment with the Union in the upper Canton' and 'In the Centre of each Colour is to be painted or embroided in gold Roman Characters the Number of the Rank of the Regiment within a Wreath of Roses and Thistles'.

Prince Ferdinand of Brunswick and his staff officers watch the course of the battle of Minden from a commanding height. He was later to say of the action - 'It was here the conflict was most obstinate and it was here that the British Infantry gained immortal glory'. For its part in the battle of Minden, the XX Regiment of Foot was honoured by the award of a laurel wreath to be borne on its Colours and appointments 'as a never-failing memorial of its conduct in this glorious victory'. MINDEN became the regiment's second Battle Honour. In the far background of the engraving are the three bridges over the River Weser across which the remnants of the French army withdrew after its defeat. The battlefield at Minden is in an area which was to become all too familiar to a generation of Fusiliers that served in BAOR.

The five other British infantry regiments beside the XX that fought at Minden were the 12th Foot (the Suffolk Regiment, now the Royal Anglian Regiment); the 23rd Foot (the Royal Welch Fusiliers); the 25th Foot (the King's Own Scottish Borderers);the 37th Foot (the Royal Hampshire Regiment now the Princess of Wales's Royal Regiment) and the 51st Foot (the King's Own Yorkshire Light Infantry, now the Light Infantry). Also of decisive importance in the battle were Macbeau's and Phillip's Companies 1st Battalion Royal Artillery - now 12 Minden Battery and 32 Minden Battery Royal Artillery respectively. Tradition has it that on their march to the battlefield of Minden they passed through rose gardens where they plucked the flowers and wore them in their hats. Since then, it has been the custom of the six Minden regiments, except the Royal Welch Fusiliers, to wear roses in their head-dress on the anniversary of the battle each year 1 August.

The only exceptions to this rule were The Royal Regiments and the Six Old Corps which were allowed to display 'Royal Devices and Ancient Badges'. The Old Corps were recognised as the premier regiments of the line, including the 5th and 6th, which were permitted to carry St George and the Dragon and the Antelope respectively. As a royal regiment, the 7th carried in the centre of its Colours the Rose within the Garter and Crown above it, and their number in the upper quarter. As had been practice throughout the army since 1714, the regiment also wore the royal cipher of the White Horse and motto of the House of Hanover - Nec Aspera Terrent (Hardships do not Frighten Us) - but as its 'Royal Device' it carried the White Horse in the corners of its second Colour. By the Royal Warrant, the 20th was obliged to display its number in Roman numerals, XX, in the centre of its Colours. Thereafter, the regiment used these numerals in all matters as its distinctive device, even after the numbering of regiments was superseded by county names in 1782 to aid recruiting.

In 1767, the 5th Regiment of Foot introduced a medal known as the Regimental Order of Merit. It was presented by the Commanding Officer annually on the St George's Day parade. Given for good conduct and military merit, there were three classes for soldiers with 7, 14 and 21 years 'good conduct and faithful service'. It was superceded in 1856 when the Long Service and Good Conduct Medal was established, but it remains the first medal of its type in the British Army.

THE THIRD COLOUR

The Seven Years' War lasted from 1756 to 1763. The final battles in Europe were fought during 1762. Notable among them was the famous victory in the woods at Wilhelmstahl where the 5th Regiment of Foot took the surrender of almost 3,000 men drawn from several elite units of the French Army, including the Royal Grenadiers, the Grenadiers of France, and the Regiment of Acquitaine. The XX was also present at Wilhelmstahl as a flank unit. To the victor went the spoils of war and the 5th acquired one standard, six pairs of Colours, two cannon and a pet poodle; the latter remained in the regiment for many years. One of the French Colours was kept and was paraded when the occasion demanded, despite the regulations that a regiment might carry only two Colours. After the battle, the soldiers of the 5th purloined a sufficient number of the French grenadiers' fur caps to equip the whole regiment. They were worn for many years thereafter in place of the standard hats of the infantry, being officially sanctioned in July 1836 by King William IV. These were the forerunners of the sealskin caps worn by Fusilier regiments and latterly by their regimental bands.

One of the proudest traditions of the Royal Northumberland Fusiliers was the Wilhelmstahl Colour which was paraded whenever circumstances allowed on St George's Day. The Colour was carried on parade by the youngest drummer, hence it was also known as the 'Drummer's Colour'. The original was destroyed, together with the King's and Regimental Colours, by fire in Gibraltar in 1833. A replacement was presented by the Colonel of the Regiment in 1836. This in turn was replaced in 1888 at a cost of £35.8s.11d (£35.45p). In 1926, the War Office reiterated its ban on the carrying of all 'Third Colours'. However, thanks to the case presented by Maj Gen Sir Percival Wilkinson, Colonel of the Northumberland Fusiliers, in 1933 the Army Council gave authority for the regiment to parade the Wilhelmstahl banner once a year on St George's Day. This was given Royal endorsement on 13 February 1936. As shown in this photograph of a St George's Day Parade held by the 2nd Battalion Northumberland Fusiliers in India in the 1920s, the Colours bear wreaths of red and white roses and the Drum Major's staff is garlanded with red and white roses, as are the drums. Red and white roses are also worn on the headdress; in this case on the Wolseley pattern solar topee which incorporates the regimental colours in the puggaree. The current Wilhelmstahl Colour was presented to 1RRF on St George's Day 1990 by the Colonel of the Regiment, Lt Gen Sir Jeremy Reilly. During the year, it is held by the 1st Battalion.

Today they remain an item of head-dress worn by the Regiment's Corps of Drums and in the Minden Band of the Queen's Division.

Many years after the battle of Wilhelmstahl, the 5th was challenged by higher authority over the irregularity of carrying the extra Colour but, by then, the regiment claimed custom and practice. Despite official disapproval, the regiment continued to do so. The actual trophy was destroyed by fire in Gibraltar on 24 April 1833; perhaps after a particularly memorable St George's Day. It was only on 13 February 1936 that the regiment was given royal permission to carry the 'Third Colour', but only on St George's Day to mark the Battle Honour of Wilhelmstahl. Traditionally, it has been carried by the youngest drummer in the Corps of Drums, which has given rise to its alternative name of the 'Drummer's Colour'. To this day, The Royal Regiment of Fusiliers is the only formation in the British Army authorised to carry three Colours.

THE DISCONTENTED COLONIES

The Treaty of Paris of 1763 consolidated the British gains across the world won by feat of arms during the Seven Years' War. Typically, the army was reduced in numbers by almost two thirds despite the greatly increased overseas commitments that required permanent garrisons; from an army of 45,500, 16,000 were destined for the colonies while 12,000 were stationed in Ireland. With the defeat of the French in Canada, the American colonies no longer felt threatened by invasion and came to resent having to pay for their security to a distant government. Resentment turned to rebellion, and open warfare between the colonists and the mother country erupted in 1775. Despite winning several set-piece battles, the tactics of the British Army that had proved so successful in Europe were sometimes inappropriate in the terrain and against the opposition encountered in America. Coupled with inept political management, the British military campaign failed when supremacy at sea was temporarily lost, compounded by France, Holland and Spain joining the war against Britain. All four antecedent regiments fought in America but no Battle Honours were won during this unhappy episode; indeed the 7th Foot lost its Colours at the battle of Cowpens, one of which is now on display at the Military Academy West Point.

During the same period, both the 5th and 6th served in the West Indies in the war with France and Spain. Following garrison duties in Gibraltar, the 6th landed on the Caribbean island of St Vincent in 1773 to quell a native insurrection. The fierce opposition and the dreadful climate claimed so many casualties that the regiment had to return to England in 1777 to reform - a common fate for regiments serving in the region, where yellow fever or the 'black vomit' was rife. In 1782 the 6th was given its county title of the 1st Warwickshire Regiment. At the same time, the 5th became the Northumberland Regiment in honour of their Colonel, Earl Percy, later the 2nd Duke of Northumberland. These county titles were to mark the main recruiting areas of the regiments. The XX became the East Devonshire Regiment of Foot with its regimental depot in Exeter where the regiment had originally been raised. However, it was not long before it began its association with Lancashire as recruiting marches were conducted there from as early as 1797. The 7th Foot had its historic title formally confirmed as the Royal Fusiliers in 1789 when Prince Edward, the Duke of Kent, became Colonel of the Regiment.

On 18 December 1778, the 5th defeated a vastly stronger French force at La Vigie on the island of St Lucia. With some 1,400 soldiers, the British faced over 12,000 French attackers. French casualties were some 400 dead and 1,100 wounded as against only ten British killed and 130 wounded. An English artillery officer writing about the action recorded - 'I had a fine situation for galling the French Army as they marched to the attack in columns. My shot in this situation swept them off by the dozens at a time, and Frenchmen's heads were as plenty and cheaper than sheeps' heads and trotters in Scotland'. After the battle the 5th took the white plumes from the French Grenadier dead and wounded and (according to Regimental legend) after dipping them in French blood wore them in their own hats. This became yet another unofficial custom which was eventually recognised as a particular privilege of the regiment to mark the Battle Honour of St Lucia. In due course, the Grenadier Companies of all infantry regiments were authorised to wear white plumes. Accordingly, from 11 July 1829 that of the 5th was then tipped with red to make it even more distinctive. This is the origin of the hackle proudly worn by The Royal Regiment of Fusiliers to this day.

THE HACKLE

On 18 December 1778, the 5th Regiment of Foot defeated a vastly superior French force at La Vigie on the island of St Lucia in the West Indies. The men of the 5th took enough white feather plumes from the bodies of the French Grenadiers to allow every man in the regiment to wear one in his cap. Thereafter, the white feather plume was worn by the regiment instead of the red and white tuft worn by other regiments of the line, until new regulations of 10 February 1829, when all line infantry regiments, other than Rifles and Light Infantry, were authorised to wear the white feather plume. The Colonel of the 5th, at that time General Sir Henry Johnson Bt GCB, made representations to the Commander-in-Chief concerning the regimental distinction. A letter was received on 11 July 1829 giving the sanction of King William IV for the regiment to wear a feather plume of half red and half white with the red uppermost, 'as a peculiar mark of honour whereby its former services will still be commemorated'.

In 1901, the Lancashire Fusiliers' distinguished service of over 200 years, culminating in the gallantry displayed at the battle of Spion Kop, was recognised by the Royal Grant of a primrose hackle to be worn on the left side of the headdress to denote an exceptional award for war service; the yellow reflecting the colour of the original facings of the XX Regiment of Foot. King George V also gave approval for the motto 'Omnia Audax' [Gallantry in All Things] and the Red Rose of Lancaster to be borne on the Regimental Colours.

During the early 1990s, Lt Col Trevor Minter was the Military Assistant to the Chief of the Defence Staff. During the tenure of Field Marshal Sir Richard Vincent, an official visit was paid to his French counterpart, Admiral Jacques Lanaxade, in the latter's beautifully appointed office that had formerly been occupied by Napoleon in the Ecole Militaire near the Eiffel Tower. Its walls were adorned with paintings of the French army vanquishing British redcoats. An aide to the French CDS asked, "Colonel, why do you wear this feather in your hat?" The reply went, "I hate to tell you, General, but we took them from yourselves at the battle of St Lucia and then dipped them in French blood, which is why it is red on top and white below". At this the French CDS interjected "That will teach you to ask a stupid question". The real reasons are related above but the legend rightly prevails. SD

CARTRIDGES S.A.
BALL
MARTINI-HENRY RIFLE
Rolled Case
Mark III 1895

The Triumph of Empire

'The British infantry are the best in the world. Fortunately, there are very few of them' - Thomas Bugeaud Marshal of France

THE SILENT RED WALL

Throughout the 18th Century, the infantry was equipped with the Long Land Pattern Musket or similar models such as the India Pattern comandeered in large numbers from East India Company stocks. Also known as the 'firelock' and the 'Brown Bess', it was to remain in service virtually unchanged for over 100 years - a testament to a robust if unsophisticated weapon. The Brown Bess was the tool that forged an empire. A development of the 'fusil' that gave rise to the Fusiliers, the standard musket incorporated a smoothbore barrel with a nominal calibre of .760 of an inch. The projectile was a lead sphere of .701 calibre weighing one and a quarter ounces. The difference in dimension between bullet and bore allowed easier ramming down the muzzle during loading, particularly when the barrel was fouled after heavy use by burnt powder residue. However, the loose fit and smoothbore barrel compromised both accuracy and velocity and therefore the range and terminal effect on the target.

The laborious method of loading and firing was instilled by endless and repeated drills until it became second nature even in the stress of battle. With a notional range of 200 yards, it was only truly accurate to about 80, although in *The Recollections of Rifleman Harris* the author recalls being missed twice by French 'tirailleurs' firing essentially identical weapons from behind cover at 20 paces. Colonel Hanger, a keen sportsman and crack shot, wrote: 'A soldier's musket, if not exceedingly ill-bored, as many are, will strike the figure of a man at 80 yards; it may even at a hundred; but a soldier must be very unfortunate indeed who shall be wounded by a common musket at 150 yards, provided his antagonist aims at him; and as to firing at a man at 200 yards with a common musket, you may as well fire at the moon and have the same hopes of hitting your object'.

In battle, British infantry were drawn up into two lines in close order. Each line fired in turn by volley; thus, on a company frontage, up to 50 musket balls were discharged per volley at a rate of four volleys a minute. At no time during the proceedings was there such an order as - 'Take aim', and the actual command was - 'Give Fire!' whereupon the whole formation fired as one in the general direction of the enemy. At normal battle ranges, the effect of the heavy projectile on flesh and bone was shattering. This graphic account by the veteran French commander of the Napoleonic and North African wars, Marshal Thomas-Robert Bugeaud de la Piconnèrie, gives a vivid impression of what it was like to attack a British position:

'About a thousand yards from the English line, our men become excited; they start talking and quicken their pace; our column becomes somewhat disordered. The English, firm as a long red wall, are motionless with their arms at the port...They appear to ignore the storm about to break over them, although we are now less than three hundred paces from them. This is unnerving. Each of us begins to feel that it will not be pleasant when the enemy, having waited so long, decides to fire. Our ardour begins to cool. We keep up our spirits by shouting all the louder. At last, the English muskets come down - they are making ready. Appalled, many of our men halt and open a scattering fire. Then comes the English volley, precise, deadly, thunderous. Decimated, our column staggers, checks, tries to recover itself. The enemy breaks their long silence with a cheer. Then a second volley, perhaps a third. Then they are upon us, chasing us into disorderly retreat.'

'Private Andrew Robb, who enlisted in the XX Regiment at Preston, in Lancashire, in 1798, was present in all the battles inscribed on the Regimental Colour, since the above period, namely: Egmont-op-Zee, Egypt, Maida, Vimiera, Corunna, Vittoria, Pyrenees, Orthes, Toulouse and Peninsula. He proceeded to St Helena, with the Twentieth Regiment, and was one of the funeral party at the interment of Napoleon Bonaparte in May 1821. On his discharge from the Regiment, he was placed as a trusty soldier, in charge of a monument erected at Rosstrevor to the memory of his former commanding officer, Major General Ross. The latter had joined the XX as a major in 1799 and was in command for ten years during a particularly proud period of the Regiment's history. Under him the XX became greatly distinguished for its bravery, dash and powers of endurance at the Battle of Maida, the Retreat to Corunna, and in the heavy fighting of the Peninsular War. Promoted Major General and given command of the Brigade of which the XX formed part, Ross was severely wounded at the Battle of Orthes eight months later in February 1814. In the same year he achieved national fame as the C-in-C of the expeditionary force against the United States where in a short but brilliant campaign, he decisively defeated the Americans at Bladensburg, and entered Washington, destroying the public buildings by order of the British Government, including the burning of the White House. He was killed shortly afterwards in a skirmish near Baltimore.' From The Historical Record of the Twentieth Foot.

With their Colours streaming aloft, the Royal Fusiliers fall upon the French atop the slopes of Albuhera. 'Then was seen with what a strength and majesty the British soldier fights'. The British guns lost earlier in the day were recaptured and the Royal Fusiliers recovered the Regimental Colour of The Buffs, restoring it to the 3rd Regiment of Foot which gave rise to a close affinity between the two regiments. During the Graeco-Turkish War of 1920-22, the 2nd Battalion Royal Fusiliers returned to the Dardanelles as part of an Allied force to guarantee the straits as an international waterway. The Buffs were also deployed there, and on 16 May 1923 both regiments held a joint trooping of the Regimental Colour of The Buffs at Kilia to commemorate Albuhera. The original event was almost repeated in January 1991 when 1RRF replaced 1 QUEENS (successors to The Buffs) at Tidworth in Wiltshire. By some extraordinary oversight, 1 QUEENS left its Colours in the officers' mess where they were found by the Fusiliers. Once more, they were restored to their rightful owners, but only in exchange for a crate of champagne.

THAT ASTONISHING INFANTRY

The above account is reputedly of the battle of Vimiero in August 1808 where Bugeaud fought as an infantryman. By this time, Napoleon's empire stretched the length and breadth of Europe. Britain stood alone against the Corsican Tyrant, with a small army of 30,000 fighting the French in Portugal and Spain. Vimiero and Rolica were Battle Honours shared by the 5th, 6th and XX during the first Peninsular War. In November 1808, Napoleon himself invaded Spain with an army of 300,000 to crush the British Army under Sir John Moore once and for all. In an epic fighting withdrawal in the depths of a cruel winter to Corunna - where the Royal Navy evacuated the remnants of the British Army in January 1809 - Sir John Moore saved 24,000 soldiers, including the 5th, 6th and XX, at the expense of his own life. These veterans were to form the nucleus of a new army under Sir Arthur Wellesley, later the Duke of Wellington, that was to return to Iberia and expel the French from Spain in five years of bitter warfare. In the same winter, the Royal Fusiliers were in far hotter climes and took part in the capture of the island of Martinique, where they secured the Eagle of the 82nd Regiment of the French Line.

Following the retreat of the British Army to the lines of Torres Vedras in Portugal, a 'Fusilier Brigade' was formed on 21 November 1810 comprising the 1st and 2nd Battalions of the Royal Fusiliers and 1st Battalion of the Royal Welch Fusilier -; the first time such a formation had been created. As part of the 4th Division under the command of Major-General Lowry Cole, the brigade was detached in April 1811 to reinforce the army of Lieutenant General Sir William Beresford who had been tasked to lay siege to the city of Badajoz. Due to a lack of engineer materials, the siege was unsuccessful and was soon reduced to a blockade which was broken by Marshal Soult as he advanced from Seville with 25,000 men. The British deployed to Albuhera to face the relieving force. They took up battle positions on 16 May along a line of low hills, with the town itself in the front centre of the Spanish and British troops, the latter numbering about 7,000.

The Fusilier Brigade had been roused at midnight on the 15th of May, following 36 hours of picquet duty before the walls of Badajoz. Under the command of Sir William Myers, the former commanding officer of the 1st Battalion Royal Fusiliers, the brigade was ordered to join Beresford's army at Albuhera. Weary and hungry, the Fusiliers marched through the night, arriving at Albuhera after battle had been joined. The situation was desperate. Soult had attacked the Allied right in great force, outflanking and unbalancing Beresford's main body. Some Spanish units fought well, but others were reluctant. The British contingent, including the 3rd and the 57th Foot - the Buffs and the Middlesex Regiment - fought with tenacious gallantry against overwhelming odds. Ensign Latham saved the King's Colour of the Buffs with exemplary heroism, while the Middlesex Regiment became known thereafter as the 'Die Hards' from the inspiring exclamation of their colonel as he fell grievously wounded - 'Die hard, the 57th. Die hard!'. Both regiments suffered fearful casualties. With the arrival of the exhausted Fusiliers, Myers sent riders to ask permission to counterattack. General Beresford was in the process of ordering a general withdrawal. With Myers' encouragement, General Cole ordered his 4th Division to advance uphill into the heart of the action. As the Fusilier Brigade entered battle, Myers stated - 'This will be a proud day for the Fusiliers'.

'In the days of lace-ruffles, perukes and brocade
Brown Bess was a partner whom none could despise.
An outspoken, flinty-lipped, brazen-faced jade
With a habit of looking men straight in the eyes
At Blenheim and Ramillies fops would confess
They were pierced to the heart by the charms of Brown Bess.
'So she followed her redcoats, whatever they did
From the heights of Quebec to the plains of Assaye
From Gibraltar to Acre, Cape Town to Madrid
And nothing about her was changed on the way
But most of the Empire which now we possess
Was won through those years by old-fashioned Brown Bess.'

A paean of praise from Rudyard Kipling for the standard infantry weapon of the British Army for almost 150 years. The derivation of the name Brown Bess remains uncertain but 'brown' is probably from the appearance of the weapon after its treatment to prevent corrosion of the metal parts, and 'bess' is thought to be a corruption of the German word 'buchse' or 'gun', as in 'arquebus' and 'blunderbuss'. The India Pattern illustrated was the most common type of Brown Bess. During some 120 years of manufacture, approximately 5 million firelocks were made of which some 3 million were acquired by the Board of Ordnance. This was achieved in an age before mass production. Throughout its many years of service, the main modification was the substitution of a metal ramrod for the weaker wooden one which tended to break with too vigorous handling, often in the heat of battle. Royal Armouries

In one of the classic passages of British military history, Sir William Napier recounts that extraordinary turning point of the battle - 'Such a gallant line arising from amid the smoke, and rapidly separating itself from the confused and broken multitude, startled the enemy's masses, which were increasing and pressing forward as to assured victory; they wavered, hesitated, and then, vomiting forth a storm of fire, hastily endeavoured to enlarge their front, while the fearful discharge of grape from all their artillery whistled through the British ranks. Myers was killed, Cole and three colonels - Ellis, Blakeney, and Hawkshawe - fell wounded, and the three fusilier battalions, struck by the iron tempest, reeled and staggered like sinking ships.

'Suddenly and sternly recovering, they closed on their terrible enemies, and then was seen with what a strength and majesty the British soldier fights. In vain did Soult, by voice and gesture, animate his Frenchmen; in vain did the hardiest veterans break from the crowded columns and sacrifice their lives to gain time for the mass to open on such fair a field; in vain did the mass itself bear up, and, fiercely striving, fire indiscriminately on friends and foes, while the horsemen, hovering on the flanks, threatened to charge the advancing line.

'Nothing could stop that astonishing infantry. No sudden burst of undisciplined valour, no nervous enthusiasm weakened the stability of their order; their flashing eyes were bent on the dark columns in front, their measured tread shook the ground, their dreadful volleys swept away the head of every formation, their deafening shouts overpowered the dissonant cries that broke from all parts of the tumultuous crowd as slowly and with a horrid carnage it was driven by the incessant vigour of the attack to the farthest edge of the hill. In vain did the French reserves mix with the struggling multitude to sustain the fight; their efforts only increased the irremediable confusion, and the mighty mass, breaking off like a loosened cliff, went headlong down the ascent. The rain flowed after in streams discoloured with blood, and 1,800 unwounded men, the remnant of 6,000 unconquerable British soldiers, stood triumphant on the fatal hill.'

Together with the 94th, the 5th Foot under the command of the gallant Colonel Ridge won immortal fame and possibly its hardest fought Battle Honour with the assault on the walled town of Badajoz at 10pm on 6 April 1812. In Napier's words - 'Still swarming round the remaining ladders, these undaunted veterans strove who should climb first, until all being overturned, the French shouted victory, and the British baffled but untamed, fell back a few paces and took shelter under the rugged edge of the hill. Here, when the broken ranks were somewhat reformed, the heroic Colonel Ridge springing forward, called with a stentorian voice on his men to follow, and seizing a ladder, once more raised it against the Castle; yet to the right of the former attack where the wall was lower and an embrasure offered some facility, a second ladder was soon placed by the Grenadier officer, Canch, and the next instant he and Ridge were on the ramparts, the shouting troops pressed after them, the garrison amazed and in a manner surprised, were driven fighting through the double gate into the town, and the castle was won. A reinforcement sent from the French reserve then came up, a sharp action followed, both sides fired through the gate and the enemy retired; but Ridge fell, and no man died that night with more glory - yet many died and there was much glory'. The British then sacked the town. Ensign Thomas Canch joined the 5th as a volunteer in 1809. Gaining a commission for his heroism, he fought across the Iberian Peninsula until the end of the war, with 12 clasps indicating he had survived 12 battles - a remarkable achievement, especially when it included such actions as the 'Forlorn Hope' at Ciudad Rodrigo and the assault on Badajoz.

'This will be a proud day for the Fusiliers' - a print entitled 'The Advance of the Fusiliers Brigade at Albuhera May 16th 1811' by W.B. Wollen shows the Fusiliers closing with the enemy. So fierce was the attack that the French were forced back - 'giving way like a loosened cliff, fled headlong down the ascent'. British casualties were the highest for the numbers engaged of any battle of the Peninsular War, but the battle was won to become perhaps the greatest Battle Honour of the 7th Royal Fusiliers when - 'Fifteen hundred men, the remnants of 6,000 unconquerable British soldiers, stood triumphant on the fatal hill'.

Of this remarkable battle, Marshal Soult opined - 'There is no beating those troops despite their generals... I always thought them bad soldiers, now I am sure of it. For I turned their right, pierced their centre, they were everywhere broken, the day was mine, and yet they did not know it, and would not run.' In his despatches, the commander of the 4th Division, General Cole, wrote - '[The Fusiliers] exhibited an example of steadiness and heroic gallantry which history, I believe, cannot surpass'. Albuhera was the bloodliest battle of the Peninsular War. The British suffered 892 dead and 2,707 wounded; the Spanish, Portuguese and the King's German Legion approximately 2,600 casualties. The Royal Fusiliers had entered action with 1,282 officers and men of whom 706 were now killed or wounded - a casualty rate of 55 per cent. Because of their losses, the two battalions of the 7th were amalgamated and a cadre of the 2nd returned to England to recruit. The French lost about 8,000 but captured some 500 prisoners and several stands of Colours. During the battle, Sergeant William Gough of the Royal Fusiliers recaptured the Regimental Colour of the Buffs and it was restored to them. It was indeed a proud day for the Fusiliers, and 16 May is celebrated every year as Albuhera Day by The Royal Regiment of Fusiliers.

THE AFFAIR AT EL BODON

The four antecedent regiments fought in every battle that became a clasp on the campaign medal of the Peninsular War up to 1814. Each clasp denoted a Battle Honour and, although Albuhera was arguably the greatest for the Fusiliers, their names were all significant in the defeat of Napoleon's marshals: Rolica (1808 - 5th and 6th), Vimiero (1808 - 5th, 6th and XX), Corunna (1808 - 5th, 6th and XX), Talavera (1809 - 7th), Busaco (1810 - 5th and 7th), Albuhera (1811 - 7th), Ciudad Rodrigo (1812 - 5th and 7th), Badajoz (1812 - 5th and 7th), Salamanca (1812 - 5th and 7th), Vittoria (1813 - 5th,6th,7th and XX), Pyrenees (1813 - 6th,7th and XX), Nivelle (1813 - 5th,6th and XXth), Orthes (1814 - 5th,6th,7th and XX), Toulouse (5th,7th and XX) and Peninsula (1808-14 - 5th,6th,7th and XX).

All these Battle Honours adorn the Colours of The Royal Regiment of Fusiliers, but there were many other notable actions, not least of which was the battle of El Bodon on 25 September 1811. After the siege of Ciudad Rodrigo, the Duke of Wellington was compelled to retire in the face of a relieving French army. The 2nd Battalion of the 5th and the 77th Foot (2nd Battalion Middlesex Regiment), supported by cavalry of the 11th Light Dragoons and the 21st Portuguese Regiment, were holding a covering position between Pastores and El Bodon. The French attacked with 2,500 cavalry and overran some Portuguese artillery on the right flank of the 5th. Under the command of Major Ridge, the 2nd Battalion of the 5th mounted a bayonet charge against the French cavalry and recaptured the guns, an almost unprecedented tactic in recalling Minden. In the centre, the 77th drove off repeated attacks. In due course, the full

On the evening of 24 August 1811, the 5th Regiment of Foot was tasked to protect two batteries of Portuguese artillery near the village of El Bodon. The guns were covering a road that carried the advance of a French army attempting to relieve the besieged town of Ciudad Rodrigo. On the following day, a French cavalry brigade advanced towards the guns at which Wellington ordered the infantry to hold their ground prior to the arrival of Allied cavalry. Within moments, the guns were overrun and the gunners fled. Realising the gravity of the situation, Major Ridge commanding the 5th Foot called upon his men to counter the French cavalry. 'Three times they halted, fired, reloaded, and marched on; the third volley broke the French dragoons; and, with a cheer, the Fifth fixed bayonets and charged. A single battalion of infantry in line charged half a cavalry brigade'. Such unconventional tactics won a brief respite during which the 5th was able to regroup with the 77th Foot and form a square - the standard formation for infantry to fight cavalry. The square remained horribly exposed on open ground and it was soon attacked on three sides simultaneously by the charging squadrons of cavalry. The men of the 5th and 77th Foot waited until the last moment and then fired devastating volleys into the dragoons. The enemy recoiled and thereafter kept their distance. The 5th Foot then joined the retreating column of the Third Division. 'For six miles across a perfect flat, without the slightest protection from any incident of ground, without their artillery, and almost without cavalry (for what are five squadrons against twenty or thirty?), did the Third Division continue its march. During the whole time the French cavalry never quitted; six guns were taking the division in flank and rear, pouring in a shower of round shot, grape,canister. This was a trying and pitiable situation for troops to be placed in, but it in no way shook their courage or confidence; so far from being dispirited or cast down the men were cheerful and gay'. The division retired to safety to the plaudits of Wellington, who wrote in his despatches - 'I cannot conclude this report without expressing my admiration of the conduct of the troops engaged in the affair on the 25th inst. The conduct of the 2/5, commanded by Major Ridge, in particular, affords a memorable example of what steadiness and discipline of the troops and their confidence in their officers can effect in the most trying and difficult situations.'

might of the French army, with some 30 squadrons of cavalry in the van, was brought to bear on the small force, numbering some 600. The latter then formed into two squares and began to retire, with the 5th and 77th in one square and the Portuguese in the other. Despite being raked by artillery fire, the squares withdrew methodically and in good order, occasionally discharging volleys of musket fire with precision to deter the pursuit of the cavalry. This was the first occasion on record that infantry had successfully charged mounted cavalry and the Duke of Wellington praised the conduct of the two regiments to the whole army in a general order, as a memorable example of steadiness and discipline against overwhelming odds. It was at this time that the regiment became known as 'The Fighting Fifth' after the Duke of Wellington referred to them as - 'the ever fighting, often tried but never failing Fifth'.

PAX BRITANNICA

After the Peninsular War, the four antecedent regiments were dispersed far and wide and none was present during the 100 Days campaign culminating in the final defeat of Napoleon. All were summoned from overseas but none returned in time for the battle of Waterloo although a Royal Fusilier officer did fire the final shot against the French Imperial Guard using a captured cannon, while the XX acted as prison guards to Napoleon on St Helena. In the War of 1812 against the Americans, the 6th won the Battle Honour of Niagara for its courageous attack on Fort Eric while the XX triumphed at the battle of Bladensburg and occupied the enemy capital of Washington in February 1814. The 6th became the Royal 1st Warwickshire Regiment of Foot in 1832. Four years later, the 5th became the Northumberland Fusiliers. For the next two decades, the four antecedent regiments were dispersed across the British Empire.

Both the 7th and XX fought during the Crimean War, gaining Battle Honours at the Alma, Inkerman and Sevastopol. At the Alma, the 7th under the command of Lieutenant Colonel Lacy Yea made a determined assault and contributed materially to the success of the battle. Of the Royal Fusiliers, it was said - 'When, along the whole line of the Allies, there was no other regiment fighting, Lacy Yea and his people were still at work'. In the fog-shrouded battle of Inkerman, command and control was lost and it became 'The Soldiers' Battle'. In this hard fought action, the XX suffered more casualties than any other formation besides the Guards. Colonel Yea was killed by grapeshot in the first assault on the heavily-defended earthworks known as the Redan during the battle of Sevastopol in June 1855. After the capture of Sevastopol in September, the XX was the only regiment to enter the town with drums beating and Colours flying. The mismanagement of this war shocked the nation, however, and prompted wholesale reform of the army after many years of neglect. Once more, it was the fortitude and valour of the common soldier that allowed British arms to prevail in the face of adversity.

Under the command of Lt Col Lacy Yea, the Royal Fusiliers were the first troops to land in the Crimea on 14 September 1854. They were brigaded with their old comrades in arms the 23rd Royal Welch Fusiliers. Six days later at the battle of the Alma in the attack on the hilltop redoubts, the Royal Fusiliers fought the élite Kazan Regiment - 'They were both Fusilier regiments and both were highly honoured in their country. They both accepted their task with a stern devotion, and the fight they made for the mastery was one of the most terrible in the whole affair'. Although the battle was won, the success was not pursued and the Russians retired to the fortress of Sevastopol unmolested. During the winter the British troops suffered greatly, and by January 1855 over 50 per cent were ill in hospital. Matters hardly improved during the year. With the institution of the Victoria Cross, the Royal Fusiliers received five of the awards, a number only equalled by the Scots Guards. The Crimean War was one of the first to be recorded by the new medium of photography. This group of Royal Fusiliers officers was captured for posterity in 1856, as the long frock coatees and Crimea War ribbons indicate. Such group photographs that depict the comradeship and shared experience of war differ little from those shown in the final chapters of this book in the Gulf or the Balkans.

The battle of Inkerman on 5 November 1854 in the Crimean War became a Battle Honour for both the 7th and XX Regiments of Foot. Contemporary accounts describe it as 'a soldier's battle' - 'Colonels of regiments led on small parties and fought like subalterns, captains like privates. Once engaged every man was his own general'. Of the XX it was said that - 'There ensued a combat maintained for some time by the industrious use of the firelock...But a change of temper came on; and on that thought of the bayonet, these men of the XX seemed all to have but one will. Despite hostile masses on their flanks, they were glowing with that sense of power which is scarce other than power itself... After nearly a century these men once more delivered their old "Minden yell". Disregarding alike the force on their right and the force on their left, they sprang at the mass in front, and drove it down the hillside... Despite their forlorn condition, Colonel Horn's division was never forced back to the crestwork. Sometimes losing, sometimes gaining ground, it remained fighting out front.' By the winter of 1854, the conditions under which the British Army lived and fought had gone from dreadful to utterly atrocious. On 14 November, the whole of the Crimean peninsula was swept by an appalling blizzard. Offshore, the fleet of ships carrying winter stores, including all the medical supplies, boots, 40,000 greatcoats and shelters for the troops, was wrecked. Thousands of troops suffered from frostbite and related ailments. By the end of November, cholera was rife in the British lines, killing 60 men a day. A letter from a soldier of the XX was published in *The Times* - the newspaper became known as 'The Thunderer' because of its outspoken views on the war: 'We have no firing to cook with, but when we come across a tree we down it for fuel. We are poisoned with vermin and dirt; the men are dying with cold and exposure... Our officers are noble fellows, and they do all they can to alleviate the sufferings of the men.'

A commemorative postcard depicts the entry of the 1st Battalion Royal Fusiliers into the Tibetan capital of Lhasa for the signing of the peace treaty in the Potala palace on 3 August 1904 at the conclusion of the Younghusband Expedition. In the 'Great Game' that had been conducted between Britain and Russia throughout the Victorian era, there were many conflicts and surrogate wars on the North-West Frontier; but when the Russians attempted to install a 'trade mission' in the forbidden city of Lhasa, the British response was rapid and decisive. A similar trade mission was despatched supported by an expeditionary force which brooked no refusal. In an unequal contest, Tibetan soldiers clad in chain mail and wielding the kind of muzzle-loading muskets that the Fusiliers had used a century before, faced Maxim guns and bolt action rifles. The Tibetan army was shattered in minutes at a cost of six British wounded. Even the great adventurer Col Francis Younghusband, commander of the expedition, was shocked - 'I was so absolutely sick at the so-called fight that I was quite out of sorts'. A treaty was signed that excluded foreigners from the 'forbidden city', and the expedition withdrew to India.

In the meantime, the 6th was fighting in the protracted Border Wars in South Africa between 1846 and 1858 in the defence of Cape Colony where the regiment suffered the loss of the troopship *Birkenhead.* After a decade undertaking garrison duties on Mauritius, the 5th was despatched to China in May 1857 but was diverted to Calcutta following the outbreak of the Indian Mutiny of 1857-59. The regiment served with distinction at Arrah and it won its first three Victoria Crosses during the relief and defence of Lucknow. This became a Battle Honour, as it did for the XX which also fought at Lucknow and throughout the campaign, remaining in India until 1867. The 6th sailed from South Africa for India where it took part in some of the heaviest fighting during the campaign in Oude and the jungles of Jugdespore. The 7th arrived in India during 1857 but saw little action as the regiment was stationed in the Punjab on occupation duties, although it did take part in the Umbeyla campaign in 1863 on the North-West Frontier.

THE TRIUMPH OF EMPIRE

In the latter half of the 19th Century, the British Empire grew inexorably with only the occasional setback. In 1885, the Sudan was abandoned to the Mahdi after the death of General 'Chinese' Gordon at Khartoum. Twelve years later, an Anglo-Egyptian army under Sir Herbert Kitchener advanced up the Nile to avenge his death. In 1898, the Dervishes were brought to battle at Omdurman, near Khartoum, on the banks of the Nile. The Northumberland Fusiliers, the Royal Warwickshire Regiment and the Lancashire Fusiliers fought together in the 1st British Brigade. On 2 September, the Dervishes were completely routed by the firepower of the massed ranks of khaki-clad soldiers with magazine rifles, Maxim machine guns and river gunboats. With reckless courage and to the constant beat of tom-tom drums, the Khalifa's army made repeated charges with their colours flying high against the unwavering wall of weapons. Against the Lee Metford rifles of the British, some of whom had 'adapted' the copper heads of the .303in ammunition to make 'dum-dums', the Dervishes lost 11,000 dead and 16,000 captured as against 48 dead and 434 wounded Anglo-Egyptians: the Northumberland Fusiliers had three men wounded, the Royal Warwickshire Regiment one dead and seven wounded, the Lancashire Fusiliers six wounded. 'Chinese' Gordon had been avenged. It was the high water mark of British Imperialism. Lieutenant Winston Churchill fought with the 21st Lancers in the battle, which he described as 'the most signal triumph ever gained by the arms of science over barbarism'.

At the outset of the 2nd Boer War, the complacency of Victorian Britain was shattered by 'Black Week' when the British Army suffered three defeats in quick succession in December

With the emergence of an industrial proletariat and the rise of trade unionism, troops were increasingly called upon to suppress strikers and their revolutionary tendencies which were seen as a serious threat to governments of all persuations across Europe and the USA. Here, in their distinctive sealskin caps, men of D Company 2nd Battalion Lancashire Fusiliers confront workers at the Electric Power Station, following riots in Cardiff during the strike of 1911. This was a year of widespread industrial unrest leading to a state of paralysis in Britain due to strikes by dockers, firemen, railwaymen and transport workers which saw soldiers marching through the streets beside armoured cars.

1899. After such humiliation, the whole resources of the Empire were mobilised to crush a 'handful of farmers' and, by October 1900, the Boers had been beaten in the field though the war dragged on for another 18 months. Virtually every single battalion of the British Army served in South Africa during the war. Thousands of soldiers perished from disease as against hundreds in battle: 22,000 British and Colonial troops died during the campaign. All the antecedent regiments were deployed to South Africa and served throughout the war, gaining the Battle Honours of Modder River (5th), Relief of Ladysmith (7th and XX) and South Africa 1899-1902 (5th, 6th, 7th and XX).

One of the hardest fought battles was on a bare hill called Spion Kop on 26 January 1900. As part of the Lancashire Brigade, the Lancashire Fusiliers captured the feature at night only to find that it lay open to the enemy's guns by day. The exposed plateau was a death trap and through that long day, 1,300 British casualties were inflicted by the accurate rifle fire of the Boers and their field artillery. The Lancashire Fusiliers suffered 30 per cent casualties including two thirds of their officers. Unable to dig trenches in the rocky ground, almost all the dead were killed by single rifle shots to the head, such was the skill of Boer marksmanship. However, the Fusiliers did not waiver until ordered to withdraw that night. The British commander, Sir Redvers Buller, in his despatch on Spion Kop, wrote - 'The Lancashire Fusiliers, under exceptionally trying circumstances, magnificently upheld the best traditions of the British Army'. Although the cost was high, Spion Kop and the Lancashire Fusiliers' successful attack on Pieter's Hill led to the subsequent relief of their beleaguered comrades besieged in the town of Ladysmith. Such gallantry was recognised by the bestowal of the primrose hackle to be worn on the left side of the head-dress and the Red Rose of Lancaster to be borne on the Regimental Colour.

'NO DOGS, NO SOLDIERS'

Following the Crimean War, various reforms were instituted within the army to rectify its appalling administrative and supply services. During the 1870s, further reforms created regiments of two regular battalions to allow one at home and one overseas in the defence of Empire. The links with a particular county were reinforced with a recruiting and training depot in each county. In 1880, the 6th became the Royal Warwickshire Regiment. The Royal Fusiliers were given the additional title of 'City of London Regiment' in 1881. On 1 July of that year, the XX or East Devonshire Regiment became the Lancashire Fusiliers with the regimental depot in Bury. However, the life of the soldier remained dire with miserable pay and conditions. More often than not, recruits were forced into the army by destitution rather

In the halcyon days of the Edwardian era, soldiering could be an agreeable and generally leisurely pastime, as shown by this group of officers and their servants of the 1st Battalion Lancashire Fusiliers on manoeuvres in Malta in 1901. Cometh the hour, cometh the men: the two seated officers are Capt Willis and Lt Bromley, both of whom were to win the Victoria Cross at the Gallipoli landings in April 1915.

WOMEN AND CHILDREN FIRST - THE WRECK OF THE *BIRKENHEAD*

On 17 January 1852, the paddle steamer HM Troopship *Birkenhead* sailed from Cork with drafts for several regiments in the Cape engaged in the Eighth Frontier War, including Ensign Metford, Sergeant Teile and 58 men of the Sixth Regiment of Foot. In the early hours of 26 February, the ship struck a reef off Danger Point in False Bay, some 50 miles from Cape Town. Within minutes the ship was foundering. The commander of the vessel, Captain Salmond, ordered the eight life boats to be launched, a totally inadequate number for the ship's compliment. However, only three could be lowered and all the women and children who had accompanied the troopship were bundled aboard them. Captain Salmond urged the troops to follow but the Army officer commanding, Lieutenant Colonel Alexander Seton of the 74th Foot, gave the order - "Stand fast, men, or you will swamp the boats!". The soldiers stood silently on the decks while a drummer beat a slow tattoo as the sea engulfed the *Birkenhead*. Of the 638 people aboard, only 193 were saved, including the 56 women and children as well as Sergeant Teile and 11 soldiers of the 6th. The disaster shook the nation but the heroism shown provided an example to the world that gave rise to the notion of 'women and children first' in such disasters. King William IV of Prussia held the episode in such esteem that he ordered an account of such devotion to duty to be read out to every regiment in his army. Queen Victoria dedicated a memorial to the victims at the Royal Hospital Chelsea. The author William Makepeace Thackeray paid the following fulsome tribute: 'No saint ever died more simply, no martyr more voluntarily, no victim ever met his fate in a more generous spirit of self-renunciation than those who were content to be engulfed so long as the women and children could be saved'.

In his solar topee, Col Briggs, the Commanding Officer of the 3rd Battalion Royal Fusiliers and his retinue pause during a shooting party in the Sudan in 1903. The Colonel's Lady is sitting on the donkey cradling a shotgun. By 1870, the Imperialist European powers controlled two thirds of the world's land masses. By 1914, this had risen to almost 85 per cent. Britain was the most successful of these nations by far. In 1800, she held sway over one and a half million square miles of the globe with approximately 20 million subjects overseas. By the turn of the next century, this had increased in territory by a factor of seven and in people by twentyfold. Although this was the century of Pax Britannica, the British Army fought more than 50 colonial wars from the time of the Indian Mutiny to the Boer War. Due to superior technology and tactics, the British Army was rarely inconvenienced by native forces; a notable exception was Isandhlwana in 1879 when 20,000 Zulus overwhelmed 850 British (and 450 native) troops. Even so, honour was immediately restored by the defence of Rorke's Drift and the award of 11 VCs for a single action. In 1900, almost a quarter of the world's land surface was pacified by the British Army which did not exceed 100,000 in the colonies and India - less men than its present establishment. This was the triumph of Empire.

At 1,001 men, the full complement of the 4th Battalion Royal Fusiliers parades in Scarlets and Sealskin caps for the King's Birthday Parade at Aldershot in 1912; the one over the 1,000 was the RSM. On embarkation for France on 12 August 1914, Lt Col McMahon addressed the 4th Battalion with the words - 'A Royal Fusilier does not fear death: he is not afraid of wounds; he only fears disgrace and I look to you not to disgrace the Regiment'. There was to be no disgrace for the Royal Fusiliers at the battle of Mons, for which they were awarded the first two Victoria Crosses of the Great War.

than vocation, and discipline was strict. Training was reduced to simple drills undertaken by rote and initiative was greeted with suspicion. The status of the soldier within society can be measured by the sign on many pub doors that stated 'NO DOGS, NO SOLDIERS', in that order. Gradually such attitudes were changing, accelerated by the Boer War where smokeless powder and long range rifles had rendered the tactics of mass formations obsolete. No longer could a soldier simply stand side by side with his comrades as he had at Omdurman. Fire and movement became the order of the day and musketry training was paramount. The wide-ranging Haldane reforms galvanised the British Army into the 20th

An aquatint after Michael Angelo Hayes of 1839 shows the 7th Royal Fusiliers in action in Ireland where regiments of the British Army were stationed for long periods to quell the perennially-restless population. Service in Ireland was not popular as wages were reduced and garrison duties were monotonous, interspersed with moments of ferocious violence. An example of the latter was recorded in *The Illustrated London News* of a Belfast riot on Lady Day in 1872 which is depressingly familiar - 'In the evening of the next day, the two parties met for a pitched battle, to the number of several thousands, in the brickfields between the Shankill and Falls Roads. The police tried in vain to separate them and the military were sent for to force the combatant mobs apart, but showers of stones were thrown over the heads of the soldiery, and fierce howls of mutual execration were exchanged by hostile bands of Irishmen, who were prevented from slaughtering each other. The houses on the Shankill Road and in adjoining streets have been gutted by mobs who took the furniture out and burnt it in the street... It was pitiable to see families leaving their houses as though going into captivity or exile, and hear the lamentations of the women and children. Protestants living in Roman Catholic districts and Catholics living in Protestant districts have found it necessary to change their quarters and go to their respective friends for protection.'

Century in preparation for a continental war against other industrial powers, rather than the colonial campaigns of Victorian times. One of the last was fought by the Royal Fusiliers during the punitive Younghusband expedition to Tibet in 1904. With war clouds gathering in Europe, Britain's mobilisation plans slipped into effect with seamless precision; only the scale of the conflict was unforeseen. Britain was ready for war as she had never been before. As the official historian of the Great War stated, it was 'incomparably the best trained, best organised, and best equipped British Army which ever went forth to war'.

Total War

'The gates of Hell were opened and we accepted the invitation to enter'
Lance Sergeant Edward Dyke 26th Battalion Northumberland Fusiliers

DEASE AND GODLEY - THE FIRST VCs OF THE GREAT WAR

Following the assassination of Archduke Franz Ferdinand, the heir to the Austro-Hungarian throne, in Sarajevo on 28 June 1914, the nations of Europe mobilised for war in an inexorable spiral of mutual mistrust and misunderstanding. Bound by treaty obligations to neutral Belgium, Britain despatched the British Expeditionary Force (BEF) to France in August following the German invasion of the Low Countries and France. Comprising four infantry divisions and five cavalry brigades, the highly professional BEF faced overwhelming odds as the Germans fielded no less than seven armies for the invasion of Belgium and France.*

On Saturday 22 August, the advance elements of the 3rd Division arrived at the mining town of Mons, just inside the Belgian border. By now, in this the third week of the war, the French Army had lost over 200,000 men in the battle of the frontiers - over twice as many as the entire compliment of the BEF. Soon after 0900 hours on the following day, battle was joined with a fearsome artillery bombardment of the British positions by the III and IX Corps of von Kluck's First Army, a formidable force of some 600 guns and 150,000 men, against Smith-Dorrien's II Corps of the 3rd and 5th Divisions with supporting cavalry and 150 guns. The 3rd Division included 7, 8 and 9 Infantry Brigades and the latter comprised the 1st Battalion Northumberland Fusiliers; the 4th Battalion Royal Fusiliers; the 1st Battalion Lincolnshire Regiment and the 1st Battalion Royal Scots Fusiliers. The 1st Battalion Royal Warwickshire Regiment and the 2nd Battalion Lancashire Fusiliers served in the 4th Division of the BEF.

As the right-hand battalion of 9 Brigade defending the bridges across the Mons-Condé canal at Nimy, just north of Mons, the 4th Battalion Royal Fusiliers, was in a natural salient that was directly in the path of the German advance. Mustering 26 officers and 983 other ranks, the battalion was under the command of Lieutenant Colonel Norman McMahon, a dynamic and forward thinking soldier who, as commandant of the School of Musketry at Hythe, had inculcated into the British Army the necessity for every soldier to be able to fire at least 15 aimed shots a minute. In a fearful baptism of fire, the Royal Fusiliers put their thorough training to devastating effect as the battalion bore the brunt of the attack by IX Corps. Advancing in dense grey columns in a manner similar to the French army at Waterloo, the last time that Britain had fought in Europe, the Germans were cut down by the accurate marksmanship of the Fusiliers. Such was the rate of fire from their Lee-Enfield SMLE .303 rifles that the Germans were convinced they were facing a force liberally equipped with machine guns, while in fact the battalion had only two.

The two Vickers-Maxim machine guns of the Royal Fusiliers were commanded by Lieutenant Maurice Dease, and in the first attacks they inflicted considerable slaughter on the German infantry. Lieutenant K Tower recalls - 'Shortly after this the enemy started to advance in mass down the railway cutting, about 800 yards off, and Maurice Dease fired his two machine guns into them and absolutely mowed them down. I should judge without exaggeration that he killed at least 500 in the two minutes. The whole cutting was full of bodies and this cheered us all up. Soon, however, the enemy started debouching from the woods in all directions and we lay down and fired as hard and as fast as possible.' Temporarily checked, the Germans resumed the artillery bombardment with renewed ferocity and casualties among the Fusiliers grew steadily. Abandoning their rash tactics, the Germans advanced in bounds closely supported by machine guns and artillery. The battle now became ferocious and the fire from the Fusiliers' Vickers-Maxims faltered. Three times Lieutenant Dease crossed the open ground between the guns to direct the crews and replace those that fell; each time he was hit, suffering wounds to the shoulder and both legs. On the third occasion, with the machine gun crews dead, Dease manned one weapon himself and continued to pour accurate fire into the

*A British infantry division had 18,073 men, 5,592 horses with 76 guns, 24 motor cars, 876 carts and wagons, 275 bicycles and nine motor bikes.

A recruiting postcard of the early 20th Century for the Northumberland Fusiliers reveals the rates of pay for a soldier on joining the Army after all stoppages had been deducted. The illustration was drawn from life at the depot in 1913 with (from L to R) L/Cpl Page, C/Sgt Smith and Cpl McIntosh. Comparative rates of pay for other eras are shown below:-

Fusilier	1811	6d or 2 1/2p per day
Fusilier	1913	6s 8 1/2d or 33p per day
Fusilier	1954	49s or £2.45p per day
Fusilier	2000	£31.89p per day pre tax

SOLDIERS' PAY.
INFANTRY.

After all stoppages for Messing and Washing have been deducted, there remains on an average for the Soldier to spend as he chooses:—

WEEKLY.	s.	d.
On joining	6	8½
After two years' service (if proficient and serving on an approved term of more than three years) 2nd Class ...	8	5½
1st Class	10	2½

In addition to above, Lodging, Food, Fuel, and Lighting are provided.

A Soldier in Hospital for wounds or illness contracted on Field Service, or injuries on Military Duty, receives free Medical Treatment. In other circumstances a stoppage of 7d. for each day in Hospital is made, but in cases of sickness caused by Military Service one half of the stoppage is remitted.

The Messing allowance, 3d. a day, is also stopped when a Soldier is in Hospital, except from injuries or sickness resulting from Active Service.

On Enlistment, a complete new Uniform and other Kit is issued free, and after 9 to 12 months' service a quarterly allowance is given for the upkeep of Uniform and Kit. A careful Soldier benefits by any of the allowance he saves.

Men of good character are granted Furloughs annually. While on furlough no stoppage is made for messing or washing and the man receives 6d. a day in lieu of rations, the additional cash issue during furlough thus amounting to 5/6 a week.

A leaflet, shewing terms of service, standards of height, age, &c., can be obtained at any Post Office or Barracks in the United Kingdom, or from any Recruiter.

God Save the King.

Original Chit recommending Pte Godley for conspicuous bravery, thereby earning him the first V.C. of the Great War.

The original recommendation for Godley's VC was based on an account written by Lieutenant F.W.A. Steele and now resides in the Royal Regiment of Fusiliers Museum (London) at the Tower: it reads - 'In the defence of Railway Bridge near Nimy. 23rd August 1914. This afternoon Pte GODLEY of B Coy shewed particular heroism in his management of the Machine Gun: Lt. Dease having been severely wounded and each machine gunner in turn shot: I called Pte Godley to me in the Firing Line on the bridge and under extremely heavy fire he had to remove 3 dead bodies and go to a machine gun on the right under the most deadly fire. This he did and not a shot did he fire except as I directed and with utmost coolness until it was irretrievably damaged and he was shot in the head. He then left the firing line under orders to go to the rear.
23.8.1914 F.W.A. Steele Lt. C Coy. Roy. Fus.'

He also wrote an account of his friend Maurice Dease which subsequently formed the basis of the recommendation submitted by Lt Col McMahon - 'On 23rd August Dease was in command of the machine guns with No 9 platoon who were defending the bridge at Nimy. On the attack developing on the bridge he was one of the first to be hit - somewhere about the knee. He continued to direct the guns although obviously in great pain until he was again hit, this time somewhere in the body, after which he remained for a short time under cover. Shortly afterwards, the machine gunner having been shot, Dease asked why the gun was not firing and insisted on crawling to the gun emplacement in order to control the fire, another man having taken the place of the man who was shot. He then received a third wound which incapacitated him and I am of the opinion he received other wounds but on this point I cannot speak directly. F.W.A.S.'

The original pencil-written account also resides in the Royal Fusiliers museum together with the VC of Lieutenant Maurice Dease which is shown here. SD

advancing Germans. Against such overwhelming numbers of enemy, Lieutenant Colonel McMahon ordered a withdrawal at 1.40 pm; however, the only line of retreat was across 200 yards of open ground swept by fire. At this critical moment, Lieutenant Dease was hit again, shot through the lungs, and the machine gun fell silent. A close friend from Sandhurst days, Lieutenant Francis Steele, rushed forward to give succour but Dease died in his arms as Steele carried him to safety. Lieutenant Colonel McMahon subsequently reported laconically - 'I have brought the conspicuous gallantry of Lieutenant Dease to notice'. He was posthumously awarded the first Victoria Cross of the Great War.

By now both of the Vickers-Maxims were out of action and the Company Sergeant Major shouted above the noise of battle whether there was anyone else who knew how to fire a machine gun. One Fusilier stepped forward - Private Frank Godley, a large, powerful man with splendid moustaches who was a leading sportsman in the battalion as a cross-country runner and centre-half in the football team. Three years previously he had joined the machine gun section but had not stayed long after the sergeant major had told him 'as a machine gunner he would make a bloody good bus conductor'.

The sergeant major was to be proved comprehensively wrong as Godley ran forward under heavy fire and brought the Vickers into action. For over an hour, Godley manned the machine gun alone and wrought fearful execution. Bleeding from wounds to the shoulder and leg, he continued firing until, when loading another belt of ammunition, he was hit again and the water jacket of the Vickers was riddled with bullets. With the Germans less than 100 metres from his position, Godley removed the firing handles from the Vickers and threw the pieces of the weapon into the canal. His task done and the battalion safely withdrawn, he crawled back to the main road where two Belgian civilians helped him to Mons Hospital. Three months later in a German prison camp where he spent the rest of the war, Private Frank Godley learnt that he had been awarded the Victoria Cross for his heroic action. The 4th Battalion Royal Fusiliers had suffered some 250 casualties but lying in grey heaps in front of the machine gun positions were hundreds of German dead.

The BEF retreated from Mons to fight again at Le Cateau, on the rivers Marne and Aisne, at La Bassée, Messines and Armentières, until the front line stabilised around the Belgian town of Ypres - a name that was to become synonymous with the slaughter of the Great War. The Schlieffen Plan had failed and by Christmas a line of trenches stretched from the North Sea to the Swiss border. There followed a stalemate that was to last four years in which hundreds of thousands of young men were to die during costly attacks under massive artillery bombardments or cut down by the murderous fire of the machine gun. After the First Battle of Ypres, the BEF, comprising the flower of the British Army, had been virtually destroyed with 1,291 officers and 21,906 other ranks killed in action between 23 August and 30 November 1914. During the same period, the British Army had suffered 89,864 casualties including the missing. The original complement of the BEF had been approximately 84,000.

To maintain the fight, the regular battalions serving overseas were recalled, as were troops from across the Empire. Following the declaration of war, hundreds of thousands of willing volunteers had flocked to the Colours in the expectation that the war would be over by Christmas. Lord Kitchener, the Secretary of State for War, realised otherwise and laid plans for a long war involving all levels and facets of society. On 7 August 1914, Kitchener published his appeal for his first 100,000 recruits. In the first eight weeks, 761,000 joined the army including 33,204 on 3 September alone, the highest ever on a single day. By the end of 1914, one million men had enlisted with a further million from the British Empire. These were moulded into Kitchener's New Armies but it would take over 18 months to train and equip such a prodigious number of men. In the meantime, the Territorial Force of part-time soldiers and the Empire troops had to bear the brunt of the fighting on the British sector of the Western Front, enduring ghastly conditions in the many miles of trenches that offered the only protection from the murderous effects of artillery and machine gun fire. After the initial appetite for battle, the consequences of industrial warfare soon dawned on the citizen army that had been created to wage it, and it is their voices that recount the hardships and the horror.

Lance Sergeant Elmer Cotton, 5th Bn NF
'I was leaving a wife, home and friends and all I held dear to me behind and departing for an unknown destination with all the apprehension of death, wounds and hardships ahead. Packed together eight per carriage and including full equipment, with blackened railway windows and hard seats, we journeyed south to Folkestone via York, Cambridge, Liverpool St, London and Tunbridge Wells...', and so to the Channel ports and France.

Lance Corporal Roland Mountfort, 10th Bn RF
'We marched 15 miles on Wednesday. It doesn't sound much, but when you think of the heat of the day, the weight of the packs and the state of the French roads you will understand it was an amazing strain on our endurance. The French roads are horrible. Through every village and for a mile or two each side they were composed of great rough cobble stones, about eight inches square and not over carefully laid. Apart from the unevenness there is the difficulty that the nails of our boots step on them as on ice. If two villages are only a few miles apart the cobble stones carry on and join up the two, so that they stretch for miles. Our packs I cannot find words to describe. It is a cruel, unnatural weight that no man should be called upon to carry.'

Lance Sergeant Elmer Cotton, 5th Bn NF
'By the time we arrived at the outskirts of Ypres the traffic of ammunition and ambulance wagons had ceased and we were alone on the road. The only noise we heard was the echo of our own steps and the occasional roar of a gun or a bursting shell. Suddenly we came across a corpse lying across the pavement and the gutter - it was the body of a peasant - his bundle was lying some yards away having been precipitated forward when he fell. Just over the canal bridge a timber wagon and two shattered horses came into view and we walked through the blood of these noble animals as we passed them on the road. We were now in the town proper - everywhere nothing but ruins could be seen - not a house but was either shattered by shells or gutted with fire. Many walls leaned at dangerous angles into the streets and in the dim light of night each ruin seemed to me to represent the work of some grinning demon who was lurking in hiding behind these ghostly houses. On our way we passed more dead horses, which in many cases were in a state of decomposition and emitted a fearful odour of rottenness... At Ypres the trenches we were in from time to time were very poor; in some cases they had only been in existence a day or two and only resembled scratches in the ground. At Neuve Eglise and Armentières the trenches were splendid; they had been in existence for nearly a year, were very thick and deep, had lateral trenches running the full length in the rear, plenty of dug-outs, and good communication trenches which made it possible to leave during the day and return to billets in town. These trenches had trench boards to walk on, fire platforms to stand on, drains and sumps with pumps, shelters for lookouts with rifle racks, rubbish shoots, gas alarms, rifle batteries, loop-holes, periscopes,

Lt Col McMahon was the Chief Instructor at the School of Musketry, Hythe, from June 1905 to June 1909. When the Army had insufficient funds to equip infantry battalions with more than two machine guns, McMahon instituted the 'Mad Minute' whereby every infantry soldier had to be capable of firing 15 aimed rounds a minute. Cpl Holbrook (No.13599) of the 4th Battalion Royal Fusiliers was the servant to Lt Col McMahon and he recalls - 'Our Colonel McMahon, he was responsible for improving the firepower of the British Army. Wonderful man he was. Before he came to us he was in charge of the School of Musketry at Hythe. When I first joined the Army you fired at a bullseye, that was your target. He ended all that. You fired at moving figures - khaki, doubling - so from five rounds a minute you went to 15. You had to lie on the box, unloaded, with three clips of five rounds each in the pouches. When the whistle went you'd have to load your rifle and fire, tip the case out, fire fire fire... and get it all into the minute. His one craze was musketry. I was his servant, but you had to fire your course whatever job you was on. You had to fire 500 rounds a year.' Lt Col McMahon was killed in action on 11 November 1914 at Ypres - in the words of Captain Basil Liddel Hart, 'a date of prophetic symbolism' as it represented the turning point of the 1st Battle of Ypres and was the day and month of the Armistice in 1918. In a subsequent eulogy, it was stated - 'It was the foresight of an unsung hero, Lt Col N. R. McMahon DSO, of the Royal Fusiliers, who started the Musketry revival, made every British rifleman a human machine-gun, and saved the British Expeditionary Force from annihilation. It was the British riflemen who saved France in 1914, and prevented Germany from dominating Europe. It was their rapid and accurate fire with the Short Magazine Lee-Enfield rifle that changed the course of history.'

The men of A Company 4th Battalion Royal Fusiliers rest on the Grand Place at Mons on the 23 August 1914 after the battle on the Mons-Condé canal at Nimy. IWM Q70071

etc., and war could be carried on in a comparatively safe manner. Dug-outs, like trenches, varied considerably. At Ypres they were mainly holes in the ground and no cover. At Armentières they were all shell splinterproof and, in some cases the officers' dug-outs were like little dwelling houses, fitted with beds, tables, chairs, pictures and stove.

'Imagine a bright May morning and a platoon - about 55 men - busily engaged in washing, cleaning up, cooking and some sleeping. Suddenly a tremendous explosion, a deathly stillness as if all were paralysed, then fearful screams and groans and death gasps. What had happened? A high explosive German shell had fallen right into a wide part of the trench where many men had been. The sight of the wounded shedding their blood from gaping wounds and their agonised cries - one asking to be shot - would have convinced any humane man that war is an impossible way of settling national questions - or it will be in the near future. It was on May 2nd [1915] that this incident took place and this single high explosive shell killed seven and wounded 18 - yet the day before 400 shells came over and dropped immediately behind this trench within ten yards and no one was hurt - but this one shell bursting right in the trench accounted for a total of 25 men. The trench after the dead and wounded were removed presented a ghastly sight - it was red with blood like a room papered in crimson while equipment lay everywhere.'

Even at those times when the British Army was not conducting offensive operations during the Great War, it lost more men to stray shells and snipers every single day than the total number of casualties throughout the British Task Force in the Falklands War of 1982. Artillery was the cause of the greatest number of casualties on the battlefield, but the Great War brought other horrors of which poisonous gas was the most dreadful. It was first used by the Germans on the Western Front on 22 April 1915 during the Second Battle of Ypres, and both the Northumberland and Lancashire Fusiliers were early victims.

Lance Sergeant Elmer Cotton 5th Bn NF
'It produces a flooding of the lungs - it is an equivalent death to drowning only on dry land. The effects are these - a splitting headache and terrific thirst - to drink water is instant death - a knife edge pain in the lungs and the coughing up of a greenish froth off the stomach and the lungs, ending finally in insensibility and death. The colour of the skin from white turns a greenish black and yellow, the tongue protrudes and the eyes assume a glassy stare . It is a fiendish death to die...

'Propped up against a wall was a dozen men - all gassed - their colours were black, green and blue, tongues hanging out and eyes staring - one or two were dead and others beyond human aid, some were coughing up green froth from their lungs - as we advanced we passed many more gassed men lying in the ditches and gutter ways - shells were bursting all around. My respirator fell to pieces with the continual removal and readjustment - the gas closed my eyes and filled them with matter and I could not see. I was left lying in the trench with one other gassed man and various wounded beings and corpses and forced to lie and spit, cough and gasp the whole of the day in that trench.' [Whit Monday 1915]

One of those to die in this awful manner was Private John Lynn DCM of 2nd Battalion Lancashire Fusiliers whose self-sacrifice during a gas attack led to the award of the Victoria Cross, the citation for which ran as follows:
'For most conspicuous bravery near Ypres on 2 May 1915, when the Germans were advancing behind their wave of asphyxiating gas, Private Lynn, although almost overcome by the deadly fumes, handled his machine gun with very great effect against the enemy, and when he could not see them he moved his gun higher up on the parapet, which enabled him to bring even more effective fire to bear, and eventually checked any further advance. The great courage displayed by this soldier had a fine effect on his comrades in the very trying circumstances. He died the following day from the effects of gas poisoning.'

Horrified at the losses in manpower and with no foreseeable means of breaking the deadlock on the Western Front, the politicians sought an alternative strategy to prosecute the war against the Central Powers of Germany, Austria-Hungary and Turkey. At the behest of Winston Churchill, First Lord of the Admiralty, consideration was given to forcing the Dardanelles Straits with the intention of neutralising Turkey and bringing succour to Russia, the eastern ally of Britain and France. The Turkish threat to the Suez Canal would also be nullified. In March 1915, an Anglo-French naval force almost succeeded in destroying the

While Lieutenant Dease and Private Godley were the first recipients of the Victoria Cross in the Great War, the Royal Fusiliers were also to gain the last two, although these were awarded to men who served with the 45th Battalion Royal Fusiliers in the War of Intervention against the Bolsheviks. Raised at Park Royal on 8 April 1919, the 45th and 46th Battalions fought in North Russia in support of the White Armies. The VC was awarded to Corporal Arthur Sullivan, an Australian, for the most conspicuous bravery and devotion to duty on 10 August 1919 at the Sheika River where as his citation states - 'The platoon to which he belonged, after fighting a rear guard covering action, had to cross the river by means of a narrow plank, and during the passage an officer and three men fell into a deep swamp. 'Without hesitation, under intense fire, Corporal Sullivan jumped into the river and rescued all four, bringing them out singly. But for his gallant action his comrades would undoubtedly have been drowned. It was a splendid example of heroism as all ranks were on the point of exhaustion and the enemy less than 100 yards distant.'

The second was awarded to Sergeant Samuel Pearse MM whose citation reads -'For most conspicuous bravery, devotion to duty and self-sacrifice during the operation against the enemy battery position north of Emsta (North Russia) on 29 August 1919. Sergeant Pearse cut his way through the enemy barbed wire under very heavy machine gun and rifle fire, and cleared a way for the troops to enter the battery position. Seeing that a blockhouse was harassing our advance and causing us casualties, he charged the blockhouse single-handed, killing the occupants with bombs. This gallant NCO met his death a minute later, and it was due to him that the position was carried with so few casualties. His magnificent bravery and utter disregard for personal danger won for him the admiration of all troops.'

After the campaign, Arthur Sullivan returned directly to Australia without receiving his medal. On 12 July 1920, he was presented with the Victoria Cross by Edward, Prince of Wales, at Government House in Adelaide. In 1937, Sullivan was invited to London as part of the Australian Military Contingent for the coronation of King George VI. On 9 April, while returning to his quarters at Wellington Barracks, he slipped off the pavement and struck his head on the kerbstone. Falling into the road, he was hit by a passing motorcyclist and died soon afterwards in hospital.

forts guarding the Dardanelles Straits but the loss of three ships sunk and three damaged by mines was deemed too high and the warships were withdrawn. The opportunity to reach the Sea of Mamara and bombard Constantinople was lost. It was decided to commit land forces instead. A Mediterranean Expeditionary Force was created from the various contingents of troops in the region, including British, French, Indian and large numbers of untested Australian and New Zealand soldiers, soon to be known as ANZACs from the initial letters of the Australian and New Zealand Army Corps. Meanwhile, the Turks had been alerted to the Allies' intentions by the naval bombardment and had fortified many of the potential landing sites.

Gallipoli 25 April 1915

SIX VCs BEFORE BREAKFAST

In 1915, the 1st Battalion Lancashire Fusiliers formed part of 86 Fusilier Brigade of the 29th Division. The battalion, under the command of the Major H.O. Bishop, left Mudros harbour in the island of Lemnos on the evening of 24 April 1915 aboard HMS *Euryalus* with D Company on HMS *Implacable*. At 4.15am, some 840 officers and men of the battalion transferred into 32 cutters divided into groups of four; each towed by a steam picket boat as far as the shallow water off the Gallipoli beaches where the cutters were cast off. Meanwhile, the naval escorts bombarded the shoreline with no return fire from the enemy. The flotilla of small craft headed for the shore. The cutters carrying the Lancashire Fusiliers were rowed by naval ratings towards W Beach at Cape Helles on the tip of the Gallipoli peninsula. This was a strip of deep, powdery sand about 350 yards long and 15 to 40 yards wide. It was an ideal landing site and so had been heavily wired, although it was only defended by half a company of Turkish infantry and a few machine guns and snipers. No more than were necessary for the task in hand. Private W.G. Campbell recalls - 'As we approached the shore there was nothing to be seen. It was by then a lovely spring morning on that Sunday and then the uncanny silence following the naval bombardment was suddenly shattered as all hell broke loose from the Turkish positions.'

As the boats neared the shore, the Turks opened fire with a murderous fusillade from rifles, machine guns and pompom cannons that sliced through the heavily laden soldiers as they tumbled out of the boats and floundered through the wire entanglements in the shallows. Many were hit in the boats themselves, many in the water and many were drowned under the

The war artist Eric Kennington who served with the 13th Kensington Battalion London Regiment produced some remarkable images of the Great War including this charcoal and pastel drawing entitled 'A Famous Raider - Lancashire Fusiliers'. Its caption reads - 'Among men who may all be good soldiers there are many different degrees of aptitude for different sorts of fighting, and some temperaments find in trench raids exactly the congenial kind of call upon their daring, versatility and power of dominating circumstances and dealing with emergencies. Every good raider is a good soldier, but not every good soldier is a good raider. The boy here is not yet 20 and is short in stature, but a tall spirit, a great hand at bombing and patrolling, and highly valued by his officers.' Trench raiding, principally to capture prisoners for intelligence purposes, invariably took place at night and was a highly dangerous enterprise calling for great courage and cunning. An indication of the scale of the Great War and the commitment of the British people may be gauged by the fact that the antecedent regiments raised 196 battalions, each of approximately 1,000 men, from across the North of England, the Midlands and London.

Northumberland Fusiliers	54 Battalions
Royal Warwickshire Regiment	31 Battalions
Royal Fusiliers	76 Battalions
Lancashire Fusiliers	35 Battalions

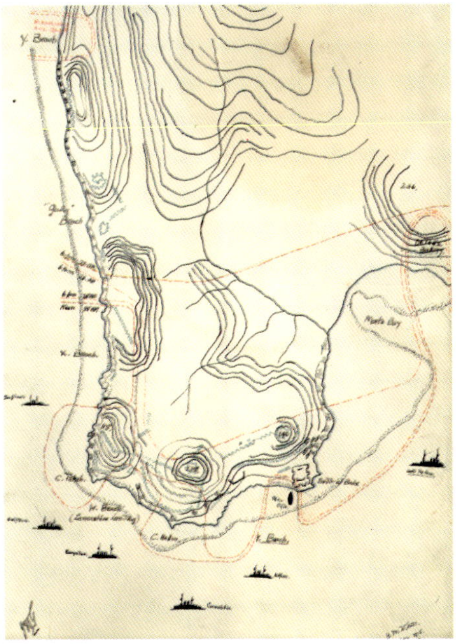

A plan of the tip of Cape Helles drawn by the 16-year old Midshipman Hubert Wilson shows the various landing beaches. He was one of two midshipmen to be awarded a Distinguished Service Cross for their part in the 'Lancashire Landings'. Midshipman Wilson recorded in his diary - 'The hands were called at 3.30 and at 4 o'clock the 1st battalion Lancashire Fusiliers were embarked on life-boats which had closed and were alongside the sea gangways. As soon as the life-boats were filled they formed line abreast & proceeded to "W" beach the *Euryalus* in company astern. The boats were in charge of Lt Bromley R.N.R. I was in the *Euryalus* Picket Boat & Mr.Williams in the steam Pinnace. HMS.*Swiftsure* carried out a general bombardment of the cliffs and trenches in the vicinity of "W" beach, whilst the *Vengeance* fired in the neighbourhood of "V" beach. The *Agamemnon* & *Lord Nelson* fired over the land from inside the straits, a net having being laid across to prevent mines being drafted down. HMS *Cornwallis* was off "V" beach being in charge of the landing there and the *Implacable* off "X" beach. 'The boats arrived off "W" beach at about 6 o clock. They were slipped about 200 yds from the shore when they pulled in under a heavy musketry & machine gun fire. The Turks, who had placed two rows of barbed wire along the beach could be seen in the trenches commanding the gully and poured a heavy fire down on the Lancashires, as did the snipers who were excellently hidden in the cliffs. The Picket boats lay off during this and I was able to obtain an excellent view of the attack. The Lancashires who rushed the trenches with the utmost gallantry must have lost about 60 killed while disembarking alone. Many were wounded while getting out of the boats and were drowned as the boats being fully loaded grounded in about 3 feet of water. Our troops also suffered severe casualties while passing through the barbed wire entanglements as the Turks had had machine guns trained on any gaps in it. The party of men who stormed the left cliff captured about 30 prisoners, who surrendered directly our troops fixed bayonets and charged their trench. 'As soon as the boats had disembarked their troops they pulled out to the picket boats who towed them out to the Fleet sweeper which had the reinforcements for the covering force on board & also the beach parties. By this time, the Essex Regiment which was supporting the Lancashires was landed the fire had greatly diminished and the beach parties suffered no casualties. By 7.30 am the beach was quite safe with the exception of a few snipers & spent bullets which were falling in the water and the removal of wounded and landing of supplies recommenced'. For the rest of his life, Hubert Wilson was a particular friend of the Lancashire Fusiliers and attended numerous memorial services and regimental functions.

weight of their 70 pound packs. Private Campbell continues - 'In the boats there was a momentary pause when someone in mine shouted "Out!". Those of us who were able, jumped into the sea. I am not particularly tall, only 5 foot 7 inches and when I felt the ground under my feet, I found the water almost up to my armpits. Almost immediately the chap alongside of me was hit and disappeared under the water. There seemed to be bullets everywhere and when I reached the beach there were men going down like ninepins all around us.'

The land attack was a sequel to the naval attempt to force the Dardanelles a month previously. This put the Turks on their guard and under the command of Mustapha Kemal, later the charismatic leader of Turkey - Ataturk - they had redeployed their forces and improved their defences. Redolent of earlier wars, 86 Brigade was a Fusilier Brigade consisting of the 2nd Battalion Royal Fusiliers, 1st Battalion Lancashire Fusiliers, the Royal Munster Fusiliers and the Royal Dublin Fusiliers. It was the first to land on the Gallipoli peninsula to cover the disembarkation of the rest of the 29th Division. Battalion Headquarters and two companies of the 2nd Battalion Royal Fusiliers sailed in HMS *Implacable* with the other two companies in a minesweeper. The battalion had been allotted X Beach, a narrow ribbon of sand about 200 yards long, with cliffs some 100 feet high rising steeply from the beach. The men were rowed to the beach in the ships' boats and, covered by the fire of HMS *Implacable's* 12-inch guns, waded ashore when the boats grounded. Scrambling up the cliff, W and X Companies quickly captured the foremost Turkish trenches. W and half of Z Companies were then ordered to capture Hill 114, 1,000 yards away to the right, in order to link up with the Lancashire Fusiliers who were landing at W Beach.

Hill 114 had been elaborately entrenched, but after a stiff fight the Fusiliers carried it at the point of the bayonet. Continuing their advance eastwards they met further strong opposition on the reverse side of the hill, but they eventually dislodged the Turks from their trenches and dug in for the night. The capture of Hill 114 tipped the scale on W Beach, and with the linking of the two beaches a foothold was established on the peninsula. Meanwhile, X Company on the left was being heavily counterattacked but beat off all assaults and the position was consolidated. The official history states - 'The success of the Royal Fusiliers at X Beach must be set down as a particularly memorable exploit.' The battalion's casualties that day amounted to nearly half their strength and included the CO, 2IC and all the company commanders. X Beach became known as 'Implacable Landing'.

Meanwhile, on W Beach the boats carrying the Lancashire Fusiliers touched the shore and immediately the Turks opened fire. Captain Richard Willis was the OC C Company which was approaching the centre of W Beach. He later recalled - 'Not a sign of life was to be seen on the peninsula in front of us. It might have been a deserted land we were nearing in our little boats. Then Crack! The stroke oar of my boat fell forward, to the angry astonishment of his mates. The signal for the massacre had been given: rapid fire, machine guns and deadly

One estimate gives the number of men who wore the Royal Fusiliers cap badge during the Great War as an astonishing 235,476 - more than twice the current establishment of the British Army. They fought in every theatre of war except Mesopotamia. At the outbreak of war, the Royal Fusiliers comprised four regular battalions, three special reserve battalions and the four Fusilier battalions of the London Regiment (Territorial Force), a total of 11 battalions. By the end of the war, including those raised for the War of Intervention against the Bolsheviks, the Royal Fusiliers comprised 76 battalions of which 45 served overseas. This was the most of any regiment in the British Army. Twelve Royal Fusiliers were awarded the Victoria Cross during the war. These two photographs show the transformation of Kitchener volunteers into soldiers of D Company 17th Battalion Royal Fusiliers or the Empire Battalion.

accurate sniping opened from the cliffs above, and soon the casualties included the rest of the crew and many men. The timing of the ambush was perfect. We were completely exposed and helpless in our slow moving boats, just target practice for the concealed Turks, and within a few minutes only half of the 30 men in my boat were left alive.'

Another member of C Company in a boat near Captain Willis recorded - 'I saw him stand up and everyone in the boats heard him above the noise of the bullets and guns, shout "Come on C Company! Remember Minden!" That was it. Whenever we were in trouble, whenever we looked like going under, the cry "Remember Minden!" brought us back to our senses. Captain Willis could not have timed it better'. Rifles, machine guns and pompoms kept up a ceaseless hail of shot. Many soldiers and sailors died in the boats; of those who struggled ashore through the barbed-wire entanglements and deep soft sand which clogged their wet rifles, few remained unscathed. One much wounded Fusilier, struggling to get through the wire, joked to a nearby officer - 'Thou'st given me a bloody job!'. D Company, on the left flank, surprised the Turks, bayonetted the machine gunners there and relieved the pressure. The few remaining officers rallied the remainder of the battalion and pressed on behind D Company. By the end of the day W Beach was firmly in British hands.

Other battalions were able to link up from the various landing places, and together they carried the high ground behind the beach. The Turkish counterattacks continued long after dark, but they were beaten off successfully. The cost was high: at the end of the day only 11 officers and 399 other ranks of the Lancashire Fusiliers remained fit for duty. Of the naval ratings who rowed the Fusiliers ashore, 63 out of 80 were killed or wounded. Six members of the battalion were subsequently awarded Victoria Crosses; Captain R R Willis; Captain C Bromley as the Adjutant; Sergeant A Richards (for leadership despite grievous wounds); Sergeant F E Stubbs (killed leading his platoon); Lance Corporal J Grimshaw (for gallantry in signalling) and Private W Keneally (as a runner and cutting the wire under fire). At the outset, the War Office would only sanction the award to three recipients chosen by their fellow Fusiliers, those being Captain Willis, Sergeant Richards and Private Keneally. Their joint citation of 23 August 1915 read:-

'On 25 April 1915, three Companies and the Headquarters of the 1st Battalion Lancashire Fusiliers in effecting a landing on the Gallipoli Peninsula to the west of Cape Helles were met by a deadly fire from hidden machine guns, which caused a great number of casualties. The survivors, however, rushed up to and cut the wire entanglements, notwithstanding a terrific fire from the enemy, and after overcoming supreme difficulties, the cliffs were gained and position maintained. Amongst many very gallant officers and men engaged in this most hazardous enterprise, Captain Willis, Sergeant Richards and Private Keneally have been selected by their comrades as having performed most signal acts of bravery and devotion to duty.'

One of the heroic images that was presented to the British public by *The War Illustrated* showed the VC action of Private John Lynn DCM of the Lancashire Fusiliers during a gas attack near Ypres on 2 May 1915. In reality, he took a day to die in excruciating agony from the effects of gas poisoning. As related in the text, L/Sgt Elmer Cotton of the 5th Battalion Northumberland Fusiliers was gassed on the same day - 'It produces a flooding of the lungs - it is the equivalent death to drowning only on dry land. The effects are these - a splitting headache and terrific thirst but to drink water is instant death, a knife pain in the lungs and the coughing up of a greenish froth off the stomach and the lungs, ending finally in insensibility and death. The colour of the skin from white turns a greenish black and yellow, the tongue protrudes and the eyes assume a glassy stare. It is a fiendish death to die'.

At the outbreak of war, the Lancashire Fusiliers comprised a total of eight regular, territorial and special reserve battalions. By the middle of 1915 this had risen to 26 battalions. During the last months of 1917, 21 were deployed in France and Flanders with one in Macedonia. A further nine remained in Britain, giving a grand total of 31 battalions. The Lancashire Fusiliers won 18 Victoria Crosses, the largest number awarded to any one regiment in the war. Here, in January 1917, Lancashire Fusiliers man a trench near 'Plugstreet Wood' in Flanders, with a Lewis gun team sitting on the muddy duckboards cleaning their automatic weapon. In the foreground is a hooter to warn of gas attack. The device above the helmet of the Fusilier on the right is a wind vane to indicate its direction and therefore the likelihood of gas attack. IWM Q4649

'Six VCs before Breakfast' - the Lancashire Fusiliers wade ashore at W Beach in the face of intense Turkish fire and barbed wire entanglements, with Capt Richard Willis urging his men on while brandishing a walking stick - it was in fact a silver-topped cane, now held at the Lancashire Fusiliers Museum in Bury.

It was not until 15 March 1917 that the other three awards were gazetted under the same citation. By then, Captain Bromley had been promoted major and had led the battalion when the CO fell ill. On 28 June, he was at the head of the Lancashire Fusiliers when he was wounded in the battle of Gully Ravine. Having survived several wounds and untold hardships on Cape Helles, Major Cuthbert Bromley was drowned when the hospital ship evacuating him to Egypt was torpedoed and sunk by a U-Boat on 13 August. Private William Keneally VC was mortally wounded in the same attack as Major Bromley and died the next day.

General Sir Ian Hamilton, Commander-in-Chief of the expedition, ordered that W Beach should be renamed 'Lancashire Landing'; it was actually renamed 'Helles Landing'. He wrote in his despatch:-

'...so strong, in fact, were the defences of W Beach that the Turks may well have considered them impregnable, and it is my firm conviction that no finer feat of arms has ever been achieved by the British soldier - or any other soldier - than the storming of these beaches from open boats on the morning of 25 April. The landing at W Beach had been entrusted to the 1st Battalion Lancashire Fusiliers (Major Bishop) and it was to the complete lack of sense of danger or fear of this daring Battalion that we owe our astonishing success...'

GALLIPOLI LANDINGS
The steam pinnaces from HMS *Euryalus* tow the ship's lifeboats carrying the Lancashire Fusiliers towards Cape Helles at the outset of the landings on the morning of 25 April 1915. A photograph taken later on in the day of the Lancashire Landings on W Beach gives a vivid impression of the difficulties in making an opposed landing against entrenched automatic weapons from open rowing boats.

Like hundreds of thousands of his comrades, the classic image of a British soldier of the Great War as he poses for a souvenir photograph a short distance behind the front lines in full battle order still with mud on his boots. This corporal of the 27th Service Battalion Tyneside Irish is depicted some time in 1917 as he is wearing '17 Pattern Webbing and has the Irish harp insignia of the Tyneside Irish on his tunic collar; previously they were worn on the shoulder straps. Both the Tyneside Irish and the Tyneside Scottish battalions of the Northumberland Fusiliers suffered grievous casualties during the first day of the battle of the Somme on 1 July 1916.

The battle of the Somme was the first real test of Kitchener's New Armies. At 7.30 am on 1 July 1916, as the whistles blow, the Fusiliers of 103 Tyneside Irish Brigade clamber from their trenches into well ordered, serried ranks with their rifles at the shoulder as they advance over the Tara-Usna ridge towards La Boisselle. The troops of the 34th Division had to march at least a mile over open ground before they even reached the British front lines, all the while under fire from German artillery and machine gun teams. As Sgt J Galloway, 26th Battalion Tyneside Irish, recalled - 'I could see, away to my left and right, long lines of men. Then I heard the "patter, patter" of machine guns in the distance. By the time I'd gone another ten yards there seemed to be only a few men left around me; by the time I had gone 20 yards, I seemed to be on my own. Then I was hit myself.' A Tyneside Irish officer writing in *The Northern Echo* stated - 'We left our trenches, the artillery lifted and the Irish were thirsting to get at the foe. The fighting was of the fiercest description, unsurpassed during this or any other campaign. The Irish advance never ceased, in spite of all the unadulterated hell they were going through. The men were fine, no men in the world could have done better. They got it in the neck - enfilade machine gun fire traversing ankle high, waist high and breast high, over that awful stretch mapped out for us.' They never really had a chance. The slaughter was appalling. The 101 Tyneside Scottish Brigade lost 70 officers and 2,440 men in a matter of hours - almost three times the total number of dead suffered by the Royal Northumberland Fusiliers during the whole of World War 2. The British Army lost 57,470 officers and men on the first day of the battle of the Somme; 19,240 of whom were killed and 2,152 missing. Approximately 60 per cent of the casualties were caused by machine gun fire. IWM Q53

'Gallantly led by their Officers, the Fusiliers literally hurled themselves ashore and fired at from right, left and centre, commence hacking their way through the wire. A long line of men was at once mown down as by a scythe, but the remainder were not to be denied...'

Vice-Admiral de Robeck, in his despatch on the naval aspect of the operation, wrote - '... it is impossible to exalt too highly the service rendered by 1st Battalion Lancashire Fusiliers in the storming of the beaches; the dash and gallantry displayed was superb...'

Sir Aylmer Hunter Weston writing about all the battalions within the 29th Division stated - 'It was an impossible task for any but high disciplined, well trained, skilfully led, heroically brave, grimly determined Britishers, animated by high ideals and upheld by the traditions of their battalions and their race. It may truly be called the achievement of the impossible'. HMS *Euryalus* signalled - 'We are proud as can be to have had the honour to carry your splendid Regiment. We feel for you all in your great losses as if you were our own ship's company, but know the magnificent gallantry of your Regiment has made the name more famous than ever.' However, the proud boast of the Lancashire Fusiliers of 'winning six VCs before breakfast' was not strictly true, as the awards were separated by almost two years and the Fusiliers had been fed on board HMS *Euryalus* before the attack. Five other battalions of the Lancashire Fusiliers fought at Gallipoli, as did many other Fusilier battalions. Gallipoli was a Battle Honour of all four antecedent regiments and Gallipoli Day is one of the proudest traditional days marked by The Royal Regiment of Fusiliers to commemorate the gallant actions of the former Fusilier regiments.

Despite the supreme gallantry of the British and Empire troops, every assault against the Turks foundered in the face of machine guns, barbed wire, artillery and snipers defending the parched, barren landscape. During the fearful heat of summer, disease ran rife through the huddled masses of soldiers. Summer turned to autumn and the torrential rain turned iron hard ground to deadly mud slides. During blizzards in November, men froze to death and thousands suffered from frostbite. At the turn of the year, the Gallipoli Peninsula was evacuated without the loss of a single man. The campaign as a whole had cost the deaths of 25,000 British, 10,000 French and 2,000 Indian; of the ANZACs, 8,500 Australians and 2,500 New Zealanders died - over ten per cent of the male population of military age in New Zealand. Of the 500,000 Allied troops committed to the Gallipoli beaches, almost a half became casualties of disease or battle. Turkish casualties were even greater. The Gallipoli campaign had failed and the main emphasis of the war returned to the only place where it would be resolved - the Western Front.

'The 1914-1918 War was the cruelest war in history. Because it was static, unyielding, relentless, it destroyed the will and it destroyed hope. In the big battalion men were reduced to mere numbers, ciphers who were pushed over the top to be killed by other ciphers 150 yards away. In such a grotesque world a man must cling to something or go mad. For all its members, the Royal Fusiliers regiment pushed out a small, frail boat into which a man could climb from the encircling ocean of impotence and frustration. There, a soldier could be together with his fellow sufferers, assured of a little humanity and friendship. There, a man could assert his individuality, blow his hunting horn with Colonel Malone, or like Jack Forster saunter into battle with a small dog under his arm. From the comfort of his regiment, the Fusilier could afford to cock a snook at Armageddon which threatened to batter him into nothingness.'

From 15 July 1916, Delville Wood was the scene of intense fighting during the second phase of the battle of the Somme, when orders were given to capture the key feature at all costs. They proved to be extremely high as it was not taken until 3 September. In the month of July alone, British casualties on the Somme battlefield were 156,000 men - more then one and a half times the present numbers of the entire British Army. Although forever associated with the South Africans, units of eight divisions were swallowed up in the carnage that the troops called Devil Wood. Amongst them were seven battalions of the Royal Fusiliers. The first of these was the 4th Battalion. It was deployed to the wood on 20 July to relieve the remnants of the Essex, Suffolks and Royal Welch Fusiliers. In a 13-day period, the 4th suffered 352 casualties without attacking once. The other battalions of the Royal Fusiliers to see action were the 12th Service, 17th 'Empire', 20th '3rd Public Schools', 22nd 'Kensingtons', 23rd '1st Sportsman's' and the 24th '2nd Sportsman's'. The battle of the Somme ground on until 19 November 1916 by when the British Army had lost 540,000 men, mainly from the New Armies of patriotic civilians who had volunteered in 1914, for a territorial gain of some five miles. Winston Churchill wrote - '...the actual battle fronts were not appreciably altered, no strategic advantage of any kind had been gained.' In the words of A.J.P. Taylor - 'Idealism perished on the Somme'. Both in his pictures and his words, the German expressionist painter Otto Dix found life in the trenches to be utterly vile and summed up the conditions under which the soldiers of all nations, on all fronts, lived and endured:- 'Lice, rats , barbed wire, fleas, shells, bombs, underground caves, corpses, blood, liquor, mice, cats, artillery, filth, bullets, mortars, fire, steel: that is war. It is the work of the devil.' It is not surprising that surrealism was born in the trenches of the Western Front. Nevertheless, the cost to the Germans was also horrendous and the history of their 27th Division that defended the nearby village of Guillemont stated - 'In the Somme fighting of 1916 there was a spirit of heroism which was never found again in the division... the men in 1918 had not the temper, the hard bitterness and spirit of sacrifice of their predecessors.' Men now fought for survival - often with valour, always doggedly - but for themselves and their comrades in arms. Therein lay the strength of the British regimental system, for a man knew where he belonged and anything beyond his battalion meant little - beyond his regiment, nothing. To Lt Charles Carrington of the 1/5th Battalion Royal Warwickshire Regiment - 'We were banded together by a unity of experience that had shaken off every kind of illusion, and which was utterly unpretentious. The battalion was my home and my job, the only career I knew.'

The 1/8th Battalion Lancashire Fusiliers returns home on 8 April 1919.

'Died, some pro patria,
non "dulce" non "et decor"
Walked eye deep in hell
believing in old men's lies,
then unbelieving
came home, home to a lie
home to many deceits,
home to old lies and new infamy'
Ezra Pound

In 1914, hundreds of thousands of willing volunteers flocked to the Colours throughout the United Kingdom. From 1916, conscription inducted many more. By Armistice Day on 11 November 1918, 850,000 British servicemen lay dead. In the following months, many healthy young men who had survived the horrors of the Great War succumbed to a pandemic of influenza that killed more people than the conflict itself. A generation weaned on the glories of Empire and patriotism had been shattered, as were the accepted social divisions of class and gender that had held sway before the war. Untold millions across Europe had been physically and mentally scarred by the conflict. Tragically, the underlying geo-political differences remained unresolved and, 20 years on, the world was plunged into Total War once more.

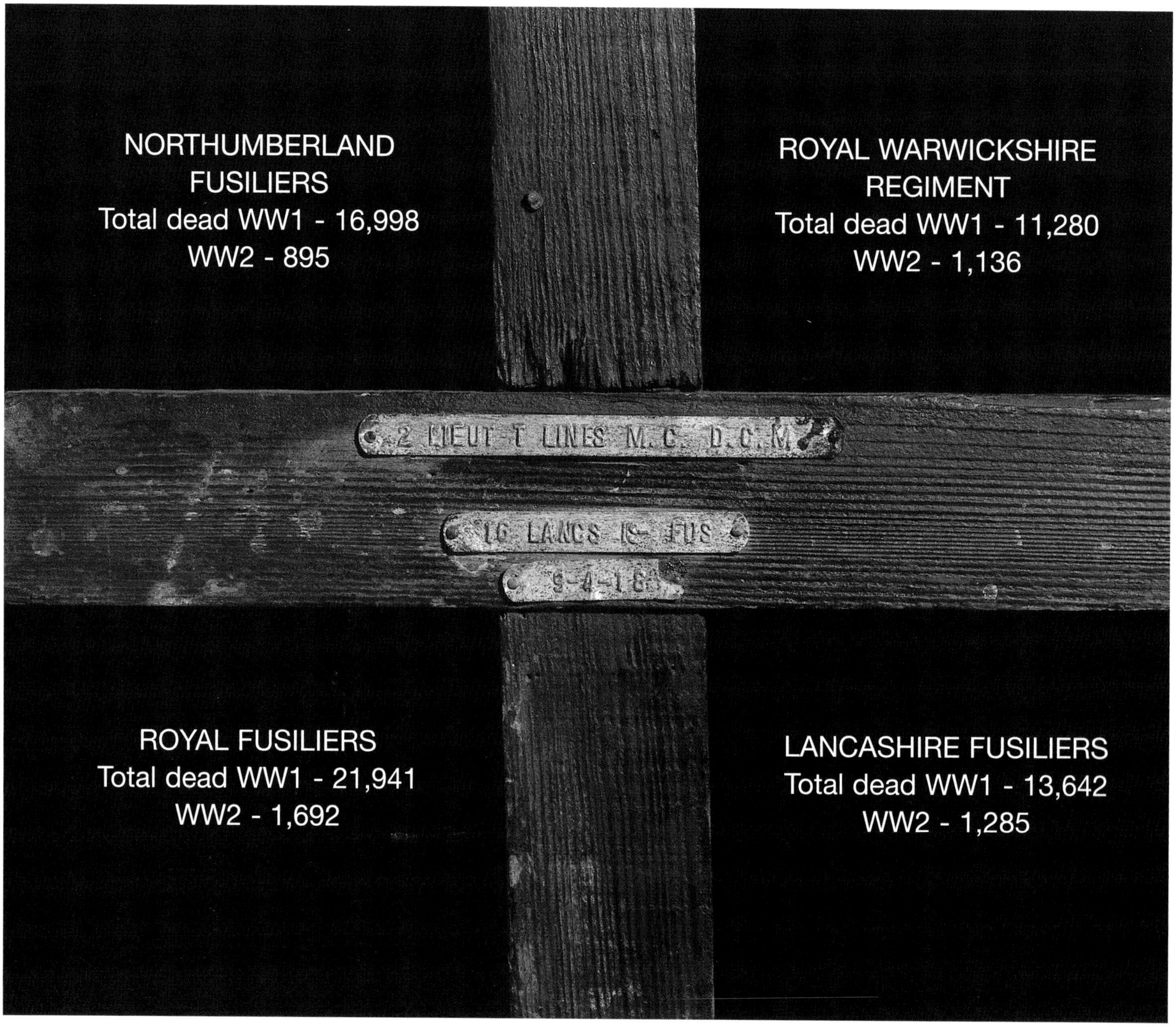

'Total War is not a succession of mere episodes in a day or week. It is a long drawn out and intricately planned business, and the longer it continues the heavier are the demands on the character of the men engaged in it.'
General George C. Marshall

WORLD WAR 2

Following the Armistice in November 1918, the extraordinary number of battalions raised to fight the War to End All Wars were rapidly disbanded. By the end of 1922, only the 1st and 2nd Battalions of the antecedent regiments remained in being. In the following year, the rank of Private in the Fusilier regiments was changed to Fusilier. In 1936, the Northumberland Fusiliers became a Royal regiment. This coincided with a rapid expansion of the armed forces and extensive rearmament in response to the rise of fascism, as despotic dictators rekindled the fires of war in Europe and Africa. The regular and territorial battalions were strengthened with many being recruited above their nominal establishments. However, many were converted to specialised roles within the Royal Artillery or Royal Armoured Corps, such as anti-aircraft or reconnaissance units.

With the outbreak of war on 3 September 1939, battalions of all the antecedent regiments were despatched to France with the British Expeditionary Force. Severe losses were suffered during the retreat to Dunkirk, particularly by the 2nd Battalion Royal Warwickshire Regiment at Wormhoudt where wounded and unwounded prisoners of war were massacred in a barn by a Waffen SS unit. After Dunkirk, the main theatre of operations for the British Army was the Middle East against the Italians and then the German Afrika Korps. Fusiliers were triumphant at the battles of Sidi Barrani, Bardia, Tobruk and Beda Fomm in the defeat of the Italians and at the siege of Tobruk in resisting German assaults. In November 1941, the breakout from Tobruk began and, during the attack on Ed-Duda, Captain James Jackman of the 1st Battalion Royal Northumberland Fusiliers was posthumously awarded the Victoria Cross for his gallantry.

In November 1942, the 8th Army under the command of General Bernard Montgomery won a decisive victory at the battle of El Alamein. The Axis forces began a long retreat until they were finally defeated in Tunisia where 250,000 Germans and Italians surrendered in May 1943. After gaining a Battle Honour at Medjez El Bab in Tunisia and fighting in Sicily, the Lancashire Fusiliers joined the Royal Northumberland and Royal Fusiliers in the long and bitter struggle up the Italian mainland, where all three regiments shared the Battle Honour of Monte Cassino. It was beneath the fortress monastery 'brooding over the battlefield like a curse' that Fusilier

In 1920, the troubles in Ireland broke out with renewed vigour when Irish nationalists waged a systematic campaign of attacks on the property of loyalists and against British forces. Both the 1st and 3rd Battalions of the Royal Fusiliers took part in operations against the rebels as did a special constabulary raised in Britain, mainly from veterans of the Great War, known as the 'Black and Tans'. Here, Fusiliers of B Company of the 1st Battalion Royal Fusiliers prepare for an operation, known at the time as 'stunting', at Kinsale in Cork during 1921. The Lancia armoured lorry on the left is emblazoned with the slogan - IF YOU FANCY YOUR CHANCE HAVE A GO AT THIS.

During WW2, both the 1st and 2nd Battalions Royal Northumberland Fusiliers (RNF) were converted to machine gun units equipped with Vickers Medium Machine Guns and later 4.2 inch (120mm) mortars. The 1st Battalion took part in all the campaigns of the Western Desert, fighting at Tobruk and El Alamein until final victory over the Deutsches Afrika Korps in Tunisia. 2RNF served with the BEF in Belgium and France before it was sent to North Africa and Italy. The 2nd Battalion landed at Salerno in September 1943, fighting as the divisional machine gun battalion of the 4th Division in many actions, culminating in the hard-fought battle of Cassino in May 1944. 1RNF landed in Italy in March 1944 and fought throughout the remainder of the bitter campaign until the German surrender in April 1945. Both battalions provided invaluable fire support during infantry operations such as this Vickers machine gun team of 2RNF during an attack by the Gurkha Brigade in late 1944.

Typical of the Fusilier formations raised during World War 2 was the 11th Battalion Lancashire Fusiliers. There is no mistaking the provenance of this Universal Carrier in the distinctive 'crazy paving' camouflage scheme peculiar to Malta - above the weapon's aperture at the gunner's position is painted the double XX of the 20th Regiment of Foot and below it the regimental Battle Honour INKERMAN. This battalion was raised at Rochdale in July 1940 and left England for an unknown destination in October 1941. After transferring from troopships to warships at Gibraltar, the 11th took part in a convoy action en route for Malta when sailors and Fusiliers fought side by side for almost 60 hours, with the Fusiliers acting as 'powder monkeys' for the ships' AA gunners. The battalion then endured 18 months of hardship at the height of the siege of Malta with constant air attacks and limited resources which called for high powers of endurance and a sense of humour - both renowned attributes of the Lancashire Fusiliers. Coincidentally, Malta was then the home base for the fifth HMS *Euryalus*, a Dido Class cruiser, and mutual visits were made between the battalion and ship. MALTA 1941-42 became a Battle Honour of the Lancashire Fusiliers. In Italy during 1944, the 11th Battalion took part in the fierce fighting for the Gothic Line, experiencing some of the toughest campaigning in the advance to Monte Cece, Monte Grande and Monte Galderaro. The battalion was relieved in March 1945 and moved to Palestine where it was disbanded in July, two months after VE-Day.

Frank Jefferson of the 2nd Battalion Lancashire Fusiliers won the Victoria Cross for halting a German armoured attack with a PIAT anti-tank weapon. Equipped with Vickers machine guns and 4.2 inch [120mm] mortars in the supporting role, both the 1st and 2nd Battalions of the Royal Northumberland Fusiliers fought in the Italian campaign, from the Salerno landings to VE Day for the 1st and until December 1944 for the 2nd when it was deployed to Greece. The 2nd Battalion Royal Fusiliers was likewise sent to Greece after it had fought side by side with its sister 1st, 8th and 9th Battalions in the protracted battles for Monte Cassino. The latter remained in Italy until the final battles of the campaign at Argenta Gap and the surrender of the Germans in April 1945. These gallant Fusilier battalions were no 'D-Day Dodgers'.

Neither were those that fought in the Far East. After a distinguished action at Steenbecque during the Battle for France and evacuation from Dunkirk, the 9th Battalion Royal Northumberland Fusiliers was despatched to the Middle East as part of the 18th Division but was diverted to Singapore following the Japanese invasion of Malaya. During the voyage, it stoutly defended the French troopship it was sailing on against a concerted attack by dive bombers. The battalion arrived at Singapore shortly before it fell and its men were taken prisoner. During three years of captivity, they suffered dreadful privations as they were forced to work on the Death Railway in Siam. Denied medical supplies and adequate food, they were brutalised by their captors and 151 of them had perished by the end of the war. The 1st Battalion Lancashire Fusiliers had been stationed in India since 1938 on the North West Frontier. In July 1943, it was selected to join 77 Indian Infantry Brigade as part of the Chindits under Brigadier Orde Wingate to fight behind enemy lines. After ten months of strenuous training, the brigade was flown some 150 miles behind the Japanese lines on 5 March 1944. The Chindits operated with considerable success before returning to India in July 1944, but suffered high casualties and complete exhaustion. The 1st Battalion Lancashire Fusiliers saw no further active service during the war.

Normandy 1944

THE LONGEST DAY

On 6 June 1944, the largest amphibious invasion in the history of warfare was launched across the English Channel in an armada of 2,700 ships and 4,000 landing craft onto the Normandy beaches of Nazi occupied France. Operation 'Overlord' was underway. In the van of the assault troops was 2nd Battalion Royal Warwickshire Regiment. As part of 185 Brigade of the 3rd 'Iron' Division, the landing craft carrying the battalion approached the most easterly of the

In a painting by Gilbert Solomon held at the Royal Regiment of Fusiliers Museum (Royal Warwickshire), the 2nd Battalion Royal Warwickshire Regiment is depicted landing on Queen Sector of Sword Beach between Lion sur Mer and La Brèche in the early morning of 6 June 1944 - D-Day.

five assault beaches of Utah, Omaha, Gold, Juno and Sword on schedule at 0955 hours, some two hours after the first troops had landed. The precise landing point was a house with a gable end on Queen Sector of Sword Beach between Lion sur Mer and La Bréche. Captain Harry Illing was the commander of A Company - '...at last we touched the beach. Down went the ramps and ashore we stumbled, lugging our kits through the last few yards of shallow sea, up breathless and anxious on to the sandy beach. Up the beach we hurried towards the "Gabled-ended house" - it seemed like an old friend by now. Down we flopped - we were ashore, then up again to get clear of the beach and under cover. Nobody much seemed hurt, we most of us seemed to be there. We were on French soil. We had made the landing anyway.'

The two LCIs (Landing Craft Infantry) carrying B and C Companies were not so lucky: one struck a mine as it beached and the other was hit three times by shellfire and mortar bombs. Fortunately, the men disembarked on the beach with relatively few casualties. The beach itself was cluttered with tanks and equipment trying desperately to negotiate the exit lanes under the constant German fire. The battalion marched half a mile inland to its prearranged assembly area and awaited further orders. The original plan called for the brigade to advance southwards on the Hermanville-Beuville-Lebisey axis to the city of Caen which was the principal objective for D-Day. Instead, the 2nd Battalion Royal Warwickshire Regiment was to move south-eastwards through Colleville to Benouville and Blainville on the banks of the Orne river, to relieve the paratroops of the 6th Airborne Division who had captured the vital bridges over the river and the adjacent Canal du Caen.

Shortly after midday, the battalion began its advance and cleared the first hamlet without difficulty, but was then held up by accurate small arms fire from the north of Benouville. A Company under Captain Illing was ordered to assault the village - 'A hasty plan was made and we formed up behind some farm buildings and a long high wall. Two lone Germans ran towards us unaware of our presence. As we moved into view, the Germans dived into the hedge for cover, but before they could open fire a very willing Sten gunner shot them neatly in a pair from over the hedge.' At that moment, as the dusk was gathering, gliders carrying reinforcements of the 6th Airborne Division descended through a curtain of flak. One glider unfortunately landed on two signallers of B Company who, wearing headphones, did not hear it coming and both were killed. Under this diversion, the battalion quickly occupied Benouville and began to winkle out the last of the hidden snipers who had exacted a heavy toll of casualties. The battalion continued the advance along the river road supported by a few tanks of the Staffordshire Yeomanry until it halted around midnight on the northern edge of Blainville. During D-Day, the Warwicks had advanced some seven miles and had incurred

Fus Frank Jefferson was the company runner in C Company 2nd Battalion Lancashire Fusiliers during the campaign in Italy; his Victoria Cross citation reads 'On 16 May 1944, during an attack on the Gustav Line, an anti-tank obstacle held up some of our tanks, leaving the leading company of Fusilier Jefferson's battalion to dig in on the hill without tanks or anti-tank guns. The enemy counter-attacked with infantry and two Mark IV tanks [StuG III self-propelled assault guns] which opened fire at short range causing a number of casualties and eliminating one PIAT group entirely. 'As the tanks advanced towards the partially-dug trenches, Fusilier Jefferson, entirely on his own initiative, seized a PIAT, and running forward alone under fire, took up a position behind a hedge; as he could not see properly, he came into the open, and standing up under the hail of bullets, fired at the leading tank, which was now only twenty yards away. It burst into flames and all the crew were killed. Fusilier Jefferson then reloaded the PIAT and proceeded towards the second tank, which withdrew before he could get within range. By this time our own tanks had arrived and the enemy counter-attack was smashed with heavy casualties. Fusilier Jefferson's gallant act not merely saved the lives of his company and caused many casualties to the Germans, but also broke up the enemy counter-attack and had a decisive effect on the subsequent operation. His supreme gallantry and disregard of personal risk contributed very largely to the success of the action.' *London Gazette* 13 July 1944. The photograph was taken two days after the event at the same time as a graves registration unit was disinterring his company comrades killed on that day. In the background, is the Sturmgeschutz III Ausf. G self-propelled assault gun which Fusilier Jefferson had destroyed with the PIAT (Projector Infantry Anti-Tank) carried over his shoulder. IWM NA15431

A Universal Carrier named DOG STAR of the 2nd Battalion Royal Warwickshire Regiment moves forward through a field of ripening barley at the outset of the successful attack against the village of Lebisey on 8 July 1944; a month after its first assault had been thwarted by the Panzergrenadiers of the 21st Panzer Division. IWM B6617

In WW2, many infantry battalions were converted to specialised roles. On 1 April 1941, the 8th Battalion Royal Northumberland Fusiliers became the 3rd Reconnaissance Regiment within the 3rd Infantry Division. Ever proud of its origins, the new formation always appended RNF to its title. However, it quickly took to its new role and as early as June of 1941 it made its mark by capturing Tilshead Airfield by the ruse of dressing an officer as the Corps Commander and escorting him into the enemy's HQ. Over the next two years, 3rd Recce Regiment took part in numerous exercises in Britain as part of its parent formation, the Reconnaissance Corps. In January 1944, the latter came under the Royal Armoured Corps, but even so it carefully nurtured its own esprit de corps as an elite unit. This was to be proved time and again after the invasion of Normandy where elements of 3rd Recce Regiment landed on D-Day as traffic controllers and Contact Detachments on Queen Beach in the Sword sector. The AFVs of A and B Squadrons landed on the night of 20/21 June with C Squadron following on 3 July. The regiment first fought in its intended role on 6 August and did sterling work in the breakout from Normandy. By September, it was in Brussels and in October on the river Maas, where it remained for some two months before conducting a raid across the river on 27 January 1945. By late March, the 3rd Recce was across the Rhine and supporting the Guards Armoured Brigade Group and the 17th US Airborne Division. On 6 April, it reverted to the Iron Division, fighting up to VE-Day. This Humber Armoured Car Mark IV, named LAUGHING BOY III, of A Squadron 3rd Reconnaissance Regiment RNF is firing its coaxial Besa machine gun at Goch in the final days of the war. Occupation duties involved much patrolling to corral DPs, prevent looting and less onerous tasks such as the guarding of a castle full of Nazi looted art treasures and a working distillery. The regiment was disbanded on 15 February 1946.

casualties of four dead and 35 wounded. The British Army was only half-way to Caen but it was safely ashore in Normandy.

THE ATTACK ON LEBISEY

On D+1, the 2nd Battalion was ordered to move through the village of Blainville and capture the wood at Lebisey which was on high ground overlooking Caen. The position was some 3,000 yards south-west of Blainville and, unknown to the battalion, it had been occupied during the night by the Panzer-Grenadiers of the formidable 21st Panzer Division, veterans of the Deutsches Afrika Korps. The attack was planned for 0845 hours without armour support in a three-company assault. However, due to unforeseen swampy ground that blocked the advance of the battalion's carriers and 6-pounder anti-tank guns - the principal weapon to counter enemy armour - the CO, Lieutenant Colonel 'Jumbo' Herdon, postponed the attack and its massive supporting artillery bombardment for one hour. Unfortunately, B and C Companies did not hear of the delay due to faulty radios and began the attack without any supporting fire beyond a pair of self-propelled guns in the vicinity. Lieutenant Kingston Adams, a platoon commander in A Company, recalls - 'It was a terrible rush to get through our recces, orders etc and when H-Hour arrived, only our company seemed to be on the start line and none of the supporting fire promised had started. We later found, I believe, that H-Hour had been postponed.'

The Commanding Officer was in a cruel dilemma but decided to commit the whole battalion without artillery support rather than leave the two forward companies to their fate. The three companies advanced across open ground towards the wood (D Company remained to occupy the bridges over the Orne and the canal). Lieutenant Adams continues - 'I have recollections of advancing up a corn field and coming under heavy fire from Lebisey wood. When we were about 100 yards short of it, my platoon was unable to make directly for its objective so I tried to work my way round to the right flank. We were heavily engaged from that direction also but we eventually got into the wood where control became very difficult and I was hit by a phosphorous grenade and burst of machine gun fire from a hidden position in front of me. This put me out of the battle, but the company held on to the edges of the wood until the rest of the battalion came up and joined in the attack, but they also were unable to move further forward.'

The battalion could make no further headway as it was pinned down under heavy fire and in desperate need of fire support. Captain Illing was wounded and the assault pioneer commander killed. Soon afterwards, the CO was cut down by machine gun fire and killed as he moved between his companies. By 1600 hours, the battalion was virtually out of ammunition and under attack from enemy tanks. Under the command of Captain A. Bannerman, the carrier platoon with its six vital anti-tank guns was approaching the battalion by a wide detour of the boggy ground when it ran into an ambush. Captain Bannerman recalls - 'So we stopped and baled out in a wild frenzy and I gave the order I had always felt certain of never giving: "Action rear!". To fire backwards! Our drill wasn't bad, though I think the language was far from the drill book. The gun was soon firing and joy, we hit and holed the tank which had poked out from a house... We got off about eight rounds while a German machine gunner sprayed the wheat round us and bullets ricocheted off the road. I remember the loader being quite imperturbable and another Birmingham lad firing the gun with a gleaming smile and a flood of obscenity. Suddenly an 88 got our range and up went our carrier in a deafening explosion with all our ammunition, knocking us all sideways'. Captain Bannerman and his men were captured. Despite a supporting attack by the 1st Battalion Royal Norfolk Regiment, the objective was too strongly held and, when darkness fell, both battalions withdrew to their start lines. The Warwicks had lost ten officers killed, including the Commanding Officer, and 144 other ranks.

Many years after the war, Brigadier Harry Illing MC and Bar, Deputy Colonel Warwickshire of The Royal Regiment of Fusiliers, recounted- 'The first battle of Lebisey was lost and it was galling that the great prize of Caen had not fallen into our hands. Lebisey could in all probability have been captured if a properly co-ordinated brigade attack had been put in instead of battalions being committed piecemeal, but this is mere hindsight, for the atmosphere within the battalion, brigade and division at the time should be appreciated. Troops were immensely fit, morale was terrific, they were probably the best trained, battle inoculated and rehearsed troops the world has ever seen, but for nearly all of them it was the first time in battle apart from a few who were at Dunkirk. There was a desire to "Seek Glory" - a term well known in the Regiment from its Peninsula days. There was a doctrine of "getting on", "taking risks" and "staking a claim". There was real determination to succeed or die in the attempt. The atmosphere was heroic.'

Lebisey was eventually captured on 8 July by the 2nd Battalion Royal Warwickshire Regiment during Operation 'Charnwood' in a sharp action lasting little more than three hours. Even so, the battalion suffered 26 dead, 98 wounded and 25 missing. A grim satisfaction was derived by the battalion in the capture of this small Norman village and its dense wood, not least of which was the opportunity to bury their comrades from the earlier battle who had lain dead in and around the heavily disputed wood for a month. The 2nd Battalion Royal Warwickshire Regiment remained in the 3rd Division in 21st Army Group until the end of the war in Europe in May 1945, having fought from the Normandy beaches to Bremen in Germany. The 1/7th Battalion Royal Warwickshire Regiment also fought in Normandy with the 59th Division from June to the end of August 1944, when the division was broken up to provide reinforcements to the depleted regiments that had suffered serious casualties in the Normandy fighting. Two complete company groups were transferred to the 2nd Battalion.

The 1/7th Battalion itself had suffered severely with 551 casualties in little over a month of fighting. It had entered combat on 8 July at the same time as the 2nd Battalion had just completed the capture of Lebisey. At St Contest, it had faced elements of the 12th SS 'Hitlerjugend' Panzer Division - fanatical teenagers led by veterans of the Eastern Front and the perpetrators of several massacres of POWs in Normandy - and was not found wanting. On 3 August, it fought alongside the 2/5th Battalion Lancashire Fusiliers in the successful attack on Villers-Bocage. At Brieux on 8 August, the battalion was counter-attacked by four Tiger tanks and forced out of the village. The battle swayed to and fro until the battalion resumed the advance at 0300 hours on 9 August. Once more it was fighting against the 12th SS Panzer Division, as the British, Canadians and Poles drove south to close the Falaise Pocket that was to mark the end of the Normandy campaign. In 1946, the Colonel of the Regiment, Field Marshal The Viscount Montgomery of Alamein, ordered the observance of 6 June by the Royal Warwickshire Regiment as Normandy Day to celebrate the regiment's part in the liberation of Nazi-occupied Europe. The Royal Regiment of Fusiliers continues to honour that memory to this day.

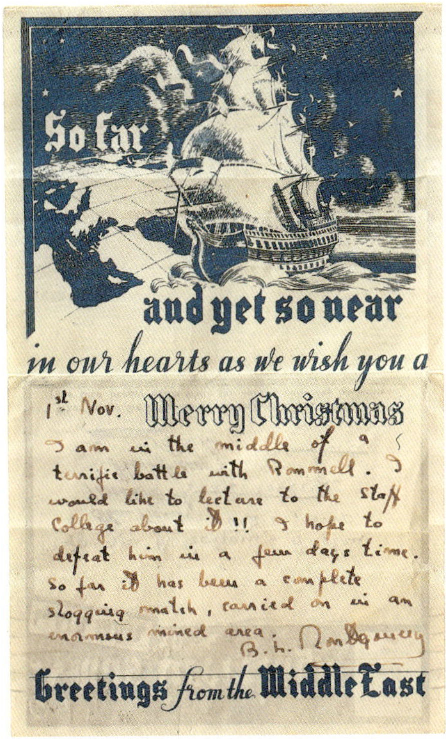
So far and yet so near in our hearts as we wish you a

1st Nov. Merry Christmas

I am in the middle of a terrific battle with Rommell. I would like to lecture to the Staff College about it!! I hope to defeat him in a few days time. So far it has been a complete slogging match, carried on in an enormous mined area.

B. L. Montgomery

Greetings from the Middle East

General Montgomery was an inveterate letter writer even during the battle of El Alamein when he wrote this Christmas Card that mentions - 'I am in the middle of a terrific battle with Rommell'. (sic)

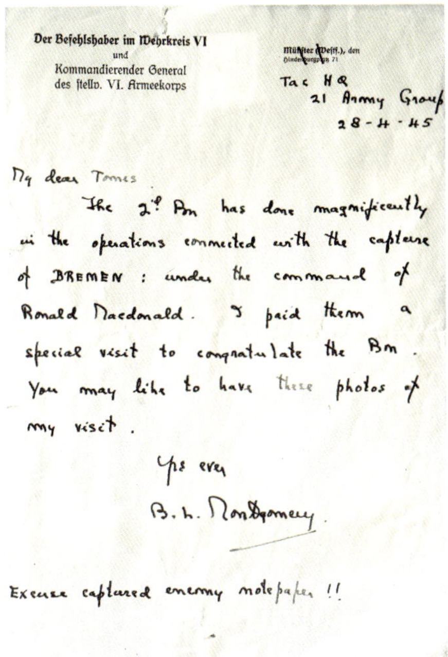
Der Befehlshaber im Wehrkreis VI
und
Kommandierender General
des stellv. VI. Armeekorps

Tac HQ
21 Army Group
28-4-45

My dear Tomes

The 2nd Bn has done magnificently in the operations connected with the capture of BREMEN: under the command of Ronald Macdonald. I paid them a special visit to congratulate the Bn. You may like to have these photos of my visit.

Yrs ever

B. L. Montgomery.

Excuse captured enemy notepaper!!

A letter written on captured notepaper praises the part played by the 2nd Battalion Royal Warwickshire Regiment during the capture of Bremen at the conclusion of the campaign in North West Europe in May 1945.

The Korean War

A 3-inch mortar fires in support of the Royal Northumberland Fusiliers during the battle for Point 217 in October 1951. In early October, the Fusiliers were tasked with the capture of Point 217 during Operation 'Commando'; the first offensive of the 1st Commonwealth Division. On 3 October 1951, the assault began against a well entrenched enemy. Over the next two days, the Fusiliers gained a foothold on the summit on several occasions but each time were forced back. The Chinese abandoned the position on 8 October. During the action, the Fusiliers suffered 113 casualties, including nine platoon commanders and 32 NCOs. As a result W Company was disbanded to reinforce the others. Three weeks later, the battalion embarked at Pusan bound for Hong Kong - Quo Fata Vocant.

On 25 June 1950, the North Korean People's Army crossed the 38th Parallel to invade the Republic of Korea. The United Nations responded by committing troops drawn from several countries, including Britain, under the command of the US Army. The first two British units to be deployed to Korea were 27 Brigade from Hong Kong; subsequently 27 Commonwealth Brigade with the addition of Australian troops. It was followed by 29 Independent Infantry Brigade comprising the 1st Battalion Royal Northumberland Fusiliers, the 1st Battalion The Gloucestershire Regiment and the 1st Battalion The Royal Ulster Rifles. On 10 October 1950, the Royal Northumberland Fusiliers were despatched to the Far East after only eight months of a home posting following 18 years continuous service overseas. The battalion landed at Pusan in Korea on 19 November 1950. Of the 970 Fusiliers in the battalion, approximately 800 were Reservists with another 60 volunteers from other regiments. Together with an attached Belgian Battalion, the units of 29 Brigade were to win lasting fame at the battle of the Imjin River in April 1951, supported by the 25-pounder guns of 45 Field Regiment Royal Artillery and the 170th Independent Mortar Battery RA as well as the Centurions of the 8th Hussars. The Chinese Spring Offensive was unleashed on the night of 22 April 1951 when some 30 Chinese divisions attacked the UN lines in western and central Korea with the intention of capturing the capital, Seoul. The 63rd Chinese Army of three divisions comprising some 30,000 troops fell upon 29 Brigade of 6,000 men. Advancing in human waves, the Chinese Communist Forces crashed against the isolated hilltop positions of the British infantry holding 12 miles of the frontline. Flanked by the Glosters on their left and the Ulsters to their right, the 5th Fusiliers fought an exemplary delaying action, as supporting defensive fires of artillery and aircraft inflicted grievous casualties on the enemy. Against such overwhelming odds, 29 Brigade was forced to withdraw after 72 hours of continuous fighting. Although the Glosters were surrounded and forced to surrender, 29 Brigade had blunted the Chinese offensive to such an extent that the line was soon stabilised and the lost ground recaptured within weeks. Having suffered horrendous losses, the communists realised that their human wave tactics were unlikely to defeat the overwhelming firepower of the UN forces and prolonged truce negotiations ensued. Here, Fusiliers of 10 Platoon Z Company enjoy the warmth from the engine decks of a Centurion tank of the 8th King's Royal Irish Hussars during a patrol on 17 April 1951, a few days before the battle of the Imjin River: subsequently the final Battle Honour of the Royal Northumberland Fusiliers.

Two exhausted Fusiliers catch some much needed sleep in a shallow foxhole with their SMLE No. 4 Rifles readily to hand on the day after the battle of the Imjin River. The Fusilier wearing the beret still has his St George's Day roses behind his capbadge. During the battle, 29 Brigade lost 1,091 men yet, after 24 hours rest, the formation was fit for further operations. The Fusiliers lost 13 killed, including their CO Lt Col Kingsley Foster, 83 wounded and 46 missing. IWM BF10225

In November 1952, D Company under the command of Maj Chard was ordered to raid an enemy strongpoint on a hill feature codenamed 'Mark' which was located some 500 yards forward of the battalion's positions on the high ground of Kigong-Ni. The purpose of Operation 'Pimlico' was to destroy enemy defences and secure prisoners for identification. Company Headquarters and 11 Platoon took up a covering position on the end of a long spur running out towards the enemy. At 0100 hours on 24 November, 10 Platoon as the assault platoon left the start line for the attack. After it had covered about a third of the distance to its objective, a large party of Chinese was encountered and a firefight ensued. As all surprise had been lost, 10 Platoon was recalled but as soon as it had disengaged it clashed with another enemy patrol. Both the assault and the covering platoons were soon being heavily attacked. Many Fusiliers distinguished themselves that night. The radio operator of 10 Platoon was particularly gallant. He kept up a running commentary of the battle over his wireless set until his position was overwhelmed. Here, 10 Platoon of D Company make their final preparations before Operation 'Pimlico' with from L to R L/Cpl Eades (KIA), Fus Hodkinson, Sgt Nash (sideways at back), Fus Gilham (WIA), L/Cpl Clark (with Sten) 2/Lt Hoare (foreground with Sten - KIA), Fus Pryor, Fus Hall and Fus Mills (KIA). For their gallantry, Fusilier Hodkinson received the Distinguished Conduct Medal and L/Cpl Clark the MM. D Company lost 14 dead, 19 wounded and eight missing. Due to various factors, Operation 'Pimlico' was unsuccessful and far too costly in casualties for the intended purpose. Such raids were not repeated. IWM HU68034

Following WW2, the 1st Battalion Royal Fusiliers undertook occupation duties in BAOR and Berlin until 1 April 1952 when the battalion returned to England to complete final preparations for service in Korea. Prior to its departure, the Colonel of the Regiment informed the City of London that he wished the battalion to exercise its ancient right of 'Marching through the City with Drums beating, Bayonets fixed and Colours flying'. On 9 June, the march took place and a few days later the battalion sailed from Liverpool for Korea. Under the command of Lt Col Stevens, the Royal Fusiliers landed at Pusan on 5 August to serve as part of 1st Commonwealth Division. The battalion was deployed on the right flank of 28 Commonwealth Brigade on the Samichon River which was a tributary of the Imjin where the Royal Northumberland Fusiliers had fought with such distinction the year before. By the time of the battalion's arrival, the war in Korea had reached a stalemate as the protracted truce negotiations at Kaesong and Panmunjon continued the while. For the infantry, this meant a war of defensive positions, constant patrolling and the occasional raid with the intention of gaining tactical intelligence of the enemy's dispositions or to capture prisoners. The battalion was usually in the line for periods of three to six weeks followed by three or four in reserve.

Suez Canal Zone and Mau Mau

Returning home from India in 1947, the 1st Battalion Lancashire Fusiliers moved to Warminster in the following year as the demonstration unit at the School of Infantry. In April 1950, it moved to Fayid near the Great Bitter Lake in the Suez Canal Zone. In January 1951, the battalion flew to Aqaba and on 21 April the cruiser HMS *Euryalus* docked at the port. There followed five memorable days of reunion, the first time the ship and the battalion had been together since April 1915. The two then undertook operational duties together during the Persian oil crisis when HMS *Euryalus*, with embarked Lancashire Fusiliers under the command of Maj Shaw, was despatched to Abadan to protect British interests. On its return to the Canal Zone, there was turmoil as the Egyptian government had abrogated its longstanding treaty with Britain and nationalist fervour was growing. The battalion was tasked with internal security duties as terrorist incidents increased. With popular unrest being fomented by the Egyptian auxiliary police, the Commander Middle East decided drastic action was necessary.
At first light, on 25 January 1952, the 1st Battalion Lancashire Fusiliers mounted an operation against the auxiliary police at Ismailia. When challenged, the police refused to surrender and opened fire on the British troops. A firefight ensued which escalated through the morning until one building, the Bureau Sanitaire, had to be stormed by force. Under the supporting fire of Centurion tanks, the Lancashire Fusiliers launched an attack and, after a brief but bitter battle, the police surrendered. Here, the Fusiliers begin their assault into the courtyard of the Bureau Sanitaire behind the Centurions of the 4th Royal Tank Regiment against stiff resistance.
Over 1,000 rifles and many automatic weapons, together with ammunition, were seized. Five Fusiliers lost their lives and nine were injured. A George Medal, a BEM and a Queen's Commendation were awarded to the battalion for this action. In October 1952, the Lancashire Fusiliers were flown to Kenya and, for the next six months, the battalion was the only British unit operating against the Mau Mau. It returned home in August 1953, having spent nearly 2 1/2 years under operational conditions. In November 1953, the battalion moved to Iserlohn as part of BAOR.

On 20 October 1952, a state of emergency was declared in Kenya by the British governor following the emergence of the Mau Mau movement. Originally considered to be a criminal organisation, Mau Mau had grown among the most populous Kenyan tribe, the Kikuyu, with the aim of expelling the white settlers through terror and murder. Under the leadership of Jomo Kenyatta, increasing areas of the 'White Highlands' came under Mau Mau control. However, the insurrection involved less then 20% of the population in less than 6% of the land area of Kenya. In late September 1953, the 1st Battalion Royal Northumberland Fusiliers flew to Kenya in one of the first strategic troop deployments by air. In April 1954, the Royal Northumberland Fusiliers, among 25,000 troops conducted cordon and search sweeps throughout Nairobi during Operation 'Anvil' which effectively cleared the Kenyan capital of Mau Mau sympathisers. 'Anvil' was followed by Operation 'Hammer' in January 1955 when 1RNF swept through the Mau Mau strongholds in the Aberdare Mountains. The latter had been declared a 'Prohibited Area', as was Mount Kenya, which became in effect 'free-fire zones' where Security Forces were allowed to shoot on sight and Lincoln bombers conducted carpet bombing raids on jungle bases. As in Malaya, the Security Forces attempted to separate the insurgents from the indigenous population. The Kikuyu Reserve was designated a 'Special Area' and, by the end of 1954, almost one million Kikuyu tribes people were moved to new protected villages where the supply of food was carefully controlled to deny succour to the insurgents. Between 20 October 1952 and 12 January 1960 when the state of emergency was declared over, 11,500 insurgents had been killed and over 6,000 captured and imprisoned. In the same period, 2,000 native civilians and 600 black members of the Security Forces were killed, often in a most gruesome manner. Thirty two white settlers met their deaths at the hands of the Mau Mau as did 63 white members of the Security Forces while 26 soldiers of the British Army died on active service. From top to bottom - Fusiliers of the Medium Machine Gun Platoon fire their Vickers machine gun in the sustained fire role during an operation below Mount Kenya. Middle - Fusiliers stand guard on the streets of Nairobi during Operation 'Anvil' in April 1954. Bottom - As in all counter-insurgency campaigns, the protection of lines of communication is vital: here, a novel type of transport is employed to patrol the tracks of the East African Railways with members of 5 Pl X Coy ready for action.

Cyprus and Aden

Sgt Hal Lofthouse of 1 RNF quells a hostile crowd single-handedly during disturbances in Aden. This was one of many dramatic photographs by the Daily Express photographer, Terry Fincher, (kindly donated to the Royal Northumberland Fusiliers Museum at Alnwick) depicting the battalion in action in 1967 during the Aden campaign. Such media interest was a foretaste for IS operations in the Province of Northern Ireland from 1969 where imagery of this sort could be used for political ends, not necessarily sympathetic to the British Army.

In August 1954, the 1st Battalion Royal Warwickshire Regiment sailed from Korea to the Suez Canal Zone where it joined 3 Brigade of the 1st Division for the last major exercises to be held in the area by the British, being encamped initially at Kabrit Point and later in Fayid. Subsequently, the battalion was tasked with guarding the massive British Army supply complex at Tel el Kebir prior to its handover to civilian contractors. Meanwhile, the impending move to Northern Ireland had been postponed due to the deployment of the battalion to reinforce the Cyprus Garrison in view of the worsening security situation there. In January 1956, the battalion moved to Cyprus which hitherto had been a leave centre for troops in the Canal Zone. Its arrival coincided with Enosis, the Greek Cypriot wish for union with Greece, which degenerated into a campaign of civil disobedience and then armed insurrection. Based at Wolseley Barracks, the 1st Battalion rotated between the Country and Town Battalion in Nicosia. As the Country Battalion, the troops conducted searches in the out-lying villages and patrols of ten men in two 1/4 ton Champs which were usually a pleasant day in the countryside as compared to duties in Nicosia. The internal security of Nicosia and central Cyprus was the responsibility of the 1st Battalion Royal Warwickshire Regiment and 1st Battalion South Staffordshire Regiment. Here, soldiers of the 1st Battalion Royal Warwickshire Regiment conduct a platoon search for a Greek Cypriot printing works which produced seditious propaganda denouncing the brutality of British forces in Cyprus.

In the long withdrawal from Empire in the post-war years, the British Army fought many hard campaigns but that in the Federation of South Arabia between 1962 and 1967 was particularly bitter; no more so than in the teeming alleyways of the Crater district in the former colony of Aden. Originally a coaling station for the Royal Navy on the trade routes to India and the Far East, Aden had lost its strategic significance but the rise of pan-Arabic nationalism in the early 1960s fomented by Col Nasser of Egypt made disengagement difficult. As in Cyprus and Kenya, a force of two infantry brigades or approximately 25,000 men was needed to contain the insurgency. Up until 1967, the British Army operated in support of the indigenous police but thereafter the situation deteriorated into civil war with the army caught between the two factions vying for power after the British departure, the NLF and FLOSY or the Front for the Liberation of Occupied South Yemen. The 1st Battalion Royal Northumberland Fusiliers deployed to Aden in September 1966 and was soon operating in the sapping heat of the humid Crater district. Between September 1966 and June 1967, the number of terrorist incidents in the Crater district included 212 grenade attacks, 308 shootings as well as 24 mines, booby traps and rockets. In the incident illustrated below, a patrol of X Coy was ambushed on the Aban Road on 3 April 1967 when a grenade exploded wounding a Fusilier before the attacker was shot dead – seen here on the ground with from L to R Fus Hume, Fus Davidge (Injured by grenade fragment), CSM Pringle and Fus Anderson. With the defeat by Israel of the Arab forces in the Six Day War in June 1967, the violence in Aden grew ever worse. This was compounded by police mutinies on 20 June 1967 when two Land Rovers of 1RNF were ambushed on Queen Arwa Road near the Aden Armed Police Barracks in Crater and nine Fusiliers were killed. During the tour a further 35 Fusiliers were wounded. The British finally withdrew from Aden on 29 November 1967. In the period 1674 to 1968, over 22,000 men lost their lives in the service of the 5th Regiment of Foot to the Royal Northumberland Fusiliers.

LANCASHIRE THE FUSILIERS

Four into One

'The British soldier can stand up to anything except the British War Office'
George Bernard Shaw

During the Normandy campaign in the summer of 1944, the British Army suffered appalling casualties and losses became increasingly difficult to replace. During offensives with such harmless sounding operational names as 'Epsom', 'Charnwood' and 'Goodwood', whole battalions were shattered in the dense hedgerows of the bocage. Severe losses continued as the campaign moved eastwards through the Low Countries. By 1945, the British Army was so desperately short of infantrymen that many of those previously classified 4F (medically unfit for service) or else still under 18 years of age were conscripted into the forces. Personnel were also withdrawn from both the Royal Navy and Royal Air Force to take up rifles. So acute was the lack of manpower that vital operations, such as the clearing of the Scheldt estuary to open the port of Rotterdam, were compromised and delayed. Battle weary units were broken up to provide reinforcements for others; famous regiments lost battalions as their personnel were absorbed into other formations in order to provide the necessary numbers for the final offensive into the heartland of Nazi Germany.

In the euphoria of victory, demobilisation was swiftly implemented, but so extensive were the overseas commitments of Empire and occupation that the rate at which soldiers were returned home had to be curtailed. Indeed, some men had to be recalled to the Colours to fulfil particular specialised roles. Perversely, the quest for reduced defence expenditure led to the loss of the second regular battalion of each infantry regiment in 1947. They were 'placed in suspended animation' - the first of many euphemisms for cuts in the army. However, the demand for manpower in the armed forces remained such that National Service had to be introduced in Great Britain in 1949 for the first time in peacetime (except for a few months in 1939 from May to September). The lessons of the war did not go unheeded however and in 1946 the Army Council determined that Infantry Regiments of the Line were to become part of Brigade Groups created on a territorial basis with a shared depot. This had been advocated as early as 1942 by Major General Sir Claude Auchinleck.

The main aim was to allow mutual reinforcements between regiments in each Brigade Group (an ability that the German Army showed with such telling effect throughout the war to form ad hoc units in short order) and the cross-posting of personnel to fill particular positions and appointments. Such moves necessitated a change of regimental cap badge, anathema to many, but an individual regular soldier would resume his own when he returned to his parent regiment. Although such enforced moves between regiments had happened with increasing frequency during World War 2, they were very unpopular as John Newmark of the Royal Warwickshire Regiment affirms - 'At some point during 1943 or 1944, I was transferred to the Shropshire Light Infantry, very much against my will. Most of my platoon were transferred with me and we all refused to "dog trot" on parade. We kept to our regulation pace of 120 to the minute or whatever it was. Furthermore I refused to wear an SLI cap badge, keeping my Warwickshire cap badge up, despite my CO telling me to change it. One day General Montgomery appeared on the scene and congratulated me on wearing the Warwicks' badge - his old regiment - and my CO avoided me thereafter.'

Following the introduction of this measure, the antecedent regiments were disposed as follows with the Royal Northumberland Fusiliers in the Yorkshire and Northumberland Brigade Group; the Royal Warwickshire Regiment in the Midland Brigade Group; the Royal Fusiliers in the Home Counties Brigade Group and the Lancashire Fusiliers in the Lancastrian Brigade Group. Despite these groupings little actual integration occurred during this period except during the Korean War when reinforcements between regiments were commonplace. Both the Royal Northumberland Fusiliers and the Royal Fusiliers received intakes from various units as well as Z Reservists and National Servicemen during their operational tours. Shortly before the ceasefire, the Royal Warwickshire Regiment was deployed to Korea with a significant complement from the Royal Lincolnshire Regiment and the Royal Leicestershire Regiment of the Midland Brigade Group. Similarly, the demands for manpower during the

With all four hackles of the antecedent regiments on display, the Colonel of the Regiment, General Sir Kenneth Darling, inspects the Old Guard at the Depot of the Fusilier Brigade in Sutton Coldfield on St George's day 1968 at the formation of The Royal Regiment of Fusiliers. The Fusiliers were the first infantry regiment in the British Army to establish a truly new Regiment based four-square on the four former regiments and their respective counties and cities. Others were soon to follow the lead of the Fusiliers.

Malayan Emergency necessitated a high turnover of battalions with many National Servicemen being drawn from other regiments.

After the Suez debacle and the Defence Review of 1957 which radically pruned commitments in the Far East, the emphasis focused on the expansion of nuclear weapons at the expense of conventional forces. The army was to be reduced by over half from 373,000 to 165,000 men with a proposed reduction of 60 infantry battalions of which 49 would belong to the Regiments of the Line. Since World War 2, there had been some influential advocates for a Corps of Infantry in place of the regimental system which hitherto had been at the heart of the British Army. The perceived benefits were greater flexibility and easier administration which would reduce costs. This was firmly rejected by the Chief of the Imperial General Staff (CIGS), Field Marshal Sir Gerald Templer (formerly Royal Irish Fusiliers), who endorsed the concept of larger formations through the amalgamation of regiments to reduce overall manpower if necessary rather than losing them through disbandment . Amalgamations had first been used on a significant scale in 1922 as a means to preserve famous regiments - particularly the cavalry. Although the process had been difficult at the outset, time proved to be a great healer and such august regiments as The Life Guards and the 17th/21st Lancers had prospered as a result of successful unions.

To provide greater flexibility and the capability of reinforcement between regiments which had not improved markedly with the introduction of Brigade Groups, the latter were to be superseded by a more formalised brigade structure. Again, the Brigades of Infantry were to be formed on a territorial basis with separate entities for the Fusiliers (thanks to the influence of the CIGS); Light Infantry; Riflemen; the Foot Guards and the Parachute Regiment. Each brigade was to contain either three or four Regiments of the Line in groupings similar to the organisation introduced in 1946. Thus, the Royal Warwickshire Regiment retained two of the same companion regiments - the Royal Leicestershire Regiment and the Sherwood Foresters - but the Midland Brigade Group became the Forester Brigade. The 5th, 7th and XX were withdrawn from their previous territorial Brigade Groups to form the new Fusilier Brigade. Within the Army, the whole process was to take five and a half years. However, as the antecedent regiments did not have to suffer any amalgamations, the Fusilier Brigade was swiftly formed in April 1958.

No sooner had these brigades been formed and a gradual process of integration begun, including a common depot and cap badge for the Fusiliers (its main emblem being St George, the patron saint of England, which was adopted on 7 January 1959), the War Office set up a committee to reorganise the infantry once more in an attempt to resolve the demands for force reduction and the problem of recruiting sufficient manpower, which was to

With Windmill Hill in the background, new Colours are presented to the 3rd Battalion at Gibraltar on Albuhera Day 1970, before some 2,000 spectators and 120 Old Comrades. The Royal Regiment of Fusiliers was the first of the Large Regiments to be presented with new Colours. In late 1971, 3RRF was succeeded as the resident battalion in Gibraltar by 1RRF. By chance, the Quartermasters of the two battalions were the twin brothers, Majors George and Tom Connolly. It is reputed that the handover included an AF 1033 form completed with the words - "1x Rock, last entry".

become even more acute with the ending of National Service in 1962. The Bower Committee was tasked to recommend an infantry organization that permitted, 'with the minimum disturbance', a reduction of up to ten battalions which, looking to the future, 'would remain viable, after the total number of regular battalions had been reduced, should a further reduction be necessary.' In its hidden agenda was the suggestion, should the trend to larger regiments be endorsed that, if a three-regiment brigade had to be sacrificed, it was to be the Fusilier Brigade on account of the geographical separation of its individual regiments which was thought to be inefficient administratively and for recruiting across the brigade.

Perversely, the committee considered that a four-regiment brigade was necessary to allow for contraction yet still remain viable. It further determined that the recently-introduced brigade structure was insufficiently flexible and recommended that the brigades should evolve into what was termed 'Large Regiments' of four battalions each. It was deemed simpler and less traumatic to reduce a regiment by one battalion rather than a brigade by one regiment with the attendant loss to the Army of its heritage and traditions. The concept of the 'Large Regiment' was adopted as policy by the Army Council; as was the interim organization of the four-regiment brigade. Accordingly, the existing three-regiment brigades had either to be augmented or disbanded, and the latter was ordained for the Fusilier Brigade. For territorial reasons, the Royal Fusiliers and the Lancashire Fusiliers were then to rejoin the Home Counties Brigade and the Lancastrian Brigade respectively. In an extraordinary decision, the Royal Northumberland Fusiliers were to join the Royal Green Jackets. The reason for the latter proposal was that there was no existing brigade they could join on a geographical basis - although this was deemed essential for recruiting purposes; whereas the Royal Fusiliers and Lancashire Fusiliers were not to reinforce three-regiment brigades but to join those which had four regiments already. Thus the committee was prepared to sacrifice the Fusilier Brigade and scatter it willy-nilly for reasons that completely defied the logic of its own arguments.

To add insult to injury, it also decreed that the rank of Fusilier be abolished and the soldiers of the 7th and XX become 'Privates', and those of the 5th, 'Riflemen'. In an afterthought, as the term Fusilier had considerable historical significance, the committee suggested that the rank should apply to those soldiers in the anti-tank platoons of all infantry battalions - a feeble compromise guaranteed to offend everyone. To the Fusiliers in their foxholes or APCs, and to the 6th returning from Hong Kong to Germany, such deliberations were beyond their ken, but copies of the committee's report were sent to the infantry regiments for comment before its submission to the Army Council. Not surprisingly, Major General Cosmo Nevill, the Brigade Representative Colonel of the Fusilier Brigade, and its Council of Colonels took grave exception to the report. Learning of Bower's recommendations while fly-fishing in Ireland, General Nevill commandeered the local Donegal telephone exchange, much to the bemusement of its staff, to fire verbal broadsides at the War Office before forsaking his holiday to return, via a hastily convened Council of Colonels, to London on 12 June 1962 . On the following day, General Nevill went to the War Office to present their views to the Bower Committee. There he encountered the former CIGS Field Marshal Templer in an irascible mood leaving the committee room, who greeted him with a curt- 'Your turn, Cosmo; Good luck and give those buggers stick'.

In the event, Nevill not only persuaded the committee to rescind its decision to scrap the Fusilier Brigade but also to consider its enlargement, with the addition of the Royal Warwickshire Regiment as its fourth regiment since the Fusilier Brigade Depot at Sutton Coldfield was in the heart of Warwickshire. In a telephone conversation some days later, General Bower informed General Nevill that the committee had accepted his arguments in full; subject to the agreement of Field Marshal The Viscount Montgomery of El Alamein - the senior serving Infantryman of the Army, the Senior Colonel of Regiment in the Infantry of the Line, the first Brigade Representative Colonel of the Forester Brigade and, last but not least, Colonel of the Royal Warwickshire Regiment. As such his views were decisive and, after consultation with the CIGS, General Sir Richard Hull, and the Colonels of Regiment of the Fusilier Brigade, he concurred with the proposal. General Nevill only learnt of the decision sometime later when he was approached by General Cassels and told cryptically - 'He has agreed'. As a keen advocate of the Large Regiment, Field Marshal Montgomery was no doubt influenced by the strong opposition from elements within the Forester Brigade to the concept and perhaps by his time in command of the 17th Battalion Royal Fusiliers after the

Maj Gen Cosmo Nevill CB CBE DSO was one of the leading luminaries in the formative years of the Fusilier Brigade, which gave rise to The Royal Regiment of Fusiliers. Commissioned into the Royal Fusiliers (City of London Regiment) in 1927, he spent several years with the 1st Battalion in India where he rose to the rank of Lt Col. On his return to the UK in 1943, he was given command of the 2nd Battalion Devonshire Regiment which he led with great gallantry on D-Day and during the Normandy campaign until he was severely wounded in July. After the war, he served at the UN in New York before he became the Chief Instructor at the School of Infantry at Warminster at the same time that 1st Battalion Lancashire Fusiliers was the demonstration battalion. He remarked to its CO, Lt Col Bamford, that - 'In 20 years, all the Fusiliers will be in one regiment'. He was correct to within one year. Lt Col Nevill commanded 1st Battalion Royal Fusiliers between 1950-52. As a Brigadier, he commanded 6 Brigade in BAOR and the School of Infantry at Warminster. He was promoted to Major General in 1956 and commanded the 2nd Division at Hilden in BAOR. Sadly, as one of the most talented soldiers of his generation, Gen Nevill was obliged to retire owing to ill health in 1958. Nevertheless, through his stalwart endeavours before the bureaucratic machinations of the Bower Committee, he saved the Fusilier Brigade from disbandment. Accordingly, the stage was set for the formation of the RRF in 1968.

The Royal Warwickshire Regiment became Fusiliers at the instigation of Lt Col Illing with the full support of FM Montgomery of Alamein. One of the high points of the parade was the donning of the new hackle of orange and blue. Here, the new hackles are marched on by, from L to R, C/Sgt Franklin, RQMS Hoare and C/Sgt Carter. At first, the colours of the hackle were orange over blue but they were reversed at the suggestion of FM Montgomery.

Great War which he remembered with affection. Thus, the Fusilier Brigade was saved and the Forester Brigade doomed. The Brigade Representative Colonel of the latter, who was a longstanding personal friend of General Nevill, never spoke to him again.

In the outcome of the Bower Committee's deliberations, it was no coincidence that there were ten four-regiment brigades (each with a regiment under the threat of disbandment) and three brigades with three regiments to give a grand total of 49 battalions of infantry. Of the presumed unviable three-regiment brigades, the Welsh and North Irish perhaps had some political justification in the interests of a national Army, but the other being the Royal Green Jackets caused widespread resentment, as they were perceived to be immune from reduction for less enlightened reasons. For the Royal Warwickshire Regiment, the new circumstances meant yet another cap badge. Having lost their own Antelope cap badge, which they had worn since the early 18th Century, on joining the Forester Brigade, the 6th now had to adopt the Fusilier badge but with their own distinctive hackle. Following regimental colours, a design of blue over orange was chosen, with the blue denoting the regiment's Royal connections and the orange (or, as regimental tradition insists, 'old gold with a touch of Dutch pink') as a mark of its origins in the service of Holland. Originally, the colours were to be orange over blue but they were reversed at the suggestion of Field Marshal Montgomery who, as Colonel of the Regiment, had the final decision. The regiment's title of the Royal Warwickshire Fusiliers was approved by the Sovereign in November 1962 and a formal parade was held on 1 May 1963 to mark their joining of the Fusilier Brigade.

It was Field Marshal Montgomery's wish that, first and foremost, his regiment must establish themselves as Fusiliers and then for the brigade to become a Large Regiment in accordance with the Army Council's policy. He was convinced that this was the only realistic way forward, both to secure the future of his own regiment and of the regimental system itself. The Field Marshal's views, and those of the other Colonels of Regiments, were codified in a policy statement of 1 May 1963 to coincide with the entry of the Royal Warwickshire Regiment into the Fusilier Brigade. While the way forward was agreed by all parties, the conditional tense in the last sentence of the final paragraph is indicative of the lingering doubts and the difficulties that lay ahead, particularly as there was no specific time scale: 'All Officers and Other Ranks are liable to serve in Regiments of the Fusilier Brigade, other than their own, and cross-postings will be normal. Furthermore, by evolution and the gradual integration of all ranks, the Fusiliers could eventually become one Regiment, should circumstances dictate this change.' With the position of his regiment now secure, Field Marshal Montgomery relinquished the Colonelcy of the 6th on 28 October 1963.
Despite such declarations from on high, the majority of Fusiliers neither wished for, nor

Lt Gen Sir Kenneth Darling, as Commander 1 British Corps, takes the salute at the parade to mark the occasion of the 1st Battalion Royal Warwickshire Regiment becoming the Royal Warwickshire Fusiliers at Hameln in West Germany on 1 May 1963.

regarded, the concept of a single regimental entity as a goal at all. The immediate business of soldiering and the problems of recruiting did not allow for such considerations, and any discussion on the subject tended to highlight the seemingly intractable difficulties of resolving the loss of regimental titles, traditions and accoutrements. In July 1964, a committee was formed to address just such problems and the implications for the brigade of a single regiment. Its findings were considered by the Council of Colonels on 9 July 1965 and, with Lieutenant General Sir Kenneth Darling assuming the appointment of Brigade Representative Colonel on the same day, a consensus emerged as to the manner in which the four regiments were to become one. The fundamental decision was for none of its putative battalions to have any county or territorial affiliations, but for the single regiment as a whole to preserve and foster links with the existing recruiting areas. The battalions were to be numbered from 1 to 4 and all were to perpetuate the combined traditions of the four antecedent regiments. This ran counter to the methodology adopted by other brigades which became Large Regiments at the time. In the Royal Anglian Regiment, the first Large Regiment of Infantry to be formed, its battalions were identified by former regimental titles; for example the 2nd Battalion (Royal Lincolnshire and Northamptonshire) The Royal Anglian Regiment. This was little more than the Fusilier Brigade had achieved already and would still mean the loss of complete regiments and their traditions when the time came for a battalion to be disbanded.

Various titles for the new regiment were considered including 'The Queen's Fusiliers', 'The Queen's Royal Fusiliers' and even 'The Royal Fusiliers', although all of these suggestions were soon to be overtaken by events. It was proposed that to avoid discrimination an entirely new hackle be adopted of Royal Blue; however, there remained a strong sentiment for the Primrose Yellow hackle of the Lancashire Fusiliers as it had been awarded in recognition of the regiment's gallantry at the Battle of Spion Kop and, although not a battle honour as such, it was a singular distinction that deserved to be perpetuated.

Once again there was pressure from the War Office/MOD to accelerate the process of conversion to Large Regiments and although the Fusiliers had by now developed something rather different, its concept was perfectly acceptable to the Army Board.* However within the

*In the major defence reforms initiated by the new Labour Government of 1964, the War Office was superseded by the Ministry of Defence (MOD) and the Army Council became the Army Board.

Field Marshal Bernard Law Montgomery, 1st Viscount Montgomery of Alamein, KG, GCB, DSO. He joined the Royal Warwickshire Regiment from Sandhurst in 1908 and is shown in his guise as the Commanding Officer 17th Service Battalion Royal Fusiliers in 1919.

The Tower of London has had long associations with The Royal Regiment of Fusiliers both as its present Regimental Headquarters and as the birthplace of 'The Royal Regiment of Fuzileers' in 1685. It was also the RHQ and depot of the Royal Fusiliers from 1949-68. At the bottom left of the photograph is the area of the moat that now houses Bobby, the Black Buck antelope Regimental Mascot; close to where the Royal Menagerie was situated in former times.

Fusilier Brigade itself, attention focused on the Territorial Army whose problems had to be addressed following the departure of thousands of National Servicemen in 1965 - National Service required two years in the forces and three in the reserves. In consequence, many TA units were now understrength, with ageing officers, obsolete equipment and inadequate training, although there remained considerable enthusiasm among the dedicated band that formed its core. In the Fusilier Brigade there were six TA infantry battalions - the 4th/5th; 6th and 7th Battalions Royal Northumberland Fusiliers; the 7th Battalion Royal Warwickshire Fusiliers; the City of London Battalion Royal Fusiliers and the 5th Battalion Lancashire Fusiliers. These were shortly to be reduced to three. Up until this time the Fusilier Brigade had been absorbed with the problems of its regular regiments, perforce to the exclusion of the TA battalions which hitherto had not been led to feel part of the brigade at all.

These problems fell squarely in the lap of the new Brigade Colonel, Colonel Bill Etches, late of the 6th, who took up his appointment at the beginning of January 1966. For much of the year, the TA was to be his principal concern, with the creation of the Fusilier Volunteers comprising a rifle company from each of the four regimental homelands, in Territorial Army Volunteer Reserve II, as well as two territorial battalions of Royal Northumberland Fusiliers for Territorial Army Volunteer Reserve III. Of interest, the Fusilier Volunteers exactly replicated the organisation of the proposed regular regiment. Furthermore the soldiers of the new Territorial Army Volunteer Reserve II battalions were to be trained to much higher standards on a par with regulars. This demanded younger and fitter men with more spare time for training than many of the contemporary TA who enjoyed its social and recreational aspects fully. As Colonel Etches observed - 'Efficiency and competence were to increase in inverse ratio to bar profits and avoirdupois'.

During his first year as Brigade Colonel, Colonel Bill Etches also visited each of the regular battalions and to his consternation discovered widespread resistance to the single regiment concept. Many believed that the changes in hand were but the thin end of a wedge designed to create a Corps of Infantry with a single cap badge and thus the end of the regimental system. This prospect was deemed so awful that a hardcore, particularly among the younger officers and the more senior other ranks of the Royal Northumberland Fusiliers and the Royal Fusiliers, had simply closed minds to the whole matter. So disturbed was Etches by this attitude that he wrote an article for publication in the four regimental journals at the end of 1966. In it, he reiterated the vital necessity of closer integration at all levels and the

Recruits for The Royal Regiment of Fusiliers, together with those for The Princess of Wales's Royal Regiment and The Royal Anglian Regiment, were trained at the Depot The Queen's Division, grouped together at Bassingbourn Barracks in Hertfordshire. The Queen's Division is the successor to 17 former county regiments that have been amalgamated over the years to the present three. Bassingbourn replaced regimental depots at Canterbury, Sutton Coldfield and Bury St Edmunds. Recruits underwent 21 weeks of training and some 100 soldiers passed out every four weeks. As an Army Training Regiment, Bassingbourn now accepts recruits from the Royal Engineers and Royal Signals as well, for 11 weeks of basic training before recruits move to their Special to Arm Training. Here, recruits go through body strengthening exercises against the backdrop of a wartime hangar. Formerly an RAF base, Bassingbourn was a World War 2 US Army Air Force airfield of the 91st Bombardment Group (Heavy) and home to the famous B-17 Flying Fortress 'Memphis Belle'. Bassingbourn Barracks was also used as the location of a US Marine Corps facility in the Stanley Kubrick movie, 'Full Metal Jacket'. One of the palm trees from a Vietnam scene was subsequently planted in a Catterick garden as a gift from one RRF RSM to another!

recognition of a common purpose by each regiment to work in a coordinated manner so that - 'If, for reasons outside our control, we have to change to one Fusilier Regiment we will be in the best possible position to do so'.

The ink was hardly dry on this document before rumours began to circulate that there was to be yet another reorganisation of the Army following renewed pressure for defence cuts from the government. However it was expected that there would be extensive consultation throughout the infantry, with a generous time scale for implementing any further changes. Of the former there was none and of the latter very little indeed. On 21 April 1967, the Chief of the General Staff (CGS), General Sir James Cassels, wrote to all Colonels of Regiments that the Army Board had decided on a new structure for the infantry. At a conference held on 8 May at the Old War Office, the CGS dropped several bombshells, not least of which was the need to reorganise the infantry in order to implement 'an early reduction in the number of battalions' against 'a background of a substantial degree of contraction of the armed forces'. A second shock came with his declaration that the Army Board had decided to create yet larger formations by the amalgamation of the existing brigades and Large Regiments into 'Divisions'.

The Deputy Chief of the General Staff (DCGS) then gave a presentation of the new divisional organisation which was deemed to be necessary because the scale of the reductions envisaged would result in the Large Regiments becoming too small for efficiency and economy; indeed, it might even be necessary to amalgamate the Large Regiments. Six divisions were to be formed comprising the Queen's Division (including the Fusilier Brigade, the Queen's Regiment and the Royal Anglian Regiment); the King's Division; the Prince of Wales's Division; the Guards Division (later the Household Division); the Scottish Division and the Light Division. These were to be formed between 1 January 1968 and mid-1969. All officers would henceforth be gazetted, and all soldiers enlisted, into a division, being placed on common rolls to allow free movement between the regiments therein. Such an organisation, the DCGS stated, would survive the immediate - and any future - contractions envisaged. Furthermore, it had been approved by the Army Board 'only after very careful thought, much deliberation and considerable consultation'. Fifty-five Colonels looked at each other in bemusement and wondered whom had been consulted, for they certainly had not.

The second part of the conference was concerned with the method of achieving the reductions required, given that the overall scale was as yet unknown. Government was still to decide the number and the Army Board the particular battalions to be cut. However, at the very least six battalions were to be lost by 1971. The DCGS continued by stating that the the previous policy of forming Large Regiments had now been superseded by that of divisions and those brigades now undergoing change must have completed the process by mid-1968 when the divisions would begin to take over responsibility from the brigades. The day's final bombshell came with the statement - 'No particular measures will be authorised which would run counter to the new divisional plan. For example, no new cap badges will be allowed: it would be wasteful and unnecessary as a divisional badge will eventually be introduced.'

Most Colonels left the conference in a state of shock but they hastily consulted their respective regiments to determine their response. It was apparent that each brigade was to lose one (possibly two) battalions. To many the prospect of a divisional cap badge was the ultimate insult and spelt the end of the regimental system, despite the DCGS's assertion that the 'the new divisional system was designed to preserve all the essential and valuable features of the regiments'. However, it did focus minds sharply. In the Fusilier Brigade, the Colonels were immediately tasked to garner the views of their regiments forthwith. A clear majority restated the agreed policy of proceeding to a single regiment without delay. Even so, the risks of such a course were plain and there was every likelihood that the plan would be overtaken by the reorganisation into divisions when the identity and individuality of regiments might well disappear altogether. However, not all acted with the necessary vigour. Despite being provided with a 1st Class return air ticket, the Colonel of the Royal Northumberland Fusiliers summoned the CO and RSM of the 1st Battalion from Aden for consultation: they were obliged to fly to England by RAF transport plane on 15 May during the midst of an operational campaign.

General Sir Kenneth Darling retired from the Army on 11 November 1969 after 40 years distinguished service. He joined the Royal Fusiliers from the RMC Sandhurst in August 1929 and was the adjutant of the 1st Battalion in India from 1935 to 1938. During World War 2, after a period on the staff, he commanded the 11th Battalion Royal Fusiliers from 1942 to early 1944 when, on the disintegration of the battalion, he was seconded to the Parachute Regiment as Second in Command of its 12th Battalion. He dropped with the battalion in France and was wounded soon after D-Day. In December 1944, he returned to command the same battalion in North-West Europe, including the Rhine crossing. After the war, he took the Battalion to Java. Subsequently, he commanded 5 Parachute Brigade and, from 1948 to 1950, he was Commandant of the Airborne Forces Group. He commanded 16 Independent Parachute Brigade from 1950 to 1952. Thereafter, he held various senior staff appointments in BAOR before becoming the GOC in Cyprus between 1958 and 1960 during the emergency. He was the Director of Infantry from 1960 to 1962 and commander of 1 British Corps from 1962 to 1963. He was then GOC-in-Chief of Southern Command/Strategic Command from 1964 to 1966 and his last active-list appointment was as C-in-C Allied Forces Northern Europe from 1967 to 1969. He retired from the Army in 1969.

He was appointed Colonel of the Royal Fusiliers (City of London Regiment) in December 1963, an appointment he held until 23 April 1968. He was Colonel Commandant of the Parachute Regiment from 1965 to 1967 as well as Representative Colonel of The Fusilier Brigade from 1965 to 1968. It was in this latter appointment that he and his fellow Colonels of the Fifth, Sixth and Twentieth carefully prepared and laid the foundations for The Royal Regiment of Fusiliers, of which he was subsequently appointed the first Colonel. Throughout his Colonelcy and in the years thereafter, his tireless efforts on behalf of the Regiment were an inspiration to all Fusiliers and his contribution to its unity and strength has been without peer. General Sir Kenneth Darling GBE KCB DSO died in 1998.

The Royal Fusiliers were the only one of the four antecedent regiments not to have fought at the battle of Omdurman but soon after they had returned from Korea, they were deployed to Egypt in 1953 and to the Sudan in 1954. Here, the CO of the 1st Battalion Royal Fusiliers, Lt Col Harris, discusses the performance of the Mortar Platoon with its commander, Capt Teague, as the 3-inch mortar team stands by for orders in the desert close to where the battle was fought. In the background is the Gebel Surkab from where the Khalifa watched his army being annihilated during the battle of Omdurman in 1898. In 1956, the battalion deployed to Suez but arrived after the ceasefire. Thereafter, it served in the Persian Gulf and Kenya before spending two years in Malta between 1959 and 1961. Afterwards, the Royal Fusiliers spent most of the following years at Osnabruck in Germany as part of the BAOR.

A Regimental Council was held on 24 May 1967 to respond to the CGS's question to each Brigade how it would choose to effect the loss of any one of its battalions. There were three possible courses open, namely; the disbandment of one existing regiment; the amalgamation of two; or to form a new regiment of four battalions with the expectation of losing one battalion in due course. The latter had been the long stated policy of the council and the four regiments since 1963 and the meeting was held to endorse this as the united response to the CGS. It was therefore all the more astonishing when the Colonel of the Royal Northumberland Fusiliers announced that the 'Fifth Fusiliers' no longer wished to be part of any amalgamations and that to form a new regiment within the permitted time scale would be 'untidy, incomplete and bad for morale'. Moreover, the further change of joining the Queen's Division was equally unacceptable. Above all, his regiment wished to remain 'Fifth Fusiliers', both in title and in fact. While fully supporting the Fusilier Brigade, they had 'always been of it, but not with it' and therefore would choose to remain as they were and accept disbandment of the Royal Northumberland Fusiliers if so nominated. These sentiments, he went on, were those of his serving and retired officers and many senior other ranks.

The other Colonels were flabbergasted and immediately dissociated themselves and their regiments from this proposition which fatally undermined the long-held policy of the brigade. General Darling asked if the 5th fully appreciated the likely consequences of their choice, but on receiving no satisfactory reply he continued that there was grave disappointment with the views of the 5th. He tasked the Brigade Colonel to examine urgently the implications of forming a new regiment from three battalions instead of four. The 5th became the object of considerable bitterness and resentment in the other three regiments in what became known as the 'Defection of the Fifth Fusiliers' which was put down to Geordie stubbornness and the fact that they were currently enjoying widespread publicity and plaudits for their part in the Aden conflict; so soon to be overshadowed by tragedy. General Darling continued to lobby hard and in the following weeks the 5th came under intense pressure from the MOD. In a meeting with the DCGS and the Director of Infantry on 14 June it was made plain to the Colonel of the 5th that they were highly unlikely to survive the first round of cuts. On the following day, Colonel Etches, who was spending the week with the Fusilier Volunteers on their first annual camp at Sennybridge in Wales, was ordered by the Director of Infantry to drive to Camberley and persuade the Colonel of the Royal Northumberland Fusiliers to reconsider his decision. In a difficult interview, during which he was met with only monosyllabic responses, Colonel Etches spelt out the stark choices facing the 5th and reassured him concerning the plan to form a new Regiment. Two days later, a letter of contrition was sent to General Darling seeking his permission for the 5th Fusiliers to return to the fold. This was duly given.

As a former soldier of the Royal Warwickshire Regiment, the Regimental Colonel, Colonel Bill Etches OBE MC, contemplates his Minden Rose before eating it on the first Minden Day celebrations after the formation of The Royal Regiment of Fusiliers. The rose is marinaded in champagne before consumption to make it slightly more palatable. This ritual is necessary only once in a Fusilier's career. Col Etches was the Brigade Colonel from 1966-1968 and Regimental Colonel from 1968-1969; thereafter he was the Regimental Secretary until his retirement in 1985. His tenure of office was renowned for his firm guiding hand in regimental affairs. His penetrating gaze and ferocious interviewing technique are remembered by many regimental officers. He was a truly outstanding servant of the Regiment.

Events then moved quickly and on 14 July 1967, at the 23rd Regimental Council, General Darling indicated that there was considerable back-pedalling with regards to the implementation of the new divisional organisation and, in particular, the imposition of a single cap badge. Following this welcome news, the Council agreed several fundamental decisions including the regiment's title; the regular battalion designations and the design of regimental badges, buttons, emblem and flag. It was decided to adopt the red and white hackle of the 5th as these were also the colours of England and St George and that the colours of the new regiment were to be the rose and primrose yellow of the Twentieth. The most potentially contentious issue of the regimental title was agreed amicably after the earlier proposals were quickly dismissed, because the regiment was to be part of the Queen's Division and any inclusion of the word 'Queen's' in the new title would be a recipe for confusion; particularly as the Queen's Regiment was also part of the division. A further choice of the Royal English Fusiliers was rejected because of the football connotations of its initials. In the event, the title of 'Royal Regiment of Fusiliers' was chosen because it had been the original title of the 7th between 1685 and 1688. Since it had historical significance and yet was not associated exclusively with one regiment for any great length of time, it was therefore the most acceptable to the Colonels. Its shortened name was to be the Fusiliers which was commendably distinctive. Finally, it was agreed that the new regiment's birthday would be St George's Day 1968.

However, on the same day at the brigade cricket week at Hurlingham, some crowing by a coterie of the 5th Fusiliers that their hackle had been chosen for the new regiment was heard. Comments were also passed by some of the diehards in the Royal Fusiliers with regards to the title. General Darling, who had overheard these remarks, became extremely angry at this petty-minded attitude. Some pertinent advice was passed down the chain of command with the result that the most reactionary elements within the Royal Northumberland Fusiliers and the Royal Fusiliers, mainly young officers, were obliged to keep quiet or reassess their commitment to the Regiment. Between eight and ten subsequently resigned their commissions or transferred elsewhere.

The General's humour was not improved on his return to his command at Allied Forces North in Oslo on 18 July when he received a letter from the CGS stating that 'it was his unhappy duty to inform him that the new regiment was to lose its fourth battalion by the end of 1970'. The CGS continued 'how very distressed he and his colleagues were to have to order the disappearance of such a fine regiment as the Lancashire Fusiliers after almost three hundred years of distinguished and gallant service'. Although the sentiments were sound, the CGS and the Army Board thereby displayed little understanding or appreciation of the Fusiliers' aim and purpose in forming the new regiment over two years before the reduction was necessary by which time the fourth battalion would have lost its Lancastrian trappings while its members, traditions and recruiting area would be an integral part of The Royal Regiment of Fusiliers.

As this statement had been released to the press before the letter had even been sent to General Darling, there was nothing to be done to redeem the situation. It caused much resentment in Lancashire and indeed was damaging to morale across the Fusilier Brigade. It was all the more insensitive as the CGS had given his formal authority for the formation of the new regiment on 12 July - the day after he wrote the letter to General Darling. Matters hardly improved through the summer and autumn as bureaucratic red tape conspired to delay and stifle its birth. Forsaking summer leave, regimental staff worked long hours to expedite matters: past favours were called in; old debts redeemed and strings pulled to further the cause. As Colonel Etches wrote in exasperation to General Darling - 'It is quite extraordinary how hard one has to work to get recognition of even the simplest facts of regimental life into some heads in MOD'. Various committees sat to resolve the many practical problems such as the location of the regimental headquarters or those particular regimental customs that could not be readily observed by all of the new battalions such as the Drummers' Colour of the 5th or the Antelope mascot of the Sixth. All these matters were considered on 13 January 1968 at the final Regimental Council held before the birthday of the new regiment on 23 April. Their deliberations were codified in a regimental handbook published before vesting day.

As if the Fusilier Brigade did not face enough problems in forming the new Regiment, the imposition of a further level of organisation with the introduction of the Queen's Division only

The Regiment is fortunate in having its own sea-going yacht, the first of which was a 32-foot Contessa named *FUSILIER* shown here in the early 1980s. During her long and distinguished career, she conveyed many Fusiliers, their families and friends, as well as being available for charter to other Service personnel. This boat was superseded by *BOLD FUSILIER*, a Sadler 34. This in turn was replaced in 1999 by a Vancouver 34 which has reverted to the original name of *FUSILIER*. The new yacht was officially commissioned by the Colonel of the Regiment, Brig David Biggart OBE, and christened by Mrs Carol Biggart on 5 May 1999. *FUSILIER* is based at HMS *Excellent* on Whale Island in Portsmouth harbour.

Cpl Almond instructs Fus Locke and Simpson in the use of the Self Loading Rifle (SLR) on the 50 metre range at the Depot Queen's Division in 1977. At that time, the Depot had a full establishment of nine adult recruit platoons, as well as junior soldiers, which produced over 120 Fusiliers for the regular battalions during the year.

exacerbated them. Many of the responsibilities formerly undertaken by the regiments, such as career management; postings and allocation of recruits, were to be borne by the division. Furthermore, all communications from a regimental level to the MOD were to pass through the Colonel Commandant of the Division who was to be of two-star rank. If the system was to work, such a man would have to be of an exceptionally temperate, patient and impartial nature to satisfy all the conflicting demands of the post. Not surprisingly, none of the major generals from the existing or proposed Large Regiments of the Queen's Division volunteered for the position and the first incumbent was drawn from the Parachute Regiment, although originally Queen's, who was also the Director of Infantry which posed certain conflicts of interest. Those who had served with him previously had not known him as being either patient or temperate.*

Within short order, many Fusiliers had been antagonised by the initial issues considered by the new organisation to be paramount when attempts were made to 'rationalise' orders of dress across the regiments; implement a divisional cap badge and subsume the authority of the Colonels of Regiment. All these measures were resisted diplomatically by General Darling. Many divisional initiatives were introduced with indecent haste and inadequate planning which created a feeling of considerable mistrust in the minds of many regimental officers; warrant officers and NCOs - a legacy that has undermined the acceptance of the divisional concept to this day. One issue that proved particularly vexing was the distribution of recruits across the division. Although cross-postings had been one of the fundamental reasons for the introduction of the brigade groupings, it assumed greater difficulties when applied throughout the Queen's Division. The Fusiliers had traditionally been successful at recruiting soldiers (officers less so), and indeed in the years 1964 and 1965, had been first and second respectively in the infantry.

Of all those tasked with recruiting none was more successful than Major Terry Shaw who achieved the extraordinary rate of attracting on average 15 regulars a month from the Lancashire region in his capacity as Regimental Area Secretary - a remarkable record by any standards which the Queen's Division used to its own ends. Much confusion arose among new recruits who, on joining the Lancashire Fusiliers, were despatched to the depot of the Queen's Division where, before realising what was happening, they could be assigned to the Queen's Regiment thinking they were still in the same organisation. Following the demise of the 4th Battalion The Royal Regiment of Fusiliers in 1970, many more Lancastrians were seduced into the Queen's Regiment whose main recruiting area lay below the 'Fortnum and

* In the best traditions of English fair play, *The Fusilier* provides a kinder assessment in No.1 Vol.5 - page 433.

Leaning against a Daimler Armoured Car Mark 1 outside Linaskea RUC Station in County Fermanagh, Capt Balcon and DI Meharg discuss a suitable route for a mobile patrol along the Northern Ireland border with Eire during the IRA Border Campaign of the late 1950s. In 1957, the 1st Battalion Royal Warwickshire Regiment was stationed in Ballykinler in County Down in what was supposed to be a quiet rural posting after three operational tours overseas. The IRA campaign involved cross-border raids to harass the British presence in the north and to steal arms from RUC police stations and army barracks; the one against the armoury of the Royal Irish Fusiliers at Gough Barracks in Armagh yielded 250 Lee-Enfield rifles, 30 Sten guns and nine Bren LMGs but the IRA failed to steal any ammunition. The campaign, codenamed Operation 'Harvest', began in earnest on the night of 11 December 1956 when a BBC relay station at Rosemount near Londonderry was destroyed, followed by the TA depot at Enniskillen and the county courthouse at Magherafelt being torched. The RUC police stations at Linaskea and Derrylin in County Fermanagh were attacked. Internment without trial swiftly followed in Northern Ireland. Some days later, an abortive attack on the RUC station at Brookeborough in County Fermanagh resulted in the deaths of two IRA men, Sean South and Feargal O'Hanlon. Two new martyrs for the cause were born. By Christmas 1956, the Royal Warwicks were spread widely with a company based at Enniskillen with other platoon deployments and a patrol programme in support of the numerous isolated RUC stations in the border area. They also advised the RUC regarding the defence of the police stations and their fortification with sandbag emplacements and barbed wire entanglements. The campaign continued into 1957 and on 4 July the IRA attacked the RUC police station in Forkhill, South Armagh, killing one constable and wounding another. Public outrage in the south allowed the introduction of internment in the Republic of Ireland; the only way for it to be successful. By the end of 1957, 167 IRA activists had been interned. The campaign limped on with sporadic nuisance attacks until another raid against the RUC in South Armagh resulted in the death of one RUC officer and the wounding of three others at Jonesborough on 12 November 1961. Once more public outrage against the IRA allowed the reintroduction of Military Tribunals in the north and long prison sentences were meted out. IRA morale was shattered and a ceasefire was announced on 26 February 1962. No arms were surrendered and their weapons and explosives were hidden away in dumps for another day. The five-year campaign had resulted in the deaths of 12 men; six RUC and six IRA (four of the latter in one premature explosion), and 38 wounded. Operation 'Harvest' had been crushed and the IRA decisively defeated but the problems remained.

Based at Palace Barracks Holywood, the 1st Battalion Royal Northumberland Fusiliers served in Belfast between 1955 and 1958 during the IRA Border Campaign hence this patrol is armed on the streets of Belfast. Note the officer at left is wearing a side hat.

Mason Line' (ie South East England) where a high employment rate discouraged a career in the armed forces. Indeed, during the 1970s so many recruits from Lancashire were allocated to the Queen's that they were obliged to form a Manchester branch of their regimental association.

Unfortunately, this policy diminished the Lancastrian composition of The Royal Regiment of Fusiliers which fundamentally undermined one of the basic tenets of their formation. Similarly, many of those with City of London roots who had formerly joined the Royal Fusiliers were assigned to the Queen's which over the years has significantly reduced the number of Londoners in the Fusiliers. For a regiment with its headquarters at the Tower of London this was and remains unsatisfactory. At the instigation of General Nevill, the problems of recruiting the right calibre and number of young officers had been addressed by creating a network of regimental officers who were tasked to liaise closely with their old schools in order to introduce candidates for commissions to the Fusiliers at an earlier stage of their education rather then waiting until they arrived at Sandhurst, by which time many had already made up their minds as to which regiment or corps they wished to join. It became the responsibility of the Regimental Secretary to pursue this policy and, from 1971 to 1985, this was Colonel Bill Etches. Many a prospective young officer has enjoyed a generous gin and tonic or glass of sherry at his hands in the salubrious surroundings of the Tower, regimental funds providing a constant supply of liquor to this end. The first officer to be granted a regular commission in The Royal Regiment of Fusiliers was 2nd Lieutenant Roy Wilde.

Parades to mark the Regiment's birthday were held by all battalions and at the depot on St George's Day 23 April 1968. At the time the battalions were deployed as follows with the 1st Battalion (1RNF) at Kirton-in-Lindsey in Lincolnshire; the 2nd Battalion (1R WAR F) at Watchet in Somerset; the 3rd Battalion (1RF) at Sharjah in the Persian Gulf; the 4th Battalion (1LF) in Hong Kong and the 5th Battalion (The Fusilier Volunteers) in their home stations. At all of them, the Special Order of the Day from the Colonel of the Regiment, General Sir Kenneth Darling, was read and the changes of title and of the hackle, except of the latter by the 1st Battalion, were observed. In the 1st Battalion, a St George's Day parade was held. In the 3rd Battalion, a full Trooping of the Colours was conducted in a temperature of 45°C or 114° Fahrenheit. In Hong Kong, St George's Day was observed as the Sovereign's official birthday so the 4th Battalion held a special Fusilier parade to mark both occasions. In the 2nd Battalion and at the depot, a simple parade, including a symbolic changing of the guard ceremony, took place to mark the transition to The Royal Regiment of Fusiliers which is admirably described in the last edition of *The Antelope* and in the first ever issue of the new Regiment's journal *The Fusilier*:-

The Colours of the Royal Fusiliers are trooped for the last time at Sharjah on 23 April 1968 to mark the formation of The Royal Regiment of Fusiliers and the 3rd Battalion. Accompanied by Maj Woodford, OC No. 1 Guard, the Colour Party comprises from L to R, Capt Jones, C/Sgt Welfare, WO2 Coward and Capt Botwright and Sgt Fenn. Captains Jones and Botwright were former RSMs of the 1st Battalion Royal Fusiliers. The ceremony was conducted in temperatures as high as 114°F (45°C) but by then the Fusiliers were well acclimatised and nobody fell out.

'The parade was handed over to the Commanding Officer and the Colours were marched on, the Regiment receiving them with presented arms. There was time for the pensive to reflect that as well as elsewhere in the UK, similar ceremonies had already taken place in Hong Kong and Sharjah and that the names of other famous Regiments were likewise passing into history. Still other names came to mind - Namur, Minden, Lucknow, Khartoum, Sevastopol, Ypres, Dunkirk, Normandy, Burma, Korea - "Royal Warwickshires, Present Arms". The reverie was over, and we were very much back in the present with our thoughts perhaps more on the future than in the glorious past.

'The Colonel of the Regiment had mounted the saluting dais and now stood returning the compliment of his men. The Commanding Officer reported the parade and then accompanied the General on his inspection of the Battalion. Back at the dais, WO2 Sandland was presented with the Long Service and Good Conduct Medal after 18 years' service. The Colonel of the Regiment then addressed the parade and said:-
"Royal Warwickshires past and present assembled here today, in a few moments of time another page in the history of the British Army will have been written. After 294 years of dedicated and distinguished service the name of the Regiment will disappear from the Army List. This is a very solemn moment and I, the last in the line of 33 Colonels, salute you. Your reputation is a glowing tribute and those of you standing on parade today have lived up to it in every way - the Army and the Nation can be proud of you. We will now join together with three other distinguished Fusilier Regiments and form a New Regiment. As my final word I charge you to take with you all your fine traditions, honours customs, and possessions - add to them your unswerving loyalty, and a strong and worthy successor will emerge and enable us all to continue to enjoy the British Infantryman's most precious heritage - that of belonging to his own Regiment."

'Next followed the most symbolic and, for many, the poignant part of the proceedings. On the orders of the RSM, himself a Royal Northumberland Fusilier, the new Brigade Call was sounded to herald the Guard Changing Ceremony. The Old and New Guards had emerged from their positions in rear of the parade and now stood facing each other in front of the dais. The highlight of the ceremony was undoubtedly the moment when the Old Guards slow-marched from parade to the plaintive air of "Auld Lang Syne". Above the heads of the crowd the last we saw of them was the old gold and blue of their plumes and soon they too had disappeared from view. With their passing went the name of the Royal Warwickshire Fusiliers.

Mad dogs and Englishmen - members of C Company wade through the tough 'lallang' grass as they climb a 'bukrit' during a patrol out of Paradise Camp, the British Army training base at the town of Kota Belud in Sabah Province in Borneo. The 1st Battalion Royal Warwickshire Regiment served in Borneo between July and September 1966 after a stop-over in Hong Kong for acclimatisation and the Chinese New Year when civic disturbances were prevalent. The battalion was due to take over an operational area in Sarawak from 40 RM Commando but with the advance party already deployed this was cancelled at the time the ceasefire was declared; with a repetition of their experience of the Korean War and another opportunity for operational service was lost. In one of the most efficient counter-insurgency campaigns ever conducted, the British Army decisively defeated the Indonesian forces of President Sukarno at a cost of 71 soldiers' lives in four years of jungle warfare.

'Nostalgia was however nipped smartly in the bud by fresh words of command and further activity as the New Guard took post on the right flank of the parade. We soon noticed that during the ceremony the new flag of The Royal Regiment of Fusiliers had been broken almost unnoticed at the masthead. The new Regiment was officially in being and its birth was formally announced by General Macdonald, who read the Special Order of the Day and a Loyal Message to Her Majesty The Queen. The Padre read the new Regimental Collect and short prayers of rededication and thus the links of continuity in our traditions had all been quietly but firmly restated.

'The first act *en masse* of the new battalion was an impressive Advance in Review Order crowned by a General Salute, first to General Macdonald then to Field Marshal Montgomery, which was a fitting first gesture of respect by the new unit. During the salute, the Regimental Colour was dipped in recognition of honour done to the Battalion by the presence of the Field-Marshal. In return the Field-Marshal addressed the Battalion. All that then remained was for the parade to march off in column of route to the strains of "The New Fusilier" and "The British Grenadiers". As they came past the saluting base, echoes of commands to the "The Second Battalion The Royal Regiment of Fusiliers" were still ringing in our ears and yet there were the same old faces of the men we had known minutes before as Royal Warwicks.

'The operation had apparently not been so dramatic and painful and indeed this was another milestone rather than a tombstone for the Regiment after all.' Thus the four famous former regiments came together to form yet one more manifestation of the British infantry that had served the crown so faithfully for almost 300 years; indeed the combined total of service of the antecedent regiments was 1,151 years. The Royal Regiment of Fusiliers was determined that there would be many more years yet.

With a Sterling SMG to hand, Lt Milsom disembarks with members of 2 Platoon from a Royal Navy Whirlwind helicopter during Exercise 'First Flight' in November 1960 when the 1st Battalion Royal Warwickshire Regiment was stationed in Hong Kong. Of interest, the soldiers are armed with a mixture of SLRs and No. 4 Lee Enfields.

At the parade to mark the formation of The Royal Regiment of Fusiliers, the 1st Battalion Royal Northumberland Fusiliers presents arms after the advance in review order against a backdrop of FV432 APCs at Kirton-in-Lindsey in Lincolnshire on St George's Day 1968. As the first of the Large Regiments, The Royal Regiment of Fusiliers takes precedence as The 5th in the Infantry of the Line thanks to the seniority of the Royal Northumberland Fusiliers.

Playing Fields
ANDERSONSTOWN
La Salle Boys' School
Holy Child Primary School
St Genevieve's Girls' School
Library
St Agnes RC Church
ANDERSONSTOWN ROAD
St. Joseph's Training College
St Michael's RC Church
St John the Baptist Primary School
Alterations in Progress
Playing Fields
RIVERDALE
LIFT ON SIGHT
Thomas Gorman
24 Carrigart Ave
14.05.45
Francis Quigley
45 Glenalina Rd
29.09.52
Robert Storey
8 Riverdale Pk Sth
11.04.56
Sean Adams
105 B/Murphy Rd
26.06.57
Martin Lynch
89 Stewartstown Pk
22.10.58
B15
RESTRICTED
Army Code No 70771
INSTRUCTIONS FOR OPENING FIRE IN NORTHERN IRELAND
General Rules
RESTRICTED

BAOR Banner and Brandy Sours

'Pride of Regiment is the oldest and brightest weapon in the British soldier's armoury' Sir Arthur Bryant

THE EARLY DAYS

On Vesting Day, the 1st Battalion was stationed at Kirton-in-Lindsey as the UK-based Armoured Personnel Carrier (APC) battalion equipped with FV432s. In March, the Royal Warwickshire Fusiliers had returned from a six-month unaccompanied tour in Gibraltar to their base in Watchet with under four weeks to prepare for Vesting Day. They became the 2nd Battalion as part of 24 Infantry Brigade which was roled for amphibious warfare within the 3rd Infantry Division, The Iron Division. Similarly, the 3rd Battalion returned from Sharjah to Shorncliffe during July and August after almost a year in the Middle East before moving to Gibraltar in the autumn of 1969. As was customary, the three home battalions provided the necessary manpower to fill the ranks of any battalion within the Regiment on an operational deployment, so several were transferred to the 4th Battalion in the Far East.

Despite much sadness at the demise of the famous Fusilier regiments, the parades to mark the forming of the new Regiment had gone according to plan with only minor hitches. There had been no overt displays of tribal intransigence and any demonstrations had been stifled at the outset; the only one of note being the determination of a handful of Royal Fusiliers to go on parade retaining their white hackles. This was thwarted by the RSM, WO1 Jack Hall, who pronounced that the new hackle of red and white - 'were the colours of England and St George and just as importantly, the colours of Arsenal'. A sentiment reinforced by the fact that when he arrived at Sharjah as RSM, WO1 Hall had soon emptied the gaol which was situated in the air-conditioned battalion headquarters building. The miscreants henceforth were imprisoned in a deep hole in the desert with only a canvas tilt for cover. Within days, there were no more defaulters.

In Hong Kong, the Vesting Day of The Royal Regiment of Fusiliers on 23 April was also the official birthday of the monarch so both occasions were celebrated in suitable style. With due regard for the traditions of the former regiments, 25 April was the cause for further commemoration as it marked the anniversary of the Gallipoli landings. For only the second time since 1915, the contemporary HMS *Euryalus* was in port to join the battalion in a combined pageant tracing the history of the XX since its formation in 1688. Once the celebrations were over, the 4th Battalion returned to its operational role of Internal Security (IS) duties throughout the colony and sealing the border against the waves of refugees trying to flee the Cultural Revolution in the Republic of China. One arrival was the British Chargé d'Affaires to Peking, Sir Donald Hopson, who was forced to seek refuge following the sacking of his mission by Red Guards when he refused to kowtow to a portrait of Chairman Mao. During his brief stay in Hong Kong, he only accepted one official invitation. That was for lunch with the 4th Battalion at Gun Club Hill Barracks where he arrived wearing his Lancashire Fusilier tie; one of his few possessions to survive his expulsion. Other activities included Exercise 'Minden Rose' when the battalion flew by C-130 Hercules to the Jungle Warfare School in Malaysia; protecting the populace against the effects of Typhoon Shirley in August and providing an Honour Guard to the United Nations Command for a three month tour in Korea.

During the autumn of 1968, the 1st Battalion undertook training in its mechanised infantry role for two months in BAOR at Sennelager and Soltau. At the same time, the 2nd Battalion conducted a major seaborne assault landing in Northern Ireland from HMS *Fearless*. Exercise 'Swap' involved 6,000 troops of 24 Infantry Brigade roled as the Amphibious Brigade, supported by 45 Royal Marine Commando. They invaded the country of 'Downia' - in fact the rural countryside of County Down. The initial objective was Bishop's Court Airfield where the RSM tried unsuccessfully to evict some SAS troopers from the control tower for his accommodation. The battalion then fought a series of engagements from the beachheads at Ballyhornan southwards. With the SAS acting as the forward reconnaissance element, the brigade made such rapid progress that the whole exercise had to be stopped and reorganised. The battalion was then airlifted to the Mountains of Mourne to engage 39

After Vesting Day, the 4th Battalion Royal Regiment of Fusiliers continued to undertake Internal Security duties in the Crown Colony of Hong Kong. The guarding of the border with the Republic of China against the infiltration of economic migrants and political refugees was a major task, particularly at the height of the Cultural Revolution. Here, Lt Hampton and L/Cpl Roberts conduct a patrol during border duty in the first operational deployment of The Royal Regiment of Fusiliers. The battalion was based at Gun Club Barracks in Kowloon with two companies on the Sai Kung Peninsula. Due to the humidity, acclimatisation took some considerable time and the copious consumption of 'San Mig' beer. In February 1968, the 1st Battalion Lancashire Fusiliers was embarked aboard the Landing Platform Dock HMS *Intrepid* and conducted the first beach landing as a complete battalion since Gallipoli in 1915 during Exercise 'Cherry Blossom'.

The hackle has opened many a conversation and friendship across the world as well as being useful currency for barter. Here, Cpl Williams borrows some transport from a new recruit during Exercise 'Caper' in Cyprus during May and June 1972 while the 1st Battalion was stationed in Gibraltar where training areas were at a premium.

The officers from TAC HQ of 1RRF assemble to celebrate Minden Day under the shadow of the Peace LIne in Belfast with from L to R 2/Lt Allen, Capt Youll, Lt Col Guy, Cpl Kennedy and Lt Col Piggins on the first Operation 'Banner' tour of Northern Ireland conducted by The Royal Regiment of Fusiliers.

Infantry Brigade; the resident British Army formation of some 2,400 men with a party from the 3rd Battalion acting as umpires. However, on account of a rising mist, the helicopters dropped the companies some five miles short of their objective resulting in a gruelling approach march up the mountains. At the conclusion of the exercise, Corporal Tony Reddy of 9 Platoon C Company remembers being somewhat bemused when, returning towards the coast in open Bedford 4-tonners, the Fusiliers were pelted with empty beer cans by the locals. It was a portent of things to come.

OPERATION 'BANNER' - MILITARY AID TO THE CIVIL POWER

In the same month, on 5 October, a parade organised by the Northern Ireland Civil Rights Association in Londonderry degenerated into violence with rioting breaking out in the city and across the Province over the weekend. It was the culmination of months of rising sectarian strife that had stemmed from a campaign of protest and civil disobedience on the part of the Catholic minority and the resulting violence and intimidation against the demonstrators by Protestant factions and elements of the police. The situation deteriorated during the New Year. In April, the first terrorist bombs planted by loyalist extremists exploded destroying water pipelines in the Silent Valley; the area where the 2nd Battalion had conducted Exercise 'Swap' in the Mourne Mountains. Rioting became a daily occurrence in Belfast and Londonderry. By the time of the marching season in August to affirm the Protestant ascendancy, the police of the Royal Ulster Constabulary and its partisan auxiliaries, the 'B Specials', were no longer able to contain the violence as both Catholic and Protestant properties were torched by the opposing mobs. Hundreds of inhabitants were forced to flee their homes. The first troops to be deployed as Military Aid to the Civil Power on the embattled streets of Ulster were 80 men of the 1st Battalion The Prince of Wales's Own Regiment at Waterloo Place near the Bogside of Londonderry at 1700 hours on 14 August 1969. On the following day, the 2nd Battalion Queen's Regiment and a company of the 1st Battalion Royal Regiment of Wales marched into the riot-torn areas of Belfast. It was the start of a campaign that the British Army was to wage for over 30 years during which the Fusiliers were deployed to the Province for a tour of duty on an average of once a year.

During the spring and summer of 1969, the 2nd Battalion participated in Exercises 'Bold Adventure' and 'Canterbury Tales' in Germany, Denmark and France before moving to Berlin in October. In the same month, the 3rd Battalion deployed to Gibraltar for a two year tour with Bobby V arriving from the 2nd Battalion in November. November 1969 was also a sad month for The Royal Regiment of Fusiliers. It saw the retirement of General Kenneth Darling from the Army, although he was to continue as the Colonel of the Regiment, and the disbandment of the 4th Battalion. After their return from Hong Kong to Weeton Camp near Blackpool, the 4th Battalion ceased to exist from 1 November and the majority of its personnel were distributed among the other three battalions. The New Year saw the opening of the Queen's Division Depot at Bassingbourn, near Royston in Hertfordshire, which henceforth acted as the Depot The Royal Regiment of Fusiliers. 1970 also marked the Presentation of Colours to all of the battalions; The Royal Regiment of Fusiliers being the first of the new large regiments to be presented with Colours. The 1st Battalion and 5th (Volunteer) Battalion received theirs on St George's Day from the hands of the recently appointed Colonel-in-Chief, His Royal Highness The Duke of Kent. The 3rd Battalion was given its on Albuhera Day in Gibraltar by the Governor and the 2nd Battalion its on Minden Day in Berlin by the Colonel of the Regiment, General Sir Kenneth Darling. The old Colours of the 1st Battalion Royal Northumberland Fusiliers were laid up in the new regimental museum in The Abbot's Tower at Alnwick Castle on 2 May when the museum was officially opened by the Duke of Northumberland. Those of the 1st and 5th Battalions Lancashire Fusiliers were laid to rest in the parish church in Bury on Gallipoli Sunday.

On 6 May 1970, the 1st Battalion underwent a change of role from mechanised infantry to an airportable battalion within 5 Infantry Brigade which was part of the Strategic Reserve. From the same date, the battalion was put on stand-by for duty in Northern Ireland. The four month emergency tour in Ulster began on 16 June with the battalion moving to Belfast at a time of increasing violence. The battalion was deployed along the east of the Peace Line, around the city centre with part of the Shankill to the north and the Divis Street Upper Falls area to the south; names that were to become depressingly familiar to a generation of Fusiliers. The area of responsibility embraced Catholic, Protestant and mixed parts of Belfast. At first, all groups welcomed the British Army, including much of the Catholic populace which was grateful for some semblance of law and order in the face of the sectarian violence and police intimidation. However, the living conditions for the troops were disgraceful. The TQMS, WO2 Bill Pringle recalls - 'At the beginning, the local population were quite friendly towards us and they kept us supplied with coffee and cakes. Sleeping conditions were deplorable, the men spent the first two nights kipping in doorways - I was in the comparative luxury of a vehicle inspection pit in a garage. Battalion Headquarters and Command Company moved into a disused mill in Hastings Street and I eventually got a room in Hastings Street police station.' These drab buildings were a marginal improvement over the streets. They contained areas known as 'The Pit' where 70 Fusiliers slept and 'The Zoo' where the officers had their quarters. WO2 Pringle continues - 'Before long, the political climate began to change and we were greeted with riots and missiles'.

Through the summer, the riots continued. Reinforcements arrived from the UK and BAOR until eight battalions were stationed in the Province. By July, there were 11,000 soldiers in Ulster as against a peacetime garrison of 2,400. The many arms searches conducted by the Army alienated the Catholics when their homes were ransacked. The situation deteriorated further when the marching season was allowed to proceed by the new government in Westminster against the wishes of the Army. Wherever the Orange marches encountered Catholic territory, fighting erupted. The opportunity for any political settlement was lost. With the Army stretched to the limits, it was unable to protect every Catholic enclave. On the night of 27 June 1970, the small Catholic ghetto of Short Strand in the east of Belfast was attacked by loyalist extremists. A gun battle ensued that lasted all night. Unlike the year before when the IRA did nothing, giving rise to the graffiti 'IRA - I Ran Away', gunmen lurked in the shadows. Five people died, four of them Protestants. The Provisional IRA (PIRA or the Provos) had emerged as the guardians of the Catholic community. The latter began to express their deep resentment at the presence of the British Army as an occupying force to perpetuate Unionist domination. By the time that the 1st Battalion left in October, the PIRA had initiated full scale urban guerrilla warfare following the trend of numerous revolutionary factions across the world. The time of tea and cakes was over. As the Regimental Journal recorded at the time - 'We arrived in June, uncertain what the future held. We shall leave sadder, more experienced people. The problems are great, the solution so doubtful. The response from all ranks of the Battalion has been of the highest order. However it is tragic to have to perform such duties within the United Kingdom. One can only pray that the good sense of all will prevail soon enough to end this tragedy.' Thirty years on, the future of Ulster remains uncertain.

L/Cpl Porter and L/Cpl Wiltshire of Y Company guard the end of a street during a search of the Falls Road area in July 1970. Tactics for riot control at this time were basic as was the personal equipment for such duties comprising little more than a visor for the GS Mark 4 helmet, respirator and the rifle sling looped to the wrist to prevent it being grabbed by a rioter.

Maj N Robinson, Lt Col Webster, RSM Pringle and Sgt Foster confer during a 1st Battalion cordon and search operation on 21 Feb 1971. Serious rioting broke out in the first weeks of February resulting in one soldier killed, another dying of wounds and a third seriously injured. During February, 1st Battalion mounted two operations in the Belfast area. The first was conducted near Drumore with armoured cars of the 17th/21st Lancers in support. The haul from this operation was one ancient rifle, 33 pounds (15kg) of gelignite, 200 rounds of ammunition and sundry para-military equipment of the Ulster Volunteer Force (UVF). In these early days in Ulster, the only concession to combat dress was the wearing of 'flak jackets' - in this case US Army M-1952 Body Armour, and respirators.

Throughout 1970, the 2nd and 3rd Battalions continued to undertake the many ceremonial and public duties associated with postings to Berlin and Gibraltar. These were interspersed with military training in BAOR and in Cyprus and Morocco. The latter became the chosen venue for exercises for the Gibraltar battalion, following the end of training facilities in the Western Desert with the assumption of power of Colonel Gaddafi in Libya. At 1400 hours on Wednesday 13 January 1971, Lieutenant Colonel Bryan Webster took over command of the 1st Battalion. Four hours later, the battalion was warned that it was to be deployed to Belfast on Saturday. Once all the preparations had been completed, the move was cancelled. At 0115 hours on 4 February, the order was resurrected and within 36 hours the battalion had moved to Palace Barracks, Holywood, where 1RNF had been stationed from 1955 to 1957 during the previous IRA border campaign. The tour lasted only three weeks but the situation was tense with the battalion acting as brigade reserve. Soon after arrival, Support Company were attached to the 1st Battalion The Royal Regiment of Wales and Z Company to the 3rd Battalion The Parachute Regiment at the North Howard Street Mill. The remaining companies were on stand-by in Holywood Barracks where they were equipped to Internal Security (IS) scales for riot control. Subsequently, Z Company was attached to the 3rd Battalion Royal Anglian Regiment and Support Company to the Royal Regiment of Artillery. The style and tempo of operations had changed from the previous summer. Riots were now more orchestrated with IRA gunmen using them as cover to shoot at the Security Forces (SF). Although several in the battalion had experience of IS duties from Aden, the use of the box formation had become outdated by the new terrorist tactics. During the tour, the battalion mounted two significant cordon and search operations for terrorist weapons and ammunition in and around the city of Belfast.

The battalion returned to Kirton-in-Lindsey on 25 February and began their preparations to take over from the 3rd Battalion in Gibraltar, one of the last remaining outposts of the British Empire. However, as the infantry battalions of the British Army were quickly learning, Northern Ireland was never far away. The RSM of the 1st Battalion, WO1 Bill Pringle recalls - 'On 16 June with the impending posting to Gibraltar uppermost in our minds, we were ordered back to Northern Ireland to cover the Protestant White Rock march. This must have been the shortest emergency tour on record. We spent three nights under canvas at Long Kesh where it rained for most of the time. At 10 o'clock on the morning of 23rd June the Commanding Officer instructed me to parade the Battalion and shortly after the GOC, Major General Farrar-Hockley, arrived by helicopter. He thanked us for our assistance and told us we would be returning to Kirton-in-Lindsey almost immediately. As we were leaving Long Kesh in convoy we met the Quartermaster Major Tom Connolly with several vehicles full of internal security equipment, shields and flak jackets etc. He had collected these stores from Kinnegar Depot.

RRF BANDS

On 23 April 1968, The Royal Regiment of Fusiliers inherited four regular bands from the antecedent regiments which provided each battalion with its own band. In November 1969, the band of the 4th Battalion was merged with the other three bands when the 4th Battalion was withdrawn from the Army's Order of Battle. Each battalion continued with its own band until 1 April 1984 when the authorised establishment was reduced. The Regiment decided to have two full size bands rather than three smaller ones. These were entitled The Duke of Kent's Band and the St George's Band. The 5th and 6th TA Battalions each continued to have a Territorial band. The two regular bands served with the various battalions as required until January 1994 when they combined while retaining the title of The Duke of Kent's Band. In August 1994, the latter was subsumed into the two bands created for The Queen's Division following a further reduction in the complement of bandsmen. Entitled the Minden and the Normandy Bands, one was based at Catterick and the other at Colchester. With the demise of the Regimental Band, the Corps of Drums within the two battalions have ensured the continuation of the Northumbrian Pipers within the Regiment

Anyone who knew Tom can guess what his reaction would be on being told to return the stores! After a string of choice Anglo-Saxon words he about-turned his vehicles and headed back to Kinnegar.' While this was possibly the shortest Operation 'Banner' tour of Northern Ireland and was dubbed the 'Long Kesh Weekend', the 2nd Battalion claims to have undertaken the longest which was between 24 July 1991 and 20 February 1994.

Before moving to Gibraltar, the 1st Battalion conducted another short tour of duty in Belfast between 11 and 19 August following internment. On 9 August, the mass round-up and detention without trial of republican paramilitary suspects led to widespread rioting and shooting. Catholic support for the IRA rose greatly On arrival, X and Support Companies were attached to the 2nd Battalion The Parachute Regiment in the Ballymurphy area. The remainder of the battalion, with a company of the Green Howards and a squadron of 15th/19th The King's Royal Hussars, was allotted to the Ardoyne district. It proved to be the most arduous tour to date. The bitterness of the people was more apparent and both sides had become polarised beyond redemption. The task of the Fusiliers was more frustrating with the threat of personal danger greater than had been apparent previously. Constant patrolling quickly became monotonous, but always there lurked the very real threat of being shot at, petrol bombed or attacked by proxy bombs that were initiated in a variety of ways. Nevertheless, there were many examples of the kindness and hospitality of the Irish people. Equally, there were innumerable occasions when the Fusiliers were met with a tirade of abuse and obscenities followed by stones and missiles.

Due to faulty and outdated intelligence, internment did not succeed. From September, the PIRA began an indiscriminate bombing campaign against commercial targets. Shootings became an almost daily occurrence. Far from containing the violence, internment led to wider terrorist activity. It was through its lack of an intelligence organisation or sources among the terrorist factions that the British Army remained on the defensive and purely reactive to events. The breakdown in law and order was by now almost complete as police authority had collapsed entirely in many areas. The Army was no longer acting as military aid to the civil power as the latter no longer held sway in the nationalist and loyalist ghettos of Ulster's grimy cities.

FOUR MONTHS IN WINTER

It was against this dismal background that the 2nd Battalion moved from Brooke Barracks in Berlin to Alma Barracks Catterick in North Yorkshire, with notice to deploy to Belfast for a four month tour. All three battalions were to change stations in 1971 but that of the 2nd Battalion was severely compromised by a serious fire in the motor transport section where much of the battalion's baggage was stored prior to its move to Catterick. As a result some 211 single Fusiliers and 80 families lost all or most of their possessions and very few were insured. The total value of private items lost in the fire amounted to £81,118 with a further £49,373 worth of military stores. The move to Catterick coincided with a change of command when Lieutenant Colonel Jeremy Reilly took over from Lieutenant Colonel Alan Wooldridge on 16 July. The battalion now came under command of 24 (Airportable) Brigade, for whom the battalion were obliged to provide manpower for a military tattoo to mark the 1,900 th anniversary of the City of York. This seriously impinged on the comprehensive training programme instituted by the new Commanding Officer. Among the original measures he introduced was the use of slum areas in towns of the North East to replicate the streets of Belfast. Shortly to be demolished for new housing, Exercise 'Crumlin Down' was held in the slums of Darlington and Northallerton. It was made all the more realistic by the participation of the local population and police as well as reporters from the local newspapers and camera crews from Tyne Tees Television. The CO also made sweeping changes of personnel across the battalion in preparation for the rigours of Belfast. As NITAT (Northern Ireland Training and Advisory Team) had not been formed as yet, the Commanding Officer of each battalion had considerable latitude to prepare his men as he saw fit.

Among the most radical innovations was the creation of a dedicated intelligence cell which was despatched to Belfast some weeks prior to the battalion's deployment to Ulster which was completed on 19 October. As part of 39 Infantry Brigade, the battalion were responsible for the predominately Catholic enclaves of New Lodge and Unity Flats together with the staunchly Protestant area of Tiger Bay. Battalion Headquarters was in the Glenravel Street

NORTHERN IRELAND CHRONOLOGY

At the beginning of 1969 there were 2,400 garrison troops in Northern Ireland and the HQ NI officers mess had a grand total of 14 resident officers.

24 April 1969 2 QUEENS deployed to guard key points.

14/15 August Troops deployed onto streets of Londonderry and Belfast.

7 September CS gas used by troops for the first time.

April 1970 Ulster Defence Regiment established.

3 July 1970 First RRF casualties when a grenade explodes in Northumberland Street among 4 Pl X Coy - 8 injured.

9 August 1971 Internment.

30 January 1972 'Bloody Sunday' Londonderry.

31 July 1972 Operation 'Motorman'
largest operation conducted by British Army since Suez with the intention of establishing a permanent presence in all 'no-go' areas in order to dominate extremists and thus neutralise their ability to influence events until a political solution was achieved. 2RRF in Belfast and 3RRF in Londonderry

By the end of 1972, there were 21,000 British troops in Northern Ireland and 9,000 of the Ulster Defence Regiment. The cost of troop deployment to Ulster was £51 million a year.

The walls of every street in Ulster are a canvas for the distorted history of its inhabitants and a means of free expression to convey their political dogma. Much of the graffiti is directed at the British soldier but Fus Galland of 1 Platoon A Company 2RRF shows suitable disdain for the advice on this Belfast street during the battalion's Banner tour of October 1974 to February 1975.

Lieutenant Colonel Jeremy Reilly was the Commanding Officer of 2RRF during its operational tours in Belfast in 1971 and 1972. On the first tour, from October 1971 to February 1972, the battalion was responsible for the Unity Flats and New Lodge areas of North Belfast. Thanks to thorough pre-deployment training and the emphasis on intelligence driven operations, the battalion dominated this area through a combination of aggressive patrolling and targeted operations against the IRA. By the end of the first tour, 2RRF had recovered over 30 weapons and brought IRA activity in their area to a virtual standstill. The second tour was part of the preparation for Operation 'Motorman' when the battalion found themselves sent to Northern Ireland at 24 hours notice in mid-July 1972. Deployed into the Andersonstown area in south west Belfast, the battalion had to live and operate on the streets for the first week as there were no proper Security Forces bases available; but they quickly established themselves as the dominant force in the area. One particular aspect of the battalion's operations was the approach taken with the local community leaders. The battalion's actions were clearly, politely but firmly explained to them at every opportunity, so helping isolate the IRA from the everyday Catholic Community in Andersonstown and once again forcing the IRA to curtail their terrorist activities. By the end of the tour, the battalion had arrested more terrorists than any other unit in Northern Ireland. As a result of his battalion's two highly successful tours, during which he had himself had come under fire several times, Lieutenant Colonel Reilly was awarded the Distinguished Service Order. It was, he is at pains to point out, an award that recognised the achievements of all the Fusiliers he was privileged to command.

police station. By dint of redeploying every single man in the battalion including placing the Corps of Drums in Support Company, 14 rifle platoons were created with a 15th available in an emergency by reducing the administrative tail yet further. Having established themselves in their cramped quarters, the companies began operating in the nationalist areas where the PIRA had complete influence and freedom of action. The opposition had been identified as C Company 3rd Battalion PIRA in the New Lodge area and B Company 1st Battalion of the Official IRA which operated from North Queen Street and Unity Flats. Both were active at the time and responsible for numerous bombings. They were supported by a small unit of the Auxiliary IRA and the youth movement or Fianna as well as *Cumman na Bann*, the female section of PIRA

The objective was to counter both wings of the IRA by mastery of their own areas with constant patrolling and systematic searches based on carefully collated intelligence. This was obtained by various means both overt and covert. The intelligence gained was fundamental to all the offensive operations to eradicate the IRA and reconcile the Catholic community thereafter. Battalion operations were commonly carried out in nationalist areas and were designed to dominate and then search selected areas within a close cordon, both for arms and 'players' of the IRA. Company operations were legion and encompassed every facet of Internal Security duties from riot control to sewer searches as well as constant street patrols. Recurring tasks were the protection of economic targets against bomb attack such as the Gallaghers tobacco factory, one of the only sources of mixed employment in the area; the protection of Catholic schoolchildren using the Antrim Road; the escort of Protestant football supporters up Royal Avenue and past Unity Flats every Saturday; the defence of RUC police stations; the escort of explosives to the quarries at Glengormley or Post Office vans carrying large amounts of money; the guarding of Key Points (KP) such as the Crumlin Road jail or the city docks, and the close protection of bomb disposal teams or Sapper search teams as they undertook their hazardous tasks across the area of operations. Escorts were also provided for Army assets such as water cannon, the mobile library and the mobile fish and chip shop. All the while, street patrolling continued with the innumerable 'P checks' and vehicle searches: B Company examined over 10,000 vehicles during the four month tour of duty.

The 2nd Battalion claimed its first success on the night of 3/4 November when A Company fought a three hour gun battle in Unity Flats. The incident began when a Pig (Humber wheeled APC) of the 1st Battalion Royal Scots came under automatic fire on Upper Townsend Street at 2055 hours. A platoon was deployed to cordon the area, while a second began the search of four suspect houses. This caused a crowd of 60 to assembleand stone the Fusiliers on the cordon, to the accompaniment of women banging dustbin lids. This was met in turn by a volley of rubber bullets until the crowd parted when two gunmen engaged those on the cordon

A mobile patrol passes the Grand Central Hotel during Operation 'Segment' with Sgt McDonald in command, L/Cpls Robinson and Mcloughlin in the back, and Fus Agbadabunia as driver, during the second tour of Belfast by 2RRF in 1972. Operation 'Segment' was intended to reduce the incidence of bomb attacks in the city centre by sealing particular areas and searching all pedestrians wishing to gain entry.

with Thompson sub-machine guns soon after midnight. 1 Platoon returned fire with eight rounds of 7.62 and one of 9mm. One gunman was seen to fall but no follow up was possible because of the hostile crowd. The search continued and once more gunfire came from the flats. Fire was returned but no casualties were observed. At 0113 hours, an ambulance was seen leaving the other end of the flats complex. Followed to the Royal Victoria Hospital, it carried one man who had died of gunshot wounds to the head (Christie Quinn) and one who was seriously injured. He and another suspect were subsequently arrested. During the course of the night, the terrorists fired some 60 rounds and threw three bombs at the Fusiliers who suffered no casualties. The remainder of November passed relatively quietly although the level of bombing did not diminish. Within the battalion area, the hours of patient observing and patrolling were beginning to provide concrete intelligence. On 25 November, a screening operation in New Lodge uncovered three IRA volunteers and an officer from a Fianna company.

With the Christmas season underway, a bomb exploded at 2047 hours on 4 December in McGurk's Bar, a public house on North Queen Street frequented by nationalists. It was completely devastated by a PIRA bomb that had been in transit and had exploded prematurely - 'an own goal' in the jargon of the time.* Fifteen people were killed and 21 injured. Major Jeremy Snow, the OC of C Company, was on the scene immediately and took control of the rescue operation. Many Fusiliers showed considerable bravery that night as they clawed at the rubble with their bare hands to extricate the injured as did the rescue services and scores of civilians. Notable among them was Fusilier Gittens who, acting on his own initiative, burrowed himself into the rubble to a depth of two metres and extricated two survivors while a third died. He was awarded a GOC's Commendation for Bravery. For the first time in many months, Catholic women provided the Fusiliers with cups of tea but as one of them said - 'You may as well drink this now because tomorrow I will be throwing the cups at you'. Four hundred metres away, Major Snow was trying to control two opposing crowds which had gathered, with Protestants from Tiger Bay cheering at the slaughter and the Catholics from New Lodge anxious to retaliate. As he stood in the road between them, a gunmen shot him in the throat and he fell seriously wounded. Although his injuries were grave, they did not appear to be life threatening but he died four days later. Two RUC policemen were also wounded in the incident. In the same evening, the CO's vehicle was fired upon in Halliday Road. Major Jeremy Snow was the first member of The Royal Regiment of Fusiliers to die on active service.

Further tragedy occurred on 8 December when Lance Corporal John Burke was shot in the chest by a sniper as he kept watch on the funeral processions of the victims of McGurk's Bar. The bullet lodged in his spinal column and he was paralysed for life. Thus the cycle of violence continued. On 11 December, the battalion uncovered the largest arms cache of the current emergency in a ground floor flat in Clifton Park Avenue. Large quantities of ammunition, explosives, timing devices and weapons were found. Later in the month information from the Special Branch led to the arrest of the OC of C Company 3rd Battalion PIRA who was the principal bomb maker in the area. A few days later, the explosives officer and quartermaster of B Company 1st Battalion IRA were captured followed by the whole command structure of the Auxiliary Company 3rd Battalion IRA and the majority of the Newington Fianna Company as well. Further arrests were made in the first weeks of the New Year with the result that IRA operations were severely compromised in the battalion's area of operations. Information gleaned from interrogation of those arrested led to further arms finds in a wide variety of places including the boiler room of a Roman Catholic junior school. The weeks of painstaking intelligence gathering had come to fruition so that by the time the battalion left on 16 February, the IRA had been effectively neutralised in the New Lodge area of North Belfast.

As the 2nd Battalion departed, the 3rd Battalion had just arrived for its first four-month Operation 'Banner' deployment to Ulster. Unlike the urban tours of the 1st and 2nd Battalions, the 3rd Battalion was committed across the Province, with A Company and Battalion Headquarters in the lush countryside of County Tyrone on the border with Eire; B Company was attached to the 1st Battalion The Queen's Lancashire Regiment in the Ligoniel area of

* Between 1969 and 1994 ceasefire, the IRA incurred 105 fatalities due to the premature detonation of their own IEDs according to RUC sources.

3RRF OPERATION MOTORMAN

3RRF had hardly finished unpacking from its first tour in Ulster in May 1972 when it found itself back in the Province again as the Spearhead battalion on 11 July after a mere 36 hours warning. Initially the order was for a short deployment to cover the 'Marching Season'. It lasted two months. Deployed to Londonderry, 3RRF was soon in action, taking the war to the IRA which had established itself in 'No-Go' areas, particularly in the Bogside where the IRA believed itself to be immune to the Security Forces. This belief was shattered on 20 July when a carload of IRA gunmen raced to join a gunbattle against one of C Company's patrols. Unfortunately they deployed under the gaze of the recce platoon which had just returned from winning the Sniper Cup at Bisley; all the car's occupants were neutralised at over 1,000 yards. The patrol withdrew intact and 3RRF subsequently conducted operations deeper and deeper into the Bogside. On 24 July 1972, a further heavy gunbattle occurred near the centre of the Bogside involving a B Company patrol that accounted for at least one gunman and a nail bomber. 3RRF was withdrawn from Londonderry on 29 July 1972 before returning to take part in Operation 'Motorman' two days later. Mounted in 34 Saracen APCs, 3RRF invaded the Bogside behind a Centurion AVRE that cleared the barriers en route. After some initial finds of weapons and explosives, the area gradually returned to normal although the rifle companies were working long hours; typically six hours on and six off. The rapid deployment from UK also meant the QM's staff had precious little spare clothing and equipment with which to replace worn out kit. It was also very hot and bathing facilities were limited. On 17 August 1972, Fus Wilkinson of A Company on patrol in the Bogside suddenly felt very tired and had to sit down. He had been shot in the back by a sniper's Armalite with the bullet passing through his flak jacket and body, bouncing off his heart en route. Miraculously he survived and was fit for the next tour in Northern Ireland some five months later. On the next day, LCpl Reilly of B Company was hit in the ankle, again by a sniper armed with an Armalite but his wound was not serious. Sadly, on 24 August 1972, LCpl Davis of the Anti-tank Platoon was shot dead by an Armalite. The Scots Guards who took over from the 3RRF eventually caught the sniper involved. 3RRF left Londonderry on 2 September 1972, moving by ferry from Belfast to Liverpool and troop train to Colchester – then marching from the station to the barracks behind the Regimental Band.

The callous nature of the conflict in Northern Ireland is revealed by the slogan painted on the pavement in red letters - 'ONE IN THE HEAD AND TINGY WAS DEAD'. Soldiers were constantly taunted on the streets of Ulster's towns and cities with the vilest of abuse yet they had to show complete restraint at all times, even in the face of such provocation. Fusilier Alan Tingey was shot by IRA gunman on Kennard Avenue in Andersonstown, West Belfast, on 23 August 1972. In the background is a Saracen APC in desert camouflage. Many of the tropical variants of Saracen that had been returned to the UK after the British expulsion from Libya were employed for Operation 'Motorman' to clear the 'No-Go areas' of Belfast and Londonderry where 2RRF and 3RRF were deployed respectively.

Belfast before moving to Londonderry while C Company joined 16th/5th The Queen's Royal Lancers in County Armagh as they patrolled almost half the length of the border. Support Company was stationed in Lisdhu House which was a country house with delightful grounds but, as in most of the Province, the accommodation for soldiers was deplorable. On arrival it was found that for the 110 Fusiliers of the company there was only one lavatory, two wash basins and virtually no water, no electricity, no gas, no drains and no contractor willing to work there. All three battalions had now experienced the frustrations, the hate and the hopelessness of Ulster while enduring the inevitable quota of casualties. Within months, both the 2nd and the 3rd Battalion had returned to Ulster. On 31 July 1972 they undertook Operations 'Motorman' and 'Carcan' to clear the 'No-Go' areas of Belfast and Londonderry when the British Army presence in the Province rose to an all time high of 21,266 soldiers: yet still the violence continued.

2RRF - OPERATION 'MOTORMAN'

On 10 July, the 2nd Battalion was summoned back from a weekend leave to find themselves promoted to Spearhead Battalion and moved to Belfast within a 12 hour period. The expected four-day deployment to provide additional security to the Orange Day marches soon turned into a four-month tour as the breakdown of the Lenadoon cease-fire, the increasing pressure upon the nationalist 'No-Go areas' and the eventual mounting of Operation 'Motorman' grew in momentum. Rifle companies conducted several relief-in-place operations under fire as they consolidated the previous No-Go area of the Lenadoon Estate and carried out pre-emptive patrolling into West Andersonstown. During a three-week period of intense activity there were several major firefights with exchanges of up to 500 rounds. On 14 July, Fusilier Ian Canham of A Company was killed after he was shot through the rear door of a Pig and another Fusilier wounded. The Fusiliers wounded five members of the IRA whilst they were subject to catapulting and stoning, blast and firebombs throughout three weeks of intensive rioting and sniping.

At dawn on the 31 July, the battalion was the south-western cornerstone of 39 Brigade's part in Operation 'Motorman' - the largest military operation ever conducted in the UK, and at that time, the largest British military operation since Suez. At dawn on that day, the Security Forces seized all the nationalist 'No-Go areas' throughout Northern Ireland, re-imposing the rule of law for the first time in nine months. During the following three months of operations, the battalion tightened its grip upon West Andersonstown and the south west corner of the City, in the process arresting more than 70 Provisional IRA volunteers, including the perpetrators of the Bloody Friday bomb outrage. Throughout this intense period, Fusiliers were rocketed, subjected to small arms attack and faced numerous riots. Tragically, Fusilier Alan Tingey was killed by a sniper in West Andersonstown on 23 August. A PIRA volunteer of 1st Battalion stated on interview that 'the Fusiliers are a professional lot who gripped the area. Its not been gripped before. They are quick with their shooting - and accurate. They are decent too'. During the tour, 87 major incidents occurred, 24 weapons, 21 bombs and more than a ton of explosives were found. In addition to the terrorist arrests, 12 terrorists were hit in firefights and over 80 youths were charged with riotous behaviour and assault. Under Lieutenant Colonel Jeremy Reilly's leadership the battalion was recognised across the Army as the most successful in Northern Ireland and the exemplar for counter-terrorist operations for the years ahead. As a result of these two tours, and a further one in 1973, the success of the battalion was recognised by the award of one DSO, one MC, one MBE, two DCMs, two MMs, two BEMs, four Mentions in Dispatches and five GOC's commendations for bravery.

1974 TERCENTENARY

Despite the growing commitment to the conflict in Ulster, conventional military training continued regardless with the 1st Battalion stationed in Gibraltar undertaking company exercises in the Persian Gulf, Morocco, Cyprus and the south of France during 1972. The 2nd Battalion conducted Exercise 'Pond Jump West' in Canada between their various Belfast tours. All three battalions returned to Ulster in 1973 with the 1st Battalion embarking upon a two year residential tour in Londonderry from June. The 2nd Battalion went twice and the 3rd Battalion once. 1974 was notable as the tercentenary of the Regiment and marked the 300th birthday of two of the antecedent regiments, the 5th and 6th. The event was appropriately

During the border referendum of March 1973, 2RRF was deployed to Belfast in case of further trouble. Here, Fus Ridings, Bridgeman, Bland, McMillan and Downton conduct a patrol in the grounds of the Floral Hall where the votes were counted.

marked and celebrated in the four regimental areas of England with His Royal Highness The Duke of Kent, The Colonel-in-Chief, taking a leading part in regimental affairs. One of the highlights of the celebrations took place on Monday 8 July when the Regiment marched through the City of London with Colours flying, bands playing, drums beating and bayonets fixed. The column comprised the Regimental Bands of the 2nd and 3rd Battalions, the Drums of the 3rd Battalion and three divisions found by the 3rd Battalion and by C (City of London) Company 5th Battalion. The Colours of the 3rd and 5th Battalions were carried. This was the first occasion that The Royal Regiment of Fusiliers had exercised their Privileges in the City of London; an honour inherited from the 1st Battalion Royal Fusiliers which was first granted such Privileges in 1924 by the Council of Aldermen of the City. The battalion also mounted the guard at the Tower of London. Other tercentenary celebrations took place over the Gallipoli weekend in Bury, Rochdale, Salford, Swinton and Ramsbottom. In Northumberland, the occasion was marked under the name Exercise 'Geordie's Pride'. At both venues, the 2nd Battalion exercised their Privileges in Bury and Newcastle-upon-Tyne as well as Berwick-upon-Tweed and Morpeth.

The year was still young when tragedy struck. In the early hours of Monday 4 February, a party of Fusiliers and their families, who were returning in a coach along the M62 motorway from weekend leave in Lancashire, were the victims of an IRA bomb placed inside the luggage compartment. In this dreadful murder, Corporal Clifford Haughton, his wife Linda, and their baby sons Robert and Lee; Lance Corporal James McShane and Fusilier Jack Hynes lost their lives. A further five soldiers died in the explosion. Fusilier Stephen Whalley died of the injuries he sustained three days later in hospital at Dewsbury. All served with the 2nd Battalion. On Armistice Day, General Sir Kenneth Darling relinquished the Colonelcy of the Regiment. A true Fusilier, he had been the principal architect of the Regiment. Employing diplomacy, guile and a forceful temper, he had laid the firm foundations of The Royal Regiment of Fusiliers despite some internal resistance and the external machinations of government and Whitehall. He oversaw the difficult formative years and remained an inspiration throughout his tenure as Colonel of the Regiment. He was succeeded by Lieutenant General Sir George Lea.

Against the backdrop of the notorious 'Free Derry Corner', Fus Strong and WO2 Ryan of Y Company conduct a street patrol in the Bogside in September 1973 during the 1RRF 1973-75 residential tour of Londonderry. On 29 September, Fus Shipley of Y Company was shot in the throat during a patrol in the Bogside and seriously injured.

On 4 February 1974, a coach carrying soldiers and their families exploded on the M62 motorway, killing nine soldiers including four Fusiliers of the 2nd Battalion. The wife and two sons of a Fusilier also died as a result of this IRA bomb attack. The following list records the names of those members of The Royal Regiment of Fusiliers who were killed due to terrorist outrages associated with the conflict in Northern Ireland during the 20th Century:-

Major Jeremy Snow 8/12/71 - Shot and mortally wounded in an IRA gun attack on North Queen Street in North Belfast following the explosion at McGurk's Bar in which 15 people were killed on 4/12/71.

Fusilier Kenneth Canham 14/7/72 - shot by IRA gunman in Lenadoon, West Belfast.

Fusilier Alan Tingey 23/8/72 - shot by IRA gunman on Kennard Avenue in Andersonstown, West Belfast

Lance Corporal John Davis 15/9/72- died from wounds after being shot by IRA gunman in the Bogside on 22/8/72.

Fusilier Charles Marchant 9/4/73 - died from wounds suffered after being shot in the back by an IRA gunman in Lurgan on 26/1/73.

Corporal Clifford Haughton 4/2/74 - killed in M62 coach bomb.
Lance Corporal James McShane
Fusilier John Hynes
Fusilier Stephen Whalley- killed in same incident.

Fusilier Anthony Simmons 15/11/74 - shot in an IRA ambush in the Fountain Street area of Strabane.

Corporal David Gleeson 9/10/75 - killed in IRA culvert mine attack at Lurgancullenboy near Crossmaglen.

Sergeant Simon Francis 21/11/75 - killed by IRA booby trap near Forkhill, South Armagh.

Fusilier Michael Sampson 22/11/75 - killed in an IRA attack on covert OP at Drummuckavall.
Fusilier James Duncan
Fusilier Peter McDonald- killed in same incident.

Corporal Donald Traynor 30/3/76 - killed by IRA booby-trap in Ballygaran Orange Hall near Porrtadown in Armagh.

Corporal Philip Barker 25/1/81 - died of wounds sustained having been shot by an IRA gunman the day before in Belfast city centre.

Corporal Thomas Agar 18/5/84 - killed by an IRA bomb placed under car while off-duty at a fishing competition.
Lance Corporal Robert Huggins - killed in same incident.

Lance Corporal Peter Gallimore 18/10/84 - died of a heart attack brought on by traumatic injuries sustained in an explosion at Enniskillen on 18 May 1984.

Corporal Terence O'Neill 25/5/91 - killed by IED at North Howard Street SF Base in West Belfast.

Fusilier Andrew Grundy 1/5/92 - killed by massive IED at PVCP Romeo 15 at Killeen, South Armagh.

Lance Corporal Michael Beswick 9/2/93 - killed by IRA IED while on foot patrol in Armagh City.

IRA fatalities during the same period were 319 according to the republican newspaper *An Phoblacht*

SPEARHEAD TO CYPRUS

As the residential battalion, the 1st Battalion continued operations in Londonderry and Strabane with the tempo rising markedly with the Ulster Workers Council general strike from 1 May 1974 when the battalion learned such new skills as dispensing petrol. The 3rd Battalion returned from their third tour of Armagh in time for the tercentenary celebrations in London before becoming the Spearhead battalion on Wednesday 17 July. As part of the Strategic Reserve, the Spearhead Battalion was on standby for deployment by RAF C-130 Hercules. Three days later, the Turkish army invaded northern Cyprus following the coup against Archbishop Makarios, the President of Cyprus, after internecine fighting had broken out between the Greek and Turkish Cypriot populace. Shortly before becoming the Spearhead Battalion, the 3rd Battalion had been informed that they would not be deployed to Cyprus as there were sufficient British troops there but that a return to Ulster was most likely. Lieutenant Colonel Ian Cartwright, the CO of the 3rd Battalion, recalls - 'On Thursday 11 July, my 2IC [Major John Rigby] briefed me on his visit to HQ UKLF and we discussed the probable deployment to Northern Ireland. The battalion continued the routine preparations associated with Spearhead duties. That night I dined with the Light Infantry, our neighbours in Colchester. Near midnight I was called to the telephone to be told by someone claiming to be the UKLF duty officer that the 3rd Battalion were to come to 24-hours notice to move to Cyprus. Because of the time, the circumstances and what we had been told, I assumed it was a practical joke. I did nothing.

'Next morning I asked the adjutant if we had received any notification about possible deployment. He knew nothing. I held a conference to discuss our Spearhead preparations, but continued on the assumption that the telephone call had been a joke. That lunchtime A Company, commanded by Major George Curtis, started a long weekend. They were to be the "First Away Company" when we started our Spearhead duties. The rest of the battalion worked normally. The majority of the battalion were on a weekend pass. At about 1730 hours I arrived at my married quarters to receive a telephone call from GSO1 Staff Duties at HQ UKLF. He told me "Last night you seemed to think it was a joke when you were warned off for Cyprus. The battalion will be deployed to Cyprus before you start Spearhead next Wednesday. You are now to come to 24-hours notice to move".' This time I took it seriously! I asked for his telephone number and called him back to confirm the news.

'A mild panic set in when I realised the situation. I called for an 'O' Group in the officers' mess for 2000 hours and got the adjutant and operations officer to start thinking about the problem. The 'O' Group assembled except for the quartermaster and OC A Company, who was sailing in the Solent and not contactable until Sunday. The adjutant telephoned the quartermaster to be told by his wife that George [Major George Connolly] had not come in because she thought it was just another excuse for the Colonel to have a party!

'Obviously the main topic at the meeting was how to recall the battalion. We were forbidden to use the BBC or make any other public announcements. Telegrams could be sent out from Cambridge on the Saturday morning, but would not be delivered until the following Monday. With the co-operation of the local police and through telephone contacts we started spreading the word around Lancashire and Northumberland where most of the Fusiliers were on leave. The meeting adjourned until 0800 hours the next day.

'I had a domestic problem, my two sons were on a barge on the Grand Union Canal with a group of scouts from school. I was due to pick them up on the Saturday afternoon. I decided I had to find them that night. By about midnight I had located them and picked them up.

'On the Saturday morning it was obvious the word was getting around the regimental areas. Fusiliers were calling in to find out what was happening, and some had already started drifting back. Mid morning I received another call from HQ UKLF stating that we should expect to move sooner rather than later. When would the battalion be ready to move? I told them we would be ready to move by midday on Sunday. Fortunately we were reasonably ready to move as companies had packed their stores before the weekend. The only trouble was we had about half of the battalion missing. This situation improved throughout Saturday and Sunday morning as more and more drifted back, but it was not until Monday that we were complete - even absentees had rejoined. But by midday on Sunday we were reasonably ready.

'At lunchtime on Sunday there were parties in the various messes as we prepared to say farewell to our families. During a curry lunch in the officers' mess an apparition had walked in. It claimed to be our new RMO. Major Eustace had been on a caravan holiday on the Essex coast from Edinburgh when he was told to report to us. He only possessed some very casual civilian clothing. The quartermaster had just kitted him out with brand new KD uniform and a large blue floppy beret. He looked like a music hall joke for a soldier. Later he was to prove invaluable and a great asset.'

Among the officers hastily preparing for the Spearhead deployment was the intelligence officer, Captain Richard Mills. He had just returned from HQ UKLF at Wilton with the Top Secret operational maps of the battalion's deployment to Cyprus. Like most Army officers, he had been transported to field exercises by aircraft and had experienced the vagaries of the RAF air movements staff. However, he recalls that he and the operations officer were flabbergasted to receive a telephone call from the RAF inquiring where the battalion would like to fly from to which the operations officer, Captain David Spackman, replied that RAF Wattisham was the most convenient - a Lightning fighter station only 30 minutes down the road. The RAF agreed immediately to fly in the Hercules aircraft to transport the advance party. On its arrival, the operations officer asked about the paperwork and was told not to worry as it was an emergency.

Colonel Cartwright continues - 'Headquarters 19 Brigade had been exercising in Cyprus when the Turks invaded. They had taken over responsibility for the defence of the Episkopi and Akrotiri Sovereign Base Areas. The battalion was to rejoin the brigade in Episkopi. The deployment started on the evening of Wednesday 17th from RAF Wattisham. I travelled ahead of the main body in my staff car with the adjutant and a company commander. On arrival we were met at the guardroom by a smiling Wing Commander Flying. They had been due for a NATO Tactical Evaluation Inspection, but that had been postponed because of the operational move. He invited me to join him and the station commander for a drink in the officers' mess. Sending the adjutant off to sort out the move, I went to the mess with the company commander. We had been there some time when the station commander, to my surprise, asked me what time my flight was. I had assumed he would tell me. A quick call to the movements section indicated the flight had been delayed waiting for me to turn up. We were not popular when we checked in.

'During the flight we received information that we would not be deploying with 19 Brigade, and would be rebriefed on arrival. We speculated that we would go to Nicosia where the Turks were threatening a combined British and Canadian contingent. Our reception and briefing on arrival at RAF Akrotiri was very professionally organized by Headquarters 19 Brigade. We were briefed to relieve 41 Commando in Dhekelia and would move there by air later that morning having transferred from strategic aircraft to in-theatre aircraft.'

Against the backdrop of a refugee transit camp, Fusiliers of 3RRF patrol the perimeter of the Eastern Sovereign Base Area at Dhekelia during the Spearhead deployment to Cyprus following the Turkish invasion in July 1974. IWM MH33820

DUN 22/04
R 220540 Z MAY
FM 3 RRF
TO AIG 1352
AIG 6252

BT
UNCLAS
DIG RTT
FAREWELL TO ARMS IN AREA K
A POX ON ALL THE IRA
GOOD LUCK TO EVERYONE NEAR AND FAR
BE THEY JOCKS IN OLD ARMAGH
OR DUKE OF BOOTS DOWN AT T'MILL
OR SAPPERS GRAFTING AS SAPPERS WILL
OR HUSSARS AND LANCERS ON THE HOOF
(THAT VOICE PROCEDURE - MY HOW SMOOTH)
OR GUNNERS DOING VERY WELL
WITH LOTS OF SHOT BUT DAMN-ALL SHELL
OR THE UDR AND THE RUC
WHOSE HELP-MATES WE HAVE AIMED TO BE
OR BRIGADE HQ AND ALL THEIR SIGS
WE SHALL EVEN MISS OUR DEAR OLD PIGS
AND THE DOE WILL SURELY SEEM
IN RETROSPECT A PLEASANT DREAM
ENOUGH, ENOUGH, WE'RE ON OUR WAY
THISTLES THEN LEEKS WILL SOON HOLD SWAY
JUST ONCE AGAIN WE'D LIKE TO SAY
A POX ON ALL THE IRA
BT

NNNN
TOT 0554
ZEV DP AR

Signal sent on the departure of 3RRF from Northern Ireland in May 1972 by the CO 3RRF Lt Col David Woodford.

In 1674, in the reign of Charles II, ten companies of soldiers were raised in England under the command of Sir Walter Vane to serve with the Protestant States General in the Low Countries against the French armies of Louis XIV. Shortly after arriving in Holland, they were formed into various regiments and fought with great gallantry in the wars against Catholic France. Eleven years later in 1685, two of these regiments were recalled to England by James II at the time of the Monmouth Rebellion. In those days, regiments were known by the name of their Colonel. Monck's and Bellasyes's Regiments were brought on to the English establishment as the 5th and 6th Regiments of Foot; their respective seniority being dependent on which disembarked first on their arrival from Holland. In the same year, the 7th Regiment of Foot or the Royal Regiment of Fusiliers was raised by Lord Dartmouth at the order of James II. Similarly, the 20th Regiment of Foot was raised three years later in 1688 by Colonel Peyton at Exeter at the order of William III on his arrival from Holland. The 5th, 6th, 7th and 20th served continuously and independently for 290 years until 1968 when they were united as The Royal Regiment of Fusiliers. The Regiment celebrated its Tercentenary in 1974, the 5th and 6th Regiments of Foot both having been formed in Holland in 1674.

In the event, the advance party continued its journey in the C-130 and arrived over Dhekelia to find the airstrip deserted. After flying a low pass to determine that the runway was clear, the pilot executed a tactical landing. The Fusiliers unloaded their two Land Rovers and drove to the garrison headquarters to find it deserted as well. As it was the afternoon, the working day in Cyprus had finished at 1330 hours despite the emergency. Eventually, someone was found and the advance party was accommodated in a tented encampment on the playing fields to await the rest of the battalion which arrived within the next 36 hours. The Fusiliers immediately began to patrol the garrison as a visible reassurance to the families and refugees sheltering there. As a further measure, Lieutenant Colonel Cartwright insisted on holding a series of parties to which many of the locals were invited with the officers holding theirs on one evening and the NCOs and then the Fusiliers on successive days.

The 3rd Battalion had arrived in Cyprus on 25 July. A ceasefire was declared on the 30th of the month. With the majority of the British dependents safely evacuated from the Nicosia area, there was little for the battalion to do and so they settled into the comfortable routine of the Dhekelia garrison. In early August, the battalion were warned that they were to be relieved by the 10th Gurkha Rifles and returned to the UK to continue their Spearhead duties. On the day of the battalion's scheduled departure on 14 August, the Turks began the second phase of their offensive with armoured thrusts eastwards from Kythrea towards Famagusta. The 3rd Battalion were stood by 'for any eventuality'. A Company deployed to Ayios Nikolaos on the eastern tip of the Dhekelia Sovereign Base Area (SBA) in the defence of 9 Signal Regiment which was only two miles from Famagusta; the objective of the Turkish offensive. The remainder of the battalion soon followed but they also guarded key installations and conducted numerous patrols in the overall defence of the SBA and the radio monitoring sites. The latter were sufficiently efficient that the British high command were aware of every movement of the Turkish forces in advance of their execution. Accordingly, B Company was able to evacuate British service families from Famagusta before the arrival of the Turks or the bombardment of the port by the Turkish navy and air force with high explosives and napalm.

Once the evacuation of Famagusta was complete, the 3rd Battalion continued to improve the defences of the SBA. The battalion had half of A Squadron 16th/5th The Queen's Royal Lancers equipped with CVR(T) Scorpions under command. For political reasons, the Scorpions were not allowed outside the perimeter of the SBA but even so this was the first occasion that these AFVs had been deployed on active service. Elements of the Greek National Guard retreated in face of the Turkish army and attempted to withdraw through the Dhekelia SBA towards Larnaca and Limassol. The battalion did not allow the passage of any foreign troops through the SBA unless they were disarmed; their weapons being collected and returned once they had been escorted through the base. On 15 August, the Turkish offensive

After a Turkish tank had fired on a British OP position within the British Sovereign Base Area, Colonel 'Biffo' Cartwright converses with the senior Turkish officer that had flown in from Nicosia by the Huey helicopter in the background. Capt Mills is standing on the right of the group of the Turkish helicopter crew and interpreters.

reached the outskirts of Famagusta but as the battle developed, an observation post manned by A Company on the SBA perimeter was engaged by three rounds of 90mm from a Turkish tank, together with several bursts of machine gun fire. Nearby, a television crew was filming the Turkish advance. Fortunately, nobody was hurt but the incident was sufficiently serious for a pair of Phantom fighter bombers to be scrambled from RAF Akrotiri as a show of force. However, the armoured column of 30 M48 and M47 tanks and 30 APCs remained facing the SBA. Realising the gravity of the situation, Lieutenant Colonel Cartwright ordered the Scorpions of the 16th/5th Lancers to pull back to hull down positions as they were no match for the Turkish armour.

In one of those quintessential moments of British bravura, Lieutenant Colonel Ian Cartwright draped a Union Flag over the bonnet of his Land Rover. He, his driver and an interpreter then motored across the open ground with the CO standing upright in the vehicle with his hackle to the fore to demand an explanation from the Turks. One eyewitness reporting for *Soldier Magazine* wrote: 'At this point at 1700 hours today I saw two squadrons of Turkish tanks with armoured personnel carriers drawn up in battle formation in a shallow valley. Lieutenant Colonel, Ian Cartwright, CO of 3rd Battalion, The Royal Regiment of Fusiliers, drove his Land Rover over the 1000 metres to the Turkish squadron and met the unit commander. After pointing out how close the tanks were to the British base, the battle tank formation turned and left. During the 15-minute conference an enormous pall of smoke rising from stricken Famagusta formed a backdrop to the proceedings'. The report in the *Daily Mirror* of 16 August went further: 'A diplomatic British colonel took the tension out of a tricky situation yesterday - with a bit of chat. Lieutenant-Colonel Ian Cartwright, of The Royal Regiment of Fusiliers, strode unarmed across a Cyprus no-man's-land to confront a Turkish tank unit which had opened fire on his men...He said later: "It was the only thing to do. If I had not chatted, terrible things might have happened. When the tank commander saw me coming, he and his unit thundered off. He told another Turkish officer the whole incident was just not on".'

Colonel 'Biffo' Cartwright is too modest a soldier to give but the most cryptic of accounts - 'The Turks fired at an A Company OP on the perimeter. At the time a TV party arrived including Jonathan Dimbleby. A Ferret scout car was also there of 16th/5th Lancers. We got them all out on the back of the Ferret. Later I drove to within about 100 metres of the Turkish formation and then walked to them with an interpreter. The Turks summoned a general from Nicosia who arrived by helicopter. At that stage Richard Mills also arrived with my Rover Group including Dimbleby. This was the first of many contacts with the Turks over the next few weeks. They were not easy people to deal with.' He was assured that the incident had been a complete accident and that the Turks had no intention of entering the Dhekelia SBA. The account in *The Guardian* provides yet more colour to the event: '...The tanks then halted their advance. Lieutenant Colonel Ian Cartwright, commander of the 3rd Battalion, Royal Regiment of Fusiliers drove out to confront the Turkish commander. A helicopter with a Union Jack on it watched from aloft and was joined by a Turkish helicopter from Nicosia. The crews of British Scorpion tanks took up positions and watched Cartwright through field glasses as he walked the last few yards to the Turkish column. "He looked like an advertisement for a deodorant," one of them remarked. "All the Turks were moving away from him".'

Flying in the Sioux helicopter adorned with a Union Flag was the intelligence officer, Captain Richard Mills. Qualified as a Fighter Ground Attack forward air controller, he had been tasked with directing the bombing runs of the Phantoms if the Turks broached the SBA perimeter, which was being marked by the helicopter. When the Turkish tank fired on the Fusilier OP, the shock wave of the projectile buffeted the Sioux helicopter. The pilot immediately dived to ground level and flew nap of the earth through an 'aerial farm' which Captain Mills found somewhat disconcerting. In the event, the Phantoms did not make any bombing runs and Captain Mills landed in the helicopter to join Colonel Cartwright in his meeting with the Turkish senior officer from Nicosia. To forestall a repeat of the misunderstanding, Major Rodney Buckton was attached to the Turkish formation as a liaison officer.

Meanwhile, almost 8,000 Greek Cypriots had been accommodated in a refugee camp in the Athna forest and the Fusiliers were called upon to run it; a task that fell to C Company under Major George Carter. Following the Turkish offensive, the battalion returned to Slim Barracks in Dhekelia and began a four task cycle. The companies were rotated with one guarding

Fusiliers of the 3rd Battalion and the Drums of the 10th Gurkha Rifles provide some entertainment to the Greek Cypriot refugees in the Athna Forest during the Turkish invasion of 1974. The Gurkhas replaced the Fusiliers after the initial Spearhead deployment.
The Royal Gurkha Rifles

The principal Battle Honours of The Royal Regiment of Fusiliers are proudly displayed on a drum bedecked with roses on Minden Day 1984. The distinctive dogged tooth rims of the drums were inherited as a traditional custom of the 5th Regiment of Foot. On 23 April 1968, The Royal Regiment of Fusiliers inherited four regular bands from the antecedent regiments which provided each battalion with its own band. In November 1969, the band of the 4th Battalion was merged with the other three bands when the 4th Battalion was withdrawn from the Army's Order of Battle. Each battalion continued with its own band until 1 April 1984 when the authorised establishment was reduced. The Regiment decided to have two full size bands rather than three smaller ones. These were entitled The Duke of Kent's Band and the St George's Band. The 5th and 6th TA Battalions each continued to have a Territorial band. The two regular bands served with the various battalions as required until January 1994 when they combined while retaining the title of The Duke of Kent's Band. In August 1994, the latter was subsumed into the two bands created for The Queen's Division following a further reduction in the compliment of bandsmen. Entitled the Minden and the Normandy Bands, one was based at Catterick and the other at Colchester. These two bands continue to serve the Regiment to this day.

Ayios Nikolaos, one at the refugee camp, a duty company at Dhekelia SBA and one training or on recreation. Following the end of hostilities, the battalion was anxious to return to the UK as they were scheduled to play a major role in an exercise in the Caribbean. However, the RAF were not so cooperative on the return trip as it was now impossible to fly out of Dhekelia which necessitated a laborious trip by truck to Akrotiri. Similarly, it was quite impossible to fly to RAF Wattisham and the battalion had to return via Lyneham and antiquated coaches to Colchester: the outward journey had taken only seven and a half hours while the return took almost as many days.

The Caribbean exercise involved three rifle companies and most of Headquarters Company. It was designed to practise the deployment of a battalion of infantry by air over long distances. Unlike Cyprus, there did not seem to be the same sense of urgency and the battalion spent long hours waiting at the terminal at Brize Norton. Eventually, the battalion flew to St.Lucia; a name redolent with regimental history. From there, the companies were deployed by the frigates, HMS Eskimo and Tartar, and RAF Andovers to various of the British Virgin Islands. With names dating from the time of the Spanish Main such as Cooper, Salt, Ginger and Peter, the islands appeared to be the idyllic setting beloved of travel brochures but looks were deceiving. Behind the white sandy beeches, the hinterland comprised thorn scrub and cactus plants of the most vicious nature. There the companies chased and captured dissident rebels in the guise of the Reconnaissance and Drums Platoons. Equally vicious were the mosquitoes which Captain David Spackman remembers as 'being as big as crows'; indeed one Fusilier had to be medically evacuated because of multiple mosquito bites. Nevertheless, much useful training was achieved and a similar scenario was to be put to the test for real only three years hence when the 1st Battalion was deployed to Bermuda on Operation 'Orchard'. The battalion returned to England via St Lucia There the Fusiliers toured the battlefield where, in 1778, the 5th Foot had won a famous battle honour and adopted the hackle from the vanquished French that the Regiment wears to this day.

OPERATION ORCHARD - BERMUDA 1977

On 2 December 1977, serious rioting broke out in the British colony of Bermuda following the execution of two local men convicted of the murders of two shop managers and of a former governor, Sir Richard Sharples, and his ADC, Captain Sayers, in 1974. These were the first executions on the island for 30 years. Buildings were fire-bombed as mobs went on the rampage and shops looted, destroying much of the island's foodstocks. Such public disorder posed a significant threat to the island's principal industry of tourism. As the Spearhead Battalion, the 1st Battalion Royal Regiment of Fusiliers were alerted late on 3 December. Urgent telephone calls went out to all personnel with many having misheard the instructions and believing that they were deploying to Belfast, not Bermuda. Within 24 hours, a reinforced company under the command of the CO, Lieutenant Colonel David Betley, had arrived on the Caribbean island. The leading Fusiliers were Z Company plus 7 Platoon of Y Company with a command and logistic element. Although 62 men of the 1st Battalion The Royal Regiment of Wales had deployed there from Belize some hours before, the Fusiliers immediately took up positions around the key installations of Hamilton, the capital of Bermuda, to relieve the pressure on the police and the part-time soldiers of The Bermuda Regiment.

Thereafter, the 186 men of the Spearhead units maintained a low profile and generally only appeared at night to mount guard at Government House; the police headquarters and other civic buildings as well as the power station, oil refinery and the airport. A curfew was imposed from 1800 to 0600 hours. By day, they returned to their quarters at Warwick Camp, the quarters of the Bermuda Regiment. After several nights of guarding KPs, order was restored with only isolated incidents of stoning and petrol bombing. By the end of the first week, the curfew was reduced to nine and then six hours. During the day, the Fusiliers now went to the beach to swim - an event recorded by the local press as no tourists swam during December. In addition, the Fusiliers became the recipients of overwhelming hospitality and numerous gifts, including barrels of beer, 60,000 cigarettes, 12 colour TVs and invitations to the world premiere of 'Star Wars' which was first screened in Hamilton in aid of charity. Much of this was seen as inducements to keep the Fusiliers on the island over Christmas and the New Year in order to safeguard the busy holiday season. In the event, the Fusiliers returned to the UK on 18 December but not before all of their IS equipment, vehicles and combat rations had been purchased by the Bermuda government. Z Company went on leave for a few days before joining the rest of the 1st Battalion on Boxing Day undertaking firefirighting duties during Operation 'Burberry'.

A newspaper article published on 6 December 1977 gives a vivid description of the arrival of the Fusiliers and their reception at the hands of the American press -
'No matter how many obituaries are written on Britain's imperial role, there are bits of it that refuse to go away. There is always some part of the globe that calls for the presence of British armed might at a moment's notice to douse a niggling bit of civil disorder. Whether it is Aden, Northern Ireland, Cyprus, Anguilla or, as is in this case, Bermuda, the chaps bring with them a refreshingly simple philosophy, enunciated yesterday by Major John Varley, of the Royal Regiment of Wales, soon after he and his men had stepped from their aircraft. He said he had heard the rioters and arsonists in Bermuda were rather young. "A little more show of a disciplined body of men will be rather like having their parents start to discipline them", he declared.

'Major Varley's 80 men, many themselves still in their teens, were the first to arrive last night. They had come from Belize where, for the moment, there is a slow season for peace-keeping. The other 180 men, from The Royal Regiment of Fusiliers, came in two aircraft from RAF Brize Norton, Oxfordshire, a few hours later.

'It was a deeply impressive arrival, even if the sense of colourful grandeur was diminished by British troops having to fly into an American naval base, the only suitable military facility on the island. The chubby and cheerful base information officer, called with little warning from a relaxing day by the pool, fussed about in his Bermuda shorts, organising emergency urns of coffee and Kool Aid, a soft drink, for his NATO allies.

'For Commander David Aldrich, a naval officer who is the senior British serviceman in Bermuda, it was also a rare weekend stint. Usually, with only ten men under his command, he can count on untroubled duty hours.

'But this was an emergency as was indicated by the purposive way in which the Fusiliers trotted smartly off the aircraft into the balmy night, setting their faces that little more firmly when they came within range of the television cameras. They looked like a football team coming on to the field for a cup tie, except they wore camouflaged battledress and black berets with red and white plumes they call hackles, earned by defeating the French at St Lucia in 1778.

'All this intrigued the American correspondents who are reporting this skirmish in as large numbers as the British. Most of all they took to Lieutenant-Colonel David Betley, commander of the Fusiliers, whom they saw as an archetypal British officer from the best kind of war films.

HIS ROYAL HIGHNESS THE DUKE OF KENT GCMG GCVO COLONEL-IN-CHIEF

The Colonel-in-Chief receives a demonstration in riot control techniques from L/Cpl Kennedy during a visit to 3RRF at Catterick on 7 May 1985 prior to the battalion's deployment to South Armagh in August. His Royal Highness The Duke of Kent honoured The Royal Regiment of Fusiliers by accepting the appointment of Colonel-in-Chief from Her Majesty Queen Elizabeth II in June 1969. The connection of the Regiment with the House of Kent originates in the year 1789 when His Royal Highness Prince Edward, later the Duke of Kent and the father of Queen Victoria, was appointed the twelfth Colonel of the 7th Royal Fusiliers on 9 April in that year. On 24 February 1790, he arrived in Gibraltar, being received with the honours due to his rank. Prince Edward, who was a Colonel, was Governor of the Fortress and Commander of the Garrison. His Regiment, The Royal Fusiliers, arrived in Gibraltar in August 1790. He was in active command of the Regiment in Gibraltar and later in Quebec from 1790 to 1793. He remained Colonel of the Regiment until 1801. In 1802, Prince Edward, then the Duke of Kent, returned to Gibraltar as Governor and Commander-in Chief. On 11 July 1900, His Royal Highness Prince George, Duke of York, was appointed the first Colonel-in Chief of The Royal Fusiliers by Queen Victoria. He continued as Colonel-in-Chief on becoming Prince of Wales and, later, on his accession to the throne in 1910, as King George V. He held the appointment until his death in 1936. The father of the present Duke and the youngest son of King George V was appointed Colonel-in-Chief of the Royal Fusiliers in March 1937. He was tragically killed on active service in an air crash on 25 August 1942. His Royal Highness The Duke of Kent, the Colonel-in-Chief of The Royal Regiment of Fusiliers, is thus the great-great-great-grandson of the Duke of Kent who was appointed as the Colonel of the Royal Fusiliers in 1789.

As the Spearhead Battalion, elements of 1RRF were deployed to Bermuda in December 1977 at a time of civil unrest to support the local police and the soldiers of the Bermuda Regiment. *SOLDIER Magazine*

After the worst of the disorder during Operation 'Orchard', the Fusiliers had a brief opportunity to see the sights of Bermuda. Here, a Fusilier chats with a couple of fishermen on the sea front. *SOLDIER Magazine*

'Indeed, with his lean, spare appearance, his clipped accent and, most of all, his neat military moustache, it might be suspected that he was chosen for this mission as much for his bearing as for his undoubted military skills.

'Although not fully briefed on the role of his men, he said he assumed, on the basis of his experience in Northern Ireland (seven tours) and other trouble spots, that this was another "sort of meet-force-with-force situation". The troops would take their cue from the local police and politicians and use only the level of force the situation demanded. He exuded confidence, competence and calm.

'While the commander went off for high-level talks, his men climbed into pink school buses and headed for Warwick Camp, where most of them will be billeted. The Bermuda Regiment, who are normally there, have moved into a hotel, which was closed to tourists on Friday after a fatal fire.

'The British forces have brought with them all they need, from their own Land-Rovers and rubber bullets to a public relations man flown out specially from the Defence Ministry.
'Ideally, while no one was unmilitary enough to admit it, a stay of about a fortnight would be most convenient. This would get the men home in time for Christmas, but would mean they missed a stint of London firefighting due to start on December 20. For a soldier, even for a soldier of a declining imperial power, life is full of surprises.

The piece above appeared in *The Times* under the headline - 'A Soldier finds himself far flung in the remnants of the Empire'. In one of his many trenchant witticisms, Oscar Wilde observed that - 'Of all the far flung parts of the British Empire, Ireland was the one part not flung far enough'. A sentiment shared by many Fusiliers but Northern Ireland was to form a central part of the life of all the battalions of The Royal Regiment of Fusiliers from the time of its inception to the end of the 20th Century and beyond. To recount every one of the 33 tours so far undertaken would require several volumes and perforce be repetitive. Thus, it is the intention to describe only some representative tours and one in detail. The latter was that undertaken by the 3rd Battalion at the time of the IRA hunger strikes of 1981.

THE HUNGER STRIKE TOUR OF 1981

Ostensibly, the prisoners at the Maze Prison began their hunger strikes to coerce the government into granting political status to those criminals convicted of terrorist offences. By chance, the MP for Fermanagh and South Tyrone died unexpectedly. The first hunger striker, Bobby Sands, was proposed as the republican candidate for the seat against the wishes of the IRA leadership. His subsequent election to Westminster due to popular sympathy and a split in the Unionist vote persuaded the IRA to pursue a new strategy. Their continuing attempts to oust the British by force were now twinned with political dialogue - the bullet and the ballot. To the Fusiliers on the grimy streets of Belfast and Londonderry or struggling through the thorny hedgerows of South Armagh, such a debate meant little as they returned to the Province time and again to face the discomfort and dangers. However, few Fusiliers would forsake a deployment to Ulster as it was a chance to escape from the routine of soldiering in garrison towns such as Colchester or Paderborn. In Northern Ireland, everyone in the battalion down to section level and the youngest Fusilier had an important part to play in the scheme of things. He was at the centre of the stage and no bit player waiting in the wings. Ten years on, the British Army was by now highly experienced in the skills of Internal Security duties and was equipped accordingly. The IRA had also honed its skills and had reduced its numbers to a hardcore of professional terrorists operating in small, secure cells. Both sides were prepared for a long war.

One of the perennial tasks for the soldier is Aid to the Civil Authorities of which fire-fighting duties during industrial disputes is a recurring assignment. Such deployments are codenamed Operation 'Fresco' in the north of the country and Operation 'Burberry' in the south. Here, Fusiliers of HQ Coy 1RRF pose for a local newspaper in front of one of the antiquated Green Goddess fire appliances they are obliged to use at the Bromley T&AVR Centre in December 1977.

'The familiar sight of Belfast from the Liverpool Ferry was welcoming on that early morning in mid March. I was arriving as part of the advance party to take over from our sister 2nd Battalion and I was the Regimental Sergeant Major. It would be a challenging tour, our recce visits and briefings had shown that with the lowering of tension and a limited deployment of a company to McCrory Park, our worst problem would be the boredom of our non-deployed soldiers. However we had made a number of plans for an intensive round of courses, adventure training, ranges and cadres. We had a major success in most of the families agreeing to accompany their husbands to Belfast. This was mostly due to the innovative idea of allowing a wives recce party to visit some months before, but I was worried that the

restrictions of living behind “the wire” would eventually lead to many wanting to go home to mum.'
WO1 Alan Jones RSM 3RRF

'The 3rd Battalion relieved the 2nd Battalion in Palace Barracks in March 1981. It was a time of considerable optimism in the Province, with an expectation of troop reductions and lowering of the military profile in the City. This optimism probably stemmed from a lack of momentum in the republican campaign. The failure of the 12 year military campaign was becoming apparent. However, this was the stage at which the influence of new thinking in the republican movement, in which Gerry Adams was to play a prominent role, was beginning to make itself felt. Armed struggle alone, represented by the Armalite, had failed to force a decision, and the politico-military strategy of 'the Armalite and the ballot box' resulted. As Adams stated in the Summer of 1981:

> “the concern has always been to assert the political nature of the struggle in which the IRA has been engaged”.*

'This strategy required mass mobilisation to recover the loyalties of a weary population which was being increasingly attracted to support of the SDLP. The brilliant tactic of the hunger strikes - over the issue of political status for republican terrorist prisoners - was the result, and was to form the backdrop to the 3rd Battalion's tour. The battalion initially deployed with a single rifle company in McCrory Park under command of the West Belfast roulement battalion (1st Battalion Royal Welch Fusiliers to begin with, followed by 45 Royal Marine Commando) on a one month rotation. A Company (Major Rodney Buckton) was the first to deploy - the hunger strikes were to keep them deployed there for several months. At the outset of the hunger strikes in April, as Bobby Sands thinned and civil unrest increased, West Belfast was split into two AORs. 1RWF ran the east of the City, based on Springfield Road RUC Station, with bases at North Howard Street Mill, New Barnsley, Fort Whiterock and our own 3RRF company at McCrory Park. 3RRF moved into Woodbourne, taking command of D Company 1 RWF, B Company 3RRF (Major David Spackman) also moved into Woodbourne, and C Company (Major Paul Bibbey) which was based at Andersonstown and the neighbouring bus station. As the hunger strikes wore on, a third battalion was deployed. The Spearhead Battalion, 1st Battalion The Royal Regiment of Wales, was deployed to increase force levels in West Belfast.'
Lt Philip Stack Pl Comd and 2IC C Coy

'Once we were settled in, our principal role was to provide reinforcements when needed for the roulement battalion of the day. We also provided specialist intelligence personnel, with a high level of experience and expertise, to assist the battalion's intelligence effort. In particular, we assisted the RUC Special Branch in terrorist recognition training, and the COP carried out a wide variety of uniformed surveillance tasks.'
Lt Col Geoff Youll CO 3RRF
**H Block/ Armagh Bulletin* Aug 14, 1981, p2

During any urban patrol, it is vital to be aware of what is happening all around so walking backwards for short distances becomes second nature on the streets. At the start of the hunger strike on St David's Day 1981, 2RRF was deployed in Belfast on an Operation 'Banner' tour of duty; it was replaced by 1st Battalion Royal Welch Fusiliers. Here, Fus Ricketts and a companion patrol warily in the Clonard district of Belfast.

A delightful study by Capt David Perry of the Second Fusiliers captures the two most famous accoutrements of The Royal Regiment of Fusiliers - Bobby and the Hackle. David Perry

'When 3RRF were taking over from 2RRF, I was attached to a 2RRF platoon. We were sent to the Divis Flats so that I could shadow the actions of the platoon commander. I was assigned as his "close protection". This meant I got to carry a baton gun. Needless to say, there was trouble and we soon found ourselves being stoned from the first floor balcony of the Flats. I decided to have a go with the baton gun so I loaded a round, raised the gun to my shoulder, looked up to the first floor, stumbled backwards and fired. The round sailed off, hit the underside of the second floor balcony, and rebounded on to a yob's head who was promptly knocked out. The troops looked at me in awe, as it was an incredible shot, achieved by being completely off balance with both eyes shut. I can remember exclaiming to Adam Farnsworth, the platoon commander, "Well, at least all the NITAT training paid off!" It was the first rubber bullet I had ever fired.'
Lt Andy Harris Pl Comd 1 Pl A Coy

'We spent most of our active service carrying out tours of operational duty under the control of the roulement battalions in the nationalist parts of West Belfast. The deployments varied in intensity. The pace, sometimes slow, measured, even soporific, could accelerate with blinding speed. After days, sometimes weeks, of patrolling without any major incident, a sudden shoot, a bomb, a vicious riot, a mortar attack, a rocket propelled grenade, could explode any latent boredom or complacency. At times the tension on the streets was almost palpable, but this was the normal routine for the frequent minor patrol actions that went on in the murky back streets. These were the actions that made up the staple of a soldier's everyday experience. Everyone tried to ensure that alertness was kept at a constant pitch, but it was never easy.

'As most patrols were of only four men spread out over more than ten or 20 yards, a dangerous situation could arise very quickly. Initially only one riot gun was issued to each patrol, but we soon decided to carry two or even three during the summer aggro season. If a patrol was mobbed in this way, the only solution was to come together rapidly to lend one another mutual support and use the riot guns. If things got out of hand, we planned to take refuge in the nearest house - knock down the door, if necessary - and hold it as a fort until the cavalry arrived. Such action, we believed, was preferable to killing members of the public in an act of self-defence.

'The large number of riot guns had another purpose. When a riot exploded on the streets, our aim was to contain it, disperse it, and then restore order by vigorous patrolling. Riots in West Belfast had a particular pattern all of their own. The baddies would form up in the same old places, and attempt to confront the security forces on ground of their choosing. The RUC were old hands and many a time they would sniff the air, declare we were in for a bit of aggro, and then promptly nip any incipient unrest in the bud by the simple expedient of rushing a

In a most unusual scenario, the COs of the three Fusilier battalions 'return' to the Springfield Road SF base from a patrol of the streets of Belfast in early 1981 during the handover between 2nd and 3rd Battalions with (from L to R) Lt Col Tarver (2RRF), Maj Tomes, RSM Rowland (1RRF), Lt Col Youll (3RRF) and Lt Col Robinson (1RRF). Note the Pig with the 'paddy-pusher' bars on the front. This photograph was taken to mark the fact that elements of all three RRF battalions were in Northern Ireland at the same time.

couple of armoured Land Rovers or Pigs to dominating ground. Often, though, the enemy infantry would infiltrate cunningly, usually under cover of some other ostensible purpose, such as coming back from a football match, and then ignite the evening's recreational activities by setting fire to cars and lorries. Our initial response was probably predictable to the seasoned rioter, hardened as he was by years of practising. We would choose a place to stand and attempt to drive the mob back.

'This did not mean we necessarily formed a base line, but we would dominate streets and junctions with groups of patrols, and attempt to catch rioters by use of snatch squads. We would try to manoeuvre behind and to the flanks of the riot, with the simple aim of snatching slower members of the opposition. A technique we developed was battery and assault. We would try and entice the leading edge of rioters to come closer, by giving way. Instead of using three or four riot guns, we would have a battery of eight to 12, all of which would be fired instantly at one tiny sector of the riot frontage. The purpose was to hit a small handful of rioters, perhaps knock some over, and simultaneously loose the dogs of war. This particular tactic used our own mobsters - the company boxing team. Fit, fleet of foot, fearless, and fighting mad, this pride of lions would rocket out, determined to close with the enemy - who fled.

'Of course it didn't always work, but it was aggressive, exciting, and - dare I say it - deeply satisfying. There were dangers. It was possible that the riot was deliberately staged to entice us forward. Petrol bombs, paint bombs, blast bombs, acid bombs, all were used to exact retribution on any unwary manoeuvre by us. One of our platoons was bombarded by more than 300 petrol bombs at New Barnsley after the death of one of the hunger strikers. On another occasion we lost count of the number of blast bombs that rained from the heavens. There was also the ever-present threat of a concealed sniper. The best defence against a sniper is another sniper. We would hide marksmen in covering positions, and every snatch squad -wearing no equipment and armed only with a baton, for lightness and speed - would be accompanied by riflemen.

'Another technique we developed was the "surge". During the summer, the battalion would occasionally be deployed into the city centre to block particular routes that were being used by nationalist marches. A platoon would draw up its Pigs across the road to provide a physical block to the initially peaceful demonstrators. We would deploy the Pigs with their wings out (steel nets that gave protection against thrown missiles), and position a second line of Pigs in depth 20 or 30 yards behind the front line group. The demonstrators would lap right up against the leading Pigs and get frisky. To deter them, the drivers of the leading Pigs would rev their engines and surge forward a few inches, putting the fear of the Almighty into the front. This simple tactic, kept the boyos at a respectful distance, and deterred them from trying to set fire to the Pigs, or from trying to clamber onto the bonnet or roof and to inflict damage on us. The surge never actually hurt anyone but it proved effective.

'Sometimes Fusiliers were employed on special guard duties. Two of our soldiers were lucky to survive assassination attempts in separate incidents when deployed away from their platoons. An RUC Constable injured in a bomb blast was under guard in hospital. One Fusilier on duty with an RUC Constable guarded the injured man inside a locked single ward. A gunman, posing as a doctor, shot dead the RUC guard who opened the door, and escaped in seconds before the Fusilier could react. On another occasion a Lance Corporal and a Fusilier were guarding an elderly UDR soldier in hospital after he had had a heart attack. The Lance Corporal was just inside the entrance corridor to the ward kneeling down behind semi-opaque, semi-rigid plastic doors that overlapped at the centre. The Fusilier was a few feet to the rear. Suddenly, an Armalite rifle, pushed between the plastic doors and just above the head of the lance corporal, fired rapid shots indiscriminately into the corridor. The gunman disappeared within seconds. Luckily, no one was hurt. These two attacks were well planned and executed with daring against armed and alert guards. Such incidents proved that the terrorists lacked neither boldness nor tactical intelligence.

'There's so much more to tell about operations. It's worth recalling, though, that because we were a resident unit, based in the Province for two years, battalion life had to go on regardless. Postings, training, leave, and all the usual activities took place. A few snippets to illustrate. During a month's tour in the base at Woodbourne, our arrival coincided with the death of another hunger striker that provoked riots. Throughout this period sporadic aggro and a spate

ONCE A FUSILIER ALWAYS A FUSILIER
Members of the Fusiliers Association, including Mr Harry Hart, the Secretary of the 8th/9th (Service) Battalions branch, prepare to lay a poppy wreath from The Royal Regiment of Fusiliers at Nimy Bridge on 22 August 1980 to commemorate the VC actions of Dease and Godley in 1914. At the nearby St Symphorien Cemetery where Lt Dease is buried, Remembrance Crosses were laid at the graves of the men of 4th Battalion Royal Fusiliers who fought at the crucial holding action on that day. In the same cemetery in the Fusilier Corner, a memorial was erected by the German Army in recognition of the gallant men who fought against them in the distant days of 1914. The Fusiliers Association is very much an integral part of the Regiment. It is the main way in which former soldiers of all ranks keep in touch with comrades after leaving the active list. Each of the four Regimental areas has an Honorary Chairman (usually a retired senior officer) with the Assistant Regimental Secretary in the area as his secretary. There is a total of nearly 40 branches organised on a basis of town or area, battalion or central registers. Most branches are thriving, holding monthly meetings and other activities. Inevitably, as time passes, those branches based on World War 2 battalions are beginning to struggle but as they fade away, new branches open for new Fusilier members. There are 2,500 active members of branches country wide with many hundreds more who receive branch information but take little part in activities. Each year the Regiment holds the Fusilier Gathering which is open to all members of the Regiment, past and present.
It is hosted in turn by the two Regular Battalions and the various Regimental Area Headquarters. It is usually attended by 300-400 of the Association members. It starts on a Saturday with lunch, then a different activity depending on location (for example, with a Regular Battalion it is often a display of current weapons and equipment, football and sports). In the evening there is a dinner/dance and on Sunday morning a parade and Drumhead Church Service and lunch. Branch activities vary widely from an informal get-together in a local pub to annual dinner and dances. They include branch visits to the Regular Battalions and places of military interest or visits to battlefields where members can see modern trends in the Army or honour the graves of fallen comrades.

1RRF BELFAST 1976 -
A TYPICAL OPERATION BANNER TOUR
On its sixth tour of Ulster, the 1st Battalion were deployed to the 2nd Battalion's old stamping ground in West Belfast patrolling the nationalist strongholds of Ballymurphy, the Lower Falls and Beechmount Estate. With 544 Fusiliers, Battalion HQ was in the Springfield Road with company bases at Henry Taggart Base, a former community centre; Broadway Camp, a former mortuary and McCrory Park, a children's playground. In four months, the 1st Battalion discovered 341 pounds of explosives; 15 incendiary bombs; 28 timing devices; one mortar bomb; 2,000 rounds of ammunition and numerous weapons. 59 people were arrested and charged and 300 apprehended. One Fusilier was killed and three others shot and injured. Eight others were injured by IEDs. For this, they were paid an 'environmental allowance' of 50 pence a day extra.

of car hijackings and occasional shooting kept us at full stretch. Yet during that month the company won the battalion athletics competition, fought and won the inter-company boxing, won the rifle match in the skill at arms meeting, and produced six successful candidates at the grade 1 soldier board. We also painted Woodbourne camp and Fusiliers Peszel and Robins painted a mural 10 feet high depicting a B Company Fusilier. Life was busy, challenging, exciting, tiring, rewarding, in about equal measure.'
Maj David Spackman OC B Coy

'We arrived just in time for the hunger strike, which gave rise to the longest period of brutal and vicious rioting seen since the early 1970s, accompanied by an upsurge of bombings, shootings and sectarian murders. Within a few days Battalion HQ was deployed to Woodbourne Hotel [3 May 1981], reopened for the purpose, and given a Tactical Area of Operational Responsibility which included the Twinbrook, Poleglass, Ladybrook, Suffolk, Lenadoon, Riverside, Andersonstown, Turf Lodge and the Ballymurphy. Under command were A Coy 1RWF, C Coy 3 RRF, and eventually, Support Company 1RRW (from the Spearhead Battalion), plus our own COP, Drums Platoon, RMO, REME, Chefs, etc. This gave us the opportunity to make up a joke sign, 3 RR(W)F - 3rd Battalion Royal Regiment (Welch) Fusiliers. We were also regularly reinforced by bricks from our own Headquarters Company, known as either Oscar Sierra (Old Soldiers) or P Company (Pensioners).'
Lt Col Geoff Youll CO 3RRF

'I was the 2IC of the battalion, so was therefore mainly responsible for the general training of the battalion during the two year tour, primarily to ensure that the troops were properly trained for their next role in Germany. We maintained an approximation of the training required to enable the career patterns of the young Officers, SNCOs, and the JNCOs to be maintained. We also had to ensure that we retained those skills within the battalion necessary for low intensity conflict. The CO had charged me with ensuring the well-being of the soldiers as regards adventurous training and extra-mural activities. Each were mutually exclusive, and were difficult to achieve while we were involved with the IRA.'
Maj George Molyneux-Carter 2IC 3RRF

'For ourselves and our families, the facilities "behind the wire" were relatively good, with a swimming pool, riding stable, coffee shop, Plastic Pub and of course, the three messes. We even had our own mobile Fish & Chip Van, called "The Irish Potato", run by two of our battalion wives. Once we were back in barracks, and running the normal roulement and deployments downtown, we settled down into being a sort of self-contained small town or village.'
Lt Col Geoff Youll CO 3RRF

'Once the rioting started in earnest, it was necessary to deploy the whole battalion downtown - it is probably unique but we moved downtown lock stock and barrel for a month. Shut down everything we could and sent everyone, so only a few storemen were left to get the food downtown and a small guardforce. Messes were closed, just pocketed the key and off we went as it was necessary to have all hands to the pump to reinforce the rifle companies. A fourth company was formed equipped with riot equipment but, although derisively named Oscar Sierra Company for Odds and Sods or Pappa Company for Pensioners by the other rifle companies, its members had a tremendous amount of experience through the older NCOs who preferred to be called P Company for obvious reasons. There was also an under-18 platoon which was not allowed downtown and they were used as guards, together with the band whose instruments were locked away as they were required to man the sangars. HQ Company sent every possible man so even the "base rats" such as the company clerks went downtown.'
Maj Richard Mills OC HQ Coy

'We all thought when the hunger strikes started that they wouldn't go the distance as before, but it became apparent that things were changing. It was almost as if there was a honeymoon period. Initially the local people appeared to tolerate us being in their midst but they turned to despising us. The IRA PR machine was good. There was political march after political march involving all the residents associations. I sensed they wanted death. They are a nation who love death, they're professional mourners. I can imagine how disappointed the people of West Belfast in the Falls, Andy Town, Turf Lodge and Ballymurphy would have been if those people had come off hunger strikes. We all remembered when Bobby Sands died but who can remember the second or third let alone the fourth or fifth.'

Sgt Bob Broadbent Bn Int NCO

'As Sands weakened, tension mounted. As far as C Company were concerned, the Turf Lodge was almost a no-go area. The inhabitants had barricaded all of the access routes in and out. This was a double-edged weapon for them. It impeded our access in but we were content to hold them behind their barriers and keep the major routes open. Most barricades were formed from burnt-out lorries and cars obtained through hijacking. Hijacking was particularly prevalent on the link road to the west of the Turf Lodge, and 8 Platoon under Lt Mark Hawkins were tasked to do something about it. The platoon moved into the Oliver Plunkett School and established an OP which gave a good view of the areas where hijackers operated. After about 12 hours two youths were seen stopping traffic, and the Platoon Sergeant [Sgt Sean 'Jock' Reilly] led a section to intercept them, whilst Lt Hawkins maintained observation from the OP, Sgt Reilly [plus Fusilier Andy 'Bush' Bushell] worked himself into a position just some 40m from the hijackers and waited until the OP told him that a lorry had been stopped. Appearing in the open they saw the two youths, one of whom was pointing a handgun at the cab of the lorry. Sgt Reilly's challenge was a little unorthodox but none the less effective - "Drop it or I'll blast you". The terrorist with the gun threatened the patrol and was shot twice. The same stretch of road continued to be used for intermittent hijacking. A partially burnt-out refrigerated lorry was subjected - with the owner's approval - to immediate salvage by the CQMS (C/Sgt Hilton) keeping C Company in gourmet puddings for several days! Sgt Reilly was shot later in the tour outside the shops on the Glen Road by Robert Storey, one of the most wanted terrorists in Belfast. Corporals Legge and McCarthy dragged Reilly out of the line of fire into a butcher's shop. The chase that ensued after Storey had shot Sgt Reilly led to his arrest and conviction for terrorist crimes. Cpl Matt McCarthy and L/Cpl Paul Legge were subsequently Mentioned in Despatches for their actions. Sgt 'Jock' Reilly was also awarded an MID.'

Lt Philip Stack Pl Comd and 2IC C Coy

'We were sitting in Whiterock when we were crashed out [7 Platoon] in three Pigs to Turf Lodge to clear some barricades which had been set up as a no-go area but as we came down the hill it was too quiet and everybody had disappeared which was a sure sign that something was going to happen. Everybody was on edge. Then from out of a side road came a crowd in balaclavas throwing petrol bombs by the score. Little 'Titch' Wright was our baton gunner at the time and he was blatting away and other people joined in with baton rounds everywhere. Suddenly there was the crack of high velocity rounds and the Scooby-Doo [Royal Engineer mechanical digger] was hit. The Sapper reversed off and he was gone - back to

THE GREEN BOOK - IRA TRAINING MANUAL

1. A war of attrition against enemy personnel which is aimed at causing as many casualties and deaths as possible, so as to create a demand from their people at home for withdrawal.

2. A bombing campaign aimed at making the enemy's financial interest in our country unprofitable while at the same time curbing long-term investment in our country.

3. To make the Six Counties as at present and for the past several years ungovernable except by colonial military rule.

4. To sustain the war and gain support for its ends by national and international propaganda and publicity campaigns.

5. Defending the war of liberation by punishing criminals, collaborators and informers.

By now it is clear that our task is not only to kill as many enemy personnel as possible or to cause as much economic damage as possible but of equal importance create support which will carry us not only through a war of liberation which could last another decade but which will support us past the 'Brits out' stage to the ultimate aim of a Democratic Socialist Republic.

The Five Demands for which ten men starved themselves to death in their quest for political status in the IRA's war against the British government in the spring of 1981. Apart from ten of the 23 hunger strikers, another 67 people died in associated violence during this period comprising 15 policemen, 15 soldiers and 37 civilians (including an unknown number of IRA volunteers). More than 750 were injured. There were 1,205 demonstrations which were attended by an estimated 355,000 people.The paint bomb was courtesy of a Fusilier. Philip Harris

EXTRACTS FROM THE DIARY OF FUSILIER EDDIE CROSSLAND 3RRF

TUESDAY 5 MAY 1981

At 0117 hours Bobby Sands died.

0130 hours Falls Road population heard the news and started blowing whistles, horns and banging dustbin lids to wake everybody up.

0140 hours Majority are up now. The Broadway barricade has been built up to about 6 feet high

0155 hours A builders yard has been broken into and lorry loaded with bricks was stolen and used as part of the Broadway barricade.

0215 hours Cars are being hijacked in the Falls and set on fire. The fire engines are being stoned and bottled by about 400 people and troops are firing baton rounds every minute, everything is chaos in the Falls Road.

0600 hours Rioting has been continuous. Troops fired 250 baton rounds at rioters.

0630 hours A youth was shot in the leg by an SLR when he tried to throw a petrol bomb at troops.

0730 Everything has died down now as it has got light.

0745 hours Returned to McCrory to wash, shave and breakfast.

1400 hours Went to TAC to do 48 hours guard.

WEDNESDAY 6 MAY 1981

Left TAC at 0111 hours to return to McCrory Park to assist in removing a huge barrier that was blocking the Beechmount. This was to happen at 0300 hours but they didn't do it as it was dark. We slept until 1200 hours and then had lunch. We have had a lot of Scots Guards and Royal Engineers arrive here at McCrory to put our numbers up. There was a briefing for NCOs at 1230 hours. We're going out to the Beechmounts to take down the big barrier. The barrier was taken down and we returned to McCrory. On the way back across the school fields we all got in a straight line and went up a hill and approached stone and bottle throwing youths. It looked great as about 30 of us came over the hill at them. I fired one baton round at one guy throwing bottles but he dropped to the floor and I missed him (close though). Later on we went cruising up and down the Falls Road with 3 Baton Guns sticking out the back of the Pig, We stopped and got out for a bit and about 15 kids started stoning us so for a laugh we started stoning them and they went crazy. No one was hit but there were a lot of people and press spectating.

THURSDAY 7 MAY 1981

Bobby Sands is to be buried at 1300 hours today. It has now started. On the news they said there were a lot of people from Londonderry that arrived in coaches to attend the funeral. They erected scaffolding around the cemetery for news men from all around the world. There are two buses near the cemetery full of B Sands mourners one from Dulwich one from Southampton. Two of the lads from our platoon went on leave today so our brick 31 Delta had to split up, I am now in 31 Bravo until they come back. There was a contact and we went to assist on the Falls. When the hot pursuit went into a house in the Iveaghs there was an explosion. When we went down the Falls Road all the lights were out and it was deserted. As we passed Daleys Garage we were fired at seven times by a pistol, six of the shots hit the side of the Pig, no one was injured. We all piled out and cocked our weapons and took up fire positions. A group of Scots Guards had a petrol bomb on the front of the Saracen they were in and crashed into a wall at the garage. As they were sorting themselves out they heard weapons cocking all around them. It's reckoned we could have saved them.

▼

camp. We were left for three or four hours, fighting these blokes off this barricade. A guy came out of his house and was standing in his doorway giving us all kinds of verbal abuse from about 15 yards away. 'Titch' Wright loaded up and put one baton round through his front window, another through one upstairs window and then one through the other. That shut him up. For a couple of hours we kept firing, they kept throwing. The crowd was getting bigger and bigger and in the end we had to fight our way over the barricade to form a baseline on the other side so we could clear it. It probably took about a week to clear Turf Lodge or to get it back to some normality although there was no such thing there. It was a mess. It was brilliant.'
Fus 'Scouse' Jones 7 Pl C Coy

'Lots of burning cars, the stench of burning rubber, it went on night after night after night. Once we recaptured a no-go area we had to stay there to dominate it because as soon as we moved away they returned. However if you stayed there living in your Pig you became a target so you had to patrol constantly. Operations were conducted at company strength with a typical platoon task being to clear a barricade so we were given a Scooby Doo and my four Pigs. Firstly, you had to get the bad guys off the barricade with baton rounds. We got through box loads of them as we shot them off the top. There were petrol bombs flying everywhere so you had to be careful not to go up in flames. We used both 25 and 45 grain baton rounds - there were no restrictions at the time. If the blokes' lives were in danger which of course they were, we were given dispensation to use the 45-grain and because of the distances we had to cover. So you would eventually clear them off the top and the Scooby Doo would come charging up and create a hole which you exploited in order to dominate inside while the Scooby Doo cleared the rest of the barricades into dumper trucks which took it all away.'
Lt Philip Macey Pl Comd 2 Pl A Coy

'It was during one of many riots that the main differences between the RUC and us became very clear to me. Our front line was taking a beating, mainly petrol bombs, with a sprinkling of bricks. Lt Col Geoff Youll gently advised the senior RUC officer that if we withdrew to the next corner we would be in a much better position to identify the petrol bombers and deal with them, as they would have no cover. The response was firm "that would leave the library unprotected" as with police everywhere, property was obviously much more important than people at that time.'
WO1 Alan Jones RSM 3RRF

'Bobby Sands died on 5 May 1981, and his funeral followed two days later. The procession started in the Twinbrook estate and made its way through Andersonstown to the Milltown Cemetery, the front entrance of which was exactly opposite C Company's base in Andersonstown RUC Station. The funeral procession comprised 100,000 people, and the chances of trouble in C Company's exposed location was high. The boxes of 45-grain baton rounds were broken open and I was sent to Lisburn to collect our secret weapon - an attack dog of exceptional ferocity. This beast had bitten off its own tail and used to operate with its lead on a drum attached to its handler with a harness. Nothing ever scattered a crowd faster than this dog, which was worth at least a platoon of baton gunners and snatch squads. In the event, Sands's funeral passed off relatively peacefully, with the great majority attending out of peer pressure or simply a desire to be there out of a sense of occasion. However, for the Republican movement, Sands had acquired a legitimacy by being elected to Parliament and the issue had achieved political mobilisation on a scale not achieved since the days of the Northern Ireland Civil Rights Association marches in the 1960s. The hunger strikes continued.'
Lt Philip Stack Pl Comd and 2IC C Coy

'The opposition knew the capabilities of the FRG [Federal Riot Gun] to the yard and came to riots equipped to counter the effects of baton rounds with cricket pads and boxes, shin pads and extra thick anoraks to absorb blunt impact trauma. They also used bin lids, bread baskets and corrugated iron as shields, with one holding the sheeting as another threw projectiles at the troops in an identical manner to a soldier with a short shield protecting a baton gunner. Baton rounds were used against specified targets identified by the brick commander such as "Identify green parka, blue jeans and black balaclava!" As a baton gunner, I carried ten rounds of baton ammunition in two '58 Pattern water bottle pouches. You needed permission to fire 45-grain rounds but authority for their use had been passed down from the brigade commander to company commanders to use as they saw fit, which in the event meant it was at the discretion of individual baton gunners, without it the situation would have been impossible. 45-grain had an effective range out to 100 yards and would knock down a rioter whereas a 25 grain would merely wind them.

'On the day of Bobby Sands' funeral [7 May 1981], we were working out of Woodbourne on the interface between Doon Road and Lenadoon Avenue with Pigs stationed on the corners. It was between 2000 and 2200 hours and the Drums Platoon had been under concerted attack with acid and petrol bombs - the acid was melting the rubber compound between the concrete roadway causing smoky fumes and an acrid smell. It was raining. As the baton gunners, Corporal Gary Carter and I were firing volleys at identified bomb throwers. We were about to fire another volley so I raised the visor of my Cromwell helmet for better visibility in the persistent drizzle when Corporal Carter gave the fire order - "On the count of two - fire". At that moment, a brick struck the barrel of my baton gun and ricocheted into my face. As I was flung backwards, the baton gun fired into the air. Carter looked over to see the inside of my visor splashed with blood and thought that the firing of the weapon was a rifle shot that had hit me in the face. As I writhed on the ground, a Welch Fusilier demanded to know what my Whisky number [Casualty identification code] was but I had no idea and anyway was unable to speak through the broken teeth.'
Fus Dave Griffiths Drums Platoon

The vehicle park at North Street Mill is crammed with the AFVs and Royal Engineer plant equipment most commonly used on the streets of Belfast during the hunger strikes of 1980-81. These were assigned to 2RRF with in the foreground Saracen Armoured Ambulances, an armoured Land Rover, RE dumper truck and the Humber Pigs. On the left are the front buckets of two RE Scooby-Doo mechanical diggers and another dumper truck.

'Bin-lidding was used as a means to indicate the presence of troops, a constant counter-point to house searches. In retrospect, these were quite appalling - we would search a whole street and completely destroy these people's homes. We just completely dominated them. At the time though, that is how we did things. Five o'clock in the morning was the time for lift operations. You'd have your list and off you'd go and lo and behold you'd knock on someone's door and then kick it down, straight up the stairs, grab him and arrest him, fling him into the back of the Pig and drive straight to Springfield Road police station and hand him over to the tender mercies of the RUC.'
Lt Philip Macey Pl Comd 2 Pl A Coy

'We suffered casualties, the main one being Fusilier Harrison of the Drums Platoon who was shot in the chest. Others were burned, several others had slight acid burns and several were injured by an assortment of weapons. Fortunately all of these casualties are now back on duty (with the exception of Corporal Hartley, a short account of whom appears later). 1 RWF and 1 RRW also had several casualties but luckily none serious.'
Fusilier Journal Volume 4 Number 2

'There were several RPG-7 attacks at this time and mostly policemen had been killed or maimed. During this period I hated going out in Pigs. There was much debate as to whether we should drive round slowly with the "windows" open and FRGs or rifles bristling to deter petrol and acid bombers but make ourselves an easier RPG-7 target or otherwise drive like stink to make a rocket attack harder but get petrol and acid bombs smashing through the window. I recall on one occasion down the Monagh by-pass we slowed for the roundabout at the bottom and a bottle came through that didn't ignite. We all joked and breathed a sigh of relief thinking we'd been lucky until Fusilier O'Brian 68 started screaming in the back of the Pig - the bottle contained acid and it had splashed over him - and me - as the bottle broke coming through the window.'
Lt Malcolm Johnston Pl Comd 9 Pl C Coy

Drummer Brian Harrison was shot through the chest from a high angle near Lenadoon Avenue on 9 May 1981. Fortunately the bullet passed through his body cleanly. Three days later, Lance Corporal Paul Thompson was also shot. As a Battalion Intelligence NCO, Sergeant Bob Broadbent was on the streets of Lenadoon that evening when he noticed a foreign TV crew jump hurriedly into their car after filming some minor incident. He flagged them down and asked where they were going. They replied that they had been told of a shooting incident in Ballymurphy. Sergeant Broadbent reported this on the net but was told nothing had occurred.

'I hadn't heard any shots, hadn't heard a contact report whereas we normally heard them all. Ten minutes later a patrol coming out of Whiterock down the funnel was shot up. Corporals Thompson and Wilkinson, one of my CONCOs, were hit although Wilkinson was still involved

FRIDAY 8 MAY 1981
On immediate today. Went out on Op Satellite to the Beechmounts. There was a contact up the Whiterocks and we went up but were not needed, so when we got back we had to go straight out to assist 3 Platoon when they saw youths with pistols and people wearing paramilitary clothes. We proceeded to ram the barrier and a petrol bomb hit the front of the Pig, the flames came into the drivers cockpit and engulfed him for a few seconds, a bottle of paint was thrown and an acid bomb hit the rear side of the Pig and splashed a couple of muckers in the back. Nothing too serious though, we were ordered to get out and back to camp as soon as possible, as we reversed Cpl R (Bob) was firing baton rounds out of the front at the yobs. As he fired I grabbed the empty FRG and gave him a live one, it was quite warry. Later on we were coming down the Falls Road and a few bricks were thrown. Three baton rounds were returned and 1 hit was seen (goody).

SATURDAY 9 MAY 1981
At 0010 hours as we were going down Whiterock and turned right up the Falls we were heavily petrol bombed, a bit close for comfort really, we replied with two baton rounds and scored one hit in the chest (Bob). Not much happened after that with us but B Coy were shot at and one soldier was shot in the chest and was critical but he is now said to be alright and breathing on his own.

SUNDAY 10 MAY 1981
On patrols today did a taxi run to MPH in the morning, I had changed to L/Cpl H's (Geordie) brick as Fus H (Ian) is on leave. Did a couple of White routes, these are driving around on the major roads needed to get in and out of camp, we do this to make sure they are not blocked or barricades have been started, if they have we can bust through them.

MONDAY 11 MAY 1981
I slept in sheets last night, first time in 20 days, was it nice, supposed to go on a taxi run to MPH to pick up two RUC. I got ready and was not needed (I could have stayed in bed). Later on in the day we took down all the barricades in the area of the Whiterocks, there was a bit of a scuffle and a few aggressors got hit with hard things on their heads. On a white route at 2055 hours. I wish we could go back to Palace as I am getting a bit weary but I think we are going soon. Nothing happened. Hughes the hunger striker is said to be very weak.

TUESDAY 12 MAY 1981
Hughes has gone into a coma. We the Battalion, Scots Guards, Royal Engineers and the Welsh [Fusiliers] went into the Beechmounts and took down all the barriers.
1740 hours Francis Hughes the 2nd in line of the hunger strikers died. We were crashed straight into the Beechmounts area, rioting started and we got out to repel, I almost immediately got half a brick right in my shin of my left leg and it bloody hurt, it bled quite a lot until I got back to camp and saw the medic, but I could only get a bandage on it as there was a soldier badly burnt by acid.
While we were at the Westrocks clearing a barricade and rioters we heard five high velocity rounds from an automatic weapon. I personally think it was an Armalite from its deep sound. At the moment I am waiting to be called out again. I have to go and see the medic again in the morning.
L/Cpl T (Thomo) was shot at and wounded in the leg tonight. 1 Platoon are on a lurk and immediate tonight. The lurk went OK. They said they heard a ▼

in the follow up and walked back into Fort Whiterock for treatment of fragments in his knee and a flesh wound to his upper arm. You can draw your own conclusions.'
Sgt Bob Broadbent Bn Int NCO

'The CO had been injured while in Germany before moving to Belfast but he was a man of boundless energy and humour and was liked by the Fusiliers. He hated the idea of some "worthless sh*t" (his words, not mine) terrorist hurting one of "his Fusiliers". I was often at great pains to remind him that "his Fusiliers" were well able generally to take care of themselves. The Fusiliers knew of his injury, and whenever he appeared at the scene of a riot, which was almost every time there was one, they would surreptitiously detach a couple of minders to ensure that he was OK. I can not recall who was more concerned for the other. I do recall though, seeing him weak with laughter, at the humorous antics of the Fusiliers in mid riot, particularly when a rioter had caught fire from one of his own petrol bombs.'
Maj George Molyneux-Carter 2IC 3RRF

This occurred on 13 May on the day after the second hunger striker, Francis Hughes, had died. There was widespread rioting across West Belfast during which one petrol bomber was hoist by his own petard and set alight. Fusilier Steve 'Geordie' Hills has cause to remember the incident - 'During a riot at the top of Turf Lodge, I was part of a snatch squad. I gave the order to Fusilier Wilmott to fire on a petrol bomber dodging behind a car but there was this little Yorkshire terrier running around as well. I shouted "Fire now!" Wilmott totally missed the bloke and hit the Yorkshire terrier which jumped into the air as the petrol bomber was about to throw a bottle and hit his arm. The bottle smashed and both caught alight. I ran forward to help and patted the fire out on the Yorkshire terrier as I'm partial to dogs. I then put the petrol bomber out. He was arrested by the RUC and charged with riotous behaviour.'
Fus 'Geordie' Hills 9 Pl C Coy

'It was the adrenalin once the riot started. Depending on what the platoon was doing, you could be put into the snatch squad. Two blokes without webbing on but with baton sticks and two FRG blokes to protect you. Your job would be to snatch someone the commander picked out who was throwing petrol bombs whatever. The barrier shields would open and you rushed out with the FRGs giving cover and you'd bring back the villain and pass him to the Rucksack [RUC] and he was lifted straight away. Because the adrenalin is flowing you are totally focused on the job and you ignore the bottles and bricks but it was knackering. After two whole days on the streets without sleep, a baton gunner was in a riot when he heard the distinctive sound of glass on glass so he just turned and fired thinking it was a petrol bomber. It was an old man putting out his milk bottles on his doorstep in the middle of a riot. Fortunately, the baton round missed.'
Fus 'Fish' Fisher 4 Pl B Coy

'When acting as a support platoon to the Welch Fusiliers in Turf Lodge where no security forces had been for a couple of weeks, a large crowd came round the corner wearing balaclavas and carrying sticks and wriggly tin. The platoon commander took one look and turned to the three teams and gave the order - "Run away!" We began to run for Whiterock firing FRG rounds to cover the retreat. Somehow Willie Wilmott got stuck in a garden hedge. An old woman of about 80 came out and started to batter him with a coal shovel. "Help! Help!" he was calling and as the crowd was getting near we ran back to save him from this aged grandma.'
Fus 'Geordie' Hills 9 Pl C Coy

'Five to ten year olds were used to shield stone throwers and petrol bombers in many riots on the basis that soldiers would not fire a baton gun for fear of hitting children. Young children were also made to lie on the rear parcel shelf of hijacked or stolen cars to prevent soldiers from firing when the vehicle crashed through a VCP. Such a situation put a young Fusilier under enormous pressure - it was his finger on the trigger.'
Fus Scouse' Jones 7 Pl C Coy

'Whilst on duty on the Falls Road/Beechmount Avenue junction one evening, I was dozing in the front seat of the Pig. A shot was fired very close by. Bundling out of the Pig, I sent a contact report and tried to establish what was happening. After some confusion, I found that Cpl Richardson had been on stag by the Pig. A youth had appeared round the corner with a petrol bomb and was about to throw it. Cpl Richardson shot at him, range about 25 yards.

Fusiliers form a baseline behind the wing of a 'Flying Pig' during Northern Ireland training at Sennelager before the 3RRF deployment to Belfast in early 1981.

He missed, and the youth scarpered. However, the round went on down Beechmount Avenue, finally embedding itself, about 150 yards away, in a kitchen wall while the occupier was washing up. He was quite rightly a bit annoyed and came storming down the road to find out who was in charge. Me! About three minutes had passed now, and I was involved in the full shooting follow up radio transmissions, and was a little busy! This man found me, explained who he was, and was very, very shaken and not a little cross. I must have been so pumped up with adrenalin, and I can remember telling him that we were in the middle of a battle - with Coy HQ as it happened, he should look on the positive side - i.e. no one was hurt, and he should go away because we were all busy and had a job to do. To my surprise, he apologised and left - just like that!'
Lt Andy Harris Pl Comd 1 Pl A Coy

At 1900 hours on 22 May 1981, shortly after the death of Patsy O'Hara, Corporal Phil Hartley was travelling in a Pig on the way to Woodbourne when it was hit by an RPG-7 in Andersonstown Road. It was also carrying his OC, Major Paul Bibbey. The latter was riding in the back with Sergeant Major Ian 'One-Eye' Hilton and Fusiliers 'Chuck' Berry and 'O.G.' O'Grady who recalls - 'The Pig was hit in the front wing and the projectile exploded inside the engine block causing fragments to fly into the front compartment wounding the RCT driver and Corporal Hartley. The latter suffered only minor injuries to his legs but the driver was lucky to survive since he had failed to do up his flak jacket and a fragment had lodged in his chest cavity barely an inch from his heart. We jumped out of the back into a hail of automatic fire. As I leapt from the vehicle I slipped and fell. Fusilier Berry, thinking I had been shot, dragged me unceremoniously across the street into the cover of some shops. By now the Pig had come to rest against some railings and a crowd had gathered to cheer and jeer - although not unduly hostile it was apparent that they were aware of the situation. At that moment, Sergeant Major Hilton appeared in the middle of the road clutching a box of baton rounds demanding to know the whereabouts of the baton gunner - me. Meanwhile the injured Hartley had sent a situation report and the Quick Reaction Force (QRF) was soon on the scene with a Sarrican [Saracen ambulance]. Corporal Hartley and the RCT driver were taken to hospital for treatment while the rest of us went to Woodbourne where we were given a glass of whisky and a pat on the back. The next day we were back on the streets.'

'During the five weeks of this particular deployment, Security Forces (SF) in West Belfast (excluding 1st Battalion Scots Guards north of the Shankhill) saw over 120 riots, received in excess of 200 petrol bombs, 82 acid bombs, 6 hand-grenades, 8 booby-trapped vehicles. SF were engaged by RPG7 (resulting in one RUC casualty [There were in fact four casualties -

Even in the darkest hours of the hunger strike, there were humorous incidents in Belfast as this account by Captain Chris Mears affirms -

'At the height of the hunger strike - 24 hours before Bobby Sands died - 90% of the battalion were deployed in and around Belfast - this left just the cooks, bottle washers, sick, lame and lazy and essential administration personnel in Palace Barracks. Amongst the essential administration personnel were the RQMS - Nigel Whitfield and myself - I was TQMS. We both stole a window of opportunity to visit the local Supply Depot - via Carnlea Golf Club!. Whilst strolling down the sixth fairway, sandwiched between Belfast Lough and the main Bangor/Belfast railway line, we both reflected on the fact that our fellow Regimental golfers were unable, through active duty, to enjoy our dual contentment. It was at precisely that moment that a group of drunken Belfast yobs ambling down the railway line took umbrage and decide to stone us with rather large missiles obtained from between the tracks. Nigel, never the most patient of golfers immediately grabbed a seven iron, leapt the fence and set off in hot pursuit bent on teaching the offending rabble a lesson. Golfing shoes not being the best footwear for railway sleepers meant the mob soon gained a sufficient lead to evade both capture, limb and organ confiscation and other punishments too dire to relate. After a brief delay where I learnt at least three new swear words and was given an interesting solution to the Northern Ireland problem, play resumed. On returning to Palace Barracks later that afternoon, we both visited the Operations Room for a sitrep and found the only disturbance in the whole of Ulster that day had been at the golf course. Naturally we decided it was too insignificant to mention to anybody and retired hastily to the Sergeants Mess!'
WO2 TQMS Chris Mears

weapon being cocked 20 metres in front of them but could not see at all.

WEDNESDAY 13 MAY 1981.
The Pope was shot today and seriously injured. There are some stupid people about. We are on Op Satellite now watching for Prots coming across to sort out the Cats. Not much has happened today.

THURSDAY 14 MAY 1981
Tonight an RUC man was killed and three seriously wounded when they were attacked by an RPG-7 rocket, it took the top off their Landrover but didn't explode for quite a distance. The IRA claimed responsibility. We now have to wear our Flak Jackets everywhere we go. A gunman who was shot has died. We went over to the Protestant side on a patrol. We were given tea and cakes, we also went to a Fish and Chip shop and a had a lovely fish dinner.

FRIDAY 15 MAY 1981
Not much happened in the early hours of the morning except we got quite cold. Later on Cpl R (Bob) was on the Prot side and a load of kids were on his Pig, He got them all off and started down the road and apparently one of the kids jumped on the side of the Pig while it was moving and fell under the Pig he was rushed to hospital but was dead on arrival. The gunman who was shot had his funeral today, There were four IRA in full combat uniforms at the front of the procession and eight all dressed in black with black hoods leading the funeral procession of about 100 people.
At 0130 hours we were escorting the tipper truck from a dump back to McCrory when we thought we had a blast bomb thrown at us. We shot up the Donnegal road, sharp left and right and up the Whiterock road towards camp. As we turned left at the junction of Donnegal and Falls Road we were very very heavily attacked by bricks, bottles, petrol; bombs and acid bombs. As we were turning into camp we realised the tipper truck wasn't with us, it had turned right after the barrier on Donnegal Road. we found out later that it was in fact a shot that went through the side window of the truck and into the leg of the driver. He was not badly hurt.

SATURDAY 16 MAY 1981
We went to the Beechmounts to relieve a call sign that had been there all night, we are on a stag basis of two hours on and four hours off. We had to stay on the Beechmounts all night patrolling on foot and guarding the Pig. In the early hours of Sunday morning Fus J was talking to a man at Daleys Garage on the Falls Road when the man said he was a member of the IRA and was going to shoot J, he then proceeded to get out a gun, J cocked his rifle and shot him in the leg. *My brick was on the ground just round the corner and we all s**t ourselves and cocked our rifles, we were ready to shoot anyone with a rifle (lucky we heard on the radio that J's call sign was there, as we thought we were the only ones in that area) I reckon one of that call sign could have been shot by us.
At 0345 hours I was on the corner of an entry on Beechmount Road, Falls Road junction when I heard a weapon being cocked, it sounded like a pistol, I also heard what sounded like a rifle being cocked in the same place, it went on for about ten minutes and the IRA knew we were there so we thought it was a come on and didn't react to it and have a look, we just reported it to our camp.
*Fus J was also racially abused on account of his colour during this encounter. His measured reaction was in accordance with the rules of engagement existing at the time.

▼

one dead and three injured], and two members of 'C' Company slightly hurt) and shot at 64 times, mostly by Garand and Armalite, but also by M60, .30 Browning, Woodmaster, M1 Carbine, .22 and pistols various. Catapults with ball bearings and cross bows were used; beer kegs with petrol in them were rolled under pigs and land-rovers; believe it or not, during one session at the Divis Flats, a patrol was bombarded with:- one chest of drawers, one bedstead, one fridge, and one live dog (which is still alive) and two TV sets, all dropped from at least three floors up... The most cheering news for the Fusiliers is that to date the CO and three Rifle Company Commanders have all been engaged by the enemy. Major Buckton was missed, Major Spackmans's walking stick was shattered and Major Bibbey's Pig was destroyed.'
Fusilier Journal Volume 4 Number 2

'The windows of the Divis Flats were hinged in the middle and milk bottles etc could be lined up along the leading edge. By sitting underneath, the window acted as a mirror so it was possible to see when troops were walking along down below and it was a simple matter of tilting the window to drop the bottles onto the soldiers beneath. Engine blocks, starter motors and old TV sets all made admirable bombs from multi story tower blocks - anything to hurt the blokes in green.'
Fus Dave Griffiths Drums Pl

It is interesting to note that one of the design parameters for the GKN AT-104 IS vehicle intended to replace the Pig was for the roof to withstand the impact of a washing machine from a height of four floors.

'Very early one morning we were involved in a search op in the Divis area - I was a search adviser and we had one search team in the platoon. I remember a tinge of excitement as we approached these huge and ugly tower blocks. The Divis was infamous and very dangerous. We managed to get into the flats having run through what could only be described as a rubbish tip and sewage farm. The stench here and in the stairwells was unbelievable. Many of my lads came from pretty rough areas of Manchester and London but none of them could believe the squalor these people created and in which they seemed happy to live. The searches of individual flats all took place simultaneously and I remember Fusiliers having to come out for "fresh" air as they were gagging from the smell of human detritus they found during the search. Knowing the way in which the Army searched, the residents would often leave surprises in nooks or crannies knowing the soldiers would find them - used sanitary towels, excrement, fish hooks and razor blades were quite common. I cannot recall if anyone found anything on this occasion but I do recall us all having to have our clothes taken from us and burned then all taking a good shower to lessen the chances of catching nits, lice or any manner of disease that festered in the Divis. The smell took much longer to get out of our nostrils.'
Lt Malcolm Johnston Pl Comd 9 Pl C Coy

'My first patrol was on a Sunday evening, a relatively quiet time down the Whiterock Road to the Falls Road and then across and south towards the Belfast Portadown motorway. I was enthralled by the pre-patrol briefing, taking every detail down, most of which meant absolutely nothing to me, and then felt very grown up as we set off. My ignorance, naivety and excitement all ensured that fear never entered my head. As is often the case there was a light rain, making the grey slates of the old red brick terraced housing shine. The patrol was totally uneventful, no shootings, bombings or rioting. The odd kid with a foul mouth, but nothing else. As far as I was concerned it was the thrill of my life. Finally commissioned, in an operational theatre, walking along roads which had been plastered across the TV for the past 13 years or so. Not yet in command, but that would come soon. This was all that I joined for. Little did I know how much fun it could be at times and after nearly two years, how tedious it could become.'
2nd Lt Ted Coates Pl Comd 5 Pl B Coy

'Martin Hurson, an INLA hunger striker from Cappagh in Tyrone, died at 0430 on 13 July 1981, and the bin-lidding started immediately. It was clearly audible in the Mill where C Company were waiting in reserve for this event. My Platoon, 9 Platoon, were on patrol in the Clonard within half an hour amidst the clattering bin lids, which all seem to be wielded by middle-aged and elderly women who would scream abuse at patrols. They were mostly ignored, although some were occasionally sent sprawling by a well-aimed kick or suffered crushed knuckles as

Bin-lidding, foul gestures and vile abuse were a part of every day life on the streets of Belfast during the Hunger Strike of 1981 - 'Whenever we had a civpop confrontation in the day, the women would be at the fore. Horrible, smelly, foul-mouthed and hateful, they would bang dustbin lids, push you, spit on you, abuse you...'. Philip Harris

they gripped their bin lids. Petrol bombs were seized, prepared for use in empty crates, and we pre-empted the next batch by smashing every empty milk bottle that we could find on the estate. The finesse of 'hearts and minds' was missing at this time, we were patrolling to dominate the estate, and that was interpreted as including the domination of the population. Everyone was subject to stopping, searching or questioning, and there was no question of allowing "back chat" or complaint. "Dominate through suppression" may not have been the stated mission, but it was the concept of operations that we were employing. It was no different to the approach employed in Aden just 13 years before, and it was campaigns such as Aden which had provided the formative experiences of the Army's commanders at company level and above.'
Lt Philip Stack Pl Comd and 2IC C Coy

'On the day before the local elections, 1 Platoon was sent to secure the school in the Whiterock estate, quite close to McCrory Park base, as a polling station. The mistake we made, although it couldn't be avoided, was to move in just as the school day ended. The result was that all the kids saw us as they left school, went home, got changed into riot gear, got their mates, and came back for a riot, which went on for hours and hours.

'A group of yobs were using a car for cover, standing up to fire ball bearings at us from a catapult. We could hear the ball bearings buzzing past like pistol bullets. We couldn't get at them because of the car. Somebody had the idea of using three baton guns to get them. The upshot was, just as the yobs stood to fire over the roof of the car, three baton guns fired, one after the other. The first round broke the passenger window. The second round passed through the broken window and broke the drivers door window. The third round, fired by me, went through both, now broken windows, and got the yob right in the stomach. The ball bearing firing from that area stopped.'
Lt Andy Harris Pl Comd 1 Pl A Coy

'The IRA mortar attack on B Company in McCrory Park [30 June 1981] happened about a fortnight after I joined the company. It was a Saturday night and the company commander, Major David Spackman, had arranged a dinner party for the officers of the Royal Welch Fusiliers, who were stationed in Fort Whiterock. The company 2IC, Captain Tim Cheeter, had miscalculated the number attending, under booking by one. As the new boy I was told to make myself scarce!

'It was a warm summer evening and I went for a walk around the camp. I wandered into the Ops Room for a chat with the watchkeeper. Nothing much happening. I then looked in on the cookhouse where the weekly movie was being shown, "The Longest Day". Little was I to know what an omen that was! Not really feeling in the mood for film and hoping that with

SUNDAY 17 MAY 1981
We have been on the Beechmounts for 4 hours today. Our platoon did a taxi run at 0630 hours. We are on immediate most of the day and are out to the Beechmounts at 0030 hours Monday morning.

MONDAY 18 MAY 1981
We didn't go to the Beechmounts, but there was a search on 31 Bravo were not all on it. We went on a White route at 0715 hours. We didn't find anything on the search, except a large hide big enough for a man to hide in fair comfort with weapons and food. I have just heard that five Royal Green Jackets were blown to pieces in a Saracen by a culvert bomb of about 1000 pounds of explosive in South Armagh.

TUESDAY 19 MAY 1981
We went to guard a school on the Falls Road ready for voting on Wednesday, while I was there I tried to phone Mom and Dad but I didn't get any answer. I was a bit disappointed as it was the first time I had phoned. In another school L/Cpl D and 31 Foxtrot got quite a leathering from stone, acid and petrol bomb throwers until help arrived, we went and relieved them for the night when we were relieved from the school we were in. Just as we got to the school there were some shots fired just up the road at some soldiers giving us cover to get in. Three shots were fired at the Army with no casualties and the Army fired five rounds through the window the gunman fired from. these five shots passed right through the whole house from one side to the other, passing 12 inches over months old twins. The two gunmen had seized the house and waited for an hour before opening fire. They were wearing full IRA uniforms with black hoods etc. I was told to go and direct the police to the firing point. I stayed waiting to be told to come out when I saw the troops way down the road. I then realised i was by myself in a very hostile area, but I legged it safely back to my squad.

WEDNESDAY 20 MAY 1981
We stayed in the school until 2100 hours when we were sent back to McCrory park, just as we got back we were told we had to go back to the school to cover as the stone and petrol throwers had started again when they saw us they increased and we went to about 20 feet from them and were about to open fire with riot guns when our OC told us we were in the open to get shot and to get back in the school under cover. We then went back to McCrory where we stayed all night.

THURSDAY 21 MAY 1981
Raymond Macrish the third hunger striker died this morning at 0200 hours. It took until 0430 hours for the Paddys to get the news and start to bang dustbin lids and honk car horns. We went into the Beechmount area and part of the road was blocked by Paddys yelling, so the RUC told them they had 15 seconds to clear off the road or they would disperse them with Baton rounds. Four were fired and they disperse. We left McCrory at 1215 hours to return to Palace Barracks for our month off. We are on two hours notice to move for the whole of Northern Ireland. Tonight I went to the NAAFI and had a pint and sandwiches. I felt quite pissed and went to bed at 1900 hours.'

And so the tour continued as successive hunger strikers died and rioting ensued with monotonous regularity. On 2 August 1981, Kieran Doherty was the eighth hunger striker to die when Fusilier Eddy Crossland was patrolling the mean streets of Belfast. His diary suddenly stopped on this Sunday as he was no longer able to use a pen. For reasons that will become obvious, his platoon mates promptly ▼

everyone occupied with either the film or the dinner night, there might be a chance of a washing machine being free, and I decided to get some dhobi done. Having checked the machines were available, I wandered out of the ablutions and bumped into the QRF commander, who invited me to join the QRF to go and sort out some youths who were stoning some cars on the M1 motorway. Washing or a bit of aggro - absolutely no competition. I rushed away and changed at a speed that would have impressed any Sandhurst Colour Sergeant.

'Our arrival at the motorway was met by a very rapid departure by a group of youths. Literally as we were getting out of the Pig, we were confronted by the sound of bullets cracking above our heads. Although the only time that I had previously experienced the crack of gunfire was in the butts of a range, this was unmistakable. Sadly a little knowledge is dangerous. I immediately took cover on the motorway hard shoulder. Not a good idea. It is very difficult to bore down through tarmac, but worse, very embarrassing to see the remainder of the patrol sprinting to take up cover behind a very solid brick wall! I felt very exposed and very foolish, but quickly picked myself up and ran to the same wall. Met by the knowing grins from the soldiers, they did not need to say a word. As I arrived we heard a series of pops and then large bangs come from the direction of the base. As we looked up we saw a pall of black smoke billowing into the evening sky. It was quite clear that something had gone wrong at McCrory Park. We tried the radios, but they didn't work. We later found out that the talk-through on the mast had been temporarily put out by the blast.

'We mounted up and drove back to the base only to find utter chaos, and roadblocks barring our way. We were given instructions to wait on the Falls Road until the area had been cleared by ATO. Whilst waiting, the company Saracen ambulance passed us, blue light flashing and klaxon blaring en route to Musgrave Park Hospital. With no communications we had no idea who was in there and what were the extent of their injuries. I later found out that it had been LCpl Ferguson who had been having a shower when the attack took place. Up until this point, my time in Belfast had been one big exciting game. Much to my parents consternation I hadn't considered the danger in a particularly mature way. The passage of the ambulance brought home to me the very real danger we were all in.

'After a long while, and after darkness had fallen, we got back into the base. After a very long night we all eventually got some sleep. I'm not a religious man, but there but for the grace of something, I could have been in the washrooms doing my washing had it not been for a chance encounter with the QRF commander. Who knows?'
2nd Lt Ted Coates Pl Comd 5 Pl B Coy

'... Boo...oom! When the second explosion rocked the flimsy structure of the portacabin, my long-dormant instincts as an ex-mortar officer took over - "Take cover!" ... and we all scrambled under the dining room table, scrabbling about on all fours when the next and the next and the next explosion thundered seemingly about and around us in the still of the summer evening air. My fellow hapless partners under the futile cover of the table included the COs of 2RGJ and 1RWF, and gallant members of the home team. I was worried. The Chicken Kiev had just been served and was now spoilt. The two Commanding Officers were probably not enjoying our hospitality. The surprise party to say goodbye to CO 1RWF was falling flat. In all, eight Mark 10 IRA mortar bombs exploded inside the confined space of McCrory Park, B Company's base just off the Falls Road.

'Remarkably, apart for a few minor injuries, no one in the company was badly hurt (both COs were uninjured, and sensibly had finished off a glass of wine while the rest of us went about our duties). The off-duty members of the company had been watching the film "The Longest Day" on television, and at first, amid the synthetic thunder of the film, had not noticed the real storm raging outside. Then someone had twigged.

'When it was all over, one unexploded bomb lay just inside the perimeter; it was not made safe until dawn the next morning. Afterwards, I discovered to my horror, among the wreckage of the tiny room that served as our mess, the naked Miss Ajax lying inert, her glass crack'd. Later still, we had Miss Ajax reframed, retaining the old cracked glass under the new glass as a permanent reminder of her service in the war zone, and presented it to the Officers' Mess. CO 1RWF, when writing to thank me for B Company's outstanding service under his command had one complaint. He enjoined us, at the end of his letter, to keep McCrory Park camp tidy,

Lurking in the shelter of a street corner, a snatch squad awaits the order to deploy from the NCO at left who is monitoring the situation during a civpop demonstration on the streets, while the Fusilier at right cradles a baton gun to give the squad covering fire.

as it had been in a bit of a mess when he had last visited. We were encouraged by the adjutant to claim for any kit lost in the attack. One Fusilier who shall remain nameless claimed for a hi-fi system, three Savile Row suits, a canary, and a blow-up doll: he got his money.'
Maj David Spackman OC B Coy

Nine mortars were fired at the McCrory Park patrol base from a hijacked lorry parked in Whiterock Crescent. One overshoot hit the roof of a house in Beechview Park and plunged through the bedroom of a six-year old boy, passing through the building and out through the front door before exploding in the garden. Each mortar bomb contained 40 pounds of explosives. Miss Ajax now adorns the walls of the Officers' Mess bar of the 1st Battalion.

'The republican firing parties at the funeral of each successive hunger striker were becoming more audacious and brazen. This flaunting of the impotence of the Army to intercede on these mass occasions, due to the physical impossibility of breaking into such large crowds, was certainly proving irksome at high levels. The firing parties themselves had fallen into the trap of setting an exploitable pattern, and their error provided the battalion with the opportunity to score a significant success. The Busy Bee shopping complex in Andersonstown was the site for a firing party, and troops were infiltrated into the side roads that flanked the main road. The southern side of the road was covered by C Company 3RRF, and A Company 1RWF were to the north. Battalion Headquarters monitored the procession using heli-tele, which gave a live TV downlink from a hovering Gazelle helicopter. The plan was straightforward and simple. The escaping firing party would be tracked by helicopter and assault troops vectored in by radio. The plan was executed faultlessly, as the terrorists had been lulled into a false sense of security by the absence of attempts by the Army to seize other firing parties. The terrorists fired their volley of shots and moved off the north of the road, to a house [20 St Agnes Drive] in the Andersonstown estate. A Company 1RWF was tasked to react, and C/Sgt Williams 54 quickly found the right house.'
Lt Philip Stack Pl Comd and 2IC C Coy

'This squad was a platoon of A Company under C/Sgt E.D. Williams 54, which followed up rapidly into the house. As the Fusiliers moved into the garden, a gunman was seen and arrested; almost at once, LCpl M.J. Adams saw another gunman aiming a weapon through the kitchen window: LCpl Adams immediately shot the man - who turned out to be Patrick Adams, brother of Sinn Fein leader Gerry Adams and rumoured to be the IRA's Belfast brigade commander - in the chest. Another gunman was sighted in the garden and also shot, but managed to escape into the crowd. The Fusiliers then entered the house, finding a man and a woman downstairs and two other men upstairs; three Garand rifles, with ammunition and paramilitary uniforms were also found. All six people in and around the house were arrested: they were Joseph Maguire, Peter Rooney, Geraldine Crawford, Sean Simpson, Michael Brady,

6 Platoon under the command of Lt Harris (second from right) of B Company prepares to set out on patrol from McCrory Park during the height of the Hunger Strike in the summer of 1981. Philip Harris

renamed him 'Esso' Crossland.

'We came around the corner with my vehicle in the rear heading towards Woodburn Camp, I was thinking of the brew that I would be drinking in a couple of minutes. Mitch suddenly dropped down from the hatch in the roof of the Lanny, then I heard the whoosh and as I turned to face the front of the wagon there was a bang to my head and everything went bright. The petrol bomb had glanced off the roof and smashed into the left side of my head, shattering my visor. The chin strap of the new helmet we were testing had been cut and the helmet fell from my head as I collapsed into the rear of the wagon. I could see my reflection in the gloss paint on the inside of wagon walls - I was on fire from my shoulders up. I screamed at Mitch to throw the wet blanket over me but then realised that they had been removed from the wagons earlier that day after an inspection as they were mouldy and stank. They had not been replaced. I put the flames on my hands out but when I started to slap my face, my hands caught fire again, then it hit me, the pain, the pain. I was screaming "Put me out, put me f*****g out!". The back door opened and I half fell out of the back and was covered in a jacket. The flames were out. As I tried to speak, the blood escaped from my mouth in a gush, my cheek had been cut open by the glass. With my teeth gritted I was able to breathe through the cut with my mouth shut. My head and hands were starting to sting badly. Ginge dragged me to the railings at the side of the road and said the ambulance and help were on the way. The rest of the lads were firing baton rounds towards the hedge on the other side of the road and a few petrol bombs were still coming over the hedge onto the road, whoosh whumpf and eerie light. I was screaming to the other guys, "SLR the bastards, slot them!", but the baton rounds kept being fired. The Saracen ambulance arrived with the QRF and I was taken to Musgrave Park Hospital. In casualty they started to cut off my clothes, I was not happy as I had just sewn creases in my OGs and it took me hours, but was told everything is alright as the effect of the injections for the pain took effect and I drifted off to sleep.

'In the morning I awoke with bags over my hands filled with Flamazine and a bandage covering my whole head with slits for nose, eyes and mouth. A drip was in my arm, and a nurse asked if I would like a drink. Shortly a plastic tube was placed through the slit into my mouth and I sucked cool orange juice which calmed the dry throat I had. Twelve stitches in the cut to my cheek, nine to my ear, 124 fine ones to hold the skin graft to my left hand, daily saline bed baths and visits from the guys in the platoon and six weeks later I was released on sick leave back to Coventry for the biggest piss-up in history. On return to Palace Barracks I was summoned to BHQ. The Adjutant took me into the Bn 2IC who said the CO would be free to see me in a moment. I thought "S**t, a full beard, leather jacket, black woolly hat and I'm going to see the CO". Moments later I go into his office. "Fusilier Crossland, you're off in 5 minutes in my staff car to the airport. I have arranged an indulgence flight to Canada for you to see your Mother and Father". And away I went, arriving in Canada with a small bag containing socks, underwear and a few toiletries as all my other kit was still locked away in the CQMS stores. I returned back to the Platoon after Canada and promptly signed on for nine years, feeling that if this is the way they treat you after it goes tits up, then the Army is for me.'

and Patrick Adams. All were charged with firearms offences and membership of the IRA, a serious blow to the IRA in Belfast. As a result of this action, CSgt Williams was awarded the Distinguished Conduct Medal, and LCpl Adams was awarded the Military Medal. The company commander, Major J.C.W. Williams, was awarded the Military Cross.'
[*Regimental Records of the Royal Welch Fusiliers*, Chapter XXXII Volume VI]

This incident occurred following the funeral of Joseph McDonnell on 10 July. 1RWF was then withdrawn from operations in West Belfast and on 15 July returned to Lemgo in Germany.

'As they were waiting to redeploy we invited the RWF, as one of our sister Regiments, to a formal dinner to celebrate the end of their tour. The table was bedecked with leeks and of course we challenged them to a leek-eating contest early in the proceedings. As our guests we invited them to choose first and eat from the display -the enormous size of these beasts was the result of two weeks selection by Ration Sgt Tony Taylor. Once they had finished we brought out the smallest leeks ever seen from our inside pockets and devoured them in a trice. The meal concluded with our mess wine stocks much reduced.'
WO1 Alan Jones RSM 3RRF

Against his doctor's orders as he still had a fragment in his thigh from the first RPG incident, Corporal Phil Hartley returned to duty on 2 August and was on his first patrol with his brick, Call Sign Three One Alpha.

'We were in a static position at the sectarian interface of Mackies Factory and Beechmounts. The RCT driver was whingeing that he only had 45 minutes left on his stag. Corporal Hartley decided to make a run up to the Clonards where the Pig was stoned and petrol bombed. We moved off again and stopped at the junction of Beechmounts and Falls Road. In the back with me were Fusiliers 'Chuck' Berry and Ian Scholes. Suddenly, there was massive explosion. I looked at Chuck and our immediate thought was - "Not again". We bombburst out of the back and took cover but soon realised that Phil Hartley and the driver hadn't got out of the vehicle. The Pig had been hit in the driver's door by an RPG rocket and had come to an immediate halt. We then ran back to the Pig and stacked our rifles against the side of the vehicle near the commander's door. By now a crowd had gathered which began to jeer. In the heat of the moment, Fusilier Scholes forgot about his weapon and ran around the Pig shouting - "Where's my rifle, where's my rifle?" We then opened the commander's door. The three of us just stood there. Phil was rocking backwards and forwards making a contact report. He didn't know where we were and nor did we, but he was giving as much information as he could. His face looked OK, a bit peppered. Chuck then looked up and said - "We're on Beechmount - Beechmounts and Falls Road". Phil relayed the information. Everything was happening in slow motion. I don't know whether we did it together but we just looked down - from the tops of his kneecaps to the top of his boots was absolutely nothing. There was just flesh hanging from his stumps and the amount of blood that spilled out of the door was immense. The heat had cauterised the wounds so no blood was coming from his legs. Initially I only noticed the blood pouring out of the door and not the fact that his legs were missing. We didn't say anything because he was making the contact report but we all looked at each other and thought - "What do we do?". At that moment, the driver caught me by the shoulder. I turned and noticed his combat trousers were all red, obviously from blood. I dragged him under cover behind a low wall and felt his legs. My immediate thought was secondary devices but there was such a big crowd by now I thought it unlikely. It seemed that the driver's legs were intact but I remember arguing with him - "where's your first field dressing?", but it was in his helmet inside the vehicle. [It was common practice for RCT drivers to wedge their helmet visor open with a field dressing while driving to improve visibility]. I'd been taught never to use your own field dressing on someone else so I was holding the pressure points on his legs until a Marine medic arrived with the QRF.'
Fus 'O.G.' O'Grady 7 Pl C Coy

The casualties were quickly evacuated to hospital. The Rocket Propelled Grenade had penetrated the driver's door low down and had grazed the backs of his legs as his feet were on the pedals of the vehicle. The full force of the explosive jet struck Corporal Hartley's legs which disintegrated under the impact. He showed formidable courage and fortitude in the face of his massive injuries. He was subsequently awarded the Military Medal as well as receiving the Man Of The Year Award for bravery and achievement.

The view through the front visor of a Pig shows one of the many examples of graffiti displayed on the walls of West Belfast in support of the hunger strikers in 1981. Philip Harris

As for the rest of Three One Alpha, they once more received a glass of whisky and a pat on the back and once more were on the streets the next day. However, nobody would now ride in the same vehicle as Fusiliers Berry and O'Grady but shortly thereafter Fusilier Berry was sent on an NCOs cadre and became a brick commander. Even so, to Fusilier 'O.G.' O'Grady - '7 Platoon has been the best platoon I've ever served in especially at that period because you had the support of so many lads, up and down, it didn't matter'.

'Whenever we had a civpop confrontation in the day, the women would be at the fore. Horrible, smelly, foul-mouthed and hateful, they would bang dustbin lids, push you, spit on you and, worst of all, single out my black soldiers for racial abuse. The true hypocrisy of the IRA's desire for a Catholic socialist republic was amply demonstrated by this abuse. Dominated by the Catholic church, these women could recite the scriptures no problem but hadn't the intelligence to realise that their singling out of black soldiers was against all the teachings of their Church and counter to the principles of a socialist doctrine.'
Lt Malcolm Johnston Pl Comd 9 Pl C Coy

'The stress of operations was pretty intense so, when they were back in barracks, the subalterns tended to let their hair down somewhat in the mess. As a bachelor adjutant I had to be pretty tolerant and the high jinks were generally harmless enough. One day a strange object appeared on the dining table at breakfast. It comprised arches of bones glued on to a wooden base, interleaved with slices of toast. A plaque attached read 'The Bobby Sands Memorial Toastrack'. It was only brought out on guaranteed politically incorrect occasions and was eventually destroyed by the CO's dog. On another occasion, I had been away for the weekend, returning late on the Sunday evening, and expected to find things pretty quiet. Not a bit of it: an impromptu party was in full swing to commemorate the fortieth anniversary of Operation'Barbarossa' - not renowned as a Fusilier battle honour - which eventually moved from the bar to Keith Kiddie's balcony where we ceremonially "executed" the empty champagne bottles for treason. It seemed eminently reasonable at the time, anyway.'
Capt Nick Beswick Adjutant

'Life back at the mess was just one huge party. We used to go to the Ards Peninsula which was frequented by the women from the Northern Ireland Office so, for the subalterns, women were always on tap. We fought hard and played hard - it really was a bizarre existence and we just burnt up money. Looking back it was just how we operated, how we coped - living close to the edge on the streets so when we got back to barracks all restraints were gone. We needed some some sort of release to sort ourselves out.'
Lt Philip Macey Pl Comd 2 Pl A Coy

'Frankly, the Fusiliers thoroughly enjoyed themselves because they love a good fight and

A patrol of 3RRF supports RUC policemen on the Springfield Road/Falls Road. It was near this point that the Pig carrying Cpl Hartley and Three One Alpha was hit by a Rocket Propelled Grenade causing this road to be renamed RPG Avenue.

3 RRF IN BELFAST – A WIFE'S VIEW

'That we would actually be living as a family in NI for two years did not sink in until a short while before leaving Fallingbostel in Germany. There had been plenty of preparation on all fronts as we had been given early warning of the move and knew exactly where we would be living because my husband Alan was RSM and there was a tied RSM's house. (He actually took advantage of a recce to the Province to look over the house and even measure windows etc.) There had also been a wives recce (this was almost unknown in 1980, but considering we were due to take over from the 2nd Battalion was not surprising), which had resulted in a lot of very useful and practical information being available. Although this covered the obvious e.g. schooling, housing & shopping etc. in this instance the feeling that this tour was going to be scary in some ways but mostly very enjoyable was a very real one.

'Initially this idea was derided by most of us. How could you go to live in a place where bombs were going off, where people were being killed and maimed, where you could not trust the person you were speaking to because it was impossible to be sure whose side they were on (after all they looked just like you and me!), and actually enjoy the experience? Now, 20 years later, the overwhelming memory of that tour is that it was probably the most enjoyable posting of all - but this statement seems absurd when one remembers the restrictions i.e. not being able to travel willy nilly around the Province, not being able to plan holidays sure in the knowledge that leave might be cancelled (and even when getting away having to leave a contact telephone number), being constantly security conscious (watching who one was chatting to, looking at post carefully, being very circumspect on the telephone); being concerned for one's husband, never knowing when he went out in the morning if he would come back that night. Then there were the other day to day problems; being worried about one's children: could you let teenagers have the freedom they would normally have on the Mainland? Could a five-year old ask her "best friend" from school (from a notorious estate) to her birthday party? Having to constantly open your shopping bags for security checks and pray that nothing happened while one was shopping?

'Yet these factors did not cloud our memories of that tour for reasons that might appear strange to a non-military audience. One reason was delight at our children's schooling. Schooling and housing are always on top of soldiers' family's worry list. In Belfast the housing was not perfect and some Fusiliers were forced to live in dreadful married quarters but the children were very well catered for. The local school was fantastic; both educationally and socially, under the control of a very strict but enlightened Headmaster. Most of the families on that tour admit this schooling laid down wonderful foundations for their children's future academic lives.

'But the main reason for our enjoyment of the tour was the fact that we were all to an extent trapped. We were living in a ghetto and the few jobs that were available were mostly in camp. Some managed to find work in safe areas elsewhere but they were in the minority. Consequently we were all dependent on each other in a way we had not been before. We were united by a common worry (our husbands' safety) and in a hierarchical society like the army certain prejudices were overcome because of that bond. The structure, which had always been, used e.g. a Company Commanders' wife looking after the ▶

Paddy does too. If they can't fight the Army, they'll fight among themselves. 2RRF had set up a disco - a "dog night" - once a week on Sundays at the barracks; mainly to stop Fusiliers going out and getting into trouble or worse still getting their heads blown off. It proved so successful, we ran them twice a week with another on Wednesdays so in theory everyone could go at least once a week. There were two RUC constables on the door, one male and one female, to pick out the undesirables or those who were too young. The girls were supposed to be out by midnight and there were dire threats against anyone found with a girl in their rooms but a blind eye was usually turned. The officers had a decrepit old squash court but it was taken over by the Fusiliers for serial bonking so had to be closed as the floor was being damaged beyond repair. The 2IC, George Carter, and myself were keen gardeners and took over a walled garden and a couple of greenhouses. After months of attention, we had created a soft friable tilth of superb quality but on a Monday there would be the distinct impression of female buttocks as well as knees and elbows. These discos were obviously a great success.'
Maj Richard Mills OC HQ Coy

'There was a 2 o'clock curfew and always a rush from the "Man" pubs in Bangor which held discos - the Coachmans, the Helmsman and the Sportsmans which were often out of bounds depending on the threat. The problem was it was easy for the RMPs to spot the soldiers in the pubs because of their short hair, and the coloured blokes stuck out a mile because there weren't any in Northern Ireland. Once 28 of them got done as they came through the gate after they'd been seen in the pubs - they each got 28 days.'
Fus 'Scouse' Jones 7 Pl C Coy

'I always felt that we were not well served by HQ 39 Brigade staff, except for the DCOS and Q staff, who turned everything upside down to ensure that the Fusiliers were properly looked after when they were deployed into a variety of totally inadequate bases - no washing facilities, no cooking facilities, limited water, no beds etc etc. This was not limited to our battalion, this happened to everyone. There seemed to be a concern that a unit in 39 Brigade might do something that would upset the local press, (not difficult to do!). For example, on occasions during the heavy rioting before Sands died, the Fusiliers had run out of 25-grain rubber bullets due to extended operations in support of the RUC. HQ 39 Brigade would not permit the Fusiliers to use the more effective 45-grain baton rounds which they carried for emergencies, in case the use of them led to casualties among the rioters! This allowed the rioters to move within petrol bomb and acid throwing range, and resulted in unnecessary injuries to the soldiers, who of course were deployed in support of, and were there to defend, the RUC, locals and property.'
Maj George Molyneux-Carter 2IC 3RRF

'I joined up in mid-January 1981 and went to the depot at Bassingbourn. As I was still only 17-years old I was attached to A Company since it was not scheduled to return downtown until October by when I would be 18 and therefore allowed on the streets. However I had already been on the streets with an SLR and live ammunition during NIRT with 45 Commando and had done QRFs and Mortar Base Patrols from Palace barracks already. I was attached to 2 Platoon with Lieutenant Philip Macey as Platoon Commander. But the situation was such that even under 18-year olds were deployed on the streets of Belfast and I was sent on a search operation with B Company in late August when I found myself on a baseline holding a six-foot shield with bricks and petrol bombs coming my way which I thought was fantastic at that age of life. I thought to myself - this is what I joined for. I felt secure, I felt safe contrary to the situation around me. I felt I was among people who were well trained and were there to look after each other. I enjoyed every moment of it and we always looked forward to when the riots kicked off.

'In those days the new boy was given the baton gun, and eight out of ten times on the streets you would use it - almost every patrol. Mobile patrols were much easier but the worst time for them was after the pubs shut and after school gets out - then you were in for a bricking. The children learnt from an early age and in time became extremely accurate out to 30 or 40 metres, beyond the effective accurate range of the 25-grain baton round.'
Fus Dennis Kennedy 2Pl A Coy

'The hunger strikes collapsed through pressures from the Catholic Church and the families of

prisoners. However, on 6 October, the Secretary of State, James Prior conceded most of the original demands for *de facto* political status, albeit he refused to use this actual term, which would have undermined the whole Government policy to criminalise terrorist actions in Northern Ireland. For the remainder of the battalion's tour the deployed company was based at Woodbourne, rather than McCrory Park. Mass unrest gave way to terrorism as the main threat to be contended with. Terrorists in West Belfast were well equipped and audacious, although they were always intent on ensuring a secure escape route for themselves. This was their weakness that we utilised in our patrolling techniques. A typical foot patrol would last about three hours and would comprise about 24 soldiers operating in six teams. Four of the teams would operate on foot in a mutually supporting pattern, whilst two teams were mounted in vehicles. The aim was to create uncertainty in the minds of anyone monitoring the patrol as to where the troops were at any one time, thereby having a deterrent effect.'
Lt Philip Stack Pl Comd and 2IC C Coy

'A crowd of hooligans mounted an attack on McCrory Park with a JCB tractor, ladders, grappling hooks, bricks, bottles, petrol bombs, the lot. It was just like a medieval siege. It was obvious the crowd were just plain angry with the Army and wanted to tear the base down because those in the sangars or with the surveillance devices couldn't see any weapons. I remember standing in the vehicle park with a baton gun and we were firing round after round non-stop at the top of the fence trying to knock those people down. It was eventually quelled by other members of the battalion from outside and we just held the base. Looking back on it the whole thing was probably orchestrated and the attack was more than likely a huge decoy to move equipment around West Belfast.'
Fus Dennis Kennedy 2 Pl A Coy

'One evening, McCrory Park camp was attacked by rioting yobs. It smacked of being a provocation to get us out of camp, so we stayed in. They came up the funnel throwing bottles and stones etc over the fencing and using makeshift shields of corrugated iron. We responded by opening the main gates an inch or two every now and again, to let loose a volley of rubber bullets. This was considered, at the time, good fun. I was involved in the firing of the baton rounds - I would fire, hand the gun to a loader, be handed another loaded one, fire that and so on.'
Lt Andy Harris Pl Comd 1 Pl A Coy

'During the siege of McCrory Park, Ian Gorsuch injured his hand and he couldn't carry an SLR so he led his 3rd Platoon wielding a pistol. On one occasion he rushed a barricade single-handed and leapt onto the top of it. There he stood brandishing his pistol, silhouetted against the fires of burning cars as he urged his platoon on. Normally he carried an aluminium photographic equipment case which in fact was a cocktail cabinet - one of the cocktails he created was called "McCrory Glory".'
Lt Philip Macey Pl Comd 2 Pl A Coy

'The churches deserve a special mention. Alan Brown was a brilliant padre and received a well earned MID. He was involved in every aspect of battalion life and his church was always full every Sunday. Many Catholics would finish at Mass and then move across the road for morning service. The CO and I would endeavour to be back from our visits to the Fusiliers downtown in time to make the service. The only criticism that I have is that the only free places seemed always to be at the front and, no matter what time we arrived, the "Wiggly Worm" appeared to be kept until our arrival, thus providing the spectacle of the CO and RSM bedecked in combat kit gyrating to the music much to the amusement of the children.'
WO1 Alan Jones RSM 3RRF

'Intense physical activity was also mixed with intense drinking when on stand down. Ian Gorsuch's portable cocktail cabinet being much in evidence as we tried to perfect a new cocktail to be called "The Hackle" and another to be named, "The Pan-Galactic Gargle Blaster". It took much experimentation to get these right and therefore not a few sore heads.'
Lt Malcolm Johnston Pl Comd 9 Pl C Coy

'The social life for those on a resident battalion tour was generally very good. The soldiers had a great time and many went on to marry local girls and then take them away to Berlin. We tended to work a six-week cycle. Six weeks deployed in the city, six weeks on various

wives in his company was broken down into much smaller units. We all felt responsible for each other. 'Many wives were nervous about venturing very far to begin with, so we went out on organised outings or in small groups. People went to Church more. The churches seemed to be more a part of the community than usual, mostly due to a particularly excellent C of E Padre (the Reverend Alan Brown). We congregated in people's houses or in designated places. The Coffee Pot, the Community Centre and the Messes were the focal point of most people's daily lives. The Coffee Pot was a little café run by wives for wives. Most people popped in every morning after dropping the children at school or playgroup. It was a place that immediately raised people's spirits with laughter and a cream cake. The community centre held the usual bingo nights and other entertainment and the Messes Cinema nights and various other events also provided us with a welcome break from the daily round.'

'As the tour progressed and the level of operations reduced, we became more realistic about our situation. We began to venture out to see the country and to try the many wonderful local restaurants, beauty spots and other attractions. We went into Belfast on shopping trips and tried the Theatre and Concert Halls, taking every precaution possible then leaving the rest to God. The time we had together as families was very precious so we made the most of it. Although there were no fatalities, the few very dreadful casualties suffered by some during the tour brought the battalion families' together and we raised money for the families of those involved as well as many good causes.'

'When the battalion left after two years for Berlin there were few who had not enjoyed themselves as much as the local conditions would allow, while in the process meeting lots of nice people and having a lovely time into the bargain. As often happens we were to return to Ireland again, but that tour does not conjure up the same nostalgia as the tour in Palace Barracks from 1981-1983.'

RECIPE FOR REGIMENTAL COCKTAIL

THE HACKLE

Take one cocktail shaker and pour in the following (measures to taste)
1/2 to 3/4 Full of Port
1 dash Vodka
1 splash Brandy
1 tipple Vermouth
2 drops Tobasco
2 teaspoons of burning Angostura Bitters

This cocktail should be like all Fusiliers, smooth on the outside with a fiery interior
Devised by Baron von Gorsuch

kinds of reserve duty and a further six weeks trying to conduct conventional military training, often involving a stint on the ranges at Ballykinler. When we came out of the city, the usual action was to adjourn to the bar and get, as we then called it, "Gargleblasted". This was an opportunity to unwind after the routine and boredom of a quiet stint, or let one's hair down after an eventful time. Taken out of context, immature, irresponsible and loutish. But essential to get it out of the system and make a definite break from one existence into a much more civilised existence.

'I had a tremendous time as a young officer in Belfast, saw things good and bad that I suspect many people do not experience in a lifetime. I certainly grew up. I went back for a second tour with the 3rd Battalion in 1985, as a watchkeeper in Battalion Headquarters. The most depressing thing, two and a half years after my first tour, was that nothing had changed. Not one little bit.'
2nd Lt Ted Coates Pl Comd 5 Pl B Coy

'The two-year tour we spent in Palace Barracks was long, arduous and hard - demanding constant alertness and concentration by all ranks, all day and all night, every day and every night. To make up for working so hard, we played hard too, and the barracks facilities were used to the hilt by everyone. Perhaps my most abiding memory, in hindsight, was the closeness of all ranks in the battalion, and our collective determination to enjoy ourselves in every way possible at the slightest opportunity! Very Fusilier.'
Lt Col Geoff Youll CO 3RRF

To the junior officers and Fusiliers, the attractions of the hunger strike tour were obvious and no different than those that have appealed to soldiers for generations. No doubt they will continue to do so:
'Booze birds and riots - what more could you want as an 18-year old and you got paid for it as well. Berlin afterwards was the icing on the cake.'
'You felt invincible - it was brilliant, this was just the best thing that we'd all done. Compared with other tours I've done since, the hunger strike tour was simply brilliant. You got shot at , blown up - it was all part of the game. Hard action on the frontline, great parties in the mess and women everywhere.'
'As a young Fusilier life was brilliant. You worked hard, you played hard and the comradeship was great.'
'We thought we were gods. We thought we had the god-given right to go anywhere, to do anything.'

It was indeed a memorable tour and a turning point in the sorry saga of the Troubles. There is no better summary than the classic example of contemporary Irish graffito daubed on a wall in West Belfast -

WE'LL NEVER FORGET YOU JIMMY SANDS

Over the years, the four antecedent regiments were honoured with the privilege of entry to several towns and cities with which they had long and close associations. This allowed the respective regiment to march through the streets of the particular town with drums beating, bands playing, Colours flying and bayonets fixed. These privileges have been inherited by The Royal Regiment of Fusiliers and include the City of London, the City of Birmingham, the Boroughs of Warwick and Royal Leamington Spa, the Borough of Bury, the City of Coventry, the Borough of Rochdale, the City of Salford, the City of Newcastle upon Tyne, the County of the Borough and the town of Berwick-upon-Tweed, the Borough of Stratford-upon-Avon, the Borough of Rugby, the Borough of Castle Morpeth and the Borough and Royal Town of Sutton Coldfield. Here, the Band and Drums of the 1st Battalion lead the march through the Royal Town of Sutton Coldfield after the presentation of the Deed of Grant in May 1971.

BRANDY SOUR TOURS CYPRUS

The 1st Battalion deployed to Cyprus on a two-year residential tour in February 1986. Leaving a cold and snow-bound UK, a sunshine posting was a just reward after completing two years at Ballykelly in Northern Ireland. After months of long days and innumerable checkpoints, the prospect of the Cyprus working day of 0730 to 1330 hours was indeed appealing. Thereafter, the day was your own and the sunny beaches beckoned. The 1st Battalion was stationed at Salamanca Barracks in Episkopi within the Western Sovereign Base Area which the battalion was charged with protecting. Other duties included internal security and the guarding of the RAF 'Golfballs' radar site atop the Troodos Mountains. Some conventional training for general war was also conducted at the Akamas ranges on the western tip of Aphrodite's island, but adventure training and sport had an equal priority. One company was detached under the command of the roulement battalion on UN duties in Nicosia and Dhekelia. At this time, the battalion in question was the 2nd Battalion so there were over 1,000 Fusiliers on Cyprus.

Although life continued at a frantic pace as the battalions assumed their operational roles, the troops soon discovered many of the island's attractions. The delights of the former fishing village of Ayia Napa on the eastern end of the island were well worth the long drive as its beaches were much frequented by Scandinavian women giving rise to the soldiers' nickname of 'Ayia Nipple' or 'Ayia Slapper'. Equally enjoyable were the weekly visits to the Keo Brewery in Limassol. These were usually arranged for a Friday afternoon and involved the consumption of copious quantities of free Keo and Carlsberg beer. Any money notionally saved was soon squandered on useless souvenirs purchased from the factory shop. A further Keo product consumed in large quantities was its brandy when mixed with the NAAFI's 'Margari Magic Drops Bitters', fresh lemon juice and soda water to make the quintessential Cypriot cocktail - the Brandy Sour. These were drunk by the jugful in every mess and on every occasion. They were an essential accompaniment to barbecues but nothing could compare to that gastronomic triumph of brandy sours and bacon sandwiches, a panacea for hunger or hangover.

On 15 April 1986, US Navy aircraft of the 6th Fleet in the Mediterranean and USAF F-111s flying from bases in England attacked targets in Benghazi and Tripoli. The air raids were a reprisal following the terrorist bombing of a Berlin discotheque used by US servicemen and incidents in the international waters of the Gulf of Sirte which Libya claimed as her own. 1st Battalion had recently completed an exercise defending RAF Akrotiri under full NBC conditions and contingency planning in case of terrorist attack. It was immediately put into effect to seal

The Colours remain the focal point of the Regiment as they symbolise its spirit and essence both in war and peace. In battle they were defended to the last by ensigns and a specially selected group of non-commissioned officers. This tradition lives on to this day as the Colours are carried by junior officers and escorted by chosen NCOs. Here, the Colours of 2RRF are paraded at a UN Medal Parade on the Old Nicosia Airport in Cyprus in March 1986, with (from L to R) C/Sgt Caswell, Lt O'Connell, WO2 Ramsey, Lt Merriman and C/Sgt Smith

Fus Hogan and Gibbons man a Vehicle Check Point at 'Happy Valley' in the Western Sovereign Base Area Episkopi in Cyprus during an alert, following the American bombing of Libya in retaliation for terrorist attacks against US service personnel.

Episkopi SBA against car bombs and the battalion was placed on full alert. Both the 1st and 2nd Battalions had planned to celebrate the forthcoming St George's Day in style but the terrorist alert precluded any form of parade. However, during the previous month, the 2nd Battalion had held a parade for the presentation of UN medals at the Old Nicosia Airport which had remained unused for its intended purpose since the Turkish invasion of 1974. Under the auspices of the RSM, WO1 Bill Edmonds, the parade had been held on the birthday of the CO, Lieutenant Colonel Paul Bibbey, and, as the battalion marched off, a large banner was unfurled proclaiming 'Happy Birthday Colonel'.

On St George's Day itself, the 1st Battalion was spread far and wide undertaking internal security duties. Y Company was deployed to RAF Troodos guarding the perimeter of the installation on the highest mountain in Cyprus. During the day, RAF personnel assumed the guard duties for a short period to allow the company to enjoy a small celebration. One of the problems of guarding the Mount Troodos and Mount Olympus 'retained sites' was that soldiers were not allowed to patrol outside the perimeter fences in uniform. To overcome this shortcoming, 1RRF devised horse-mounted patrols on beasts borrowed from the Episkopi Saddle Club. Soon the hills were alive with the sounds of 'Larpent's Horse' and the 'Troodos Mounted Foot'. The battalion was thus inspired to put together a polo team under the patronage of the adjutant, Captain Angus Welch, but it did not meet with great success. Having just won the inter-company drill competition, Z Company was thwarted in taking their rightful place as Guard Company on the St George's Day parade. Instead, the company was spread over the island with troops deployed guarding various installations, from HQ Land Forces Cyprus in Episkopi to the BBC rebroadcast station at Zyyi on the south coast beyond Limassol.

After several weeks at full alert, the pace of life slackened as temperatures rose with the approach of summer and the prospect of terrorist retaliation diminished. Sporting prowess now came to the fore and week-long beach camps were held for Fusiliers to enjoy the sun and the sea. The respite was all too short. On 3 August, service families were enjoying a pleasant weekend and many were spending the afternoon on the beaches near Akrotiri. There were various watersports facilities such as the ARABS club - Akrotiri Rowing and Board Sailing - where windsurfing was a popular pastime. At the scuba diving club, Corporal Paddy Mooney of Y Company heard gunfire and thought to himself - 'That's funny, the ranges aren't open on Sundays'. In the mistaken belief that the USAF F-111 bombers had taken off from RAF Akrotiri, Arab terrorists of the Abu Nidal faction sought revenge by attacking the airfield with rifle grenades. None hit the runway or the base facilities but one overshot and landed in the RAF married quarters where members of the RRF Band and Drums Platoon also lived. It exploded, wounding a woman in the chest with a grenade splinter. Their grenades exhausted, the terrorists tried in vain to shoot off the lock of a perimeter gate to gain access to the base. They then turned their guns on the innocent families at the seaside. Fortunately, the fine mesh of the fencing did not allow them to swivel their weapons and their aim was poor. Nevertheless, a party of one woman and two children in the ARABS car park was in the line of fire. The woman was hit in the foot but the children escaped when the young girl of some eight years bravely shielded her younger brother by pushing him into the car and lying on top of him. By an awful irony, they were the children of the woman wounded by the grenade fragment. The terrorists escaped unharmed.

At the time, Lieutenant Christopher Claridge, the Milan Platoon commander, was having a meal at the Kyrenia Bar on Paramali Long Beach with his fiancée, Liz, when he saw plumes of smoke in the distance. Shortly thereafter a Land Rover, escorted by a Ferret armoured car of A Squadron 15th/19th The King's Hussars, arrived to collect all military personnel. The Commanding Officer of the 1st Battalion, Lieutenant Colonel David Biggart, had also been at Paramali Long Beach at a barbecue and had returned home to be told of the incident by his neighbours. He soon received a telephone call from the Chief of Staff, British Forces Cyprus, Colonel The Honourable Nick Vivian, who ordered him to implement in full the contingency plan for counter-terrorism. As this required at least eight companies of infantry at the last reckoning, Lieutenant Colonel Biggart protested but was told - 'David, do the best you can!' Thereafter, the 1st Battalion reverted to Northern Ireland mode manning scores of checkpoints and sangars for months on end. Besides protecting the Episkopi SBA and all its various living quarters such as Berengaria, the 1st Battalion was now obliged to guard RAF Akrotiri and provide detachments to Dhekelia and the extensive 'aerial farms' on the island. In the broiling

Fusiliers of 11 Platoon of Z Company conduct military training in a deserted Turkish Cypriot village outside Paramali during the 1RRF residential tour of Cyprus in 1986-87. Due to terrorist activity and the need to guard the many key points across the island, little conventional military training was undertaken at this time.

Members of the Drums Platoon display their particular functions of bandsmen and machine gunners in the Sustained Fire role as well as riflemen for UN duties in Cyprus where this photograph was taken for publicity purposes during the 3RRF tour of 1986.

heat, Fusiliers constructed numerous sangars requiring the filling of thousands of sandbags. Many Fusiliers were surprised to witness the Commanding Officer and RSM, WO1 Bob Keating, help them in this irksome task as the CO's Rover Group toured the far-flung Fusilier positions.

By some subterfuge, the Royal Air Force persuaded the High Command that it was unnecessary to reinforce the RAF Regiment or Police contingents whose task it was to guard RAF Akrotiri but that it required military assistance to do so. As a result, it fell to the 1st Battalion to provide all the personnel to construct the new defensive measures and man them. The Fusiliers were on duty 24-hours a day across the island in section positions without electricity or water. For weeks on end, they endured a cycle of five days away from base and two days off, interspersed with innumerable patrols. During the summer months, the dust at the roadside sangars was unbearable compounded by the lack of washing facilities. Patrols were conducted in tropical uniforms and bush hats but sangar duty required flak jackets with beret and hackle. Morale did not improve when it was realised that the RAF simply continued with the normal Cyprus routine of finishing work at 1330 hours. Nothing was more galling for a Fusilier sweltering in a fly-blown sangar than to see his opposite number in the RAF saunter by in flip-flops and shorts on his way to the beach. Indeed the mutual animosity between the two services plumbed new depths and did not recover throughout the tour. Fights between Fusiliers and 'Crabs' became commonplace in Limassol discotheques. Relations between Army and RAF officers were little better.

Nevertheless as the New Year dawned, the commitment to IS duties diminished and the Fusiliers were once more able to enjoy the many facilities of Cyprus. During the emergency engendered by the terrorist attack, the Fusiliers endured more separation from their families then they had in Northern Ireland. They were determined to make up for lost time. Sport and adventure training assumed a large part of their lives and mess functions proliferated, no more so than when the 3rd Battalion arrived on the island for UN duties as part of UNFICYP (United Nations Peacekeeping Force In Cyprus) during the first week of December 1986. Two companies of the 1st Battalion continued to guard Episkopi and Troodos with its mountain radar site, while a third was on stand-by to move to Ayios Nikolaos, the home of 9 Signal Regiment on the eastern end of the island. The fourth company was devoted to training under the guidance of the battalion training officer, Lieutenant Simon Marr. In a new departure, X Company spent several weeks in the Kingdom of Jordan conducting joint training with the Jordanian army where the company commander, Major Dennis Bottomley, was unable to indulge his twin passions for rugby and beer.

The 3rd Battalion under the command of Lieutenant Colonel Jolyon Willans was divided into two halves, with a two-company detachment in Dhekelia and two companies 'on the line' in the UN Buffer Zone between the Greek Cypriot and Turkish armies. Battalion Headquarters was located just outside the buffer zone in St David's Camp where the CO presided over HQ Sector 2 with the two rifle companies known as Eastern Company and Western Company. Sector 2 stretched from the Old Nicosia Airport in the east to the outskirts of of the Turkish-occupied village of Pano Zodhia in the west, a distance of some 26 kms, out of a total length of 217 kms across the island. The actual Buffer Zone varied from 1 1/2 - 4 1/2 kms in width and from a barren, rocky escarpment with little cultivation in the east to lush, heavily-cultivated citrus groves in the west. The platoons were deployed to separate locations incorporating the OPs such as B22, B33 and B35. Duties included the manning of the OPs, preventing shepherds and their flocks from trespassing across the line, escorting farmers and their workers in the citrus groves, patrolling and liaising with both the Greek and Turkish authorities. Each month, UNFICYP held a different competition to test the military and sporting skills of the various Sectors, including day and night navigation, patrolling, shooting, first aid and endurance. Sports included tennis, volleyball and the Danish March - a 60 km hike over two days. The principal task at Dhekelia was to maintain the security of the Eastern Sovereign Base Area which covers 72 sq kms and is 22 kms from west to east with four principal areas of note: the Bulge, the Triangle, the Corridor Road and the Ayios Nikolaos Lozenge. The Bulge is almost semi-desert, strewn with boulders and interlaced with numerous wadis. The Triangle is flat and featureless scrub, providing pasture for goats and sheep and the cultivation of root vegetables. The Corridor is a ten kms long road that links the SBA with the Ayios Nikolaos complex comprising 9 Signal Regiment and 33 Signal Unit RAF. Duties involved patrols, guards, Quick Reaction Forces (QRF) and the manning of vehicle checkpoints. Both battalions took advantage of the varied courses available at the Joint Services Adventure Training Centre at Pergamos, including diving, freefall parachuting, gliding and canoeing. Many Fusiliers tried to prove that it was possible to ski in the Troodos Mountains in the morning and water ski in the Mediterranean in the afternoon.

For the 1st Battalion in Episkopi, 1987 brought several triumphs not least of which was sweeping the board at the Near East Skill-at-Arms Meeting and winning the Cyprus Walkabout Competition. The latter, despite its title, is one of the most gruelling orienteering competitions in the world, covering some 70 miles over two days from Episkopi to the top of Mount Troodos at over 6,000 feet and back again. This was achieved in the remarkable time of ten hours and 53 minutes. Victory never tasted so sweet then after 1st Battalion inflicted a stinging defeat over the RAF in the floodlit Carter Cup football competition - the first time that the RAF had been beaten for many years. This encounter did nothing to improve relations between the two services and they reached a nadir after the 'B Mess Boys' overwhelmed a party held in the officers' mess at RAF Akrotiri to which the officers of the 1st Battalion were invited. At Episkopi there were two messes, with 'A Mess' for the officers attached to the garrison headquarters and for the permanent staff in Cyprus. The 'B Mess' was for the resident infantry battalion and its supporting armoured car squadron, formerly A Squadron 15th/19th The King's Royal Hussars and now F Squadron 3rd Royal Tank Regiment (RTR). 'The B Mess Boys' were the young subalterns who exhibited all the *joie de vivre* of that ilk and were renowned for their sense of fun and frivolity as well as their capacity for alcohol.

The party in question was to be a 'German Carnival Night' with an Oompah Band, and fancy dress was optional with expectations that some guests might wear lederhosen or Heidi dresses. 'The B Mess Boys' had other ideas and borrowed the all-black coveralls from the RTR 'tankies'. They also had various accessories run up in 'Tin City' behind Episkopi so that they could go as German stormtroopers. Lieutenant Simon Marr recalls - 'My girlfriend was a teacher at Akrotiri and I went to collect her. We acted as an advanced party with me dressed in black uniform, Sam Browne belt, Boots Combat High and a swastika armband. Some of the RAF chaps thought it highly amusing but not for long. About half an hour later, a phalanx of stormtroopers burst into the mess with Alistair Cartwright leading and Matthew Shirley, one of the subbies, dressed as a Jew, complete with black hat, ringlets and yellow star of David. Ian 'Chubby' Brown, whose mother is German, was wearing a Gestapo-type greatcoat, and all of them were well lubricated with brandy sours. From there it just went downhill and the whole thing got very ugly, not least of which was Cartwright knocking over the station commander because he was boring and Shirley cavorting with one of the RAF officer's mother

Fus Etherton of W Company 1RRF keeps a look-out at OP B24 at Dhenia in Sector 2 of the multinational UN Force in Cyprus on the buffer zone between the Greek and Turkish Cypriots in 1978. To the anonymous DPM camouflage uniform and blue beret of the British forces on United Nations duties, the Fusiliers added a FUSILIERS shoulder title on the brassard to assert their identity. After the heavy casualties incurred at the battle of Hill 217 in Korea in November 1951, W Company of 1st Battalion Royal Northumberland Fusiliers was not reformed as a rifle company. Its practice of identifying companies by the letters X, Y and Z (first introduced on 3 September 1914 to overcome confusion in sound between B and D Companies) was inherited by 1RRF. With the introduction of the 650-man battalion establishment in 1976, W Company was reconstituted within 1RRF. It subsequently became the Fire Support Company.

Fus Gallimore and Linstead of Y Company stand guard with newly issued SA80 rifles during IS duties following the terrorist attack on RAF Akrotiri in August 1986. In September, Y Company was the first to receive the new weapon for hot weather troop trials. Initial impressions were favourable with marksmanship improving significantly thanks to its optical sight, but problems soon became apparent in the cold climes of Norway with 2RRF in the AMF(L) role.

in the car park. This party was the final nail in the coffin for Fusilier-RAF relations. Obviously word got back to Colonel David, who told the adjutant to sort us out in no uncertain terms. After telling us - "You have succeeded in being thrown out of the last mess in Cyprus at which we were welcome" - we were grounded for a couple of weeks.'

The A Mess also suffered at the hands of the 'B Mess Boys'. On one of their formal dining-in nights, a yellow Mini Moke belonging to one of the subalterns was driven up and down the corridors during the meal. All was well until a corner was encountered when the vehicle had to be manhandled around the obstacle, but not without considerable damage to the walls. On a different occasion, a similar fate befell the mess garden when it was used for high speed rallying by inebriated subalterns only yards from an RMP post. The excuse that they were driving on private property was a flimsy defence in law but the girlfriend of one of the accused used her influence over the judge to have the case dismissed. Forays into northern Cyprus for a long *meze* on the quayside at Kyrenia were a popular pastime, as was returning through Greek Cypriot villages in the dreaded Mini Moke wearing Turkish fezzes.

However, some military matters did impinge. Due to the terrorist incident the previous year and the two year stint in Ballykelly, the 1st Battalion had not held a St George's Day parade for some years. Both the adjutant, Captain Angus Welch, and the RSM, WO1 Bob Keating, were determined to have a traditional celebration in 1987. Preparations began weeks in advance with rehearsals for Trooping the Colour taking place on the hockey pitch in Happy Valley below Episkopi. These were held in the early morning before the heat of the day in order to hone the battalion's marching skills which had become rusty through abstinence. The Fusiliers made an incongruous sight as they marched hither and thither in their blue PT shorts, red PT vests, green Army socks rolled down, DMS boots, beret and hackle with SLRs and fixed bayonets.

As St George's Day approached, the rehearsals became more frequent and longer, as the RSM fine-tuned every nuance of the parade. On one occasion, a curious drill order was heard when the RSM, mindful of the heat, halted the parade and shouted - 'Ground arms. About turn. The battalion will march on Libya. Into the sea, quick march!' For the next half-hour, the troops gratefully cooled off in the Mediterranean Sea. On another occasion, a Greek Cypriot ice cream vendor arrived in Happy Valley, ringing his bell, towards the end of a rehearsal. By a curious coincidence, he carried sufficient ice creams for everyone on the parade ground - courtesy of the RSM and PRI funds. In the final rehearsals, 'blanket colours' were carried; these were simply Army blankets attached to a pole to simulate the weight of the real Colours which are far heavier than anyone ever expects. During one rehearsal on a Monday morning, the 'blanket colour' party approached the RSM at the climax of the parade and halted in the regulation manner. At the top of the colour pole was a teddy bear dressed in Newcastle

At the dress rehearsal for the St George's Day Parade of 1987, the officers of the Colour Party go through their paces, with (from L to R) Lt Beverley as Commander of the Escort, Lt Marr Queen's Colour Ensign and Lt Reay Regimental Colour Ensign, on the hockey pitch in Happy Valley. After a gap of four years due to operational commitments in Northern Ireland and a terrorist alert the year before, 1RRF held a St George's Day Parade as a celebration of the Regiment's birthday. The parade recreates some of the ceremonies of bygone years that would be familiar to Fusiliers during the Peninsular War. Each manoeuvre had its purpose in the days of horse and musket. Early in the parade, the officers inspect their companies in a slow march. In times of yore, the officers would have been checking cartridges and the flints that fired the muskets. Much of the parade is taken up with a slow troop of the Colours through the ranks. The Colours formed the rallying point for the battalion during the battle. It was therefore vital that every man was able to identify their Colours from those of other battalions in the smoke of war. The slow troop through the ranks allowed all the soldiers, especially the new recruits, to have a close look at the Colours before battle was joined. At the climax of the parade with all the companies organised and ready for battle, the Commanding Officer, on this occasion Lt Col Biggart, takes command of the parade and orders his battalion to advance for the general salute. In 1987, the salute was taken by Maj Gen Webster, Deputy Colonel of the Regiment City of London.

United strip. On the Saturday before, the Magpies had beaten the RSM's team, Arsenal, 4-1. The commander of the guard, Colour Sergeant Boris Spence, then asked permission to march off the teddy bear. At the dress rehearsal, WO1 Bob Keating cautioned the assembled Fusiliers that if any of them had a single drink the night before the parade or failed to eat breakfast and fainted during the parade - 'you're going to gaol!'. His successor as RSM, WO1 Mick Moran, had a completely different attitude and, before one Queen's Birthday Parade, announced - 'If you can't drink 20 pints of a night, eat a curry, sh*g a bird and march on my parade square first thing in the morning, you're not fit to be a Fusilier'. Such are the vagaries of RSMs.

In the fiercely-contested Newcastle Cup on St George's Day, Y Company beat X Company. The latter however still won the coveted Champion Company Shield while W Company won the Inter-Company Drill Competition and so gained the honour as Escort for the Colour on the actual parade. The parade itself and Families Day were a total success. As the *Fusilier Journal* (Volume 5 Number 7) recounts: 'St George's Day was celebrated in true style for the first time in years. An awesome amount of champagne was drunk in the Officers' Mess tent after the parade. The following day was characterised by the PMC wandering around in shock, clutching the wine-bill, and most Mess members demonstrating symptoms of catatonia'. The 1st Battalion returned to England in March 1988 and, for the first time since the formation of the Regiment, all three battalions were stationed in the UK.

SOUTH ARMAGH - BANDIT COUNTRY

'South Armagh is like a beautiful green snake - it looks lovely from above, but wait until you put a foot on it.' Virtually cut off from the rest of Northern Ireland by a range of hills, South Armagh was originally to be part of the Republic of Ireland according to the boundary commission of 1922. By some administrative oversight, it remained part of Ulster and has become the most lawless corner of the United Kingdom which makes a mockery of that title. This bureaucratic error has been extremely costly both in treasure to the British government and in blood to the British Army. With a population that is over 95 per cent Catholic, its people are predominantly nationalist and most are sympathetic to the aims of the IRA. From the start of the Troubles in 1969 to St George's Day 2000, over 160 members of the Security Forces have been killed, including seven Fusiliers, as against 30 of the IRA. A further 80 civilians have died. During the same period, it is calculated that South Armagh has suffered 1,255 bomb explosions, 1,158 gun attacks and 378 murders. Few who have served there can forget its beauty or its malevolence. As a company commander in the 1st Battalion roulement tour of 1989, Major Angus Welch speaks for a generation of Fusiliers -'The main recurring memory of South Armagh is of how rural, wet and dank it was. In over four months it never

The Fusiliers of 4 Platoon B Company of 3rd Battalion prepare to receive rioters on Scotch Street in Armagh City in early 1973. Under the command of Lt Col Cartwright, 3RRF was deployed to the Armagh area of mid-Ulster including the notorious trouble spots of Dungannon, Armagh, Portadown, Craigavon and Lurgan and some 50 miles of the border region. During the tour from 4 January 1973 to 4 May 1973, the battalion captured 59 weapons and over 5,000 rounds of ammunition. Over 3,000 pounds of explosives and 14 constructed bombs were recovered. Two terrorists were killed in firefights and one was wounded, with another 30 being arrested. Fusilier Marchant was killed. As a result of this successful tour, one OBE, one MBE, four MMs and one BEM were awarded to Fusiliers.

seemed to dry out. However, the countryside was transformed on the few clear, crisp days into one of stunning beauty and emptiness. Newtonhamilton was perceived as a small rural village of little consequence in the great scheme of things. The maelstrom of IRA activities and the attempts by the Security Forces to defeat them swirled around but seemed not to effect the company TAOR (Tactical Area of Operational Responsibility) very much. After some reflection on this at the time, I suspected that the IRA kept the area quiet for very good reasons. It was presumed that they used this quiet TAOR to transport weapons and explosives across the border with impunity. From the IRA's point of war, the less Army activity the better and the IRA tactic was to keep it that way, resulting in a lowering of the Army's profile, thus giving them free rein.

'The local population would talk to you when on patrol as long as they were not seen doing so by others. I met an old man of 80 plus who told me that he had spent his whole life in South Armagh and apart from war service had never left it - he had only been to Newry, six miles away, once in his life! At first we could not understand that however professional our fieldcraft the locals always knew our whereabouts. We soon discovered that as patrols passed by outlying farms, the occupants would light smoky peat fires. The thick smoke from the chimneys could be seen from any vantage point and was an effective warning system. At night, the flashing of security lights acted as the same warning system. Patrols were hard work. In particular, fighting through endless hawthorn hedges en route to a helicopter pick-up point is a lasting memory. So too is keeping a close eye on the weather, as, if the cloud base was low or the frequent South Armagh mists developed, it invariably meant a long patrol home. The RAF would not fly in such conditions - nor indeed, as rumour had it, on Friday afternoons or Monday mornings!

'It is often been said that Northern Ireland provided the Army with unparalleled training for junior officers and NCOs. The opportunities offered to these inexperienced commanders on a tour were so much better than normal field training. Commanders had to plan and lead from the front for real and they thrived on that responsibility. Occasionally they had to react to serious incidents when advice was either far away or time to act precluded seeking that advice, second opinion or other reassurance. Latterly, the use of Electronic Counter Measures (ECM) had helped to defeat the undoubted capability of the IRA to detonate explosive devices remotely. The need to protect ourselves first before trying to defeat the IRA proactively drove all our tactical thinking. It was a strange but necessary tactic which seemed to run counter to our normal doctrine for warfighting - to close with and destroy the enemy.'

DRUMMUCKAVALL

The 3rd Battalion returned to Ulster in August 1975 for their fourth operational tour in South Armagh. It was to be the most costly for The Royal Regiment of Fusiliers throughout the campaign in Northern Ireland. Even for South Armagh it was a period of exceptional violence with a concerted campaign against Protestants living in the area and particularly those associated with the Security Forces. On the evening of 1 September 1975, one of the most heinous acts to date occurred at the Tullyvallen Orange Hall on the Altnamackin Road near Newtownhamilton. The Guiding Star Temperance Orange Lodge was holding a meeting on the premises. It had just decided not to use the hall again because of security fears when the lodge was attacked by three gunmen in an attempt to terrorise the divided community further. Two gunmen burst in and riddled the hall with automatic fire, while a third smashed the high side windows of the church hall and fired downwards onto the meeting from a blind high port position. The terrorists then disappeared to escape across the border within minutes. Responsibility for the attack was claimed by the Republican Action Force, a cover name for the South Armagh PIRA.

A QRF (Quick Reaction Force) was speedily deployed under the command of Sergeant Tony Kimberley flying in a Puma helicopter. On landing, two Fusiliers, both armed with GPMG machine guns, entered the hall and were shocked by the scene of devastation they found. Twelve of the 17 people inside had been hit, many with multiple wounds. Two had been killed outright and another died, disembowelled, in the arms of Corporal 'Chippy' Wood. At the time, Lieutenant Trevor Minter was in Bessbrook Mill but he quickly arrived at the scene by helicopter with the RMO, Captain John Carter and his deputy, Sergeant Nigel Brookes. Lieutenant Minter took over as incident commander while Sergeant Kimberley supervised the

Fus Purvis of the Mortar Platoon paints the Regimental Emblem on the inner blast wall of Creggan Camp during the 3rd Battalion tour of Londonderry between July and November 1978. The emblem comprises St George within the garter, all within a laurel wreath surmounted by St Edward's Crown. The garter is inscribed with the regimental motto, inherited from the Royal Warwickshire Regiment and the Royal Fusiliers, 'HONI SOIT QUI MAL Y PENSE' - 'Evil be to him who evil thinks'.

Fusiliers giving first aid in support of the RMO. Despite having experienced terrorist outrages in Algeria, a civilian doctor who appeared was unable to assist because the scene made him physically sick. In the meantime, civilian ambulances had arrived from distant Newry. Two more people died as the casualties were being evacuated and later in hospital.

Meanwhile, Corporal Dave Llewellyn was conducting an area search when he discovered an unexploded device that had been left at the rear of the building by the terrorists to wreak further mayhem and disrupt the rescue operation . Word of this was passed quietly among the rescuers but it was realised that if the building was cleared some of the injured would bleed to death. Accordingly, everyone remained to give first aid to the wounded and succour to the dying. All were evacuated to hospital before the site was cleared for the EOD team. The Fusiliers performed magnificently that night and undoubtedly saved several lives. However five men died, the eldest of whom was 80 years old, the next 70, another 63; the eldest Fusilier was 22. In November 1977, a 22-year old Cullyhanna man, Anthony McCooey, was convicted in connection with the killings and received seven life sentences. He was also convicted of killing two members of the UDR. One of the Armalites used in the slaughter at the Tullyvallen Orange Hall was subsequently employed to kill three Fusiliers at a covert OP in November.

On 9 October, Corporal Edward Gleeson of C Company was killed while leading a mobile patrol at Lurgancullenboy near Crossmaglen when the Saracen APC that he was commanding was blown up by a mine hidden in a culvert. As a result of this tragedy, the British Army came increasingly to employ helicopters for the movement of soldiers. That however gave no greater protection to the infantryman on the ground. On 21 November, an improvised explosive device (IED) was detonated near an abandoned car as Sergeant Simon Francis of B Company approached it, killing him instantly. The IED had been initiated by a command wire from across the border with the Republic of Ireland. On the following day, a covert observation post set up some 36 hours earlier near Drummuckavall and occupied by four Fusiliers was attacked by an IRA active service unit (ASU) in broad daylight. The initial burst of fire killed Fusiliers Duncan, McDonald and Sampson. Amid calls for surrender, the IRA continued to fire into the position, seriously wounding Lance Corporal Paul Johnson with three bullets in his back and arm. As he slipped into unconsciousness, Johnson heard the gunmen shout - ‘Up the Provos’ before they ran across the border into the Republic of Ireland. To the IRA diehards of the South Armagh brigade, the ceasefire meant little beyond the opportunity to rearm and reorganise to their best advantage. This incident prompted the Northern Ireland secretary, Merlyn Rees, to declare - ‘There has never been a ceasefire in South Armagh for a variety of reasons - the nature of the countryside and the nature of the people. It is an unusual area - there is little support for the security forces in South Armagh. The government is not trying to buy off terrorism by the release of detainees as the numbers of terrorists arrested and charged shows. The release of detainees has nothing to do with the violence of the bandit country of South Armagh. There is wholesale gangsterism there.’

Towards the end of the 3rd Battalion's 1974 tour in Armagh and Tyrone, a UDR Land Rover was blown up by a large culvert bomb that had been placed under the Omagh-Dungannon road. The bomb was detonated from the high ground overlooking the road. The blast flipped the Land Rover off the road into a field where it landed on its roof; part of the belly plate and one wheel can be seen in the background above the crater's rim. The occupants were seriously injured, the driver losing several teeth on the steering wheel. The occupants of the car to the right of the picture had a lucky escape in that they nearly drove into the crater. Lt Greenwood, OC 1 Platoon, (in crater) was on a final check of the area with the CO of the UDR Battalion involved and Cpl 'Slasher' Brown, the A Coy medic.

It was an apposite phrase that was immediately picked up by the media: Bandit Country has been used to describe South Armagh ever since. Overall, it has been the most dangerous posting for the British Army in Ulster. The South Armagh brigade have had a policy of inflicting at least one death on every roulement battalion deployed to the area. It remains a priority for every Commanding Officer to return home from South Armagh with all his soldiers. The following accounts by former Commanding Officers illustrate the trials and tribulations of service in Bandit Country over the years.

2RRF 1976 - LT COL PETER SINCOCK

'The run-up to the 2nd Battalion's tour of Northern Ireland in 1976 suffered from one fundamental flaw. My predecessor, Lieutenant Colonel Danni Seidl, had devised an excellent training period to fit the battalion for duties in West Belfast. Two weeks before I was to assume command and with only minimum training time left, I received a telephone call at home in England. Colonel Jeremy Reilly (as he then was) phoned from the MOD to say that we would now be going to South Armagh instead! We would be taking over half the border, Armagh City and most of County Armagh. After rapid retraining we settled in with companies at Middletown, Newtonhamilton, Armagh and Glenanne. There is no doubt that the NITAT training system had come on by leaps and bounds since we had trained in Catterick in 1971 for our first tour in Belfast when I was OC B Company.

'Much of our operational area was dangerous for wheeled vehicles and so we made full use of helicopters. Their worth had been proved conclusively to me on extensive operations in Oman and we made much use of the Army Air Corps and the RAF. As well as insertion of patrols and OPs and the more usual eagle patrols, we did several cordon and search operations involving more than one company, with the cordon being air-landed from several different directions simultaneously. I suspect I was not one of the RAF's favourite Commanding Officers by continually demanding split-second timing! I remember one evening hearing a panic on the radio with the RUC saying they had had a vehicle blown up on a border road. Having myself (probably illegally) driven several times along that road with my Rover Group, I was able to calm them down with the knowledge that at that point a peat fire was undermining the tarmac. The tarmac had finally collapsed and their vehicle had tumbled into the hole amid much smoke and confusion! So it was Fusiliers to the rescue.

'It was a hard tour, although in lovely country and in mainly glorious weather. A summer tour in the country with some 18-20 hours of daylight meant little time for covert movement and much time in which troops had to be seen dominating the area. In spite of a number of close shaves, in IRA ambushes, bombs and shootings, thankfully everyone got back to Paderborn safely. Fusilier Philips, son of the famous sergeant major and whose brother was my signaller, was saved by his flak jacket when he was hit. The bullet was slowed sufficiently not to

The Airborne Reaction Force of the Recce Platoon flies over County Armagh aboard a Sioux helicopter to conduct a snap cordon and search during the 2nd Battalion tour of South Armagh in 1976. Thanks to his experiences in Dhofar, Lt Col Sincock, the CO of 2RRF, made great use of helicopters to conduct cordon and search operations in villages and areas that were not normally subject to close scrutiny by the Security Forces. This tactic did not make him particularly popular with the RAF.

Fusiliers of 3 Platoon of A Company, with (from L to R) Fus Thacker and Ryan, conduct a Close Protection Patrol of the permanent Observation Post constructed on the commanding heights of Slievebolea in South Armagh, on the border with the Republic of Ireland, during the 3RRF Banner tour of August to December 1985. The Gaelic name of Slievebolea was too much for many British soldiers who named the feature the Superbowl.

penetrate his ribs. It was a thoroughly rewarding tour and I believe everyone knew we had done a professional and worthwhile job. Our next tour, Londonderry, was less rewarding with far too much time wasted sorting out trouble at pub closing time and confronting small boys throwing stones only for long enough to dash home to see if they were on the 9 or 10 o'clock television news.'

3RRF 1985 - LT COL JOLYON WILLANS

'As CO, much of my time was spent providing top cover to the battalion, hosting visitors, liaising with the RUC at divisional level, attending brigade O Groups and other mundane tasks. There were few opportunities to get out on the ground, but Sergeant Hill (now Captain Jim Hill MTO 1RRF) had cause to remember one night when his foot patrol was taking off in a Wessex helicopter for a short patrol of some six hours duration and, counting everyone on board, he discovered that he had one extra - the Commanding Officer. I selected this patrol because I knew Fusilier Hill when he had been in my C Company in the 3rd Battalion in Fallingbostel, because it was a short duration patrol and it was in an area with which I was unfamiliar. Fortunately the only remarkable thing about this patrol was their unexpected guest! Almost every patrol was uneventful; it was the one that was not which one had to anticipate. Major Jerome Church, as OC HQ Company and public relations officer had a less traumatic tour than the one in Armagh in 1972 with A Company when he lost his lower right leg. With his natural *bonhomie*, he enjoyed escorting the media so it was not by chance that nine years later, Lieutenant Colonel Church was chief public information officer at SHAPE.

'A Company with Major Arthur Petrie drew the short straw as it was colocated with Battalion HQ at Bessbrook Mill. As so often it was when the CO took his R and R and was away that adventure, or in this case misadventure, occurred. A Wessex helicopter had just lifted off in the dark from the helipad at the isolated mountain top OP at Forkhill, having dropped off a patrol, when its rotor blade struck the radio mast and the helicopter crashed down, ending on its side but fortunately not catching fire. It was pitch dark except for sparks shorting out within the cabin. After the shattering noise of the engines and the crash, it was suddenly quiet. The heavily laden Fusiliers escaped injury from flying debris and machinery and set about trying to extricate the crew. The sparks and smell of fuel made this the more hazardous. Sadly the loadmaster died, though the pilot and copilot survived. There was plenty of adrenaline used that night!

'As ever it was a platoon and section commanders' campaign. Their follow-up and reaction would prove whether we were able to return fire effectively. These junior commanders' patrolling techniques and awareness would have to provide sufficient deterrence to pre-empt an attack. The multiple patrol, with four or five four-man teams patrolling independently yet providing mutual support, proved successful. Although we ended the tour having expended several hundred rounds over the barren and inhospitable terrain of South Armagh, with no hits claimed much to the frustration of the brigade commander, Brigadier Michael Rose, all the Fusiliers returned home to Catterick intact.'

1 RRF TOUR 1988–89 - LT COL ROY WILDE

The 1st Battalion deployed to South Armagh in the autumn of 1988 for the battalion's tenth tour of the Province during the present emergency. It was the Regiment's first experience of serving under 3 Infantry Brigade's concept of operations based upon the single brigade having responsibility for the complete border with the Republic of Ireland, from Newry all the way round to Londonderry. Tactics were based far more upon surveillance from both strongpoint OPs and towers, working with overt patrolling and covert static observation by the rifle companies. Each battalion retained an airmobile company free of AOR responsibilities, and practised in rapid heli-borne insertion to swamp or seal target areas. As the South Armagh task demanded 70 or more soldiers than the 5 Airborne Brigade establishment permitted, the battalion's reinforcements included more than 20 Fusiliers from the 5th and 6th Battalions and a platoon of Queen's Own Highlanders. Tour preparations exploited the battalion's high level of physical fitness from its 5 Airborne Brigade role but equally everyone was aware that the South Armagh PIRA had taken malicious joy in inflicting a fatal casualty upon the ten battalions that had preceded the Fusiliers to that corner of Ireland. For centuries, it had displayed a history of anti-government activities and, since 1922, honed by its border location into professional smuggling, banditry and extortion. Up to September 1988, 158 members of the Security Forces had been murdered in the Armagh Roulement Battalion (ARB) TAOR.

The Fusiliers were painfully aware that South Armagh witnessed and usually led the development of the complete spectrum of terrorist weapons from bomb, mortar, rocket and rifle. The South Armagh terrorist group consisted of a pool of specialists, booby-trap men, mortar specialists, sniping teams, but most particularly surveillance screens that were put together and regrouped for each specific terrorist operation. Overall direction, planning, weapons specialisation and logistic support was effective from south of the border. Despite this now being the tenth year of police primacy, the RUC writ did not run in the ARB; this greatly simplified battalion life as it allowed the CO to take the operational lead. However, unlike some other Regiments, the 1st Battalion realised the importance of using the different abilities of the RUC to maintain law and order and for the provision of background knowledge while the Fusiliers focused upon the operational imperative of less predictable operations, creating uncertainty in the terrorist mind. Lieutenant Colonel Roy Wilde placed particular emphasis upon the individual responsibilities of every Fusilier. First in proactive thinking; to exploit the fact that the enemy, although cunning and embittered was also a fallible criminal of low morale fibre unwilling to die for his cause, and hence someone who could be dominated by unpredictable offensive action. Second, that the professional inquisitive mind of the Fusilier was a vital element in the intelligence collecting cycle. Third, that courtesy and the importance of a firm but fair approach to the innocent majority of the population was vital. This immediately paid off when, on 14 December, the enemy launched a combined rocket and small arms attack upon the Newry Courthouse. Swift airborne action initiated by Captain "Buzzard" Gammons resulted in the attack team being pinned down and going to ground in the outskirts of Newry. Whilst the ATO cautiously dealt with the carefully arranged 'come on' booby-trapped firing point, our subtle local style paid dividends on the informant side and one of the trigger men and the four weapons used in the attack were captured.

This frustration of the terrorists' attempt for a quick win against the battalion then set the scene for five months of a subtle form of operational chess as the terrorist fell back upon his more insidious and reliable weapon of the radio-controlled bomb. Throughout the battalion area, but particularly in the Y Company Forkhill AOR and Z Company's Crossmaglen AOR, a cat and mouse game of overt patrol, covert static surveillance, unpredictable surge to counter the observation and plans of the known murderers with whom we had daily contact proceeded in the manner of a game of Russian roulette. Every Fusilier became a radio-controlled bomb

Minden Roses are worn wherever Fusiliers find themselves on the 1st of August even in the depths of the jungle in Belize, as Capt Charlie Bishop of Y Company prepares for an attack against 3 Para in the coastal shanty town of Punta Gorda during a 'Native Trail' deployment in the summer of 1984. Belt equipment includes a compass pouch and a 'bushwhacker' machete; the British Army issue is also called the 'tree bouncer' as it is often less than effective. Many soldiers buy whatever the locals use as they are better suited to the prevailing conditions and vegetation. Shaving is not encouraged in the jungle as any cuts can quickly become infected. At the time, 1RRF was based at Ballykelly in Ulster where preliminary training for Belize was undertaken as JEWTS - 'Jungle Exercise Without Trees'.

countermeasures expert. During the tour a total of 23 attempted attacks or preliminary moves were mounted against the Fusiliers, all of which were successfully frustrated. The most prolonged involved a combination of four different bombs laid on the Newry to Belfast railway at Kilnasaggart just north of the border, the first triggered on 16 December. Their eventual neutralisation took eight days and was not completed without the ATO being blown off his feet by the second bomb; cleverly operated by command detonation using the railway line powered by multiple car batteries from several miles away south of the border. Happily, the bomb disposal officer staggered out of the smoke, blackened and divested of his body-armour like something out of a slap-stick comedy, but uninjured. After a calming cup of tea and a cigarette, he immediately set about the rest of the clearance that eventually yielded a further 500 pounds of explosives. The professionalism of the 1st Battalion was recognised even by the IRA themselves. After the battalion's departure, the RUC Special Branch received intelligence that during the last month of the tour the Provisionals had made the decision to suspend operations against the Fusiliers in South Armagh until after our departure. Tragically our professionalism led them to look towards softer targets elsewhere and the RUC Divisional Commander and his border superintendent were both murdered crossing back into Northern Ireland after a conference with the Garda in the Republic of Ireland. Furthermore, only two days after the departure of the 1st Fusiliers, a successor battalion suffered a fatal attack.

The professionalism was recognised by a total of 12 operational awards, including the George Medal awarded to a Staff Sergeant of the RAOC. This tour was without doubt one of the most significant for the Fusiliers. Their ability to counter the South Armagh brigade both tactically and technically brought the realisation that neither side could win in this prolonged 'chess game with terminal results' and paved the way for the ceasefire of 1994. Despite some notable lapses, this remains extant to this day, even in South Armagh where the disaffected population has reverted to its principal occupation of smuggling. Over the years and with the connivance of successive Anglo-Irish governments, this lucrative pastime has made the area remarkably prosperous. However, the IRA has not gone away.

Looking every inch the part, a long range reconnaissance patrol, with (from L to R) Cpl Bateman, Sgt Flanagan, Cpl Taylor and Sgt Stiles, prepares for another mission into the jungle during an instructors course in Belize in 1995. The photograph of these Fusiliers reveals a wealth of detail for jungle operations with Stu Bateman's personalised SA80 incorporating a pace counter on the foregrip; pacing and bearing are the standard methods of navigation in the jungle. On his webbing harness are rows of beads to mark every 100 metres and each kilometre. Over his other shoulder is the plastic tubing from his 'camelback' water bottle so that liquid refreshment is constantly available. 'Spider' Taylor is wearing a privately purchased 'chest rig' whose pouches are readily accessible when marching with a bergen. His weapon has a D-ring and length of cord wrapped around the carrying handle. This allows the rifle to be attached to a boat so that it will not be lost should the boat capsise when negotiating rapids. Fingerless cycling gloves act to disguise the hands as camouflage cream is soon rubbed off in the jungle. Shirt collars and cuffs are buttoned up to minimise the amount of flesh exposed to mosquitoes. These patrols are normally undertaken by members of the Reconnaissance Platoon and are commonly of 14-days duration. As satellite imagery and other aerial surveillance devices are largely ineffective at penetrating the jungle canopy, such reconnaissance patrols are necessary to find and shadow enemy units so that larger company or battlegroup assets can be committed against them.

Although the 6th Battalion has always been one of the best established formations in the Territorial Army, recruiting was not harmed when Miss Judith Hall became Miss 6RRF, as well as Miss Tyne Tees and a finalist in the Miss UK contest. At 6 feet 1 inch in her fishnet stockings, the PR executive towers over Fus Brown at 5 feet 7 inches during a recruiting drive in Newcastle in 1982.

BOXING

'As the lights go down and the noise of a thousand feet drumming on the wooden floor of gymnasiums in many lands heralds the arrival of the contestants in the ring, to meet as gladiators of old in the most open of arenas, may those who have been there remember the test and those who are to come look forward to it.'

Sport, like Adventurous Training, is inextricably bound up with Army life. Both are used to cement teamwork and develop the intangible qualities of self confidence, leadership and resilience in adversity required of soldiers through the ages. Sport has the added advantage that it can be played anywhere and under most conditions. It is rare for footballs not to be included in someone's kit when they deploy on operations – how else can the England-Germany clash of Christmas 1914 be explained?

Every year most regiments in the British Army hold a Novices Boxing Competition which ends with one of the most exhilarating and tribal experiences for competitor and spectator alike. Tribal pride and loyalty are reinforced and forged on such occasions. Despite the introduction of head guards and other safety measures a Regiment's Novices Boxing Finals are an occasion where raw aggression and boxing skills can clash headlong. (In the run up to the finals many a platoon commander has found himself in the ring to 'show form' - usually leaving it bloody but unbowed, to the delight of the audience and the fierce pride of his platoon who would take on all comers on his behalf!) To be a spectator on such a night is a great privilege with tension and drama packed into every moment.

The Fusiliers have always accorded sport a high priority and boxing has held its own as a favourite sport within the Regiment since 1968. It can be argued that the increase in commitments that followed the collapse of the Berlin Wall has meant that no regiment can now promote one sport with any level of consistency. In the 1970s, 1QUEENS and 1RGJ, to name but 2 infantry regiments, consistently turned out boxing teams of the highest quality. No one who was there will forget the latter's consummate demolition of the 3rd Battalion's team in Dover in 1975. But Fusilier boxing, while occasionally producing individual successes, only succeeded when given the necessary backing and resources by the Commanding Officer of the day. A classic example of this was the performance of the 1st Battalion's Novice Boxing team in Minden in 1979-80.

Boxers in the 1st Battalion compete annually for the Harts Medals, a tradition inherited from the Royal Northumberland Fusiliers. In 1979, the newly commissioned RSM of the 3rd Battalion, John O'Grady (who had spent his early years in the 1st Battalion and had won two Harte Medals in his time), was posted back to the 1st Battalion and on arrival was made Boxing Officer. Following the Harts Medals Competition that year the Commanding Officer, Lieutenant Colonel David Houlton MBE, gave John O'Grady permission to train a squad for the Brigade Novices Boxing Competition. The chosen squad was moved into the gymnasium under the tutelage of Quarter Master Sergeant Instructor Leo Howson of the Army Physical

In the years of Pax Britannica, life in the Army could be very dull for fit, young men who were set apart from normal social life and kept strictly away from the company of women. They needed plenty of activity as an alternative and sport was encouraged as it kept men fit, fostered team spirit and was a suitable channel for aggressive tendencies. In 1886, the 2nd Battalion Northumberland Fusiliers was stationed in India and recorded - 'The draft that came out to replace those that had left for home, brought out to us a new game, that of Association Football. In the Sergeants' Mess we also took to a new form of exercise, Lawn Tennis. We played on a court made by smoothing over a large space of ground, and then covering the rough surface with a smearing of cow-dung moistened with water to the consistence of a paste that dried into an excellent court.' Here, as the winners of the All-India Boxing Tournament of 1923, the boxing team of the 1st Battalion Royal Fusiliers displays their trophies.

Training Corps and their monastic existence began. The team was captained by Corporal Mark Gleeson, a courageous young Mancunian who led by example and seemed to know no fear in the ring. The team won the Brigade Competition and then went on to win the Division, BAOR and the UK Novice Championships for 1979-80; a feat that has yet to be repeated by the Regiment.

Fusilier boxing provided the basic grounding for its most famous sporting son to date, Nigel Benn. Joining the 1st Battalion in the early 1980s his talent was identified and nurtured early on and, despite being an excellent soldier, it was soon clear to everyone that for him to remain in the Army would be a waste of his talent. The rest, as they say, is history although John O'Grady still laments the fact that he did not have the financial capital needed to turn Nigel professional at the time. Despite his success Nigel Benn still maintains a close interest in regimental affairs and is a great source of inspiration and encouragement to the Regiment's novice boxers.

Nigel Benn began his Army service on 11 May 1983 and joined 1RRF. He served for four years and 265 days with postings to Germany and Northern Ireland during which the Army taught him to box. On leaving the Army, he became a professional boxer and won both the WBO middle weight and WBC super-middleweight titles. Of the Army, Benn has stated - 'Joining up was the best thing I ever did, otherwise I would have been six foot under or locked up. I chose the right path. I went in a boy and came out a man. I am very proud to say I have been in the Army.' Nigel Benn is shown here between WO1 Jimmy Hill and Major Mick Moran at the Harts Medals competition of 1996 at Catterick.

During the 1979-80 season, 1RRF had a highly successful team which won the 4th Armoured Division, the BAOR and the British Army Boxing Championships. From left to right standing, the team comprised Capt. O'Grady, 'Jaws' Fairbairn (Heavy), Mark Gleeson (Light. Heavy), Stan Black (Middle), Mick Ledger (Light. Middle), WO2 Howson (Coach). Front from left to right, 'Mac' McDonald (Bantam), 'Jock' Stacey (Light. Welter), 'Doc' Hoo (Welter), Mark Holtham (Lightweight), Johnny Fulcher (Feather).

Nowadays a soldier can indulge in all manner of sports. These Fusiliers of X Company 1RRF are enjoying the thrills of scuba-diving among the reefs of Belize during in-country rest and recreation while deployed on Exercise 'Native Trail' in the summer of 1999. In the background is St Georg's Caye where the British Army's Joint Services Adventurous Training Centre is situated, some ten miles off the coast of Belize. SD

SKIING THE NORWAY

Among the numerous roles for the infantry battalions of the British Army into the 1990s was that of the Allied Command Europe Air Mobile Force Land. Whether deployed in the freezing wastes of Norway or in the arid barren hills of Greece and Turkey, it was a particularly arduous and demanding form of soldiering where fitness and endurance were vital to survival and success in the field. The 2nd Battalion was assigned this mission in 1986 and deployed to Norway each year up to 1990 when Exercise 'Hardfall' was curtailed because of the Gulf War. Major Charles Bishop participated in three of the deployments with the 2nd Battalion and his account graphically describes the rigours of the AMF(L) mission.

'The 2nd Battalion Royal Regiment of Fusiliers moved from Catterick to Bulford in the summer of 1986 to become the UK's infantry battalion for the Ace Mobile Force (Land). The AMF(L) was NATO's lead force for deployment to the northern or southern flanks of Europe in the event of imminent hostilities with the Warsaw Pact countries. This small multinational brigade sized unit was intended to demonstrate Alliance resolve during the period of 'Transition to War' and to show the solidarity of NATO nations in peacetime. During its time in this role, the 2nd Battalion completed four winter deployments to Norway and two summer ones to Denmark. During the six weeks prior to Christmas each year, the battalion's commanders and instructors went on Exercise 'Pre-Hardfall'. Once trained they would return to England for Christmas and the New Year before deploying on the main Exercise 'Hardfall' in early January when they were to train the rest of the battalion. This New Year deployment was for up to ten weeks and culminated in a full AMF(L) exercise inside the Arctic Circle in Northern Norway.

'Exercise 'Hardfall' started with basic lessons on how to live, survive and fight in an Arctic environment. There was a great deal of detailed instruction in how to pack the bergen. Everything had to be packed in a logical sequence so the items required during the day were easily accessible. When preparing to bivouac and sleep, each item was again removed from the bergan in the order they were required, in order to avoid having to empty the contents of the bergan onto the snow. Our first nights sleeping out were in ten-man bell tents. These were large and heavy tents so bivvy sites were never far from a track or road with access for the BV206 over-snow vehicles. The tents gave good shelter from blowing snow and against the cold. There was ample room to move so that the evenings were sociable and comfortable occasions. Arctic survival skills were taught by battalion Arctic Warfare Instructors, and were watched over by a Royal Marine Mountain Leader to ensure that lessons were being taught correctly.

'Preparing meals from the Arctic ration pack was a skill in its own right. Breakfast was the same every day: rolled oats and hot chocolate to drink. All the Arctic rations required large

With its home station at Bulford in Wiltshire, 2RRF joined the Allied Command Europe Mobile Force (Land) or AMF(L) for short In May 1987. Deep within the Arctic Circle, A Company of the 2nd Battalion under the command of Lt Col Gunnell parades on Bardufoss airfield with other contingents of the AMF(L) on 6 March 1988 during Exercise 'Arrowhead Express'. Such occasions at the end of a particular training phase were intended for troops to appraise each others' weapons and equipment but they often degenerated into convivial 'drinking fests', with as much competition as camaraderie. This was the first Arctic deployment for 2RRF as a battalion within AMF(L). It was undertaken with one Canadian and one Italian battalion and an infantry company from Luxembourg, together with support elements from Germany, Norway and the United States. The AMF(L), under the command of Maj Gen Angioni, was supporting the 6th Division of the Norwegian Army (NOA) against the 'enemy' provided by the 15th Brigade NOA.

quantities of water, but melting snow was time consuming and used a lot of fuel. Again when vehicles were not far away, jerry cans of water were available. These had to be carried inside the vehicles to prevent freezing. At breakfast time the drill was for each soldier to fill his individual flask to give him hot drinks throughout the day. Dehydration in this climate was a major problem due to the combination of dehydrated food and high work rates, which caused a lot of sweating. Also at breakfast you prepared rations for the day. Sweet biscuits (biscuits AB with fruit), chocolate and dextrose tablets were all removed from their wrappers and mixed together in a central monster bag which was kept in one of the lower pockets of the Arctic smock so that it was readily accessible. There was seldom a break for lunch though it was usually possible to eat biscuits AB (without fruit) and meat paste at some stage during the day. Those who required a morning constitutional would normally go at this stage. The tent flap was opened and in would come a rude blast of freezing air. Even in the mid-80s it was obligatory to use the cardboard kharzi (which contained a strengthened black plastic bag. Picnicking Norwegians in the summer had objected to being surrounded by little festering piles long after the snow had gone, thus the strict rules. One of the less enviable jobs was loading the kharzi onto the roof of the vehicle; it was a positive advantage if the contents of this bag froze. There were a few unsavoury tales of bags splitting when the contents were not frozen. At the appointed hour, all tents would pull pole simultaneously. There were then just ten minutes to pack away the tent, pack the last items in to the bergans, don skis and move off. This was the coldest part of the day and woe betide the soldier, who through poor personal skills, kept the rest of his platoon waiting.

'Much of the early days on the course was spent learning to ski at the hands of the Military Ski Instructors. Most found these skills easy enough when they were not carrying a load and on flat ground. However, it was a different matter when uphill or down hill slopes had to be negotiated or when webbing and bergans were carried. Pulling a heavy pulk between two men as well as carrying their full individual loads made it a near impossible task for all but the most well co-ordinated individuals. The soldiers' load generally made them top heavy and it was quite common that soldiers would fall over in the ostrich position in soft snow, heads buried and held down by the weight of their inverted bergans. As a consequence a company move when carrying full scales was a tortuous process. A quicker way was to don snowshoes but this often brought about its own problems.

'Soldiering in the Arctic brought with it lot of extra bits and pieces of kit, which had to be fitted into any available pocket or pouch but you had to remember where it all was. Items included: avalanche cord, toe covers, snow brush, ski waxes, scraper and cork, muzzle cover, wristlets, contact gloves, mitts inner and outer, wooden spoon (metal ones could stick to the skin).

Complete with SA80 and PRC 349 radio, a young officer signals to his platoon during Exercise 'Hardfall' - the young officer is in fact L/Cpl Oehlers posing as a 2/Lt for recruiting material, with Fus Whittaker in the background. The Fusiliers trained on both skis and snowshoes. The latter tended to be used in a final assault when skis are often too unwieldy. Arctic equipment included a mass of unfamiliar clothing including Boots Ski-March, Arctic cap, gaiters, thermal underwear, gloves white, gloves contact, gloves outer waterproof, snowsuit et al.

One of the severest tests during the AMF(L) deployments was the ice hole which everyone had to endure so as to learn how to escape if the ice collapsed while skiing. Here, Maj Kiddie, the OC of A Company, uses his ski poles to extricate himself from the freezing water. The hairs of the nostrils freeze at -11°C while exposed flesh freezes at -37°C. Survival techniques were an essential prerequisite for operating in the Arctic. The ideal operating temperatures are between -5° and -10°C when the snow remains dry but the air is not too cold.

People always carried their tooth brush close to hand in order to clean their teeth several times a day to get rid of the copious amount of sugar from the high calorie diet.

'The training included ice breaking drills in which a hole was chiselled out of the ice in the centre of a lake. This in itself was normally four hours work for four men because of the amount and weight of ice that had to be removed. Once created, each member of the company had to ski into the icy hole, throwing his bergan to the side as he went in . Then having lifted his skis out of the hole, the drill was to use the ski poles as daggers to haul oneself out of the hole. This was a chilling but useful exercise as, if ever it happened unexpectedly when skiing across thin ice, the value of this training could be life saving. After three weeks of this type of training, individuals could live and survive in this environment with total confidence. War fighting skills had to be practised due to the different conditions. The BV206 all terrain vehicles were excellent and we soon learned to get their articulated mobility into the most inaccessible of places. Sometimes it was more pragmatic for the platoon to be towed on two trailing ropes behind the vehicles. These skijoring tows were fun, extremely cold and more than a little hazardous. It only took one man to lose balance on a rope of eight or ten and this would result in the rest of the party piling in. We were also trained in the skills of living in the open without tents or tent sheets. We spent nights in snow holes and were shown how to build snow graves, shelters and igloos. Casualty evacuation would be on Hjelper Sledge; an ingenious but simple improvised stretcher. It comprised six inch pylons clamped onto the casualty's own skis, which supported a canvas cradle stretched between the casualty's own ski poles.

'Exercise 'Hardfall' was conducted in the Voss region. The companies were accommodated in youth hostels and transit camps in the Mjolfjell and Brandset valleys. Battalion Headquarters was accommodated in the plush Oppheim Hotel. It was normal for each company to have one day off a week: most soldiers went to the civilian skiing resort at Voss where the battalion had set up its own downhill ski facility. After skiing, the officers would generally meet in the luxurious Fleischers Hotel for tea and drinks after a hard day on the slopes. Each deployment culminated with a move to Northern Norway to the Tromso area, well inside the Arctic Circle. In the run up to the main AMF(L) exercise, there was cross-training organised between the participating nations, the US, Canada, Italy and Norway, the host nation. Inter-platoon competitions were part of this training and, despite being new to this form of soldiering, the battalion showed the quality of its men by winning almost all such events. The hackle was worn with pride and our reputation of professionalism mixed with the ability to enjoy ourselves was rapidly established throughout the Force. The final exercise, like many big exercises, was invariably slow moving. However, they were extremely testing in parts, and long night

With the indispensable Bv206 All Terrain Vehicles in the background, an 81mm mortar team of Fus Rocky, Brathwaite and Edwards prepares to fire at Range Valley in Norway. As part of the Air Mobile Force Land, 2RRF was also liable to be deployed to the southern flank of NATO for operations in Greece and Turkey, although this did not occur. However, as part of Contingency Operating Plans, 2RRF did partake in the mortar and artillery concentration of AMF contingents in Sardinia on the annual Exercise 'Ardent Ground'. On one occasion, the mortars of all the NATO partners were firing out to sea when a Greek fishing boat encroached into the impact area, whereupon all the mortars ceased firing except, for some inexplicable reason, the Turkish contingent.

With the snow falling, 2/Lt McDaid leads a ski patrol wearing the lightweight MT56 plastic skis rather than those known as 'NATO planks' of the previous deployments. Although the great majority of Fusiliers had never skied before, most became highly adept at skiing and regularly outperformed their NATO allies, even the specialised units such as the German Gebirgsjaeger and the Italian Alpini.

moves, both mounted and on skis, were frequent. Towards the end of the exercise everyone in the Battalion was aching to return home, not only for all the usual reasons after a long deployment away, but also because we were all sick of living in the snow and wanted to get away from the winter landscape devoid of colour.'

BADAJOZ COMPANY

When 'Options for Change' announced that the 3rd Battalion was to be disbanded and its personnel to be merged with the 1st and 2nd Battalions, there was a surplus of manpower of approximately company strength. With the 1st Battalion moving to Warminster and the 3rd Battalion from Hemer for the proposed merger, the Director of Infantry decreed that the extra manpower was to be allocated to support the 1st Battalion Irish Guards in its forthcoming deployment to Ulster; the first it had ever undertaken in the Province. At the time, the Irish Guards was not well recruited and its survival was largely dependent on this deployment to Northern Ireland as it was inconceivable to disband infantry battalions which had done repeated tours of Ulster and retain one that would not or could not, even if it was in the Household Division. Although never stated, it was deemed necessary to leaven the Irish Guards with some infantry with experience of Northern Ireland. Named after a battle honour of both the 5th and 7th Foot from the Peninsular War, Badajoz Company grouped with the Irish Guards at Pirbright from 9 August 1992; one week after the Minden Day amalgamation of the 1st and 3rd Battalions in Warminster. The 3rd Battalion had just completed armoured infantry training at BATUS in Canada; closed down in Hemer and moved to UK. Their personnel had never messed with the 1st Battalion let alone trained together. In general, the 3rd Battalion provided the Fusiliers and the 1st Battalion the NCOs. Command of Badajoz Company was assumed by Major James Sayer of the 1st Battalion who had to be recalled from Cyprus for the appointment. During NITAT training the inexperience of the Irish Guards was apparent and the Fusiliers won all the various inter-platoon and company competitions. The battalion deployed to County Fermanagh in the first week of November with the main body complete in theatre by 13 November. The IRA was waiting for them.

During the six month deployment, the Irish Guards suffered 14 major incidents as the IRA made a concerted effort against their battlegroup. The Fusiliers were the recipients of two of them. The first occurred within 24 hours of their arrival. Initially, Badajoz Company was deployed with one platoon at Mullanbridge and Gortmullan PVCP; one platoon at RUC Belcoo; one at RUC Kesh and a platoon of Irish Guards at RUC Beleek. Company Headquarters and a patrols multiple were at Grosvenor Barracks in Enniskillen. The company also had a dismounted troop of the Blues and Royals and a platoon of the Irish Guards under command. Badajoz Company had the largest company TAOR of the battlegroup, indeed in Northern

Ireland, as it included Lough Erne and a considerable length of border with the Republic of Ireland. At the outset, 6 Platoon was based at the RUC police station at Belcoo. The platoon commander was Colour Sergeant Tony Reith with Sergeant 'Paddy' Baines as his platoon sergeant. During the handover from 1 STAFFORDS, the departing platoon sergeant had said to Sergeant Baines that he was extremely wary of the road on which the police station was situated. It stood only 150 metres inside the border with a corresponding Gardai station 150 metres inside the Eire border in the village of Black Lion. On the border itself was a road bridge.

On the night of 14 November, the RUC were in the process of mounting a Sierra Patrol - a road patrol by two armoured Ford Sierra motor cars, each carrying two RUC Constables and two Fusiliers. To allow the patrol to leave Mullanbridge, a multiple of 12 Fusiliers was deployed with one team of four securing the village; one team was preparing to go on the Sierra Patrol while one team conducted a snap VCP outside the police station. The team took up positions under cover as Constable Alan Corbett and the team leader conducted the VCP by the light of the street lamps. The policeman had just completed a vehicle check and stood upright when a single shot rang out. Constable Corbett slumped to the ground with a bullet in his head. Fusilier Steve Donathy was forward of the VCP but within seconds he ran across and pulled Constable Corbett under cover. There he cradled the injured man's head and administered first aid. RUC policemen rushed out of their station armed with G-3 assault rifles and Heckler and Koch MP-5s to reinforce the Fusiliers on the VCP. No further shots were heard beyond a negligent discharge from an MP-5 which passed between the legs of Sergeant Paddy Baines. The gravely-injured Constable Corbett was gently placed in one of the Sierra vehicles with Fusilier Donathy holding his shattered head together. The two Sierra police vehicles sped through the Fermanagh countryside until they met an ambulance which transferred the casualty to Enniskillen hospital. Due to the prompt and compassionate actions of Fusilier Donathy, Constable Corbett survived for several hours; time enough for his immediate family to congregate at his bedside before his untimely death.

At Belcoo, the Fusiliers maintained a cordon around the site of the crime until daylight and the arrival of forensic personnel to examine the area for evidence. The firing point was determined to be on the border bridge, equidistant between the two police stations. By any standards, one round at 150 metres at night, with only pools of street lights for illumination, takes fine marksmanship. The assassin had been imported from South Armagh for the specific purpose of killing an Irish Guardsman on their arrival in Fermanagh. In the dim light, the fact that the policeman happened to be wearing a cap rather than a helmet like the Fusilier beside him made for an easier target. It might have been the reason that yet another member of the RUC

A Carl Gustav anti-tank team prepares to engage armour during Exercise 'Doughboy Dragon' in the FIBUA complex known as 'Doughboy City' in the American sector of Berlin during 1983. 3RRF was stationed in Berlin for two years after the hunger strike tour of Belfast. Berlin was a comfortable posting with a 'high octane lifestyle'. Military duties were mainly concerned with public displays and parades. Much military training was devoted to Fighting In Built Up Areas (FIBUA) in preparation for another Battle of Berlin in case the Warsaw Pact ever launched an offensive against the city. Beside the Carl Gustav, the infantry battalions in Berlin used the 106mm Wombat anti-tank recoilless rifle rather than Milan missiles, as there were too many obstacles for their guidance wires and engagement ranges were too short.

died in the line of duty rather than a soldier of the British Army. Three Fusiliers from 3 Platoon were invited to Constable Alan Corbett's funeral in the Mourne Mountains which they attended wearing civilian suits borrowed from the RUC. The family were particularly grateful for the actions of Fusilier Steve Donathy for which he was Mentioned in Despatches.

The second major incident occurred on 8 January 1993 when the IRA attacked the Mullan Bridge Patrol Base and its Permanent Vehicle Check Point (PVCP). Sixteen PVCPs had been created astride the main crossing points along the 303 miles of border with the Republic of Ireland. All were manned by the British Army. Militarily they were a nonsense as the IRA moved its weapons and material across the border on the multitude of minor roads, and so their greatest impact was to inconvenience the local populace. They had been created as a sop to the loyalist community and the Royal Ulster Constabulary following concerted attacks by the IRA against RUC police stations. As the PVCPs were actually on the border, they became priority targets to the terrorists in preference to the RUC posts which were now located further inland. The PVCPs relied on a sophisticated series of electronic bollards that rose out of the road to halt suspect vehicles or channel others into inspection bays. At first they had proved to be chronically unreliable as the continual rain shorted out electrical components causing the bollards to rise unexpectedly. This happened on several occasions with acutely embarrassing results, such as when a minibus full of nuns was elevated into the air, or a lorry load of fish was stranded for hours. The tyres of innocent motorists were punctured, resulting in hundreds of compensation claims against the Army.

Sergeant Paul Carr was the commander of Victor Four Zero India and he recalls - 'On that particular day, I had planned for a long range patrol by Two Zero Bravo outside the PVCP out to 800 metres which was beyond the normal mortar base plate checks. For reasons of "no-fly" because of weather, we went on foot soon after 1000 hours. We were on our way back from the south-east during the afternoon so we actually passed the mortar by no more than 20 metres but it was in dead ground. That was the last patrol programmed for that day as it gets dark around 1600 hours. A civilian contractor was repairing the road surface inside the patrol base. Myself, Corporal Brent and an RMP CONCO were in the main tower. Fusilier Wainwright was in the super sangar covering the border with a GPMG. We then heard this loud bang and saw the first mortar land about 80 metres to the north west of the base just outside the perimeter fence. We heard the launch of the second round but it never came near the base. We set off the alarm and called in the contractor who was still standing in the middle of the road. I sent a contact report and then had phone and radio calls from all and sundry. After remaining undercover for 30 minutes we then checked for blinds [misfires]'.

Lt Murray-Playfair leads the Fusilier Guard of 2RRF out of Spandau Prison in Berlin during January 1982. Guard duty at Spandau Prison was monotonous in the extreme with numerous irksome penalties such as the immaculate standard of turn-out that was required at all times and petty orders which stated that guards were not allowed to look directly at Spandau's only prisoner - Hitler's deputy Rudolf Hess. All cameras were prohibited as photographs of the aging Nazi had a market value in excess of 10,000 Dm. Guard duty at No. 3 Tower on the back wall overlooking Hess's garden was particularly unpopular as it was totally isolated and given to visits by bats in the dead of night. As Prisoner No. 7, Hess spent 40 years in Spandau until he died at the age of 93. Thereafter, the prison was razed to the ground and replaced by a NAAFI supermarket. With their inimitable brand of humour, British troops promptly named it 'Hesco's'.

No one was hurt in the attack except Corporal Steve Hornsby who had been training in the gym. He was temporarily deafened by the mortar detonating on the other side of the perimeter blast wall from his unprotected portacabin. The Airborne Reaction Force of two Lynx helicopters carrying a multiple of Irish Guardsmen was activated but as it approached at an altitude of 1,000 feet the helicopters were engaged by a 12.7mm 'Dushka' heavy machine gun which had been emplaced inside the border of the Republic of Ireland in a salient which projected into Northern Ireland. Thus the helicopters were being engaged from the flank at a distance of some 1,000 metres. The Dushka was manned by an IRA ASU. As the orange tracer rounds arced up towards their aircraft, the pilots rapidly lowered the collective and the Lynxes plunged earthwards, much to the consternation of the soldiers in the back. As the helicopters levelled out, one door gunner opened fire with a GPMG against what he perceived to be the gun emplacement. It was in fact the smoking mortar tubes. The Fusiliers in the PVCP were similarly confused as Sergeant Carr recalls - 'Some 45 minutes after the mortar attack, we saw orange tracers from a multi-weapon shoot. I ordered Fusilier Wainwright to engage the position but his GPMG sights were set to 400 metres. He opened fire but at the mortar base plate which was still smoking. However he was firing [it was subsequently discovered] on a direct line with the person who had initiated the mortars from inside the republic. The fire fell some 300 metres over the border and he was frightened off but left behind a CB [Citizen Band] walkie-talkie and a G-3 magazine.' After firing 420 rounds of 12.7mm, the ASU also fled leaving behind the tripod of the Degtyarev machine gun. By now, it was dark and too late to venture outside the PVCP. On the following day, a 'cordon and clear' operation was mounted and a Mark 10 mortar with a Mark 11 assembly was discovered ten metres inside the Northern Ireland border: to the IRA it is deemed essential that the struggle is seen to be fought on the soil of Ulster (see below). The first mortar had fired successfully but flown too far; the second had gone only half-way and not detonated and the last had not fired at all. The Mullanbridge PVCP was undamaged. In the first air to ground cross-border engagement by a British helicopter of the campaign, no casualties were inflicted save for one dead cow.

The republican newspaper *An Phoblacht* [14 January 1993] recorded the incident thus: 'On Friday, 9 January, two successful attacks were carried out by the IRA in County Fermanagh. At 4pm three mortar bombs were fired at Mullan Bridge checkpoint. Two exploded at their target. When a British army helicopter responded to this operation they were attacked by machine-gun fire. One helicopter was forced to crash-land. Intelligence reports say that the British sealed off the Stragowna Cross area. They removed the helicopter by covered lorry. Contrary to media reports all attacks were carried out in County Fermanagh.'

In The Queen's Silver Jubilee Year, the FV432s of 5 Platoon under the command of Lt. Cross drive past the saluting stand at Her Majesty's Review of the British Army of the Rhine on 7 July 1977. It was a memorable day for Peter Cross as, not only did he incur several extra duties that morning for being late on parade after a self-indulgent evening the night before, but it was also the day that he met his future wife. The parade took place on Sennelager and, besides the 72 APCs of the 2nd Battalion under the command of Lt Col Sincock, comprised three other infantry regiments, three armoured regiments and supporting arms of the 4th Armoured Division giving a total of 600 AFVs.

BALLYKINLER

Following their five year commitment to the ACE Mobile Force Land, the 2nd Battalion began a two year tour in Northern Ireland in the same area as where the battalion had first exercised after their formation in 1968. Based at Abercorn Barracks in Ballykinler, the 2nd Battalion arrived in theatre during late July 1991 as the resident regular battalion of 3 Brigade which was tasked with the security of the border region. Initially, the battalion had one company stationed in Newry, one deployed on Brigade Operations or acting as the Brigade Reserve Company, one undertaking guards and duties at Ballykinler and one undergoing training or leave. One of its first tasks was on Operation 'Bronski' when, in conjunction with the 1st Battalion, they formed the escort to Royal Engineer plant equipment and materials being transported into South Armagh for the construction and refurbishment of the Golf and Romeo OP Towers. Within short order, the battalion had operated in support of every unit within the Brigade TAOR, including 3, 8 and 2/11 Battalions of the Ulster Defence Regiment and with the various roulement battalions. Although residential tours are notionally of two years duration, this one was to be the longest of any battalion in Northern Ireland at 31 months. It was the Regiment's 30th tour of Ulster during the Troubles and one full of incidents, many of which seemed to have been directed at A Company. The most serious was the destruction of the PVCP Romeo One Five on 1 May 1992 in one of the most sophisticated bomb attacks by the IRA throughout the conflict. Romeo One Five was situated at Killeen, south of Newry on the main Belfast to Dublin Road. The PVCP had first been destroyed in 1990 by a proxy bomb driven to the site by an innocent civilian whose family had been kidnapped and threatened with death if he did not comply. Ranger Cyril Smith of the Royal Irish Rangers died in the explosion. Romeo One Five was built in its place but this time, it was protected by armoured blast walls against proxy bombs and incorporated a hardened shelter for the troops, known as the 'submarine'. After careful examination from afar, the IRA had discovered a chink in its armour.

Romeo One Five was armoured on the three sides facing the A1 road. The fact that the railway side was unprotected had been realised and work was in hand to rectify the failing. As part of the contingency planning, the base was to be evacuated when the threat level reached a certain level. At this point, the platoon would disperse into pre-ordained positions in the surrounding hills, leaving only a few people in the control sangar to coordinate matters. The threat level had almost been reached but there was pressure from on high not to evacuate the base. During the night of 30 April, an IRA ASU hijacked a JCB mechanical digger and drove it to Killeen bridge where the A1 passes over the Belfast to Dublin railway line, just inside the Northern Ireland border. After knocking down a wall and preparing an access ramp, the JCB lifted a blue Renault Master van on to the railway line. The tyres of the van had been removed and it had been fitted with an extra set of wheels so as to run on the tracks; it also contained

The remains of the Killeen PVCP ROMEO 15 on 1 May 1992. The 8-ton sangar manned by Fus Grundy was blown some 12m by the explosion. The crater measured 11m X 11m X 3.3m deep. Houses up to 500m away were damaged by the blast.

NORTHERN IRELAND
OPERATION 'BANNER' TOURS 1970-2000

1RRF

1. 16.6.70-22.10.70 Belfast
2. 4.2.71 -25.2.71 Belfast
3. 19.6.71-21.6.71 (Spearhead) Long Kesh (shortest)
4. 11.8.71-19.8.71 (Spearhead) Belfast
5. 1.9.73 - 5.3.75 (Resbatt) Londonderry
6. 1.3.76 -19.6.76 Belfast
7. 1.5.77 -12.6.77 (Op Forked) Province wide
8. 11.10.80-25.2.81 Belfast
9. 8.1.84 -29.1.86 (Resbatt) Ballykelly
10. 30.11.88-12.4.89 South Armagh
11. 21.6.91-30.6.91 (Op Bronski)
12. 13.11.92- .5.93 Badajoz Coy att'd Irish Guards
13. 28.3.97-12.5.99 (Resbatt) Londonderry
14. 10.3.00-16.9.00 South Armagh

2 RRF

15. 19.10.71-16.2.72 Belfast
16. 11.7.72 -10.11.72 (Op Motorman) Belfast
17. 1.3.73 -27.3.73 Belfast
18. 26.6.73 -30.10.73 Belfast
19. 23.10.74-26.2.75 Belfast
20. 24.6.76 -27.10.76 Armagh/Tyrone
21. 7.7.78 -7.11.78 Londonderry
22. 15.11.79-5.4.81 (Resbatt) Belfast
23. 24.7.91 -20.2.94 (Resbatt) Ballykinler (longest)

3RRF

24. 27.1.72 -22.5.72 Province wide
25. 13.7.72 -2.9.72 (Op Motorman) Londonderry
26. 3.1.73 -4.5.73 South Armagh/Tyrone
27. 3.1.74 -3.5.74 South Armagh
28. 16.8.75 -16.12.75 South Armagh
29. 9.3.76 -6.4.76 (Spearhead) County Armagh
30. 19.10.77-22.2.78 Belfast
31. 8.11.79 -7.3.80 Londonderry
32. 5.4.81 -3.3.83 (Resbatt) Belfast
33. 6.8.85 -17.12.85 South Armagh

one ton of homemade explosives. The courtesy light was switched on and second gear was engaged. The van started trundling north towards Newry with 1,800 metres of command wire spooling out of the back. At the same time, IRA teams set up roadblocks north and south of Romeo One Five to stop civilian vehicles from approaching the PVCP. At Romeo One Five the guard at the rear sangar overlooking the railway line had just changed and Fusilier Andrew Grundy had relieved his close friend, Fusilier Michael Beswick. Most of the Fusiliers were asleep in the 'submarine'.

Shortly after 0200 hours, a Fusilier in Romeo One Four, a hilltop OP overlooking the PVCP, noticed a light moving northwards along the railway line and sent a message by radio stating - 'A car is driving down the railway line'. He made the transmission twice on the company net but was met with disbelief. At the rear of the PVCP, Fusilier Grundy heard the warning and was leaning out of his sangar when he saw it approaching. He immediately realised the danger and shouted over the intercom - 'Proxy bomb - rear gate!' He then brought his rifle to bear to try and disrupt the device with gunfire. A third person was also watching the approach of the van and when he saw the telltale courtesy light draw abreast of Romeo One Five, he radioed to his accomplice at the end of the command wire. One kilometre south of the PVCP, multiples from 3 Platoon under the command of Lieutenant Peter Allanach were on patrol when they were approached by a civilian who told them that his car had been stopped by hooded men telling him to avoid Romeo One Five. Lieutenant 'Zippy' Allanach radioed a warning and then 3 Platoon began running towards the PVCP.

At 0205 hours, the bomb detonated on the only unprotected side of the PVCP. The explosion uprooted the 10 ton rear sangar and propelled it a distance of some ten metres. Inside, Fusilier Grundy was killed instantly by the blast. The first report to be received by battalion headquarters was from 3 Platoon which stated - 'Contact now at Romeo One Five. Major explosion'. The next report was even more dire - 'Contact Romeo One Five bombing. There are mass casualties - the submarine has gone!' There were 24 soldiers in the 'submarine' and this report precipitated numerous offers of assistance over the battalion net. The commander of the platoon manning Romeo One Five, Lieutenant Andrew Rawding then emerged from the debris, with blood running down his face and his rifle destroyed, and ascertained that the casualties were not severe. The submarine had survived intact and all inside were unharmed; indeed many of them slept through the explosion. The uninjured Fusiliers were deployed on the high ground around the site in case of a follow-up attack by the IRA. None was forthcoming.

Corporal Tom Sayers of 1 Platoon A Company was asleep at the time, having just returned from patrol but was still dressed for action. 'I was asleep in my pit and the next thing I knew was waking up with the roof on top of me as the whole portacabin collapsed. There were two other people in the room with me - Fusilier 'Evo' Evans and Corporal 'Stan' Boardman. Outside were the rest of the multiple in a hardened shelter. It was pitch black so I scrabbled around for my weapon, helmet and webbing. I got the radio out to send a contact report but the cryptic had been damaged so it didn't work. I then shouted out "Stan! Evo! Are you alright?" as I hadn't heard anything. Evo said, "I can't feel my legs". Stan said "My head's bleeding". So I moved to Stan but he seemed OK and then to Evo thinking Oh God what am I going to find here but it was only the GPMG lying on his legs. We eventually got outside and I got the teams out to their cut-off positions to stop anything or anyone coming in. My next task was to find out how many casualties there were. I went to find Sergeant Major 'Patch' Air but couldn't find him in his portacabin so I went to the hardened shelter, opened the door and there was Patch standing stark bollock naked with cuts all over him, going into shock. The medic, Fusilier 'Brewkit' Brewer was sorting through his bed bunk so I said to him, "What are you doing?" and he replied "I'm trying to find him a pair of underpants". I told him, "He's going into shock - get the blanket off the bed, wrap him in it and get him sorted". Lieutenant Rawding was on the net calling for the helicopter evacuation of the casualties to Newry Hospital. Whilst he was doing that I organized a guard to go with them. I then went back into the compound to the main sangar and asked 'Yorkie' [Corporal 'Yorkie' York] if there were any other casualties. He turned round and said, "I can't find Grundy". So I asked where was he - "In the back sangar". I looked round for the sangar but it had been blown at least 30 feet from where it started so I went over but couldn't see anything - there was nobody there. Grundy had to be in the sangar so I went back and saw a wooden door. I lifted it up and there was

Grundy - not a mark on him or I couldn't see anything in the torchlight. I called over four Fusiliers and we placed him on the door. Now the helipad is up a steep hill so it was quite a struggle to get him up there, but there was no hassle, no arguments - straight up to the top. By now the first chopper was coming in - a Lynx with the doc on board. We put Grundy straight into the Lynx, the doc stayed with him and off they went. Some of the blokes asked me how Grundy was; I didn't know how he was but said, "He's in the best place he can be, they'll look after him. Don't you worry about it now, let's get on with our job". The next thing I knew the OC was turning up so I had to get back to the helipad to meet him.'

Lieutenant Andrew Rawding was the commander of Romeo One Five on that night. 'I was woken by the shouting rather than the explosion itself. It seemed unusually dark and the sounds outside were remote, without the usual background noise of generators and road traffic. I could smell that something had gone wrong and when I tried to sit up I found that a table and the wall of the hut were pinning me down. Fortunately I had decided to sleep fully clothed with my boots on. My multiple was the 'Ops Multiple' tasked with patrolling the countryside around Newry and south to the border. That night we had been confined to the patrol base and were due to conduct an area patrol at 0530 hours. 3 Platoon, under the command of Peter Allanach and Sergeant Air were responsible for running the vehicle checkpoint. At the time of the explosion Peter and his team were conducting a check to the south of the base.

'I retrieved my weapon from underneath the wrecked wall, and tried to send a contact report on my radio before crawling outside. At that point I was very aware of my position as an officer and multiple commander. I felt stripped of all pretensions by the explosion; soldiers and officers were all now equally vulnerable and I was conscious that the reactions of the soldiers could go one of two ways - they could ignore me or listen to me. It was time now to earn my privileges. On emerging into the main compound my first thoughts were that the terrorists would follow up with a secondary attack, perhaps a heavy machine gun. The base that we called 'Tin City' had been blown open and we were exposed to the outside world, with the removal of the perimeter walls revealing local street lamps and the railway which ran along the eastern side of the base. I seized the first team Commander I could find, Corporal Clift of 3 Platoon, and ordered him to organise a perimeter protection force facing out towards the Flagstaff Road. We would need to win any firefight which might follow. I then asked for a head count from Corporal Sayers and Corporal Boardman. Fortunately most of 3 Platoon had been sleeping in the bomb-proof hardened accommodation; however my multiple had been asleep in Portacabins protected only by thin blast walls. Sergeant Air had been sleeping in a Portacabin closest to the blast site and it was clear he had suffered some burns. We soon discovered that we were missing one man. It took us several minutes to realise who it was and find him as the blast had lifted the metal sangar, in which Fusilier Grundy had been on sentry duty, at least ten metres from its original position. All the time he had been in the midst

THE IRISH DIMENSION

The roulement deployment of the 1st Battalion to South Armagh from March to September 2000 was the 33rd tour of duty conducted by The Royal Regiment of Fusiliers in Northern Ireland since the Troubles began in 1969. For the 1st Battalion and their forebears the 5th of Foot and the Royal Northumberland Fusiliers, this was their 33rd deployment to Ireland in their 326 history.

1690-91 Armagh, Newry and The Boyne
1698-1707 Dublin and Cork
1728-1755 Ireland
1737-1755 Ireland
1763-1787 Kilkenny, Limerick and Dublin
1806 Kinsale
1807 Cork
1810-1811 Fermoy
1827-1831 Enniskillen, Dublin and Cork
1831-1834 Fermoy and Cork
1838-1843 Galway, Athlone and Cork
1863 Cork
1865-1866 The Curragh
1881-1886 Mullingar, Dublin and Newry
1921 The Curragh and Carlow
1925-27 Ballykinler
1955-1958 Belfast
1970-2000 as opposite

Fusiliers of the Newry Ops Company stand guard in an improvised sangar at Romeo One Five after the Killeen PVCP had been destroyed by an IRA bomb with (from L to R) Fus Wallace and Marsh, L/Cpl Whittaker and Fus Sharkey. Based at Ballykinler, the Second Fusiliers tour of July 1991 to February 1994 was reputedly the longest of any infantry battalion in the current campaign in Northern Ireland.
SOLDIER Magazine

of us at our feet, hidden by darkness and tangled metal. I asked my team medic Fusilier Gardner and a couple of others to check on him and then subsequently to take him to the HLS to be casevaced. Fusilier Gardner, Fusilier Jenkinson and Fusilier Oxnard were amongst those who took Fusilier Grundy outside to the helicopter. It was probably the bravest and hardest thing they ever had to do and had a profound affect on them. A cordon operation followed. There was no respite. I still remember the shock on the faces of some of the soldiers, crouched behind stone walls at the side of the road, like hedgehogs, huddled around the comfort of a shared cigarette.

'The loss of Fusilier Grundy was a great one. He was capable, confident and very good humoured Fusilier . Earlier that night I had visited the Command Sangar to book an early call for 0500 hours prior to our first patrol. Corporal Matthews was in the sangar along with Fusiliers Grundy and Beswick. Fusilier Grundy and I always got on well together and that evening was no different. After some teasing, laughing and joking about my officer status, he made an entry on the 'Early Calls Board' and offered to bring me a cup of tea the next morning in the "Officers' Mess". It wasn't to be.'

Fusilier Grundy was flown to Daisy Hill Hospital in Newry but was pronounced dead on arrival. The other casualties had only minor injuries. It could have been far worse. After establishing that no follow-up attack was likely, the OC of A Company, Major James Murray-Playfair, boarded a Lynx helicopter at Bessbrook Mill and flew to the scene. As the Lynx approached, Major Murray-Playfair was too anxious to disembark and only the restraining hand of his Company Sergeant Major, Sergeant Abbe Forrester, stopped him from leaping from the helicopter at a height of over 20 feet. Major Murray-Playfair was met at the Helicopter Landing Site by Corporal Sayers who, shouting because of his deafness and the helicopter activity, told his OC that he believed Fusilier Grundy had been killed. After establishing that the remains of the PVCP were adequately defended, Major Murray-Playfair visited the Fusiliers on the cordon. He then sat on the hillside overlooking the smoking ruins of Romeo One Five where he was joined by Fusilier 'Thommo' Thompson. With the contents of the PVCP strewn around them, Fusilier Thompson picked among the debris and found a packet of NAAFI cigarettes. 'Nobody's going to miss one, are they Sir?' he asked. 'No Thommo, you crack on' was the reply. He offered a cigarette to his OC. Major Murray-Playfair had not smoked for over ten years but he took one now.

Following the formation of the Royal Irish Regiment (R IRISH), the 2nd Battalion Royal Regiment Fusiliers assumed control of the County Down Tactical Area of Operational Responsibility in January 1993. In the following month, a patrol of D Company operating in support of 8R IRISH in Cathedral Road, Armagh City, was attacked by an IRA command wire IED. Lance Corporal Michael Beswick was grievously wounded in the explosion. His companions rushed to his side to administer first aid. Three minutes later, another device exploded and severely wounded the four Fusiliers giving succour. Lance Corporal Michael

Troops of the Second Fusiliers disembark from a Chinook Medium Lift Helicopter during an operation in the County Down TAOR in 1992. The Chinook was employed as an Eagle flight capable of carrying four multiples of 12 men each, to allow greater flexibility for cordon and search operations, but such an aircraft was too expensive an asset for routine Eagle Flights. *SOLDIER Magazine*

Beswick died of his injuries on 8 February 1993. He was the last Fusilier to be killed on active service due to terrorist action in the 20th Century. It is fitting therefore that there is a trophy named in his honour. The Beswick Trophy was donated to the 2nd Battalion by his mother. It is awarded to the top student on the battalion's Junior NCO Cadres.

SOUTH ATLANTIC ROULEMENT INFANTRY COMPANY

Following the Falklands War of 1982, an infantry battalion became a part of the permanent garrison to deter further Argentinian attempts to occupy the islands deep in the South Atlantic. Between November 1983 and April 1984, the 2nd Battalion under the command of Lieutenant Colonel Tony Coutts-Britton were deployed to this theatre of operations. With a population of 1,800 islanders, and 660,000 sheep, the battalion was responsible for the security of both East and West Falklands but excluding the capital, Port Stanley. The Battalion Group incorporated a field battery and an air defence battery of the Royal Artillery. Each company had vast tracts of sodden ground in their respective Tactical Areas of Operational Responsibility. A Company acted as the battalion's Quick Reaction Force (QRF) and was based at Goose Green Camp, together with Battalion Headquarters. Soon after their arrival, the OC of C Company, Major James Porter, deployed with 1 Platoon to fight the fires at the scene of an RAF Harrier crash in Lafonia which had set the surrounding peat alight. B Company was accommodated on the floating hotel *Pursuivant* in Stanley Harbour. The company's main mission was to provide security for the airfield at RAF Stanley as well as reassurance patrols in the surrounding settlements. The largest TAOR was on the island of West Falkland where C Company was based at Fox Bay. Under the command of Major Roy Wilde, C Company conducted extensive patrols over the inhospitable terrain. As with all the companies, patrols involved the use of helicopters to reinforce key defensive points and boats to visit the numerous islands. Boats were also used to investigate possible landing beaches for invading Argentinian forces. D Company shared a camp on the shores of San Carlos Water with Royal Artillery and RAF personnel.

All the companies conducted reassurance patrols among the Falkland islanders and were always on hand to assist them with sheep-shearing or reconstruction of their farms, while the Assault Pioneer Platoon repaired or built new bridges over the innumerable streams crossing the waterlogged countryside. Field firing was undertaken at Rabbit (later Onion) range where all types of infantry weapons could be fired with impunity. Patrols, however, were the main task for the infantry. They commonly involved carrying loads of 80 pounds or more, similar to those endured by the British forces during the war as they 'yomped' or 'tabbed' towards Port Stanley.

Once RAF Mount Pleasant had been established as the main airhead, it was no longer necessary to have a complete infantry battalion on the islands. Thereafter, a reinforced company group was deemed sufficient and in times of heightened tension reinforcements would be airlifted to RAF Mount Pleasant where almost the complete military garrison was now based. The 3rd Battalion deployed B Company as the Roulement Infantry Company in

The Regimental mascot of The Royal Regiment of Fusiliers is an Indian Black Buck antelope *(Antilope cervicapra)* and is one of only nine authorised mascots in the British Army. Traditionally named Bobby, it is the only wild animal to hold the position of mascot. Accompanied by his two handlers, Fus Ketcher and Sgt Martin, Bobby is shown undertaking his official duties at the presentation of new Colours to the 2nd Battalion at Chester on 30 June 1995. When fully grown, the Black Buck antelope has some 18 inches (50 cms) of barley twist horns.

Despite the inhospitable terrain and often dreadful weather, the Falkland Islands afford some excellent training opportunities as demonstrated by 6 Platoon B Company 2RRF during a beach assault from a Combat Support Boat on Armed Forces Day 8 December 1983.

July 1988 and Z Company Group of the 1st Battalion followed in July 1990: both these deployments were in the depths of the southern hemisphere winters. In all these deployments, a detachment was sent to the island of South Georgia which the Argentinians had occupied in 1982, precipitating the Falkland Islands crisis and the ensuing war. Despite being even more isolated than the Falkland Islands, South Georgia has been a popular posting for all ranks but especially for those given the opportunity of an independent command. One such officer was Major Charles Bishop who served as the garrison commander on South Georgia between 31 October 1994 and 7 March 1995.

'Within a few months of finishing their residential tour of Northern Ireland in October 1994, the 2nd Battalion sent a reinforced company group to the Falkland Islands as the Roulement Infantry Company (RIC). The company commander for the RIC was Major Tim John. As part of this deployment, a detachment was despatched to South Georgia to join the permanent garrison there. I was selected from a small cast to command this garrison which consisted of 30 Fusiliers - the Reconnaissance Platoon complete, commanded by Captain Dicky Fairbairn, four RLC Chefs, ten Royal Engineers, eight Royal Signals, one RMO (Captain Linda Orr) and an RAMC NCO, as well as two Royal Marines (a Mountain Leader 1 and a Landing Craft 1). Not only was I the military commander but I also assumed civil duties, and was sworn in as the magistrate for South Georgia. This ceremony was carried out in the Governor's Residence in Port Stanley by the Attorney General, David Lang, in the presence of the Governor, David Tatham and the First Secretary of the Falkland Islands, Craig Shelton. WO2 Currie and Colour Sergeant Air, both Fusiliers, had also to be sworn in as Special Policemen by the Chief of Police of the Falkland Islands.

'Our deployment to South Georgia was on HMS *Iron Duke*, a Type 23 frigate. The first half of the three-day passage was a cruise for the Fusiliers but when we reached more southerly latitudes, the Captain ordered that two Fusiliers were to be on iceberg watch on the bridge. We stopped off at Bird Island, the most northerly tip of South Georgia, to deliver stores to the four British Antarctic Survey scientists who are permanently stationed there. As HMS *Iron Duke* brought us into the comparative shelter of Cumberland Bay, one got a feel for the scale of the glaciers sweeping down to sea level and also of the magnitude of the mountain chain which divides the Island like the dorsal ridge on a dinosaur. We took over the garrison from Major Alan Woolford of 1st Battalion, Royal Irish Regiment. They narrated stories of their winter on the Island and having to rope up just to move from one building in the Army Settlement on King Edward Point (KEP) to the next. We realised how fortunate we were to be there for an austral summer and the opportunities we would have for expeditions.

A patrol from the South Georgia detachment, including Cpl Dewis, Sgt Edward and Fus Wallace, passes the abandoned whaling boats *Diaz* and *Albatros* in the harbour of Grytviken during the 2RRF deployment to the South Atlantic between November 1983 and April 1984. Despite its isolated location, South Georgia is regularly visited by cruise ships; their passengers were ready customers for Fusilier memorabilia and their stewardesses welcome company for the Fusiliers.

'After HMS *Iron Duke* disappeared, the next time we were to see another RN vessel was not for six weeks. The feeling of being alone was only temporary. It was impossible to feel isolated on South Georgia with the number of visitors who travel the Southern Ocean to explore and see something of the wildlife there. We shared the KEP with Pat Lurcock, the Fishery Officer and Sarah his wife, who lived together next to the Post Office. The only other residents were Tim and Pauline Carr who lived aboard their yacht *Curlew*, a 28 foot Falmouth Punt, built in the late 1800s. They had been there for about three years and everybody treated South Georgia as theirs as they had explored more of the Island than many others, both by sea and on foot. The relationship between the soldiers and the civilians was good, yet respectful of each other's lifestyles. If it hadn't been for Tim and Pauline I would never have eaten dandelion salad.

'Although we were being lured away from the comfort of KEP by the landscape beckoning to be explored, I insisted that safety was my priority. All members of the garrison were to complete a three-week Mountain Movement and Survival course, before being allowed to join a patrol. This course was done under the expert instruction of the ML1; we were put through the hoops learning the theory of surviving and fighting in the mountains. This included abseiling with heavy bergens both backwards - the more conventional way, and forwards - the Royal Marine way. We were also taught knots for every occasion and eventuality, concentrating on those required for crevasse rescue. The more heart-stopping moments included abseiling from a six-inch ice screw, and practising stopping a fall with an ice axe. We also had to practise immersion drills in freezing sea (without a dry suit!), and living in a snow hole. The Royal Marine landing craft expert also ran a short course on the Rigid Raider boats, which included the donning of immersion suits and use of life jackets. While on the course the soldiers spent more time in the water than out.

'The skills learned on these courses provided invaluable training later on during the tour when we ventured out from the garrison. The Rigid Raiders were required to deploy and recover patrols, and were restricted to within the confines of Cumberland Bay. However, this massive body of water had to be respected as the wind could whip up six-foot waves within only a few minutes and the swell from the Southern Ocean outside its mouth was regularly significant and occasionally reached 30 feet. I was out on one particular four-boat deployment, and although the boats habitually travelled in a box formation with a separation of about 200m, so big was the swell on this occasion that we didn't see the other boats for nigh on one minute.

'It was impossible not to become fascinated by the history of all types of the Island. The history of human habitation, when the whaling industry was at its height, was evident from the

Fusiliers of the Recce Platoon acting as the South Georgia garrison lark for the camera during the Z Company Group 1RRF Resident Infantry Company Falkland Islands deployment to the South Atlantic in 1990 with Maj Harwood (+ teddy bear) as detachment commander and WO2 Boyd as garrison sergeant major. During the tour the average temperature was -3ºC during the South Atlantic summer. As a part of the Arctic Warfare training, the Fusiliers climbed an unnamed mountain in the area of the Nordenskjold Glacier which was then given the place name 'Griffiths Peak' after the late RSM of 1RRF, WO1 Ken Griffiths. During the subsequent tour of South Georgia by the B Company Group of 3RRF in 1988, another feature was named Fusilier Mountain. Both names were ratified by the Royal Geographical Society.

During the deployment to South Georgia between October 1994 and March 1995, members of the garrison drawn from the Fire Support Company of 2 RRF mounted an expedition to find the Wessex 5 helicopter, Yankee Foxtrot, that crashed on Fortuna Glacier during Operation 'Paraquat', the retaking of South Georgia during the Falklands War of 1982. The successful team is shown sitting on the wreckage with (from L to R) Fus Adams and Marsh, WO2 Currie, Maj Bishop and Cpl Haines.

remains. Indeed there were still huge whale bones littering the beaches, This period was coincident with Antarctic exploration and, due to a quirk of fate, Shackleton's legendary and unintentional exploration of the Island is still prominent in the Island's history. Its natural history also captures the interest of soldiers. When you are least suspecting it, a fur seal will ambush you from behind a clump of tussock grass. The massive elephant seals snore on all the beaches and rise up threateningly but ineffectually as you pass. The rats introduced by the Norwegian sealers and whalers are the size of cats and, on the way back from the multi gym, would rush past in the blackness of the night.

'For the soldiers, the recent military history during the Falklands conflict had to be studied; after all, the reason we were there was to demonstrate the British Sovereignty of the island. The conflict against the Argentinians involved engaging the frigate *Guerrico* with a Carl Gustav shoulder launched anti-tank weapon, as well as abortive attacks on Argentinian positions by both the SBS and the SAS. The latter resulted in three friendly Wessex helicopters crashing onto Fortuna Glacier; two were later recovered but one remains. We decided that we had to see if it was still there; so we launched an expedition which took a week to find it. The expedition was successful but turned into quite an adventure with soldiers falling into crevasses, icy and fast-flowing river crossings and tents being lost to ferociously high winds.

'The church is one of the few remaining buildings in Grytviken that is still maintained. Due to the lack of a padre, I conducted services on Remembrance Sunday, Christmas Eve and Christmas Day. After all, although I didn't have a dog collar, I was a Bishop. The other remaining building kept in good repair was the old Whaling Station Manager's house that was preserved as the museum. This became the focus for groups of tourists coming ashore from the cruise ships. These ships called about every ten days, bringing with them an assortment of eco-tourists, who wanted to see and photograph some wildlife. By way of other memorabilia, stamps and first day covers were particularly popular with the tourists, though we did a roaring trade in Fusilier sweatshirts and postcards to one boat.

'We got quite a few other visits from various smaller vessels as well. Most yachts passing by came in for a few days for a respite form the Southern Ocean. John Ridgway and his family were the most well known visitors. Another yacht, owned by an extrovert Frenchman, Jerome Poncet, was a frequent visitor, as he chartered his yacht to anyone who wanted to explore this part of the world. There was no other way of travelling – aeroplanes have nowhere to land. One of the visiting yachts arrived with an expedition, which aimed to climb Mount Paget, the highest mountain on the Island. It had only ever been climbed three times previously; and Sergeant Stratford, our Royal Marine Mountain Leader, accompanied the team in his military uniform and successfully made it to the top, but not without some dangerous-sounding moments.

'However, every three weeks we were visited by a C-130 Hercules that came to deliver our post and essential stores. Most of the time these victuals were fresh fruit and vegetables, but the flight between Christmas and the New Year brought a more vital commodity – additional beer to replenish our depleted stocks. The RAF crew dropped the stores on a dambuster type-bombing run, and at the right point despatched the loads, which drifted down by parachute into the sea. Most of the time the waterproofing and flotation was good and enough to keep them afloat for the vital few minutes before the Fusiliers in Rigid Raiders picked them up. For the boat crews this was an exhausting and hand numbing task but these hardships were overshadowed by the excitement and the prospect of mail.

'Communication from the Island was not as frequent. Letters were only collected on two occasions during our tour, when Royal Fleet Auxiliary supply ships visited. For the rest of the time each individual was allowed a 50 word "Famgram" three times each week. These were sent out by the military signals system and put into envelopes by a communications centre back in the UK. On Christmas Day each soldier was allowed a three-minute phone call on the satellite telephone; this was the only time they spoke to their families and friends during their time away! All the Fusiliers, with only a couple of exceptions, found the South Georgia the most challenging, physically demanding and fun tour of their military careers, such was the variety of the training and off-duty activity.'

As the former CO of the 5th Battalion and 2IC of the 3rd Battalion during the Gulf War, Lieutenant Colonel Keith Kiddie has had as varied a career as any Fusilier over the years. He is admirably qualified to recount the role of mechanised and armoured infantry in the heyday of BAOR and in its execution during manoeuvre warfare in the desert wastes of Southern Iraq.

'The popular image of the infantry soldier normally depicts him as a latter day beast of burden, trudging manfully forward towards the combat zone. Whilst this impression does have a justifiable ring of truth with memories of the Falklands conflict and, more recently, with the pictures of heavily laden infantry in Kosovo, it should not be forgotten that the infantry as a whole, and the Fusiliers in particular, have had a 'love-hate' relationship with mechanised and armoured warfare that stretches almost back to the end of WWII. The bulk of the mechanised infantry learnt its craft during decades based on the plains of northern Germany. Whilst the regular battalions, serving in the mechanised infantry (FV432) role and latterly with Warrior as armoured infantry got most of the high profile coverage; it may be prudent to remember the other theatres of operations in which the Regiment found itself. Many areas had a mechanised infantry presence, but not in such an obvious, high profile manner as in the NATO scenario of Germany.

'Many young officers' first operational experience of mechanisation was not with the venerable FV432 in Germany, but rather in Northern Ireland where, in the early 1970s, the standard mode of transport in most rural and many urban areas was the Saracen. This six-wheeled APC was the workhorse of the battalions in many situations, with the Saracen ambulance running on for a considerable period, when the original had been replaced by upgraded Land Rovers, or Saxon APCs. The Saracen is held in great affection by those who used it, often recalling those particular moments in rural Ulster where the width of the Saracen was greater than the sunken lane into which the platoon convoy had just driven! Who can forget the particular high-pitched whine of the cooling fans which could be heard for miles across the quiet night Ulster landscape, which normally preceded an early morning search/arrest operation? Running in parallel with the Saracen APC, but more regularly found in the Province's urban areas, was the even older Humber 1 ton, colloquially referred to as the 'Pig'. These APCs proved to be surprisingly robust and reliable, being used extensively in the cities of Belfast and Londonderry, where they were a familiar sight to generations of Fusiliers. Their role was ubiquitous, being used for everything from the 'post run' and general administrative traffic, to troop deployment. The vehicles were modified when the need arose, as was the case in the

L/Cpl Margiotta strides out at the head of Fusiliers of 8 Platoon Y Company 1RRF during the 4th Armoured Division Inter-Platoon Competition in April 1983 with (from L to R) Fus Hawley (waving), L/Cpl Gibbs, Sgt Phillips, Lt Bishop and Cpl Scrimshaw with the OC HQ Company, Maj Brown lying on the stretcher. They came third behind teams from 1WFR and 1RRW.

An FV432 of 3RRF ploughs through the snow during the long cold winter of 1979 at Fallingbostel with temperatures as low as minus 17°C. At this time, the FV432 was called the 'Manfred' by Fusiliers after the Manfred Mann pop song '5-4-3-2-1'. A mechanised battalion had 85 APCs of various types and one FV432 cost £46,700 or three times the price of an Aston Martin sports car.

1981 hunger strikes where the Pigs were fitted with mesh screens as crowd control vehicles. In this particular configuration they were known as 'flying pigs' – who said pigs can't fly? But they had a sting in the tail, in that they had baton gun ports cut in the mesh screens which allowed Fusiliers to form highly effective 'baselines' during the major riots. One of the interesting features of using the Pigs, was the fact that they came with an RCT driver who was responsible for the overall care and maintenance of the vehicle. Whilst this on one hand may have engendered a 'laissez faire' approach to vehicle husbandry by the infantry, it was an excellent introduction to many commanders to the 'combined arms' nature of mechanised operations. Frequently the RCT drivers became firm friends with their Fusiliers' cargo and a unique band of loyalty was created between the different arms and services; a factor which continues to play a significant role in the rather more traditional view of armoured warfare.

'In addition, those involved in these operations began to absorb the essentials of mechanised warfare, almost by a process of osmosis. Functions such as the correct packing sequence of vehicles for the mission were as often learnt in bases in Ulster rather than on the North German Plain. Similarly, the importance of route planning, ground appreciation with a view to where and what the vehicle could achieve was practised in a conceptually similar way in Belfast as it was in Bergen-Hohne. What should also be borne in mind was that Fusiliers were more likely, in the mid-1970s to early 1980s, to come under actual fire in these type of armoured vehicles than their counterparts in Germany who were facing the 'red threat' from the East. The Regiment was fortunate to be involved in other areas of mechanisation away

During April 1978, the Colonel-in-Chief paid one of his regular visits to The Royal Regiment of Fusiliers; he visits each battalion at least once under every Commanding Officer. On this particular visit to the 2nd Battalion he took part in a 'falling plates' competition together with (from L to R), the Regimental Secretary Col Etches, Maj Cook, HRH, and Lt Col Sincock CO of 2RRF - The Duke of Kent is a fine shot in his own right and his team won.

from the central core of BAOR soldiering. The 2nd Battalion was based at Catterick in the mid-1980s to become a Saxon-borne battalion. Vital mechanised skills were again learned by the Fusiliers, at all levels, as they mastered the new techniques associated with the vehicle. One major change was that the vehicles were driven by Fusiliers and not RCT drivers. This meant, of course, that the corporate driving skills in the battalion increased significantly, as did the ground appreciation skills of the commanders who were now faced with the particular problems of a large, heavy four-wheeled APC, with a limited cross country performance. One of the main lessons (re) learnt was the importance of route reconnaissance and working with the recce platoon to identify routes, assembly areas, de-bussing points etc, emphasising the old adage 'time spent in reconnaissance is seldom wasted'. This was especially true as the alternative was trying to recover one (or more) Saxons that were up to their axles in Otterburn mud! This type of experience was repeated on many occasions by other battalions in the Regiment, coming to fruition with the 1st Battalion's deployment to Bosnia as part of IFOR in the mid-1990s. In this situation, with all the accumulated knowledge, the Battalions' vehicles performed well, in a role they were really designed for, that is lots of travel on roads, giving Fusiliers decent, armoured protection whilst going from A to B.

'The Regiment almost by chance benefited from having the 2nd Battalion deploy from Catterick in the mid-80s to Bulford to take over the AMF(L) role. This meant saying farewell to the Saxon APC and taking on the new over-snow vehicle, the Hagglund BV206. Whilst this

In the highly distinctive urban chequerboard camouflage pattern of British AFVs in Berlin, the Reconnaissance Platoon, including Fox Combat Vehicle Reconnaissance (Wheeled) and FV432/30 APCs, lead the 3rd Battalion down the Strasse der 17 Juni during the Allied Forces Day Parade on 27 June 1983. The Berlin Infantry Brigade was part of the tri-partite military garrison of the Western Powers. As such, the Fusiliers conducted many flag tours of East Berlin in order to exercise their rights as the occupying power. However, the main mission of the British Forces in Berlin was the gathering of military intelligence on the Warsaw Pact as militarily their role was impossible. They remained a hostage to fortune throughout the Cold War but a posting to Berlin was always popular as, despite the plethora of public duties, there was always time for self-indulgence.

One of the most successful AFVs in service with the British Army has been the Warrior Armoured Infantry Fighting Vehicle seen here with C Company 3RRF on B Range at the Sennelager training area during Exercise 'Minden Charge' in July 1990.

tracked vehicle was not armoured, it did represent a quantum leap in mobility in Arctic Norway. In this particularly harsh and unforgiving environment, the skills of driving and vehicle husbandry assumed an even greater importance than before. It was a unique situation where many old lessons were reinforced and where some new tricks could be played. For example, in winter it was possible to use the frozen lakes as high-speed transit routes (providing the ice was thick enough!) and it was almost a paradox that mobility could be, on occasions, easier in winter than it was in summer.

'Thus it is clearly apparent that there was a considerable core of mechanised knowledge and experience in the Regiment as a whole, without considering the BAOR/Berlin postings. Over the years, all three regular battalions completed one or more tours in Germany, based mainly on AFV432 and latterly on Warrior. There can be little doubt that it was in this theatre that the skills of mechanised warfare were regularly practised and honed to perfection. Many in the Regiment can vividly recall the major autumn exercises, often at Divisional level and on occasions at Corps or NATO size. The 'Lionheart' exercises of the late 70s and early 80s were

The standard form of transport on the streets of Belfast and Londonderry for many years was the Humber 1-Ton Armoured Truck, commonly known as the 'Pig' from its heavy driving characteristics. The Pig was the principal Armoured Personnel Carrier in Ulster after the Saracen APC was withdrawn from urban patrolling, as were the Saladin and Ferret armoured cars, for being unduly provocative to Irish inhabitants. Here, members of B Company 3RRF, together with their riot equipment, cram into the back of a Pig at the outset of a patrol during the hunger strike tour of 1981. Philip Harris

of a scale and complexity that have not been repeated since, and it was on exercises such as these that members of the Regiment, whether with battalions or on the staff gained the vital experience that would be put to full use on operations later. The scale of training undertaken in BAOR should never be underestimated, being fortunate to have that well known, but little loved, area in the Luneberg Heath called Soltau. It was on this training area that all battalions exercised their mechanised formations, whether in the depths of winter or the scorching, dust filled summers. This basic training was complimented by extensive use of live firing ranges at Bergen–Hohne and Sennelager in Germany, whilst battlegroup procedures were exercised in the great open prairies of Canada at Suffield. Staff training was also catered for by the use of the Brigade and Battlegroup trainer at Sennelager.

'It is with this background of structured and extensive training that the Regiment found itself ideally placed in the late 80s to receive the new armoured infantry fighting vehicle, Warrior, and more importantly the new tactical doctrine that went with it. It was now that the Infantry could be more dynamic and get away from the old 'battle-taxi' mentality. Manoeuvre warfare doctrine laid sufficient emphasis on firepower as well as movement such that the Warrior, when handled correctly, was a potent fighting machine and not merely a £750,000 mobile kettle! It says much for the depth of experience and positive attitude of mind that saw the 3rd Battalion receive Warrior in late 1989 and a year later deploy on operations to the Gulf for Operation Desert Storm/Sabre, which was manoeuvre warfare writ large.

'It did seem somewhat ironic that the 3rd Battalion, having reached the pinnacle of manoeuvre warfare in the Gulf in 1991, should fall victim to the next round of defence cuts in 1992 known euphemistically as 'options for change'. However the great depth of manoeuvre warfare was not lost as most personnel from the 3rd Battalion was incorporated seamlessly into the other two Battalions. Since then the Regiment has continued the mechanised/ manoeuvre warfare trail in Ulster (like the poor, Northern Ireland is always with us!), Bosnia and Kosovo. The trend seems set to continue indefinitely.'

X Company under the command of Maj Whitwam is paraded at Fort George during the 1RRF residential tour of Londonderry from 1998-99. The 'green vehicle assets' are the Land Rover Armoured Patrol Vehicle with the Saxon Patrol in the background. The latter is now only deployed during serious breaches of the peace.

L/W MK1 DESERT CAMOUFLAGE
NATO SIZE 7080/1020
Part of Combat Body Armour
HEIGHT/CHEST
NAPS L1A1
NERVE AGENT PRE-TREATMENT TABLET SET L1A1
NATO STOCK No. 6505 - 99 - 225 - 2344
1. COMMENCE TAKING ONLY WHEN ORDERED BY YOUR COMMANDER
2. TAKE ONE EVERY 8 HOURS
3. IT IS DANGEROUS TO EXCEED THE STATED DOSE
PYRIDOSTIGMINE BROMIDE x 21 TABLETS
PART 2 ORDER (FIELD)
OFFICER/SOLDIER*, CASUALTY/OCCURRENCE*
P/Army Number
Surname
UIN
Rank
Initials
Arm/service
For ADP use only

Desert Warriors

'Train hard. Fight easy.'
Marshal Alexandr Vasilevich Suvorov

THE CALL TO ARMS

On 19 January 1990, soon after assuming command of the 3rd Battalion The Royal Regiment of Fusiliers at Barossa Barracks in Deilinghofen near Hemer, Germany, Lieutenant Colonel Andrew Larpent addressed his troops in the Warrior Gunnery Training Wing. In an extemporised speech, the CO stated his view that - 'Despite the collapse of the Soviet Union and the Warsaw Pact which has been the reason for the presence of the British Army of the Rhine in Germany for the past 40 years, there is no room for complacency'. With remarkable prescience, he went on to say that - 'With the outbreak of peace in Europe, the world is certainly not becoming more stable and the chances are that the friction in international relations could well result in the outbreak of conflict somewhere'. He concluded by declaring his belief that - 'We should at all times be prepared for the unexpected and it is my view there is more chance of the battalion being involved in operations during my time in command than there ever was during that of my predecessor'.

At the time, the battalion was undergoing conversion to the armoured infantry role and it became only the fourth regiment in the British Army to be equipped with Warrior, the new Infantry Fighting Vehicle that was replacing the venerable FV432 APC in the armoured brigades of BAOR. Intensive training, including a three-week firing package on the ranges at Sennelager and Fighting In Built Up Areas (FIBUA) at the Bundeswehr Infanterieschule at Hammelburg, continued into the summer. In blistering heat, the Fusiliers honed their skills for high intensity warfare at a time when the prospect of large scale operations by NATO forces in the defence of Western Europe against the threat of the Warsaw Pact became increasingly unlikely. Ever anxious to cut public expenditure, the government accordingly declared its intention to reduce the size of the armed forces in a euphemistically-named exercise called 'Options for Change'. By the end of July, rumours were rife that the junior battalions in large regiments were likely to be the most vulnerable in defence cuts.

Mindful of the effect on morale, the CO gave the battalion one of his regular briefings on 29 July to inform the Fusiliers of the latest developments. He emphasised that - 'life and politics are extremely uncertain things' and singled out the Middle East as a potential trouble spot, declaring - 'who knows what that madman Saddam Hussein might do? It is not beyond the bounds of possibility to see us deploying out of BAOR should the need arise.' Four days later, in the early hours of Thursday 2 August 1990, the Iraqi army, spearheaded by the élite armoured formations of its Republican Guard, invaded the sovereign state of Kuwait. Yet at first, life in BAOR continued as normal with many units contemplating the holiday season and block leave while the Fusiliers at Sennelager threw themselves into Operation 'Buxton', a demonstration staged for General Snetkov, the commander of the Soviet Western Group of Forces. It was declared a great success by the senior officers present, one of whom remarked - 'Operation 'Buxton' is the biggest thing BAOR will be involved in this year'.

On 9 August, the Defence Minister, Tom King, announced that further British forces were to be deployed to the Middle East. Additional Royal Navy ships would strengthen the Armilla Patrol in the Gulf and two RAF squadrons, as well as a contingent of 30th Signal Regiment, were to support the United Nations force tasked with the defence of Saudi Arabia under the codename 'Desert Shield'. With American troops arriving at the rate of 1000 a day, the operation was dominated by the United States, but on 14 September, Britain declared its intention to despatch an armoured brigade as a further contribution to the coalition of UN forces being assembled in response to Iraqi aggression and the threat it posed to the world's oil supplies. To the disappointment of the other formations in BAOR, 7th Armoured Brigade based at Fallingbostel was chosen for deployment to the Gulf under the codename Operation 'Granby'. Comprising The Royal Scots Dragoon Guards (Carabiniers and Greys), The Queen's Royal Irish Hussars and, as its Warrior mounted infantry component, the 1st Battalion The Staffordshire Regiment (The Prince of Wales's), the brigade began an intensive

The incongruity of training in the snow for operations in the desert struck many Fusiliers while they were in Germany but the temperatures were very similar at times. Here, Fus Nelson undergoes training with the Milan Anti-Tank Guided Weapon System at Sennelager during November 1990. At 0230 hours on 16 November, 3RRF was put on 14 days' notice to move to Saudi Arabia.

period of training and reinforcement before its scheduled deployment within four weeks. Although the majority of its units including SCOTS DG, 1 STAFFORDS, 40 Field Regiment Royal Artillery and 21st Engineer Regiment had recently undergone joint training at the British Army Training Unit Suffield (BATUS) in Canada, the brigade lacked the manpower and equipment to act as an independent force out of theatre.

Accordingly, vehicles and volunteers to man them were requested of the other formations in Germany, as well as all manner of other equipment to bring 7 Armoured Brigade Group up to its ever expanding war establishment. In addition, training and safety staff were sought to support the firing ranges at Sennelager and Hohne. Believing that this would be their only significant contribution, many units called upon their most experienced personnel and newest equipment to support the enterprise. For the Fusiliers, the first major demand was for nine Warriors with crews to provide not only command vehicles for the battery commanders of 40 Field Regiment RA but also section vehicles for the battle captains in the armoured squadrons of the cavalry regiments. Among the many volunteers, Corporal John Kelly of 4 Platoon, together with his driver Fusilier Micky Leech, were assigned to D Squadron of The Queen's Royal Irish Hussars. Called in by Company Sergeant Major Peter West, Fusilier Mark Pearson of 9 Platoon was asked whether he wished to be attached to 40 Field Regiment RA. Having just told his fiancée that he would not be going to the Gulf, the opportunity was too good to pass up and he and his gunner, Fusilier 'Bugsy' Malone, prepared the FV511 Command Vehicle of the battalion 2IC to join 29 (China) Battery at Hohne where 40th Field Regiment was conducting an FTX. As to vehicles, a further 14 Warriors were stripped down for spare parts by the Equipment and Main Assemblies Team in what the CO termed an 'act of wanton plunder'. In addition, the newest diesel Land Rovers and other 'B' vehicles were purloined for 7 Armoured Brigade Group.

On 14 October, the battalion was tasked to supply 229 Battle Casualty Replacements (BCR) in support of Operation 'Granby' and a complete armoured infantry company for Operation 'Granby 2', then being formulated as a roulement for 7 Armoured Brigade Group. Anxious that these should act as specific Fusilier entities, Lieutenant Colonel Larpent reorganised the battalion into a fully manned armoured infantry company under Major Patrick Vyvyan-Robinson and a separate BCR Group under Major Tim Jordan. The company was to be attached to 1st Battalion The Royal Scots (The Royal Regiment) which had been selected to replace 1 STAFFORDS in six months time should a roulement be necessary. Training began in earnest with particular emphasis on personal fitness, weapons handling, NBC drills, radio procedures and first aid skills. The whole battalion was formally placed on operational alert with 12-hour shifts, although for many it was nearer an 18-hour working day. Each began at 0630 with a battalion muster parade at which the CO would keep the troops informed of any new developments. Physical training, which happened at least twice a day, followed: once in gym kit and once in battle order. As the Fusiliers prepared for war long into the night with lights blazing and radios blaring, it was not long before they attracted complaints from local German residents. The situation was all the more bizarre as neighbouring units such as 3rd Royal Tank Regiment continued in their normal nine to five routine.

THE GRANBY GOLD CARD

To 17-year old Fusilier Darren 'Robbo' Robinson, recently arrived from The Queen's Division Depot Bassingbourn, the regime was 'all a big shock to the system - especially the Battle PT when we were required to run carrying heavy logs or 40-pound bergens'. Another new recruit, Fusilier Stephen Frisby of 8 Platoon, 'was thrown in at the deep end' and soon doing repeated debussing drills from his Warrior, Callsign Two One. As both were 'red-arses', they were each given an LSW (Light Support Weapon) - heavier and more cumbersome than the L85A1 Rifle - and jammed into the most cramped position inside the Warrior beside the turret cage; the seat was also next to the BV or boiling vessel which in use became hot and burnt the leg of the unfortunate occupant close by while its constant steaming was a further irritation. Moreover, when the vehicle brakes were applied hard, his face was forced against the metal mesh of the turret cage causing bruising and scratches, a condition known as 'turret rash'.

Individual BCR courses were conducted by the battalion at Sennelager while the reorganisation required many Fusiliers to learn new skills, particularly as Warrior drivers and gunners. By mid-November, the majority of the battalion was spread over Sennelager with a number of Warriors at Hohne to facilitate gunnery training on the 30mm Rarden cannon. All the while, rumours were rife that 7 Armoured Brigade Group was to be expanded to divisional strength as the number of US troops in the Gulf was being increased greatly after the failure of economic sanctions to dislodge the Iraqis from Kuwait and the realisation that they would have to be expelled by force. Speculation ended at 0230 hours on 16 November when the battalion 2IC, Major Keith Kiddie, received a signal stating that the Fusiliers were to form part of the reinforcement in what was known colloquially as 'Op Granby 1.5' and were now on 14 days notice to move. All the far-flung elements of the battalion immediately returned to Hemer to be reconfigured as a complete armoured infantry battalion within 4 Armoured Brigade together with 14th/20th King's Hussars and 1st Battalion The Royal Scots. All of the equipment, vehicles and spares that had been asset stripped for Operation 'Granby 1' had to be replaced from sources in Germany, UK and elsewhere.

The quartermaster's department worked round the clock to acquire seemingly vast quantities of all manner of items as well as numerous new pieces of equipment and clothing suitable for the desert. The RQMS Tech, WO2 Geoff Foggin, sent Priority One demands by signal and telephone to Bicester without formal paperwork, for kit such as the new PLCE webbing: 'We were scaled for about 700 sets but in the end we needed about 950 and they were taking my word for it over the telephone that I needed an extra 250 sets of this brand spanking new webbing and it arrived. That was basically the way the equipment was coming into the battalion'. Such was the power of the 'Granby Gold Card.' The motor transport platoon clocked up hundreds of thousands of miles as its vehicles crisscrossed Germany and the Low Countries to collect equipment, including that of reluctant allies, from depots and docks everywhere.

Personnel also had to be found to fill the war establishment that grew to a final total of 890. Fusiliers flocked back from postings and courses demanding any chance to join the battalion, including Fusilier Enion who had been AWOL for over a year and Captain Chris Long who had resigned from the army but returned for the duration to act as adjutant. Even so, the three depleted rifle companies had to be amalgamated into two while the third was formed by No 2 Company 1st Battalion Grenadier Guards based at Munster, commanded by Major Andrew Ford. Other significant reinforcements came from 1st Battalion The Queen's Own Highlanders (Seaforth and Camerons) to augment the mortar and Milan platoons, as well as various rifle sections with others from the Armoured Infantry Manning Increment; mainly from the Prince of Wales's Division. Twenty posts were filled by TA Fusiliers from the 5th (14) and

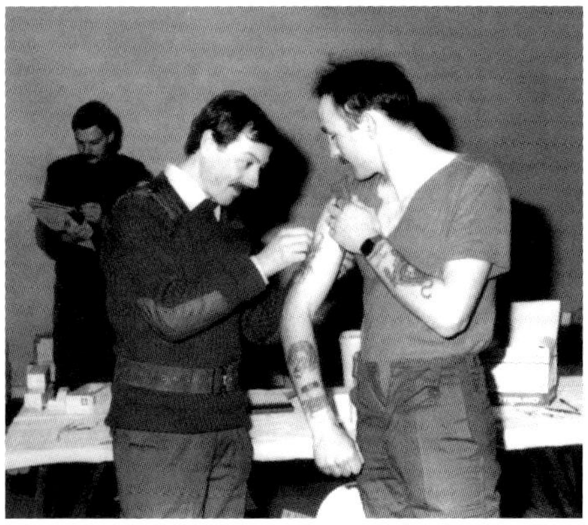

Lt Col Kempster administers one of the many inoculations necessary for military operations against the Iraqi forces, given their use of chemical and biological weapons against the Iranians and their own people.

6th (6) Battalions; one of them being Captain Jimmy Hollywood, a former RSM, who phoned the CO's office and in his blunt Geordie manner told Lieutenant Colonel Larpent - 'Colonel, if you think you're going to that f***ing war without me you can think again! I'm coming with you so what do you want me to do?' He became the ambulance controller in the regimental aid post.*

All quickly integrated themselves into the Fusiliers although each regimental contingent naturally considered its own methods to be the most appropriate in any given situation and its own cap badge to be paramount. However, all were willing to learn from the experience of others as the prospect of deployment loomed. Already in the desert with 7 Armoured Brigade Group, Corporal John Kelly constructed a GPMG range for The Queen's Royal Irish Hussars and introduced a training programme as, due to inexperience, the Hussars were suffering repeated stoppages of their dismounted machine guns. Meanwhile Fusilier Mark Pearson taught the gunners of 40 Field Regiment the rudiments of tactical driving in tracked vehicles. Inevitably, there were a few incidents but they were notable only because they were so few and minor in nature, such as when the Highlanders of Callsign Two Two attached to 8 Platoon returned to camp after an evening in a bierhaus and took exception to the flag of St George flying over the guardroom. Their comments and actions were somewhat unseemly but any difficulty was soon scotched by the RSM, WO1 Bob Broadbent.

As the days ticked away, the weather on the north German plains deteriorated with fog, rain and eventually snow impinging on the training programmes with the mortar platoon at Munster Nord; the reconnaissance platoon at Soltau and the final gunnery camp at Hohne which culminated in a series of battle runs with the Warriors passing through snow flurries in their newly-painted desert yellow livery. Problems with the feed mechanism of the co-axial Hughes chaingun persisted although on one occasion a negligent discharge happened as the CO was walking back up the range. The perpetrator was fined one month's pay. Compared to peacetime conditions, the allocation of ammunition was prodigious. Corporal Geoff Green of the mobile section in the Milan platoon recalls - 'normally when you fire live ammunition you are very restricted to the amount you have, purely due to cost, but there we were gearing up for the Gulf and we were inundated with ammunition. In three days we fired about three years' worth of Milan missiles. It was just a case of moving up to the firing point in the MCTS [Milan Compact Turret System], firing off a whole batchload of missiles and driving away as the next vehicle was coming up. It was just like a sausage factory all the way through.' Each Milan missile cost £13,000 or approximately the same as a family saloon car.

Much time was devoted to NBC training as Saddam Hussein had used chemical and biological weapons against the Iranians and dissident minority groups in Iraq. The threat was deemed so serious that each company appointed a senior NCO as a specialist in the subject while the training officer, Captain Philip Macey, attended further courses for the latest intelligence so as to act as the CO's personal adviser on NBC matters. Some Fusiliers wished to test the efficacy of their NBC suits and respirators by trying to smell the paint fumes while spraying the battalion's vehicles in desert camouflage. While there was considerable confidence in the NBC protection system of Warrior, this was not the case in the older vehicles such as the CVR(T) and FV432 families. To Corporal Green, his Spartan was - 'full of holes and the NBC system basically consisted of a rubber pipe connected to an air vent over the respirator. In the desert we started plugging the gaps with CARM [Chemical Agent Resistant Material]. That was it. Just fingers crossed.' Once their preparation was finally complete, all the 'B' Vehicles followed by the 'A' Vehicles were transported to the port of Emden under the direction of Captain Bob Keating for loading onto RORO ferries that were to take them to the Gulf; the last of which were embarked on 8 December. Throughout embarkation, Captain Keating checked and logged every vehicle being loaded; spending his nights in the back of an estate car parked at the docks close to a building that seemed to attract a lot of late night customers before he realised it was a brothel and moved his car elsewhere.

*The personnel attached to 3RRF on deployment to the Gulf as of 19 December 1990 were as follows:-
GREN GDS 146; QO HLDRS 78; GLOSTERS 3; DERR 3; D&D 5; RWF 4; PWO 6; QUEENS 2; R ANGLIAN 3; RAMC 8; R SIGS 2; REME 85; WRAC 1; RAPC 6; APTC 1; AAC 1; ACC 20; WFR 1.

With the departure of the vehicles, the tempo of activity diminished slightly, however much personal administration remained to be done. Accordingly, the Adjutant, Captain Christopher Long, set up an administrative production line in the gymnasium whereby a Fusilier would arrive at one end and be processed past a series of desks where he was documented and paid; his will and next of kin details recorded and given the first of many inoculations. The latter were administered by members of The Duke of Kent's Band in their capacity as medical orderlies in wartime, whose only previous experience had been a few practice injections into oranges. Having completed as much administration and training as possible, most of the battalion was stood down for a few day's leave with the Queen's Own Highlanders being given priority as several wished to return to their homes in places as far away as the Isle of Skye and the Orkneys. While most married men remained in Germany, the single Fusiliers were anxious to celebrate Christmas in the UK with their families and spend time with girlfriends. The battalion held its own Christmas dinner and party during a visit by the Colonel of the Regiment, Lietenant General Sir Jeremy Reilly, and Lady Reilly, followed by a moving carol service. The prospect of war was highlighted when the Battalion Colours were furled and the regimental silver was crated for safe keeping in RHQ at the Tower of London.

THE ROAD TO WAR

On 12 December, the battalion's advance party of 12 under the command of the 2IC, with Captain Bill Edmonds as the QM(T), departed for the Gulf by C-130, arriving at Al Jubayl in Saudi Arabia on the next day. As the principal port of entry into the country for British and US forces, Al Jubayl held the Headquarters Force Maintenance Area (HQ FMA) which was responsible for all administrative and logistical supply matters for Operation 'Granby'. The Quartermaster of HQ FMA was Lieutenant Colonel Frank Ramsey and its Chief of Staff Major Peter Cross so the Fusiliers were well represented in theatre, while Brigadier Peter Sincock was the Military Attaché at the British Embassy in Riyadh. The advance party was met by Lieutenant Colonel Ramsey in the reception area at Baldrick Lines before being escorted to a compound built for foreign workers of the petrochemical industry at a place called Pearl Beach which was to be the staging area for 4 Armoured Brigade. Belying its name, its buildings were in sorry disrepair and in need of thorough cleaning which was promptly organised by Lieutenant Colonel Ramsey in his inimitable and forceful style, as his nickname of 'The Screaming Skull' suggested. From there, the advance party set about its task of finding other accommodation for the battalion. The QM(T), Captain Bill Edmonds, soon acquired a suitable transit camp at Al Ventura with essential facilities such as showers and toilets, although without the illicit still that had been a prized feature of one other establishment he visited. Despite being limited in size it was preferable to the tented encampment known as Blackadder Camp that had been erected as the reception area for the troops of 1st (UK) Armoured Division.

Meanwhile, Major Keith Kiddie made several reconnaissance trips into the desert to assess the various training areas, although some proved more productive than others, as 4 Armoured Brigade Headquarters sent him to all points of the compass. He remembers - 'with the situation being very fluid; with extra troops and units arriving in theatre all the time, it was not surprising that there was a fair degree of confusion. It was not uncommon to return from a recce of some distant desert location to be told that plans had changed and that the area had been reallocated. This necessitated a further recce of somewhere else the next day. Although this was time consuming, and often frustrating, there was little point in complaining, as the whole procedure had a certain, grim inevitability about it.'

Meanwhile back in Germany, plans were well advanced but constantly changing for the flights of the battalion to Saudi Arabia. The first flight of the main body, which included the CO and members of his 'R' Group, departed on 20 December after its personnel had celebrated an early and somewhat subdued Christmas with their families. On the following day, the party arrived at Al Jubayl after a stop-over at Akrotiri in Cyprus where a final Carlsberg or Keo beer was consumed before the prohibition of Saudi Arabia. The vexed question of alcohol was to recur throughout the campaign. For Corporal John Kelly attached to the Queen's Royal Irish Hussars it had been his downfall on 21 December. Having secreted a bottle each of whisky, vodka and rum in the filter canisters of his Warrior's NBC pack, he and two companions were celebrating 1 STAFFORDS' most famous battle honour (Ferozeshah from the First Sikh War in 1845) in the back when, after two and a half bottles

The Fusiliers of 9 Platoon under the command of Lt Fairbairn display the comradeship of shared experience in the war zone as they pose for the camera shortly before the land war.

had been consumed, he was called upon to conduct a night navigation exercise. Once in the fresh air the alcohol soon took effect but by bearing and pacing he strode off with his students towards the first checkpoint where he encountered his squadron leader, Major Toby Maddison (who was awarded the Military Cross for his actions in the war). He demanded to know whether Kelly was drunk. 'Negative Sir!' was the response, as Corporal Kelly fell flat on his back at attention and unconscious. His fine of £400 was all the more galling when he witnessed the generous consumption of Bushmills by the Irish Hussars on Christmas Day.

As soon as they had been processed through Shed 5 at Al Jubayl docks, the Fusiliers moved to Al Ventura camp. On Christmas Eve, the 'R Group', comprising the CO, 2IC, the operations officer, the company commanders and the training officer, travelled 150 kilometres northwards to reconnoitre the designated training area on the Ras Al Ghar peninsula. Captain John Whitwam, the operations officer, noted in his diary - 'we visited our initial deployment and training areas today. They were nothing more than grid references in the vast tracts of sand.' On land leased from the Amoco oil company, an extensive range complex had been constructed for 7 Armoured Brigade and the US Marine Corps some months earlier. It was called Devil Dog Dragoon Range after combining a nickname for US Marines with the Royal Scots Dragoon Guards and it became the principal training ground for 1st (UK) Armoured Division where live firing of all calibres of weapons was possible. The 3rd Battalion were allotted the eastern part of the brigade's training area which was bounded to the north by the sea. Much of the ground had patches of *sabkah* which was salt marsh with a hard crust able to bear the weight of AFVs but, when dampened by rain, it turned to the consistency of wet cement with similar adhesive properties. It proved to be a serious impediment to vehicle mobility and a cause of acute embarrassment to those commanders whose vehicles became bogged.

For the Fusiliers, Christmas Day dawned bright and clear and, after the obligatory fitness session, they conducted a church service while they waited for the first shipload of equipment to arrive. The CO warned the assembled Fusiliers that the singing of Christian hymns might cause offence and attract the attention of the *mutawa* - Saudi zealots acting as an unofficial religious police force. Never before or since have carols been sung so lustily at a gathering of Fusiliers. A splendid Christmas Dinner with all the trimmings (except alcohol) was produced by the battalion cooks and those attached from the Army Catering Corps, with the officers and senior NCOs waiting on the other ranks. Visitors included Brigadier Peter Sincock and his wife Ginnie from the British Embassy in Riyadh who also visited 7 Armoured Brigade. The festive meal did much to raise spirits in the absence of alcohol and families as did the present for each man donated by the readers of the Daily Telegraph through the British Legion. The parcels contained many useful items including audio cassettes, comb, torch, sun screen and aerosols of foot spray; the latter was found to be most useful for cleaning chinagraph pencil off mapboards. Equally welcome were the many

The unloading of the battlegroup's equipment began on Christmas Day 1990 and the CO drove the battalion's first Warrior off the RO-RO ship on the following day. All the battalion's AFVs were named after Regimental Battle Honours. This one was YPRES. It was the Warrior of Lt Duxbury, the commander of 8 Platoon.

Christmas cards and supportive letters from well wishers in the UK, while those from children addressed simply 'Dear Mr Soldier' proved too poignant for many and brought tears to the eyes of grown men. At 2100 hours, the first RORO ferry arrived at Al Jubayl. Unloading of equipment continued through the night and in the morning the CO drove the first Warrior off the ship.

COLD IN MY DOSS BAG, HOT IN MY NODDY SUIT

Over the following days the remainder of the battalion arrived as did much of its equipment. To ease the accommodation problems at Al Ventura camp the first elements of the battalion, comprising TAC, Main and Alternative HQs as well as A1 and A2 Echelons, deployed to the desert on 28 December as the first of many alarms was sounded to mark the suspected launching of Scud missiles from Iraq. Contrary to the perception of many, the desert proved to be a chilly place with temperatures plummeting at night. It was equally unpleasant first thing in the morning during the PT sessions conducted by the indefatigable and merciless Staff Sergeant Alisdair Harper. The RSM, WO1 Bob Broadbent, recalls the vagaries of the weather in the desert - 'My father served in Palestine and he gave me some tips about life in the desert with the heat in the day and the temperature drop at night but I've seen sleet in the desert - my father hadn't. I've seen torrential rain in the desert - he hadn't. I've seen grass grow overnight - he hadn't. I've seen thick fog in the desert - he hadn't. I can remember it being very cold; I can remember it being warm but I can never remember it being hot.' Similarly few expected to experience the amount of rain that fell; the winter of 1990 being the wettest in 25 years. Many regretted their decision not to bring parkas with them and the acquisition of American cold weather clothing through barter became a priority. Even the issue of the desert camouflage uniforms did little to alleviate the situation although the new body armour was welcomed for its thermal rather than ballistic properties at this stage.

New Year's Eve passed with few celebrations as a combination of cold, exhaustion and a lack of alcohol was no inducement to merriment. There was also a feeling of quiet apprehension among Fusiliers as to what the fates had in store for them in 1991. For Fusilier Darren Robinson New Year's Eve meant a severe hangover following an evening of free beer at the NAAFI in Hemer courtesy of its redoubtable manageress Betty, so the fact that the RAF Tristar flight was dry did not concern him unduly, although the failure of its in-flight entertainment system made for a tedious trip. The final flights from Germany arrived on the afternoon of 11 January and the battalion was then complete in theatre although still spread between Al Jubayl and the Devil Dog Dragoon Range. At the 3rd Battalion vehicle park in Al Jaba, modifications to the Warrior fleet took several days as each had to have its powerpack removed to allow new filters and a thermal shield in the engine compartment to be fitted as well as other modifications in a programme devised by the manufacturers GKN to improve performance and reliability in desert conditions.

As the 3rd Battalion was now attached to 4 Armoured Brigade, the Fusiliers displayed their new found allegiance by adorning their vehicles and their brand new desert uniforms with its black jerboa insignia. Captain James Denny, the 2IC of A Company, noted in his diary - 'we have sewn little black rat badges onto our combats and also painted them on the vehicles. The painted ones the CO has had altered three or four times. He seems to spend a lot of time supervising the painting of the rat. It's quite amusing!' On Friday 4 January, the GOC 1st (UK) Armoured Division, General Rupert Smith, visited the Fusiliers and spoke at length on his concept of manoeuvre operations and his chosen methodology which did much to encourage and instil confidence in those who heard his address. On the same day, No 2 Company 1st Battalion Grenadier Guards arrived at the training area having been delayed by a lack of low loaders; most of which had to be hired from Saudi truck operators as the Royal Logistic Corps fleet of tank transporters was committed to other tasks; not least of which was moving the Challenger MBTs of 14th/20th King's Hussars to the Ras Al Ghar peninsula. Misfortune for the Guards continued when two days later during night training half of their company group broke through the surface of the sabkah and nine vehicles became bogged. Three Warriors were readily retrieved but five were mired over their tracks and one to the turret ring. These six vehicles required extensive recovery resources over the next 36 hours. The company commander, Major Andrew Ford, displayed remarkable sang-froid as befits a Guards officer, but he later admitted 'he felt every minute of that time go by'.

During the Gulf War, both 4 and 7 Armoured Brigades wore shoulder flashes featuring the jerboa. The insignia originated during World War 2 in North Africa with the 7th Armoured Division and gave rise to the famous title of the Desert Rats.

Soon after they had deployed into the desert, the Warriors were fitted with supplementary armour to increase protection against Iraqi crew-served anti-tank weapons. Although it increased the overall combat weight of the vehicle by almost two tonnes, performance was not adversely affected and indeed the ride was marginally improved. The task of uparmouring was undertaken by the crew and the dismounts with the aid of REME mechanics. It was backbreaking work, made all the more uncomfortable by the fact that the Fusiliers had recently received inoculations against the prospect of Iraqi biological agents such as anthrax and the plague. Here, Cpl Arch and his crew prepare Three One Alpha of A Company prior to the fitting of Chobham armour panels along the sides. On the ground at the front is the spaced amour plate for enhanced protection of the driver's position.

On 8 January, the battalion was visited by the Prime Minister, John Major, with a retinue of pressmen and camera crews with the result that the Fusiliers appeared on national television for the first time in the campaign. The final shipment of equipment arrived on 11 January. With all the battalion's assets in place, training began in earnest firstly at low level with simple section and platoon tactics, as well as driving wheeled and tracked vehicles in the soft shifting sands of the area. The fine sand particles soon taught drivers the vital necessity of cleaning air filters and to maintain their engines and tracks by the book; being assisted in the task by GKN engineers deployed into the field to advise on correct procedures. Navigation exercises and company manoeuvres followed until the battalion could move as a single entity. Training then began with other units such as D Squadron of 14th/20th King's Hussars commanded by Major Alistair Wicks which was assigned to the Fusilier Battlegroup as its armour support. Combined exercises were held so that each arm understood the operating methods of the other and the means to provide intimate support to both.

As 4 Armoured Brigade had only one tank regiment and as there would be times when the infantry battalions had no armour support, Lieutenant Colonel Andrew Larpent formed a Reconnaissance Group capable of independent offensive action. The company-sized unit, commanded by Major Corin Pearce on attachment from the Royal Anglian Regiment, included an integral anti-tank capability of four Spartan MCTS and a section of three Warrior Milan vehicles in support of the eight CVR(T) Scimitars of the reconnaissance platoon. With additional engineer; FOO and MFC vehicles as well as its own LAD and replenishment elements, the Reconnaissance group was well suited to its role of flanking and screening the battlegroup and capable of controlling indirect fire at a moment's notice. In addition, each of the rifle companies was given an attached Warrior Milan section to increase its anti-armour assets.

Originally, 7 Armoured Brigade Group came under the command of 1st (US) Marine Division as its armour support. The Marines were tasked with the frontal assault of the heaviest Iraqi defensive positions covering Kuwait City. It became apparent that all AFVs would be exposed to numerous types of infantry anti-armour weapons with many at close ranges. Accordingly counter-measures were devised to increase the armour protection of the Challenger MBTs and Warriors against these specific threats. For the Warriors, Chobham armour panels were attached to the sides with a further section over the front protecting the driver's compartment. All the Warriors were so modified except the FV512 and FV513 REME repair and recovery variants. The task of uparmouring was undertaken in the desert with REME technicians drilling the attachment points while the crews had to lift and bolt the panels to the vehicles. As each panel weighed several hundredweight, it was dangerous and exhausting work because exact alignment of the bolts to the holes was critical and it often took several minutes of straining and fine adjustment before the bolts could be screwed home. For the crews of FV511 command variants the task was even more onerous as there were fewer Fusiliers in them than in section vehicles; the nose armour alone required a complete section to lift it. The task was not made any easier by the lack of fitting instructions; the process being variously described by Fusiliers as 'a two-ton Lego kit' or 'an Airfix kit for big boys', 'with plans as useful as an MFI flatpack'. It took approximately 48-hours to complete the uparmouring of the Warriors in a company group; each vehicle taking about six hours. For C Company the problems were compounded by having to complete the task at night in driving rain which caused the generator-powered electric drills to arc and fuse repeatedly. Contrary to expectations, the extra armour did not affect performance adversely and indeed it gave a better ride for the infantry in the back as the suspension did not wallow so much, but fuel consumption was slightly impaired. Indeed, there were few complaints from the crews as the Chobham armour rendered the Warriors virtually immune from the infantry anti-armour weapons used by the Iraqis. For the crews of CVR(T), there was no added protection beyond the issue of personal body armour and they consoled themselves with bravado - 'real men don't wear Chobham'.

TRAIN HARD FIGHT EASY

Small arms practice was undertaken at a firing range devised by the 2IC and the training officer on sandy beaches overlooking the Persian Gulf in a picturesque area that became known as 'Kiddie's Cove'. With greater familiarity of the desert, training was also conducted at night. However, the total lack of ambient light so prevalent in the industrialised countries of North West Europe or when the starlight was overcast rendered the Raven image intensification sights of Warrior ineffective which, coupled with the inability to take bearings in such featureless terrain, made navigation extremely difficult. Accordingly progress initially tended to be extremely slow and tortuous until the introduction of GPS devices. The GPS or Global Positioning System of geosynchronous satellites allowed a precise point of reference to be obtained on a handheld (Magellan) or vehicle mounted (Trimble) receiver that was accurate to within approximately ten metres. For the first time in modern warfare, commanders and subordinates so equipped were able to know their exact location at all times as long as there were sufficient satellites in alignment for interrogation. Invariably triangulation was lost around 1900 hours and, as it was pitch dark at this time, all movement tended to stop until such time as the system was back on line.

Although there were never enough receivers to equip units below company level, the contribution of GPS to the successful prosecution of the Gulf War was fundamental. Not only did it allow units to manoeuvre with confidence by day or night but it also reduced unproductive radio traffic by a significant proportion. It freed commanders to concentrate on

In 1990, the white board had only recently been introduced as an instruction aid within the British Army but it was used extensively prior to the land war as a means to teach standard operating procedures (SOPs) to Fusiliers at every level. Most SOPs were rehearsed time and again so that tactical manoeuvres could be undertaken automatically under a variety of battlefield conditions such as radio silence or NBC contamination. Here, Fusiliers of C Company receive instruction from their OC, Maj Alec Bain.

The troops of the 1st (UK) Armoured Division underwent some of the most rigorous and realistic training in their preparations for war. The men of 8 Platoon conduct a trench clearing exercise on 19 January 1991 with Fus Cocker in the lead followed by Cpl Fyfe of The Queen's Own Highlanders. On the day before, the section leader of 8 Platoon, Cpl Ross QO HLDRS, had been injured by a hand grenade during a bunker-busting exercise and was medically evacuated. LCpl Fyfe was promptly promoted in the field to section leader. He was subsequently badly wounded during the blue on blue incident.

the task in hand and use the radio as a tool for gathering information rather than simply for issuing orders. Besides the FV511 Warrior Command Vehicles, the A1 Echelon and the ambulance controller had the system on their vehicles to simplify the task of finding units for resupply or casualty evacuation. Eventually more were issued which were then given to company 2ICs and every second FV432 armoured ambulance which tended to work in pairs, although Captain Hollywood preferred for all the ambulances to move in concert.

Whereas 7 Armoured Brigade Group had been deployed to the Gulf with the pick of the equipment from 1st British Corps and most of its elements had trained together at BATUS and in Germany, 4 Armoured Brigade had to make do with the remnants. Furthermore, the brigade was configured from units that had not previously worked together to any extent. Indeed, it was in reality a mechanised brigade with a 1:2 configuration of armour to infantry regiments, with an armoured brigade headquarters grafted on from which it derived its designation. Hitherto, the 3rd Battalion The Royal Regiment of Fusiliers had been part of 6 Armoured Brigade. Once in the desert, the training programme was compromised by a strict limitation on the number of major assemblies available to effect repairs because a war reserve was being created for forthcoming operations; Captain Denny noted - '...the training goes apace, but we are very restricted by track mileage and ammunition. We presume they are saving it for the big one.'

However, following the maxim of Marshal Suvorov, the Russian general of the Napoleonic era, to train hard so as to fight easy, the battalion pursued increasingly realistic exercises with the extensive use of live ammunition. The strict safety measures of Sennybridge or Suffield were relaxed to provide what was universally acknowledged as the best training any of the soldiers had ever experienced during their service with the British Army. As a case in point, the difference between Germany and the Gulf is graphically illustrated by the mortar platoon commander, Captain Simon Coatsworth, - 'At Sennelager, you had to draw all the traces properly and ensure that the mortars firing in support of the battalion had a two kilometre safety margin for the rounds falling. During the first battlegroup movement exercise in the Gulf on the Devil Dog Dragoon Range we had rounds falling 50 metres in front of Fusiliers debussing from vehicles. Safety was a matter of common sense.'

At first only small arms and grenades were used but even so casualties were inevitable. During one bunker-clearing session, 110 L2 grenades were used in 50 minutes. On 18 January, Corporal Ross Smith from A Company Queens Own Highlanders attached to 8 Platoon as a section commander was injured by grenade splinters suffering 13 puncture wounds through his helmet and body armour. The OC of C Company, Major Alec Bain, was minded to suspend the exercise but the commander of 8 Platoon, Lieutenant Brett Duxbury on attachment from the Army Air Corps, persuaded him to continue once Corporal Smith had been evacuated. Lance Corporal Peter Fyfe QO HLDRS was given an instant field promotion to corporal as section commander. Major Bain recalls - 'We thought at the time he [Corporal Ross Smith] was very badly hurt but the impressive thing to me as a commander was to see that as soon as this NCO was off the position and by that I am talking about 90 seconds, within two minutes the attack continued with even greater vigour. It was quite remarkable to watch and I think that was a watershed for me. I then realised that everything was going right. That the people were the right people and the whole process was going the right way.'

Maintenance is vital to the welfare of armoured fighting vehicles and specific maintenance days were allocated to their upkeep with every vehicle being stripped, cleaned and serviced thoroughly. Every item was removed from the vehicles and all ammunition was brushed free of sand which was also swept out of the Warriors, together with any scraps of food to avoid maggots breeding inside. The driver was responsible for vehicle maintenance of the engine and suspension, calling on members of the section to assist in heavy tasks such as 'trackbashing'. Once at the halt, trenches were dug each side of the vehicle and a shelter erected to act as a sunshade or sleeping quarter, although at this time the weather was getting progressively worse. The camouflage netting would also be spread if in a tactical hide. There was a specific hierarchy whereby the vehicle commander had the choice of sleeping place which was along the four seats on the right hand inside while the section commander took the three seats opposite. The driver normally slept in his compartment with his seat back laid flat. The gunner and the rest of the crew had to sleep outside on the ground or on the comfortable American camp beds which many Fusiliers acquired through

With complete air supremacy, the coalition forces were able to employ medium lift helicopters to move troops in theatre with impunity. The first major lift of Fusiliers occurred when the 4 Armoured Brigade moved westwards to join the US VIIth Corps. After the ceasefire, Chinooks were again used to transport A Company 3RRF deep into Iraq in order to escort military scientists in the search for the crash sites of the RAF Tornado GR1 bombers that were shot down during the air war.

barter. At the outset the Fusilier hackle was a useful currency for barter, with three hackles being worth one camp bed or four hamburgers with coke and fries. The Americans were also partial to British Army combat rations in preference to their own issue MREs (Meals Ready to Eat, but referred to by US troops as Meals Rejected by Ethiopians) and were willing to exchange almost anything for a 24-hour ration pack.

While the Fusiliers were engaged on maintenance, the officers of the battalion and of the attached units within the Fusiliers Battlegroup held a study day on 12 January which was the first occasion that all elements of the battlegroup had come together. Various tactical scenarios were discussed and a series of SOPs (Standard Operating Procedures) were devised for closer mutual cooperation. These were put into practice during the first integrated field training on 15 January at 1420 hours, which to the King's Hussars marked an auspicious start. The battlegroup undertook offensive operations that were totally different from the defensive doctrine taught for the past 40 years in BAOR. However, the weather was now vile and increasingly cold, more associated with Soltau and Sennelager in winter than the desert. Days of rain and biting cold winds made life most uncomfortable and created yet more hazardous patches of *sabkah* although greenery and wild flowers blossomed across the barren landscape. Furthermore, the Fusiliers were acutely aware of public opinion back in Britain and of events on the world stage. Almost every vehicle had a short wave radio tuned to the BBC's World Service and everyone was desperate for reliable information. Captain Denny wrote in a letter home, '...the international news does not look good, de Cuellar in Iraq (he had a lot of success during the Falklands conflict, didn't he), the Soviets killing their own in Vilnius. I also heard that there were anti-war demonstrations in Europe and England - we haven't even started yet! I think everyone is afraid and although morale is reasonable and everyone jokes - all seem worried. Hopefully if anything does happen let us hope the US airforce and artillery can do it and not us.'

Spirits were further dampened when Captain Bill Edmonds and Fusilier Leonard were both injured in a road traffic accident on Sunday 13 January which left the former very seriously ill. Confined to bed in traction and immobilised by plaster casts, Captain Edmonds was treated at the 33rd Field Hospital at Al Jubayl. Some weeks later, the city came under Scud attack and chaos ensued when the medical staff ran to the shelters leaving the patients to their fate. Across the darkened ward came a stentorian voice disclaiming 'Don't panic!' and a string of terse orders for the evacuation of the bedridden. The voice continued - 'Are there any Fusiliers here?' - to which came the answer 'Corporal Gilling, Sir!' (he had damaged his back having fallen off his Warrior). 'Gilling - come here and save my life!' Corporal Dave Gilling put a respirator on Captain Edmonds and attempted to place him in an NBC casualty bag. He then covered the prostrate quartermaster with a mattress and took shelter himself under a bed.

The intensity of training during the early weeks of 1991 inevitably led to accidents such as this Warrior, Callsign Two Zero, commanded by Lt Carmichael of A Company which came to grief while negotiating the bridge of a Chieftain AVLB of the attached Royal Engineers. During such a manoeuvre, only the vehicle crew were on board and they survived the incident unhurt although somewhat shaken. Under the command of Lt Lobb, the Sappers of 3 Troop 23 Royal Engineers gave sterling support to the Fusiliers Battlegroup throughout the campaign.

OPERATION 'DESERT STORM'

Tuesday 15 January heralded the expiry of the United Nations deadline for the withdrawal of Iraqi forces from Kuwait. Captain Denny wrote to his wife Nancy - 'Well today is the day that the deadline ran out, in fact I was listening to the World Service and they said that all the Allied troops were at a high state of alert. Well at that time I was wearing desert boots, boxer shorts, tee shirt and floppy hat with my hands in the washing - I was prepared'. As Saddam Hussein did not comply, the air war began at 0310 hours on 17 January with concerted air strikes by cruise missiles and attack aircraft against targets in both Iraq and Kuwait. At this time the Fusilier Battlegroup was practising manoeuvre warfare in the desert. The operations officer, Captain John Whitwam, noted - 'It is the 17th and the war has just started. We were woken at 0300 to be told of the cruise missile strike... We have had quite enough of waiting and training and want to get started and so finished. We will, like I am sure all soldiers on foreign campaigns throughout history have done, be fighting for survival and to get home. Turrets everywhere are covered in pictures of wives and babies in an effort to focus on something normal and predictable.'

The first day of the conflict was one of repeated false alarms of NBC and air attacks with everyone having to don respirators time and again, although they needed little encouragement to do so as the threat seemed very real. No more so than when an MLRS (Multiple Launcher Rocket System) of 39 Heavy Regiment RA fired a serial of missiles from the south of Devil Dog Dragoon Range over the brigade units without prior warning. The vapour trails in the sky and resulting explosions gave the impression of impacting Scud missiles which caused much confusion and 'an ecstasy of fumbling' for S10s and NBC suits. It was standard practice for everyone to carry their respirators everywhere they went and to be without one was an offence. For Corporal Tony Hay of C Company, 15 January was notable for his promotion to sergeant; the only Fusilier on record to be promoted on the first day of a war. At midnight on 17 January, the first Scud attack was launched against the Israeli cities of Haifa and Tel Aviv. In all, the Iraqis launched 81 Scud missiles with 38 aimed at Israel and 41 against Saudi Arabia, with a further one each towards Bahrein and Qatar, causing 32 fatalities and 185 injured.

On the following day, the prospect of war was reaffirmed with the issue of NAPS (Nerve Agent Protective Tablet System) as protection against nerve agent poisoning; one of many prophylactic measures designed to protect the troops against a variety of potential BW threats. NAPS tablets had to be taken every eight hours to be effective, even during the night which gave rise to such banter as 'Wake up for a NAP'. Such a regime was difficult to implement as Sergeant Tom Davison, the platoon sergeant of 8 Platoon, recalls - 'Running your lives around three points in the day turned out to be almost impossible in the sense that a platoon of 35-37 men could be spread over quite a large piece of real estate, with different people doing different things, some awake, some asleep and to try and guarantee that everybody took it at night-time didn't work really. It was the one at two o'clock in the morning that just didn't get taken. You got woken up nine times out of ten but you'd wake up at six in the morning and somebody would say did you take your NAPS last night but you got to the stage that you couldn't remember if you'd taken them or not.' The combination of inoculations and pills had some unpleasant side effects. In particular the vaccination against anthrax, which was given in conjunction with whooping cough to boost its efficacy, proved most disagreeable Many experienced flu-like symptoms for a couple of days which induced lethargy and weakness. One who suffered was Corporal John Kelly. During a bunker-busting exercise he had just pulled out the pin of an L2 grenade when he felt so utterly exhausted that he was almost unable to throw it and could only roll it over a sand dune where it exploded harmlessly.

Field training continued unabated with a dry battlegroup exercise known as 'A8' after the designator on the Devil Dog Dragoon Range map which was intended to test all phases of offensive operations and particularly in breaching enemy obstacle belts. The exercise ran for several days and involved the clearing of increasingly difficult positions in depth with Fire Support Company as the enemy. Meanwhile Major Keith Kiddie was despatched to reconnoitre Concentration Area Keyes to where 7 Armoured Brigade had deployed near the Wadi al Batin which forms the border between Iraq and Kuwait some 350 kilometres to the west. The route to the area was along the Tapline Road which was the only major road in the region. This dual carriageway had become the Main Supply Route (MSR) for the allied forces preparing for the liberation of Kuwait including the Americans, French, Egyptians, Saudis and Syrians as well as the British. Accordingly the volume of traffic was prodigious while the standard of driving of some nations was suspect which was the cause of many road accidents. From 3 January, 1st (UK) Armoured Division began to move westwards to join US VIIth Corps. In the next three weeks, the Royal Logistic Corps hauled 18,000 tonnes of ammunition; over 6,000 tonnes of other stores and over seven million litres of fuel, not to mention food and water, along the MSR to the Forward Force Maintenance Area known as Camp Bob, which covered 30 square miles on a desolate flat gravel plain. The Arabic word for such a featureless area is Ad Dibdibah, which seemed to appeal to British soldiers as it soon became an official operational name and an unofficial greeting among members of the Fusilier Battlegroup.

On 22 January, the battlegroup began a major live firing battle run on C Range, hence it was called Exercise 'Charlie' in which the Fusilier Battlegroup advanced from west to east engaging various static targets and clearing simulated enemy bunker systems and trenches. Breaching operations of enemy obstacles comprising wide ditches and sand berms were conducted using Giant Vipers and Combat Engineer Tractors (CET) to allow the battlegroup to move forward against successive positions. During one of these attacks in conjunction with the Challengers of D Squadron 14th/20th King's Hussars, the troop leader of 4th Troop became somewhat disconcerted at the amount of small arms striking the exterior of his tanks. With his patience exhausted, Lieutenant Andrew Harman came up on the battlegroup net stating - 'If you don't stop f***ing firing at me I will f***ing fire back, only with something much f***ing larger!' The Fusiliers desisted forthwith. With night falling the exercise became more difficult with both A and C Companies having problems in identifying targets in the dark. Despite this, both companies mounted spirited attacks against various enemy positions with much confidence and panache, given that official safety regulations had been relaxed and common sense remained the principal arbiter of safety.

After reorganisation the battlegroup underwent a maintenance period prior to the start of the major brigade FTX on 24 January that was to be the culmination of training at the Devil Dog Dragoon Range before the move west to join 7th Armoured Brigade. Codenamed Exercise 'Nessun Dorma' by the brigade commander, Brigadier Christopher Hammerbeck, his intention was to practise high intensity manoeuvre warfare under the pressure of exhaustion, hence the name of the aria from the opera *Turandot* meaning 'No one shall sleep'. To this end, the maintenance period was curtailed and a long and arduous approach march at night to the assembly area was arranged to test the troops. The route appeared to be a simple straight line between two points but in reality it ran through several quarries which were not marked on the map. Progress was slow, complicated and hazardous and, despite the efforts of the reconnaissance platoon to mark the route, tempers became frayed as one of Captain Denny's letters to his wife recounts - 'The other night we did a night firing attack after a long approach. It was very confusing and being as we were attacking Figure 11 targets it was practically impossible to find the enemy position. We attacked the wrong piece of desert by mistake. The CO then gets on the air and starts getting shirty about not finding the position - I got shirty back.'

Eventually around 0300 hours the battlegroup arrived at the appointed place. However, the brigade commander did not allow any rest by calling orders groups to modify the plans and deny sleep to his officers. For Lance Sergeant Robert Tidswell, a section commander in 5 Platoon of No 2 Company, there was to be far too little sleep in his Warrior, Callsign Two One - 'The company had just regrouped from the 14th/20th Hussars and rejoined 3RRF but it took all night. For us in the back it was cramped, hot, noisy and impossible to kip. Arrived in assembly area at 0400, just before first light - stretch legs, organise the stag, brew, shave, one hour sleep. Everyone up at 0530, orders at 0540, de-cam and ready to move at 0610.' To Major Andrew Ford, Nessun Dorma was an 'absolute f***ing nightmare' as his company had mounted the final attack and had only finished at 0400 hours. As he prepared to catch some sleep, he was called to another O group at 0500 which did not improve his humour at all.

During Nessun Dorma, 4 Armoured Brigade advanced in formation as the three battlegroups were committed to the attack in turn from the line of march. In all, six battlegroup and two complete brigade attacks were conducted, including the passage of all three battlegroups along paths cleared through a minefield under NBC conditions. The exercise concluded with the brigade advancing to contact at high speed over 30 kilometres in a fleet of hundreds of AFVs. The 3rd Battalion mounted a final live firing attack as dusk was falling with C Company on the left, A Company on the right and No 2 Company in reserve. As the companies advanced at speed, the ground narrowed causing C and A Companies to converge. Realising the danger of the situation, Major Bain in his command vehicle, Callsign Zero Bravo, moved to the right of his company but as he did the bergens hanging on the side of his vehicle were hit by three rounds of 30mm Rarden fire from A Company. At that moment with great presence of mind and at considerable personal risk, Major Kiddie interposed his vehicle, Two Two Bravo, between the two companies with a regimental flag of St George flying from his radio antenna as a clear marker to all the participants. The full retinue of weapons from the Fire Support Company added the firepower of mortars and Milan missiles to the suppressive fire of Rardens and chainguns. In Callsign Four Three, Sergeant 'Chinney' Needham fired six Milans by day and three at night; the same number of missiles that the whole battlegroup used during the land war. The 2IC of the reconnaissance platoon, Colour Sergeant Mick McCarthy, had a Milan missile pass between his Scimitar's radio antennae courtesy of Sergeant Charlie Budge in Four One Alpha; an incident that was almost replicated during the war. The final phase of the exercise was a trench clearing operation and a FIBUA attack by No 2 Company at night. By now nearly all procedures were undertaken in a series of simple SOPs whereby everyone knew exactly what to do in any given situation so that there was little chance of errors.

In No 2 Company, Lance Sergeant Tidswell recalls - 'Initially, the company is centre rear during the battlegroup's advance. 5 Platoon is always forward right within the company and we tend to move two up and one in depth. Callsign Two One is always forward left in this configuration. In this way everyone knows where everyone else is all the time. During the day we advanced, took notional prisoners, seized an obstacle crossing, secured it for the remainder of the battlegroup to pass through and then dashed 30 klicks to a forward assembly area prior to being committed to a battlegroup night live firing attack on a Soviet style trench system. We received quick radio orders and whilst the mortars adjusted onto the target we did our final checks. We had six primed grenades each, eight full magazines per rifle, 1,000 rounds for each of the two GPMGs I had in my section and a few White Phosphorous grenades. The company commander gave the countdown over the net and our Warrior accelerated forward. The 30mm cannons started firing followed by long bursts of 7.62mm chaingun. The vehicle commander was incomprehensible and suddenly the Warrior stopped. Debus! Debus! Into the darkness. Flashes, tracer, machine gun fire and explosions. The men huddle together but I can see the platoon commander. We fire and manoeuvre forward with the Warriors firing literally over our heads. We break into the trenches and using grenades and small arms fire methodically clear through the position. Two hours later we mount up, move and drive through a battlegroup replenishment site. Endex was at 0200, we leaguer up and I write a bluey home.'

Blueys and mail were the mainstay to morale throughout the campaign. The one thing above all else that sustained the Fusiliers in the field was the regular delivery of the post. However, the one thing that really angered Fusiliers was the belief that parcels were being pilfered by 'posties' back in the perceived comfort and safety of Al Jubayl. Although items addressed to individuals were rarely tampered with, those just sent to BFPO 3000 were believed to have been opened and the choice items removed - 'ragged by REMFs'. As a case in point, there was the much publicised donation by Sony UK of 1,000 Sony Walkman audio cassette players, sufficient for the frontline infantry companies, yet the Fusiliers did not receive a single one. Be that as it may, the Postal and Courier Regiments of the Royal Engineers provided a vital service that was much appreciated by the troops; according to Captain Lloyd Davies of 11th Postal and Courier Squadron RE - 'Every soldier was writing two or three blueys a day up to the war itself. That's over 30,000 troops... We actually stopped one lad. He'd written 100 blueys with 'I love you' written on each one.'

In the UK, the Regimental Area Secretaries were kept extremely busy sorting and despatching to the Gulf many of the donations that the regiment received at their respective headquarters; at first toothbrushes and toothpaste were a priority, until the troops were inundated with them; then reading matter and puzzle books helped to wile away the hours of darkness while chilli and curry sauces were always welcome to spice up the combat rations, as were the numerous bottles of shampoos that arrived with alternative instructions for application. Morale was also much enhanced by the many salacious letters from unattached women writing as penpals; Fusilier Mickey Leech maintained a correspondence with 30 girls

During training on Devil Dog Dragoon Range in January 1991, L/Cpl Whitworth takes up a fire position in an anti-tank ditch as Callsign Three One of A Company negotiates the obstacle by means of a fascine - a simple device first used by British tanks at the battle of Cambrai in 1917. Carried on the left-hand side of the vehicles, the 'mini-pipe fascines' were particular to the Warriors of the Fusiliers Battle Group. They were intended for filling anti-tank ditches so that the Warriors could cross such obstacles readily without recourse to armoured engineer assets. With a full load of weapons and ammunition inside, it was necessary to carry the crews' spare uniform and clothing in bergens suspended in C-130 cargo nets. Each crewman also had an empty 30mm ammunition container hung on the outside of the vehicle. These held personal belongings such as writing materials and cassette players. Water jerrycans were carried in brackets attached to the Chobham armour panels on the sides.

whose photographs adorned the interior of his Warrior's driving compartment. His ambition throughout his time in the desert was to return to the UK and have carnal knowledge of as many as possible - at least six succumbed to his charms before a return to duty prevented further conquests. At Barossa Barracks, Corporal Ernest Kelsall of the rear party worked countless hours for six or seven days a week throughout the campaign to ensure the smooth passage of mail between the families in Germany and the Fusiliers in the Gulf: for his selfless devotion to duty he was awarded the British Empire Medal.

THE MOVE WESTWARDS

Following Exercise 'Nessun Dorma', 4 Armoured Brigade was declared operational despite the reservations of the brigade commander who stated - 'At the end, we weren't quite there, but I thought I could begin to go to battle with what I'd got'. Considering the brigade had only been in theatre for less than a month and was not privy to how long there was before the deadline set by the high command expired, its achievements to date were remarkable and the brigadier's comments unfortunate as WO2 'Mac' Leyland, the operations warrant officer, remembers - 'I am afraid the brigade commander was not quite as patient as perhaps he might have been and although we thought we were ready he obviously did not. I personally think that we were as ready as we could ever be. Unfortunately, I don't think it was good enough for him and he did let us know and it put a bit of a dampener on our spirits. I don't think it lasted very long because we probably snapped out of it and thought - bloody hell we are good enough. It did not have to be done. It could have easily have affected morale in a big way. Thankfully it didn't.' Major Keith Kiddie further recalls - 'We were all aware of the Brigade Commander's comments but the CO and myself were entirely satisfied in the way the battlegroup had come together. The in-theatre training programme which we had undertaken could have been viewed as the logical extension of the unit's Warrior conversion which had gone on throughout 1990, especially when one considers the extensive field firing packages that the battalion had done that year. Much had been made of the fact that 4 Armoured Brigade units had not undertaken a BATUS training period prior to deployment, but with the intensity of training we had just undertaken who needed a BATUS anyway? By this stage we were all reasonably confident in our abilities and the performance of the battalion, so far, was very heartening.' To the Fusiliers in the back of the Warriors, there were absolutely no doubts as to their standard of training as most acknowledged it to have been the best they had ever had: to Corporal John Mulheran as a section commander in 7 Platoon - 'I will never ever command a group of guys who knew what I wanted to do; what I was thinking or could act almost instinctively without me having to tell them anything. I very much doubt I will ever get that level of training again.'

A brief maintenance period followed Nessun Dorma and the Warriors were emptied of any remaining training rounds to be replaced by operational ammunition on 26 January; the battlegroup being issued with 385,000 rounds of 5.56mm and 10,000 of 30mm as recorded by the RQMS, WO2 Alfie Meades. Meanwhile, the advance party under the command of Major Keith Kiddie travelled westwards to Concentration Area Keyes along the congested MSR on 26 January in foul weather which made the journey even more miserable particularly for the 2IC of A company, Captain James Denny, whose stripped down Land Rover was completely open to the elements - 'When we arrived last night it was a bright starry night. I awoke this morning to pouring rain and it rained for six hours. Not too bad if in a Land Rover. Yes, I was, but it had been stripped down i.e. no canopy, no windscreen etc. Lance Corporal Mickey Brett (my gunner) and I got thoroughly wet, right through to the skin. It was now 1705 and cold and we have not dried out.'

The movement of logistics to support 'Operation Granby' was a triumph by any standards with 1,126 aircraft flights and 126 ships carrying 5,000 ISO Containers, 35,504 passengers; 13,500 vehicles and 48,000 tonnes of ammunition to Saudi Arabia. In-theatre flights by C-130 Hercules transported elements of 3RRF westwards to Concentration Area Keyes at the end of January 1991 as 1st (UK) Armoured Division came under the tactical control of the US VIIth Corps for the major assault into Iraq. Beside the 1st (UK) Armoured Division the US VIIth Corps comprised one cavalry division, two armoured divisions, one armoured brigade, one mechanised infantry division, one armoured cavalry regiment – a force comparable in size to a World War 2 Army Group.

The remainder of the battalion and 4 Armoured Brigade followed over the next few days, with the battalion personnel being flown by C-130 to the airstrip at Al Quysumah and then by Chinook to Concentration Area Keyes, while the AFVs and their drivers were transported there by low loaders. The majority of the battlegroup arrived by nightfall but as their vehicles were still en route they were obliged to sleep out in the open in 'sleeping bag leaguers' to avoid being run over by the vast number of vehicles that were congregating at the divisional rendezvous point. The CO arrived early next day in his Toyota Land Cruiser to find his troops huddled in their sleeping bags with frost on the outsides and the zips frozen, as was the ground. In such a massive movement of men and materiel, there were inevitably some minor hiccups including Major Andrew Ford and 30 Guardsmen who were dropped off by a

4 Armoured Brigade comprised two armoured infantry battalions, 1st Battalion Royal Scots and 3rd Battalion Royal Regiment of Fusiliers, and an armoured regiment, 14th/20th King's Hussars. Cross attachments between the various units was standard practice with No 2 Company of 1st Battalion Grenadier Guards being detached to 14th/20th King's Hussars. Conversely, their D Squadron provided the tank element of the Fusiliers Battlegroup. During the land war, D Squadron provided excellent fire support during the attacks on Objectives Brass, Steel and Tungsten. Here, D Squadron is shown lined up for the commemorative brigade photograph taken after the war.

Chinook in the middle of nowhere with no grid reference; no map and no orders. In one of the very few days of blazing heat, he marched his men southwards away from the border until they met an Egyptian army convoy which was itself hopelessly lost. Undaunted, the Guards continued on their way encountering a group of US vehicles equally lost. Eventually, they came across the operations officer of the 3rd Battalion, Captain John Whitwam.

The A1 and A2 Echelons were delayed on Route Dodge, the MSR, due to the weight of traffic but by last light on 28 January most Fusiliers were reunited with their AFVs and the support vehicles had arrived at the concentration area as the sun set in spectacular fashion, to be followed by another freezing night with frost much in evidence the next morning as Staff Sergeant Harper continued his fearful regime of PT. As the battalion was now on a war footing, the Warriors carried their full scale of ammunition including 94mm LAWs (Light Anti-Tank Weapon) which were stowed along the interior walls. Accordingly there was no room inside for each Fusilier's bergen which had to be carried on the outside either in bins bolted to the sides or suspended in C-130 cargo nets as were all their other possessions such as camp beds; spare clothing and rations. Each Warrior was provided with a body bag which proved very useful as a container for items that needed to be kept dry. Others were acquired to hold a section's bergens and being waterproof they were also useful as an improvised bath; a jerrycan wedged in the engine compartment while travelling provided hot water once at the halt. After the crew and section had bathed, the warm water was used for washing clothes which were then dried on the outlet louvres of the Warrior. No personal belongings beyond those that could be contained inside a single H83 ammunition box were carried inside the Warrior together with an individual's webbing; rifle; ammunition; respirator and NBC suits which had to be readily accessible at all times. Cleanliness was indeed next to godliness and anyone who failed to make the grade could be punished by his companions. In A Company, the penalty for a dirty vehicle was for it and the crew to be banished from the leaguer until such time as it came up to standard.

Several Warriors also carried folding fabric decoys of Warrior and Challenger, each costing £1,500, which were erected well forward of a company position so that they would be engaged first by any enemy armoured attack similar to the one launched by the Iraqis against the town of Khafji on 29 January. Others carried the Mini Viper - a rocket propelled explosive line charge called RAMS (Rapid Anti-Mine System) which was designed to detonate a path through an anti-personnel minefield. Captain Whitwam describes life at the time - 'Our lives revolve around our vehicles that provide mobility and firepower, but as importantly they carry our food and are the centre of our introverted and simplified lives. They are now full of ammunition of every sort. I sit by a 700 litre fuel tank behind 300 rounds of HE cannon ammunition and on top of 50 primed hand grenades...Thank goodness we are British as otherwise we might be worried by the prospect of conflict.'

The crew of Callsign One One of 7 Platoon undertake last minute preparations to their vehicle in the final hours before the land war. The original planning called for the infantry-heavy 4 Armoured Brigade to lead the advance of 1st UK Armoured Division if Iraqi resistance on the border had been strong. In that case, the Fusiliers Battle Group would have led 4 Armoured Brigade with C Company and 7 Platoon in the van. Callsign One One was tasked with NBC reconnaissance and would have been the first to 'go dirty' if the Iraqis had used such weapons. In the event, the tank heavy 7 Armoured Brigade led the assault with 4 Armoured Brigade following. The brigades then took it in turns to be the main point of effort against the extensive fortified Iraqi positions that were codenamed after metals, such as Bronze, Copper and Steel. One One was the Warrior of Cpl Mulheran who suffered a severe injury during the attack on Objective Tungsten when his hand was shut in the vehicle's rear door.

Over the next few days, low level training and vehicle maintenance continued in preparation for the major divisional exercises to be undertaken while on 30 January battalion headquarters took part in a divisional CPX designed to assess the overall plan which had by now been imparted to all sub-units down to the level of company commander. A further round of anthrax vaccinations left many Fusiliers feeling awful and with extremely sore arms and, although the comprehensive issue of NAPS, morphine and atropine was welcome, it was another clear indicator that a ground war was now inevitable. Overhead an unceasing procession of aircraft with the unmistakable vapour trails of B-52 bombers high in the sky flew northwards to pound targets in Iraq and Kuwait. On clear nights the flashes of the explosions could be seen over the horizon with a sound like distant thunder. The likelihood of war was reinforced on 2 February when the battalion was visited by the brigade commander who emphasised the need to prepare mentally for the battle ahead and the possibility of heavy casualties. On the following day, the weather was foul with high winds and minimal visibility in which the padre, Captain Adrian Pollard, manfully conducted a service and Holy Communion. Thereafter, low level training continued but not without incident including when Warrior Callsign Two Zero of A Company was negotiating a No 8 Tank Bridge and fell sideways dragging the bridge on top of itself.

On 4 February, the battalion deployed early in the morning as part of the first complete exercise of 1st (UK) Armoured Division which had been declared operational three days earlier. Codenamed Exercise 'Dibdibah Drive', the object was to rehearse the procedure for crossing a breach created by the 1st (US) Infantry Division (Mechanized) and the passage of lines through it into enemy territory. The entire division and its thousands of vehicles were deployed into a series of staging areas with AFVs to the fore in a formidable mass that was only possible with total air superiority. The 3rd Battalion waited in its staging area all day until called forward as night fell and just at the time that the GPS satellites failed to function. Without its promised guides, the battalion moved forward along a vaguely marked track towards a gap in a simulated minefield. Fortunately, the American guides appeared but any relief was shortlived because it was soon apparent they also had little idea of the location of the breach as they led the column in a figure of eight until eventually finding the correct route which was marked with tape and coloured lights. The whole exhausting process took nearly seven hours, all of which was at night and in full NBC kit. The exercise then entered its mobile phase as the division swept across the desert in a series of dramatic manoeuvres, with battlegroups crossing each others paths in response to ever-changing orders while their wheeled fleet of supply vehicles tried desperately to keep up and causing further confusion. By midday, the exercise had finished and was deemed a success with several valuable lessons having been learnt which were duly incorporated into the master plan. In 4 Armoured Brigade, a further exercise was conducted with an advance of some 60 kilometres by night during which each battlegroup attacked objectives sequentially off the line of march as they would during the land offensive. Captain Denny wrote - 'Well we have finished the last set of manoeuvres before we do it for real. That involved driving some distance, waiting (for us about 18 hours) and then driving through the night, stopping and then driving on an advance for the morning. It was like something crossed between Wacky Races and the Paris-Dakar Rally.' Thereafter there was a period of less frenetic activity with only low level training and maintenance of the vehicles including the application of large black chevrons as a mutual recognition device of the coalition forces.

Various study periods were held on a range of operational aspects including refinements to the obstacle crossing procedures; logistical support and the dissemination of the latest intelligence which indicated that the air campaign was succeeding admirably. Furthermore, it appeared that the Iraqi air force had ceased to be effective; many of its planes having fled to Iran while the remainder were being systematically destroyed in their hardened shelters. During this period, the regimental padre, Captain Adrian Pollard, held several discussion groups to address the prospect of casualties in battle and the need to provide what was termed 'critical incident stress debriefing'. Some officers welcomed such a contribution; others remained sceptical. During one session, Corporal Dave Satchell of 2 Platoon inquired how he would be informed if his brother, Stephen, in C Company became a casualty. He then asked if he could serve along side his brother. He was advised that being separated from him was probably for the best. Satchell was one of three sets of brothers in the battalion. By a terrible misfortune, three soldiers in the battlegroup who had serving brothers were to die during the war.

On 14 February, Major General Rupert Smith, GOC 1st (UK) Armoured Division, visited the battlegroup and briefed each company from the lance corporals upwards. He stayed with A Company for lunch which was cooked by Captain Denny - 'I cooked lunch for the Divisional Commander and selected guests (chicken curry and Aunt Irene's fruitcake) and got complimented - it is amazing what one can do on a petrol cooker. GOC's talk was very frank and open. He allowed any questions to be asked and gave some sensible answers even to the daft ones. He gave the company a good deal of confidence.' On the same day, the division undertook Exercise 'Dibdibah Charge' as it moved 150 kilometres westwards from Concentration Area Keyes to Assembly Area Ray, while testing the organisational mobility of 1st (UK) Armoured Division and its administrative elements. At Ray, the battlegroups formed up in extended lines behind the proposed breach site along the Iraqi border but beyond artillery range. The next few days were spent in final preparations with yet more ammunition being crammed into the vehicles and any extraneous items being burnt or buried.

The Fusiliers of C Company march past during a parade at Area Keyes for a Fusiliers Battlegroup photograph just prior to the land war. During the air war which began on 15 January 1991, 2,700 coalition aircraft flew 130,000 sorties over 43 days and expended 87,679 tons of air-to-ground munitions while consuming 1.9 billion litres of aviation fuel.

Meanwhile, the air war continued unabated at the rate of 2,000 combat sorties a day augmented from 18 February by a series of artillery raids along the Iraqi border as further futile political negotiations were conducted at the United Nations. The weight of ordnance fired during these raids and in the subsequent bombardment of the Iraqi positions by VIIth US Corps was equivalent to 75,000 Scud warheads. As operations officer, Captain Whitwam noted - 'Our affiliated artillery battery [127 'Dragon' Battery Royal Artillery] was in action yesterday for the first time since Borneo. They were part of a bombardment that focused on two enemy batteries and a headquarters that had been previously identified. In four minutes of fire, 1,100 rounds of 155mm artillery fell on each position.'

INTO THE BREACH

G Day, the day of the start of the ground offensive, was set for 24 February following the expiry of the final ultimatum to Saddam Hussein at 2000 hours local time on Saturday the 23rd, when the reconnaissance platoon moved out of the concentration area to join the other divisional reconnaissance elements. The Fusilier Battlegroup, including the Forward Observation Officers (FOO) of 127th Battery RA and 3rd Troop 39th Squadron RE, was placed on one hours notice to move but G Day itself was a quiet day for the battalion. Among the Fusiliers there was a high level of confidence in their training and equipment with only a modicum of apprehension for the task ahead; the principal concern being the use of chemical and biological weapons by the Iraqis particularly against the mass of vehicles now concentrating in staging areas or when the battlegroups funnelled through the breach in close order. Captain Whitwam recorded in a bluey home - 'The great adventure has begun; we are moving towards the breach in the Iraqi defences that is being made by the Americans as I write'. In the same letter, he observed with awful foresight - 'The mood is still one of rising excitement and confidence. We are still entirely untested by fire and all our training and sophisticated weaponry will come to naught if the men are not prepared to stand while casualties are taken and destruction given and received. We have large, fluorescent panels tied to the rear of our turrets to prevent fratricide from over eager US pilots.' Following a final orders group to confirm the first objective, the CO and his rover group moved forward to the tactical headquarters of Colonel David Wiseman, the commander of 3rd Brigade of 1st US Infantry Division (Mechanized) as it launched its initial assault against the Iraqi 26th Division under a massive artillery barrage at 0530 on Sunday 24 February. Against expectations, resistance was spasmodic, with many Iraqis surrendering at the first opportunity.

A painting by David Rowlands depicts the Fusiliers Battlegroup passing the Commanding Officer, Lt Col Andrew Larpent, as the 4 Armoured Brigade crosses the border into Iraq at the outset of Operation 'Desert Sabre'.

Reproduction courtesy of the artist David Rowlands

Originally the intention had been to move the AFVs by low loaders to the staging area during the evening of G Day but the battlegroup was called forward soon after 1400 hours on tracks with only 45 minutes notice to its start point from where it was to follow Route Green to Staging Area 1. From there the battlegroup was to negotiate the passage of lines through the breach and into Iraq but, as night was falling and the Americans were inundated with prisoners, the plan was put on hold with the Fusilier Battlegroup on 30 minutes notice to move in full NBC clothing with all their vehicles jammed nose to tail in columns that could not be more vulnerable to air or artillery attack. Because of the initial success, General Rupert Smith ordered the tank heavy 7 Armoured Brigade to lead the assault into Iraq followed by 4 Armoured Brigade. Soon after midday on G+1, the Fusilier Battlegroup moved out of its assembly area towards the breach where it encountered the Commanding Officer, Lieutenant Colonel Andrew Larpent, standing beside his Warrior command vehicle, One One Bravo, which was emblazoned with a large handpainted sign proclaiming 'GOOD LUCK AND GOD BLESS YOU ALL'.

Following in the footsteps of his grandfather and father who had both served in the Royal Northumberland Fusiliers during the First and Second World Wars respectively, Colonel Larpent was to lead The Royal Regiment of Fusiliers into its first conventional war since its inception in 1968. In extended column the battalion passed him and every Fusilier acknowledged his sentiments with shouts of bravura or the waving of Newcastle United scarves, and the hackle in the colours of England and St George. In an unforgettable atmosphere, Captain John Whitwam, the operations officer in One One Bravo, witnessed the scene - 'It was a remarkably emotional moment when he stood beside his vehicle and waved as his battlegroup went by with the Fusiliers waving, saluting, cheering and doing thumbs up as they were so pleased to see him. Then came No 2 Company with Major Andrew Ford, the officer commanding, standing upright in his cupola seemingly oblivious to the CO but as his Warrior came level with Colonel Andrew, he and the vehicle commanders in the following Warriors gave perfect Pirbright salutes in immaculate Guards style.' Far from being unaware of the CO, Major Ford had spotted the banner through his commander's sight from a distance and gave instructions over his company net - 'Charlie Charlie One, this is Niner. To your front you will see Sunray Callsign. On my Up I expect all vehicle commanders to salute... 5-4-3-2-1 Up!'

In the rear of Callsign Two Two of 8 Platoon, the section of Highlanders was singing 'Flower of Scotland' at the tops of their voices to relieve the tension, when the sight of the CO caused them to burst into a loud round of cheering. Music was also being played in Callsign Three One of 3 Platoon but after six weeks in the desert the only audio cassette still working was Kylie Minogue. Sergeant Paddy Baines, its section commander, had never in his wildest dreams believed that one day he would go to war to the strains of - 'I should be so lucky...'. In the front compartment, in his NBC clothing Fusilier 'Gillie' Gillibrand was wrestling with the driver's controls as the temperature rose inexorably due to the heat of the V8 Perkins diesel engine beside him. He was not to leave his position for the next 26 hours until the battlegroup reorganisation before the attack on Objective Tungsten. With virtually no time to doze or even eat, he drank on average a litre of water an hour to ward off the effects of the heat. However from the troops in the back there was little sympathy as 'the driver had the best seat in the house and the best bed'.

Once across the border berm codenamed Phase Line Vermont, the Fusilier Battlegroup was escorted by American Humvees bearing large illuminated signs stating 'FOLLOW ME' for some 17 kms to Line Cherry. Thereafter, the battlegroup was led by the Reconnaissance Group commander, Major Corin Pearce, to FUP [Forming Up Position] Green at the limit of the breachhead on Phase Line New Jersey where the Reconnaissance Platoon was waiting, having marked the route with mine pickets topped by green Cylumes. After reorganising and replenishing from the fuel cans that each vehicle carried, there was some confusion as to where to leave the empty fuel cans because the FUP was strewn with sub-munitions and personnel were forbidden to dismount from their vehicles after the reconnaissance platoon commander, Captain Paul Nanson, had driven over a bomblet in his Scimitar which exploded and blew off a track pad. It was a salutary lesson as to what might happen to an unwary footstep. Corporal Geoff Green of the Milan platoon was halfway between his Spartan MCTS, Four One Delta, and that of his friend Corporal Dave 'Jugs' Allen in Four One Charlie when the order was given to stay on the vehicles. He immediately stopped walking only to hear Jugs shouting to him to pose for a photograph. On inquiring why, Allen told him that he wanted a before and after photo of him being blown up to send to Geoff Green's wife. Corporal Green carefully returned to his vehicle by retracing his footsteps. Such is soldier humour in adversity.

THE ADVANCE TO CONTACT

At 1930, 4 Armoured Brigade began its advance to contact in asymmetrical formation with the 14th/20th Kings Hussars Battlegroup leading followed by that of the 1st Battalion Royal Scots and the 3rd Battalion bringing up the rear in reserve. The mission of VIIth US Corps was 'to destroy the capability of the Republican Guard Force Command' and that of 1st (UK) Armoured Division was to protect the Corps' right flank by defeating the enemy's tactical reserves. The divisional plan called for the two brigades to attack Iraqi formations sequentially with each being supported by the full firepower of the artillery group as they overran the objectives in turn; the latter were named after metals with those tasked to 4 Armoured Brigade being Bronze; Brass; Steel and Tungsten. As one brigade attacked, the other reorganised and was replenished by the divisional support elements. Thus, General Rupert Smith's concept of operations was to employ the brigades in the division - 'like a boxer's fists with each bite-sized objective being consumed by the brigades one by one.' The aim was not to capture ground but to destroy all enemy materiel to prevent its use against the division's rear elements and then continue the advance vigorously. The brigade and divisional administrative areas were particularly vulnerable in their soft-skinned vehicles as they followed the armoured formations.

OPERATION DESERT SABRE

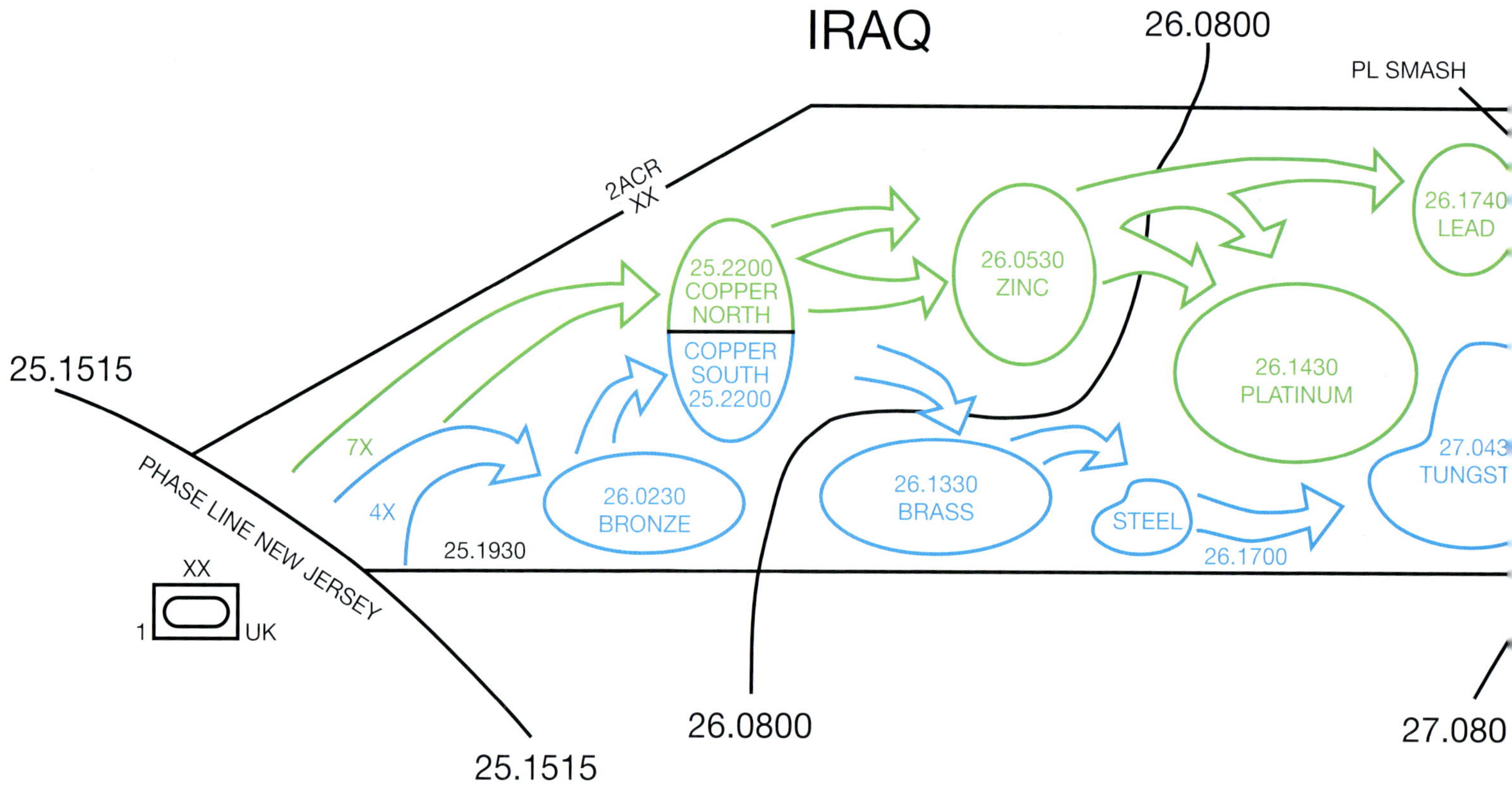

Cpl Green, the commander of Callsign Four One Delta, holds his beret and hackle aloft in acknowledgement of his Commanding Officer as the Spartan MCT(S) passes One One Bravo at the border crossing into Iraq. Nicknamed 'Appetite for Destruction', Four One Delta was heavily engaged at 'The Battle of the Pipeline' on the advance to Objective Tungsten during the last night of the war.

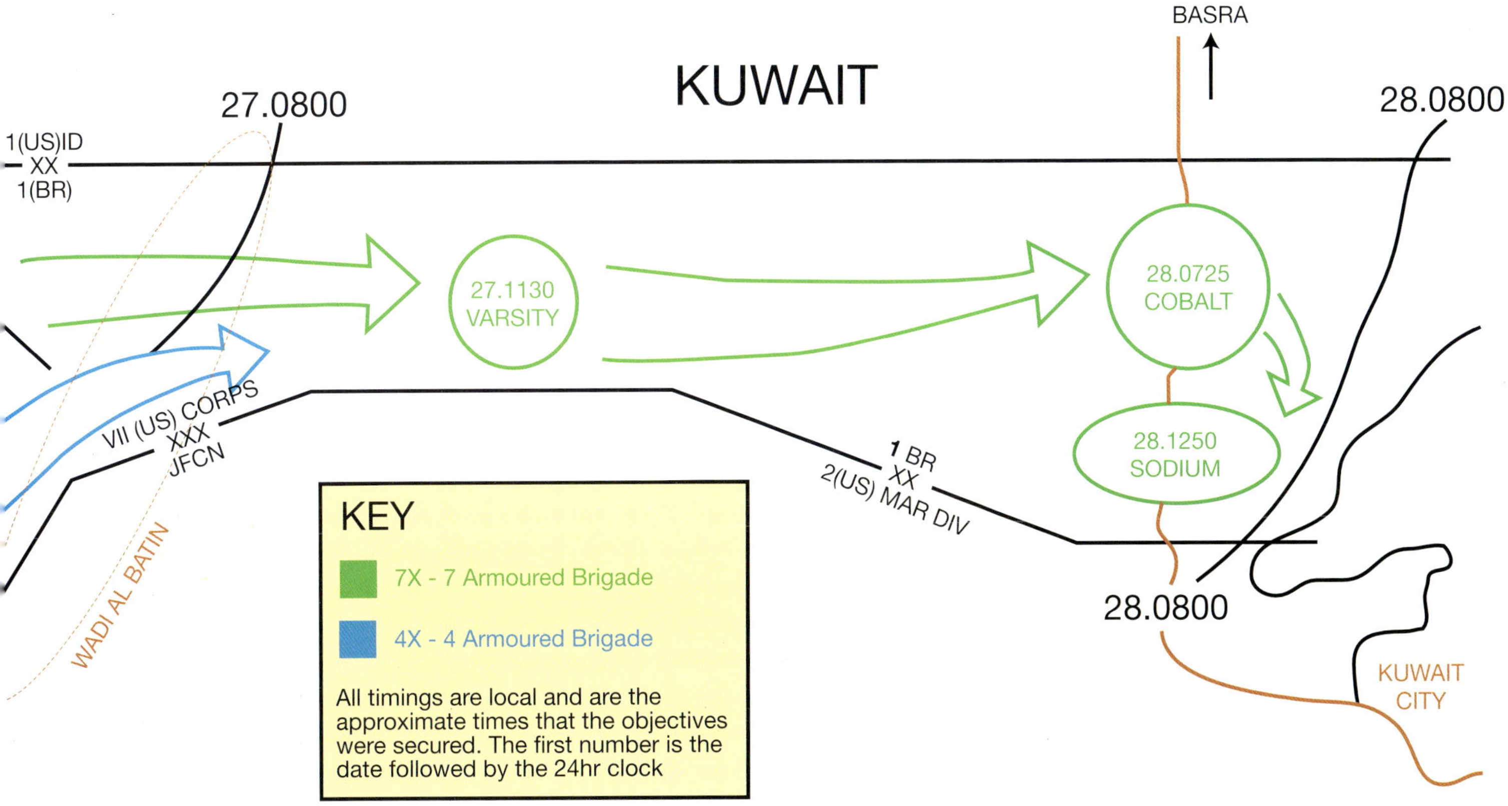

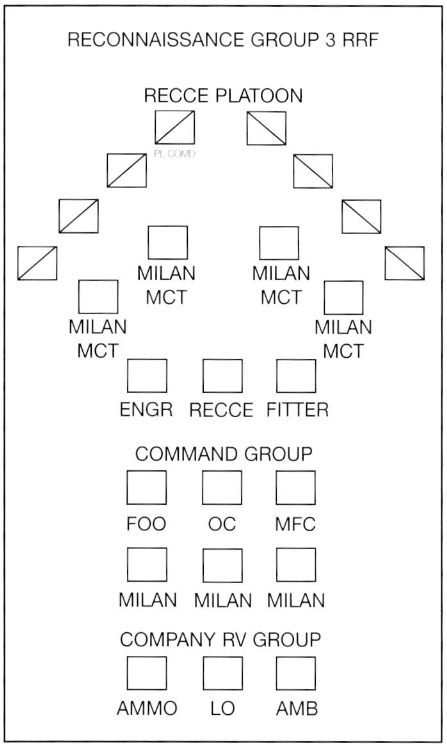

At the head of the battlegroup was the reconnaissance platoon in their CVR(T) vehicles whose image intensification sights were inadequate for the prevailing conditions. Its commander, Captain Paul Nanson, had to rely on GPS but, not far into the advance, the system ceased to function. He recalls - 'It is difficult to describe the feeling of desolation when the system showed "GPS BAD". You either had to sit and wait for the satellites to return or press on with a Silva compass and hope for the best.' Calling TAC HQ, he reported - 'We've lost the satellites', to which Colonel Larpent responded - 'Keep going, you're doing a great job'. Progress was further compromised by the foul weather with driving rain reducing visibility to virtually nil. Captain Nanson in Callsign Two One led the column, with Sergeant Ian Oliver in Two Two some five metres to his left, and Corporal Dave Stanier in Two One Alpha to his right. Sergeant 'Ollie' Oliver recalls - 'The weather was so bad that even with NVGs [Night Vision Goggles] I could hardly see the end of the Rarden cannon', so he was all the more surprised when Corporal Stanier reported on the radio that he could see some vehicles at a distance of one kilometre and found that he was using his OTIS (Observer Thermal Imaging System) sight fixed to the turret roof which was only supposed to be mounted when the vehicle was stationary. However any form of vision was vital to maintain the advance but even thermal imaging was seriously degraded in such conditions.

The Raven image intensification sights of the Warriors were rendered almost useless because of the total lack of starlight and their commanders had to travel with their heads out of the turret to be able to see anything. They were soon sodden and chilled to the bone despite their body armour and NBC suits, and periodically they had to wipe the gunners' optics to allow them some vision. As to the drivers, their periscopes were soon totally obscured by caked sand which the wipers were unable to dislodge. To steer they had to be directed by their commanders whose only sense of direction was provided by the triangle of red lights on the back of the vehicle in front. Corporal John Mulheran of 7 Platoon recalls the first night of the advance - 'Wet, cold, raining, windy, lots of bangs and flashes, explosions and smoke with everyone on tenterhooks but really confident as they knew what they had to do. It was just when you had to do it. Sometimes we opened the door or top hatches to show the lads burning tanks or points of interest. All the same, we knew after the first night that we had them on the run.'

In the rifle companies, the only vehicles with thermal imaging were those of the Warrior Milan section which travelled on the flanks of the battlegroup to protect it against armour attack. On the left flank of C Company, Sergeant 'Chinney' Needham spent the whole night with his eye glued to the MIRA sight of the Milan firing post on the pintle mount above the turret of Callsign Four Three. Soaked to the skin from the lashing rain, his vigilance was vital to the safety of the battlegroup, as was that of the Milan gunners of his two companion vehicles with each carrying a firing post above the turret and one mounted on the open roof hatches. Accordingly the crew in the rear compartment were open to the elements and soon were equally wet. Every two hours the lithium batteries and cooling gas bottles of the MIRA sights had to be changed to keep the system working. Meanwhile, in the packed troop compartments of the Warrior section vehicles most Fusiliers dozed in their 'fart-filled fug' oblivious to the drama unfolding outside.

On the northern axis of the divisional advance, 7 Armoured Brigade was attacking Objective Copper North which was secured by midnight after a two hour battle. To the south, The Life Guards Squadron of 14th/20th King's Hussars and 1 Royal Scots cleared Objective Bronze without casualties; a fact that was greeted with disbelief in the Fusiliers Battlegroup and then with pure relief, as it indicated that the Iraqis were probably unwilling to fight with determination. Throughout the night, The King's Hussars Battlegroup fought against entrenched tank companies on Objective Copper South in an action they later called the Battle of Al Hanniyah. It was in this scene of devastation that The Fusiliers Battlegroup found itself at daybreak on G+2 which Major Keith Kiddie describes - 'As the light came up, it was like being on the set of a Hollywood movie, all the war films you've ever seen rolled into one. Depth fire was in progress and there were tanks on their sides on fire, hulks of things burning and exploding in a very theatrical way.' It was the first occasion that many Fusiliers were able to dismount since the start of the offensive and even in the midst of such destruction there were sights to gladden the eye. Major Kiddie was somewhat circumspect when he heard his driver, Fusilier Dave Greenhaugh, say 'Boss, come here and look at this'.

Not known as 'Lord Wellhard' for nothing, Major Kiddie expected his driver to have found some hideously mutilated Iraqi but in fact he was shown an exquisite flower that had blossomed in the desert after the night of rain.

As the battlegroup paused on Copper South, the Reconnaissance Group moved forward to screen the formation and set up the FUP for the forthcoming attack on Objective 'Brass'. During the move eastwards, half of the reconnaissance platoon, comprising four Scimitars and two MCTS Spartans under the command of Colour Sergeant Mick McCarthy, was screening the left flank when it encountered the battlegroup's first moving Iraqi AFV as an MTLB tried to escape across their front. Corporal Pete Cockerill in Callsign Two Three reacted with alacrity and cried 'Sabot on!'; Colour Sergeant McCarthy shouted 'Fire!' and three rounds struck the MTLB. It shuddered to a halt. At the same moment, a Milan missile from Four One Alpha screamed past Two Three and hit the MTLB causing it to burst into flames. Over the net was heard - 'Two Three, this is Four One Alpha. Thanks for the spotting rounds. Target's destroyed.'

Soon thereafter, the first Iraqi infantry began to surrender to the reconnaissance platoon. However, not all the Iraqis were willing to capitulate without a fight. Corporal Derek McManus of The Queen's Own Highlanders in the CVR(T) Scimitar Callsign Two Three Alpha encountered an English speaking Iraqi close to a command bunker. Ordering him to tell those inside to surrender, McManus lost patience when he returned after ten minutes and simply shrugged. Under the covering L37 machine gun of Corporal Dave 'Gatling' Weaver in MCT(S) Spartan Callsign Four One Bravo, McManus threw an L2A2 grenade into the bunker doorway while taking cover behind his Scimitar. After the explosion, both McManus and Weaver moved forward of the vehicle to see the result. As they did, the sand around their feet began to spurt. At first, McManus thought that Weaver had had a negligent discharge but when the 30mm Rarden cannon cracked just inches from his head he realised that they were under fire. Despite wearing his helmet and noise attenuating headphones, McManus was to suffer a severe headache for the rest of the war. The gunner, Lance Corporal Russell Turner, had engaged a trench from where the Iraqi had opened fire with a Kalashnikov but the sabot round ricocheted away. Corporal McManus then tried to eliminate him with a CLAW rifle grenade but the fire from the trench continued and both he and Weaver rushed back to their vehicles.

In MCTS Spartan Callsign Four One Delta, Corporal Geoff Green witnessed the scene - 'It was like the Keystone Cops. There were the two NCOs running around their vehicles trying to get back in, trying to get on the radio and let everyone know what was happening but they were panting so much it was impossible to hear what they were saying.' With considerable presence of mind, the driver of Callsign Four One Bravo, Fusilier Anthony Cassar, stood up in

At dawn on the morning of 26 February, the Fusiliers Battlegroup found itself in the midst of utter devastation on the Iraqi position codenamed Objective Copper South. During the previous night, the position had been over-run by the Challenger 1 MBTs of the 14th/20th King's Hussars Battlegroup. Objective Copper South is shown beneath the 120mm main armament of a Challenger 1 MBT of D Squadron. The latter was the armour support for the Fusiliers Battlegroup throughout the campaign. Despite the intensity of the air campaign the Iraqis remained a formidable force, on paper by any standards. As the coalition launched the land war, the Iraqis had a total of 42 divisions comprising approximately 570,000 personnel, 2,865 tanks, 1,995 APCs and 1,772 artillery pieces.

his hatch and returned fire with his rifle, shooting the Iraqi soldier dead. As McManus jumped into the turret of Two Three Alpha head first, he ordered his driver, Lance Corporal Dougie Young to reverse away from the trench line for fear of RPG anti-armour weapons. Unfortunately, without direction from the commander who was trying to right himself in the narrow confines of the turret, Young reversed the Scimitar into the side of the Spartan, Four One Bravo. Confusion turned to panic, as the radios in the rear of the turret fell on McManus and Turner and both felt a wet warmth on their legs. Thinking it was blood, they were relieved to find that it was only the BV (Boiling Vessel) which had burst open in the collision, covering them in warm water.

Close by, the Reconnaissance Group commander, Major Corin Pearce, followed the action over the radio. He was only too aware of his orders to prosecute the advance as quickly as possible However, there were some soft-skinned echelon vehicles of the 14th/20th King's Hussars nearby, which were highly vulnerable to any entrenched Iraqis. He decided to clear the enemy trench system with ground troops. Calling his Milan Platoon commander, Captain Guy Briselden, he ordered him to deploy his Milan detachments as infantry; almost all of whom were Queen's Own Highlanders. As his three Warriors approached the position, Captain Briselden conferred with his platoon 2IC, Colour Sergeant 'Jazz' Barrie in the turret of their Warrior, Callsign Four Four. Unfortunately, they had no radio communications with their companion vehicle Four Four Alpha nor did they have radios to converse with troops on the ground. Captain Briselden then said - 'I'll go first'. Barrie replied - 'No, I'll go first'. They decided to dismount together. After firing a six round clip of HE and sabot at the trench line, they flung open their hatches. In moments, Captain Briselden found himself standing on the rear of the Warrior alone, listening to Barrie swearing volubly and struggling to free himself after his body armour had snagged inside the turret.

Laughing the while, Briselden jumped down to the ground and opened the rear door. Grabbing a bandoleer of grenades, he divided off the men in the back into pairs with himself and Private Low as one and Lance Corporal Symes of the Devon and Dorsets and Private Pearson as the other. Meanwhile, Sergeant Barrie ran some 75 metres across open ground to brief the other two vehicle commanders and deploy their troops on the ground. As the other two Warriors put down suppressive fire, Briselden briefed his men and then, with a sense of deep apprehension at the unknown, he and Low left the reassuring armour protection of their Warrior and moved off down the side of the vehicle. As he ran forward, Briselden cursed as he realised that his webbing with his bayonet and ammunition pouches was hanging from the driver's mirror. After some 15 metres, he and Private 'Titch' Low dropped to the ground and began to advance by fire and movement towards the trench line. Grasping a hand grenade, Briselden leapt up and ran forward to hurl it over the trench parapet. With a resounding crack, the grenade exploded sending up a fountain of matter that arced over Briselden and splattered Low who declared - 'Aye boss and thanks for that!'. The grenade had landed in an Iraqi field latrine sending up a shower of excrement. With the adrenalin still pumping from their initial charge, both fell about laughing.

By now, Sergeant Barrie had organised the Highlanders from the other Warriors into two fire teams, each of five men, under the command of Sergeant Brian 'Scouse' Lammond and Corporal Alan Wicks. Without radios, it was difficult to co-ordinate the assault but by taking Briselden's four-man team as the centre line, the other two sections moved forward on each side and began to clear the trench system. Meanwhile, 'Titch' Low's rifle had jammed and Captain Briselden proffered his own as he also had a pistol, but Low was soon able to clear his weapon and their team continued the assault. Having purchased a Beretta Model 92FS, in Germany before deployment to the Gulf, Captain Briselden decided to use his pistol to clear the next bunker they encountered as it was easier to handle in the confined space and he wished to conserve his rifle ammunition since the extent of the position remained unknown. By posting a grenade through the embrasure followed by several rounds of pistol fire, Briselden cleared several bunkers as he and the Highlanders moved through the extensive trench system. As they advanced, the supporting fire of the two Warriors was becoming uncomfortably close, particularly from Four Four Alpha. Realising the danger, Sergeant Lammond valiantly ran back to his vehicle, opened the rear door and used the intercom to adjust his gunner's fire onto targets in depth as the assault reached its climax. In this first encounter with the entrenched enemy who had had many months to prepare the

Citation for the Military Cross awarded to
Lieutenant Anthony Guy Briselden
The Royal Regiment of Fusiliers
The London Gazette
28 June 1991

'For conspicuous gallantry in Southern Iraq on 26 February 1991. Lieutenant Briselden, Battle Group Anti Tank Platoon Commander, was deployed with one of his Milan sections as part of a reconnaissance screen to the flank of the Battle Group as it advanced. The Reconnaissance Group encountered an occupied enemy defensive position. On orders, Lieutenant Briselden led his small force to conduct a dismounted assault against the fortified enemy position. The situation was confused, and sporadic enemy fire from the position was impeding the progress of the advance. On dismounting from their Warrior Armoured Personnel Carrier, the section took cover and were reluctant to move forward. Assessing the situation, and realising the need to take effective action to seize the initiative, Lieutenant Briselden crawled forward alone over 30 yards of exposed ground to clear single handedly the first enemy bunker. This he did successfully by the use of grenades. He immediately continued his attack on a second bunker with complete disregard for his own personal safety. By this time the men of Lieutenant Briselden's platoon, inspired and motivated by his exceptional personal example, had moved forward to support him in clearing the remainder of the position which was subsequently rendered inactive. Lieutenant Briselden's actions were in the highest traditions of the Service and resulted in a successful action. That success at the early stage of the Battle Group's operation had a significant effect on morale throughout the unit and inspired all those who heard about it.'

position, the men of the Milan Platoon showed considerable fortitude and commendable spirit. Many Iraqis subsequently surrendered. For his inspirational leadership in this exploit of arms that delayed the advance only momentarily, Captain Guy Briselden was awarded the Military Cross.

THE ASSAULT ON OBJECTIVES BRASS AND STEEL

As this action was underway, the remainder of the battlegroup was poised behind the Reconnaissance Group, waiting for the opportunity to attack its first target of the eastern half of Objective Brass. This was an extensive position covering about 40 square kilometres and containing approximately a brigade of G5 155mm artillery pieces. By now the weather had deteriorated once more with visibility reduced to less than a few hundred metres because of gusting sandstorms. With the wind blowing strongly from the south, the line of advance to contact onto Objective Brass was into the teeth of the wind. As there were still fears that the Iraqi artillery positions on Brass had gas shells, some of the Warrior commanders wore their respirators as they travelled with their heads out of the turrets. In Callsign Two Two Bravo, Major Keith Kiddie remained concerned that the preliminary artillery bombardment might hit the stockpiles of chemical shells 'and stir up clouds of mustard gas'.

The attack by the Fusilier Battlegroup was scheduled for 0945 hours following the clearing of the western half of Objective 'Brass' by the 14th/20th and Royal Scots Battlegroups. However, due to the delay in regrouping D Squadron 14th/20th King's Hussars to The Fusiliers Battlegroup, as the tanks had to retrace their tracks some 20 kilometres and reorganise, the attack did not begin until almost midday. After a quick O group from Lieutenant Colonel Larpent at the rear of One One Bravo where the sandstorm lacerated the exposed flesh of his face, Major Alistair Wicks formed up for the assault with his 14 Challenger 1 MBTs in line abreast, followed by the Warriors of the Fusiliers with C Company on the left and A on the right, with No 2 Company in depth. Originally the artillery plan was to last two hours but in the event it was reduced to approximately 15 minutes from six 155mm batteries with several MLRS serials. The FOO attached to C Company, Captain Edward Grace in his Warlord OPV named 'The Highlander', recalls the moment - 'As the guns started firing, all fear instantaneously disappeared as, suddenly, absolute concentration was required. No time for worrying. No time for thinking about myself. Go. Go. Go. We roared forward into the sandstorm, tanks leading. Here we come. This is real.'

After approximately 1,500 metres, the tanks suddenly stopped and began engaging targets with main armament rounds. As the Warriors came to a halt behind them, the battlegroup commander, Lieutenant Colonel Larpent, demanded to know what was happening but the tanks continued their reconnaissance by fire until they had subdued the positions to their front and then continued forwards. At times visibility was down to 50 metres as the sandstorm continued unabated but then cleared again to reveal targets of opportunity and abandoned gun positions all aligned uselessly to the south. In the words of Major Keith

At the forefront of The Fusiliers Battle Group throughout the land war was the Recce Pl. Once in the desert, it became part of the Reconnaissance Group which was formed from various elements of Fire Support Company to provide a force with an integral anti-tank capability. Such a unit was able to act independently and defend itself, should the need arise. Here, the first Iraqi prisoners encountered by the Fusiliers Battle Group are surrendering, seen from the turret of Callsign Two Three Alpha, the CVR(T) Scimitar of Cpl McManus of the Queen's Own Highlanders. His vehicle is working with a second Scimitar and a Spartan Milan Compact Turret System. Derek McManus

Kiddie - 'We rocked up out of the gloom and did a Singapore on them with their guns all pointing in the wrong direction'. Lieutenant Iain Hallam, the commander of 7 Platoon, continues - 'As we went in we could still not identify their exact positions but we did see some trucks to our left flank. 7 Platoon was detached to destroy these which we did with some fairly reasonable gunnery skills. Whether these had been abandoned or had already been destroyed seemed immaterial as it allowed the release of tension and raised morale as our guys had at last fired in anger.' The commander of 9 Platoon, Lieutenant Dickie Fairbairn, whose platoon was in depth takes up the account - 'The fire plan went in and we moved off keeping a bound behind Zero Bravo but there was no sign of any enemy. 8 Platoon identified a position to its left so we moved onto the flank and moved forward with Zero Bravo but all the positions were empty so we went firm. Zero Bravo rejoined the rest of the company which I thought was continuing through the desert. When we went to rejoin as well, I went the wrong way following A Company. Two kilometres later I realised my mistake and after confirming this, we reversed back towards the company.'

To No 2 Company following behind, the sight of Warriors reversing at speed out of the gloom was disconcerting to say the least especially as the radio nets were surprisingly quiet at this time despite the warning of T-62s being in the vicinity. It seemed as if they might be retiring in the face of such a threat. Clarification was sought on the battlegroup net and, although none was forthcoming, Major Ford decided to continue straight on regardless towards Objective 'Steel'. After taking up position as the forward left platoon, Lieutenant Fairbairn continues - 'Fusilier Jenkins [his gunner] spotted three barrels with berms around them and when I confirmed this, we were ordered to destroy the guns. Three Zero and Three One moved off first some 200 metres and engaged while Three Two and Three Three moved up. From 600 metres Jenkins hit one of the barrels and it snapped! At 300 metres I realised they were dummy positions, so we moved back to rejoin the company. We moved through 7 Platoon and advanced 500 metres, then 8 Platoon moved up and 7 Platoon moved through again. Challengers were firing at bunkers to our front causing huge explosions which many crews thought was something much larger.' Lieutenant Hallam of 7 Platoon takes up the account - 'About another two kilometres on 7 and 8 Platoons came across the real positions. As planned after a short artillery barrage we stood off and shot up the target for a while. We moved in and identified the guns as G5 155mm.' In *The Highlander*, Captain Grace recalls - 'Through the dust we saw our objective. Abandoned. There was nothing there apart from empty berms, empty trenches, no enemy. I yet again had mixed feelings of relief that I was still alive and regret that we did not have to prove ourselves in a real fire fight.'

Although many Warriors did not fire at all on Objective Brass, others had several engagements. As was the SOP, the vehicle commander of Callsign Two Two of 8 Platoon, Sergeant Trevor Smith, was giving a running commentary to keep those in the back of his Warrior informed about the terrain and potential targets in case they had to dismount - 'We're sticking one in a bunker at 2 o'clock', and the gunner, Fusilier Kevin Leech, fired a three round burst of HE. Each time a target was hit, the rifle section gave a resounding cheer. After several engagements, the Rarden cannon had a stoppage and the chaingun was then used to suppress the bunkers and induce any occupants to surrender. Sergeant Smith soon realised that the Iraqis were so bedraggled and pathetic that they posed no threat. He instructed his gunner - 'Don't shoot the people'. During the assault, the CO's vehicle, One One Bravo, fired on five different targets including a T-62. As the battalion master gunner, Colour Sergeant John Mickleson shared the turret with the CO and the two of them had decided that gunnery was to be the responsibility of Mickleson who recalls - 'The CO had lots of other things to do in the turret and with the hatches closed my concern was scanning for targets. What we had agreed was to leave the gunnery to me. If I saw a target, then I took it and if he was busy I loaded as well. On Objective Brass we first took out a bunker with six rounds of HE. We then traversed a trench and saw Iraqi troops in the bottom so we reversed to straddle the trench and I rotated the turret right and left to engage them but they were discarding their weapons and equipment so we moved off again. We came over a ridge and 800 metres ahead was a T-62 with the commander's hatch open. My first reaction was to fire so I put three rounds of APDS into the commander's cupola. We both realised after firing three rounds and no fire was returned that it was probably abandoned'. Indeed, most of the positions and guns on Objective Brass had been abandoned by the Iraqis.

Major Bain describes the next part of the assault on Objective Steel, which in the event was really an extension of Brass - 'The first objective was the eastern side of Brass where, having moved through the night, we assaulted from north to south to take out a series of gun positions. This actually went remarkably well. The point to note here was that it was done with visibility limited to 200-300 metres at a time. The three companies attacked through the objective, one beside the other, and then swung east. What was quite a remarkable feat was that we had to swing onto a new line of departure for Steel so, having run north to south, we had to swing through 90 degrees to run west to east. Just minutes before we were released from this by the CO, the wind died and the visibility improved dramatically and we suddenly discovered that we were all in the right place over several kilometres. All of this was solely due to GPS, which I think was a particularly good example of the benefit of the thing. Steel was a peculiar objective in that it was predominately logistic units with some gun positions and a small infantry squad. C Company was on the left, A Company on the right, No 2 Company and a squadron of tanks in the centre. A very wide frontage for the battlegroup of about five kilometres. We fired and manoeuvred the two forward platoons in 500 metre bounds and basically we did a tactical drill which we had never trained for. This was reconnaissance by fire and with the gunners dropping fire two to three kilometres in front of us. We were using main armament on anything that didn't look right. We shot it and continued to move quite fast because we did not want to lose contact with the tanks who were right forward of us in the centre of mass.'

In the centre of the attack was No 2 Company Grenadier Guards and Major Ford recalls - 'The whole area of Objective Steel consisted of dug-outs, trench systems and artillery pieces and an enemy that could not surrender fast enough, although the latter point was not immediately obvious to the crews of closed-down armoured vehicles travelling at pace'. Attached to No 2 Company was the Royal Artillery OPV of Captain Grace - 'I left C Company and regrouped to No 2 Company for their attack on Objective Steel. I had exactly the same feelings of fear and confidence on the start line and yet again, as we moved forward, there was no time for anything but total concentration. This objective was much bigger than C Company's and contained not only guns, but enemy. Again we did not fire a round but we did take prisoners. It was an amazing feeling having so much command over other members of the human race, as we trained the chaingun on 12 Iraqis as they came out of their bunker. Later we picked up another six and the one thing that struck me most was how happy they all were to have been captured. Those that spoke English kept saying "Thank you for saving our lives". That really choked me'. In A Company, Captain James Denny in Callsign Zero Charlie recalls that the first Iraqi who approached his vehicle to surrender was carrying a Tesco supermarket plastic bag containing a single bottle of water; he had returned to Iraq from his studies in England and had been conscripted into the army.

The Fusiliers Battlegroup pauses during the course of the land war somewhere in southern Iraq. In the centre is St George, the FV511 command vehicle of Lt Col Larpent. Behind him is St Edward, the FV511 of his 2IC, Maj Kiddie, whose vehicle is flying a regimental flag. This acted as the centre of mass to the battalion during training and during the war.

Major Bain was also concerned by the numbers of Iraqi PWs - 'The Iraqis were making themselves apparent everywhere but because of the speed at which we were moving we could actually do nothing about them. We just kept rolling as it was fairly evident these guys were not terribly dangerous, but it did cause us some concern because following us there were soft-skinned vehicles and we weren't terribly sure as to whether or not they would then become nasty towards these much more vulnerable folk. We stopped on three occasions and the Sappers got out to use hay ricks [demolition charges] on the gun barrels and cut them off.' Each time, an infantry section dismounted to act as close protection to the Royal Engineers and to herd the PWs to the rear for collection by following units; in all approximately 800 were captured.

At 1445 hours, the battlegroup halted around the final Iraqi gun positions on Objective Steel and waited for the Royal Engineers to complete their destruction. The Warriors of C Company were spread out, line abreast, facing eastwards with the Challenger MBTs of D Squadron forming an arc some 500 metres to the south. Mindful that his Warriors had been in a sandstorm for the last hour, Major Bain ordered the crews to ensure that the air recognition panels on the tops of the vehicles were clear of sand and readily visible. Everyone was then ordered into their vehicles and the doors shut so that the Sappers could detonate the charges attached to the artillery pieces, but a 15 minute delay was then announced. Turret hatches and rear doors were opened for better ventilation and to allow personnel to relieve themselves.

Corporal John Mulheran was standing on the turret of Callsign One One of 7 Platoon as a REME articifer repaired his 30mm Rarden when he looked up and saw A-10 ground attack aircraft at which he said to another REME craftsman - 'We've got some air cover, that's good'. At that moment, one of the A-10s dived and banked sharply dispensing flares as a counter-measure to heat-seeking missiles. Corporal Mulheran thought to himself - 'Why the f**k did he do that?'. Corporal 'Chinney' Needham also saw the A-10s circling from his Warrior Milan vehicle but thought nothing further of it as he was busy scanning the horizon for enemy armour. Captains Briselden and Nanson were standing behind their OC's Warrior enjoying a cup of coffee and watching the A-10s striking targets to their front. After several attack runs, they looked to their right and saw two A-10s circling above the Fusilier Battlegroup. One of the planes then flew a low pass over the stationary vehicles and released decoy flares. It then rose to altitude before diving once more.

In Callsign Two Two of 8 Platoon, Private John Lang had got out of the Warrior and was relieving himself as he chatted to the driver, Fusilier Gary Hunt. Having just done the same, Fusilier Leech was about to step back into the turret while Sergeant Trevor Smith was observing to his front through his commander's sight. The weather was now fine, clear and dry with no cloud cover. Visibility was excellent and he could see AFVs crossing from right to left at a distance of some three kilometres. In the rear, Private Howard 'Scouse' Finnan stood

Sgt Floydd and Cpl Stoddart man the turret of the Warrior MFC, Callsign One Three Alpha. The Cross of St Andrew on the radio antenna indicates that this Mortar Fire Control vehicle is crewed by Queen's Own Highlanders. On the rear top hatches, the driver, Pte McDonald is chatting with one of the ITN video team of Paul Davis and Nigel Thomson that was carried by One Three Alpha throughout the land war. The Chieftain MBT stowage bin on the vehicle side held much of their filming equipment.

up to clamber out of the vehicle while beside him, next to the door, Private Martin Ferguson was reading a letter from his fiancée, Rachel. Glancing up from his bluey, he asked his section commander, Corporal Peter Fyfe, what the time was to which the response was - 'Six minutes past three'. His watch was four minutes fast.

BLUE ON BLUE

At 1502 hours, an AGM-65D Maverick infrared imaging missile was released from stores pylon nine of a United States Air Force A-10A Thunderbolt II. It was fired against a target identified by the flight leader as 'T-54/55 tanks and associated support vehicles'. The missile struck the left-hand side of Callsign Two Two and Private John Lang standing near the point of impact was blown to pieces. The 125-pound shaped charge warhead of the Maverick missile tore through the side of the Warrior into the troop compartment where Private Neil Donald was sitting and decapitated him. Beside him was Private 'Scouse' Finnan who recalls - 'It was hot and sweaty and the air was stale. We had opened the door to get some air. John had jumped out to have a piss and we were waiting for him. Suddenly there was a sharp impact. I was thrown out and landed about four metres away. I must have been unconscious for about 15 seconds. When I came round I couldn't see much because my eyes were burnt and blurred - to open them was unbearable. There was a lot of smoke. I had several shrapnel wounds on my shoulders and arms, but apart from that, there was not a scratch on me. It seemed like a miracle.'

Sitting opposite to Private Finnan was Private Ali Meechan who escaped serious injury beyond badly damaged eardrums and flash burns. Beside him, his section commander Corporal Fyfe suffered serious wounds with fragments in his body and burns to the face, hands, genitals and lungs, while the blast overpressure expelled part of his intestines out of his rectum. He also felt severe pains in his legs and feet and on glancing down he saw a spare GPMG barrel protruding through his left thigh while the toes of his left foot were fused together by a metal fragment. On looking up he saw that Private Ferguson had been killed instantly as half of his head was missing and there was a large piece of metal through his neck. In the appalling heat of the fireball, Fyfe's hair and uniform caught fire but he was unable to move as he was pinned to the seat by the barrel through his leg. Beside him, Meechan was saved by the GPMG he was holding vertically between his legs as the roof of the vehicle collapsed. In the turret, Sergeant Smith experienced a bright flash of white light but heard no sound. He knew immediately that the vehicle had been hit and looking down saw a deep wound in the top of his right thigh. In shock but believing the vehicle had taken fire to the front, Smith shouted - 'Open the turret cage and get me into the back! Pull me out! Pull me out!', but when he heard nothing from the troop compartment, he hoisted himself out of the turret by his elbows as his hands were badly burnt.

Some 200 metres to the south, Major Alistair Wicks was observing the scene through his tank's periscope when he saw the Warrior explode and a body [Fusilier Kevin Leech] being flung upwards from the turret to disappear in a ball of fire. With awful clarity, he watched helplessly as another crewman [Sergeant Trevor Smith] slowly clambered out of the turret while the driver [Fusilier Gary Hunt] was seen trying to extricate himself from his compartment but his hatch was jammed. Private Finnan was on the ground behind the Warrior - 'I was really worried about the two phosphorous grenades which I had attached to me. Once they go off there's nothing you can do to put them out. I was the only person who was thrown out. I went over to look into the remains of the Warrior - there was a hell of a lot of ammunition in there so I didn't hang around. Inside I could see dead bodies and black metal. One of my best mates was in there. I started to hobble away; something in my head told me to move away in case there was another explosion.' As he did so, Finnan saw - 'One man [Sergeant Trevor Smith] then came off the top of the vehicle and started crawling on the floor. His leg had a big hole in it.' Temporarily blinded by flash burns, Smith continues - 'I pulled myself up onto the top and then rolled off the side of the vehicle. I crawled round to the back and looked inside.' Because of his wounds, he was unable to raise himself above the tailgate of the Warrior but he saw that Donald and Ferguson were beyond help. To the sound of Fyfe and Meechan screaming, Smith crawled away disorientated and half-blind with a passage from the Bible ringing in his mind. Moments later, Meechan managed to bundle Fyfe out of the back of the Warrior.

The Warriors of 8 Platoon pause after the attack on Objective 'Steel' with the platoon commander's vehicle Two Zero of Lt Duxbury in the foreground. Callsigns Two Two and Two Three are in the middle distance. On the horizon are the Challenger MBTs of D Squadron 14th/20th Hussars which are facing southwards as is the Iraqi 155mm G-5 howitzer forward of Two Zero's 30mm Rarden cannon. At the extreme right is the nose of the Royal Engineer Spartan as it moves up to destroy the G-5 with explosives. Accordingly, all the Fusiliers are sheltering inside their Warriors with the rear doors open. An air recognition panel is visible above the turret stowage basket of Two Zero. This photograph was taken moments before Callsign Two Two was struck by a Maverick missile.

Over the company net came the anguished call of Lieutenant Brett Duxbury, the commander of 8 Platoon, who managed to state in a calm and collected voice - 'Hello Zero Alpha, this is Two Zero Alpha. My callsign Two Two has just exploded.' 'Two Zero Alpha, this is Zero, say again'. 'My callsign Two Two has just f***ing blown up. Wait out,' Duxbury replied before climbing out of his Warrior and running towards the burning vehicle. As he did so he saw Corporal Fyfe staggering about with his hair and uniform on fire. Duxbury then came across Sergeant Smith crawling over the ground on his elbows, his face blackened and his eyes fused shut. Within moments, the radio net was alive with calls as to the possible cause of the explosion, with most believing that a mine had been detonated. In the confusion, 7 and 9 Platoons moved off some 500 metres and set up an all round defensive position in case RPG teams were still lurking behind or there was an unnoticed tank. In Callsign Three Two, the vehicle commander Sergeant Tony Hay ordered his driver to advance but the latter was paralysed with fear until the torrent of invective from Sergeant Hay galvanised him into action. The Warrior moved forward and engaged a large bunker system with 62 rounds of 30mm Rarden and bursts of chaingun.

A lone Iraqi soldier was seen to the left front of 7 Platoon. He moved around as if he was looking for something with what appeared to be an RPG round in his left hand. Lieutenant Fairbairn in Callsign Three Zero ordered his gunner to open fire but after only five rounds the chaingun jammed, whereupon the Iraqi surrendered by raising his hands to reveal that he was carrying a water bottle. Another Iraqi was dragged out of a trench and roughly handled by some Fusiliers. On being grilled as to what had caused the explosion and whether they were in a minefield, the Iraqi replied that there were no mines and it was one of their own planes that had caused the explosion. At this point, Major Alec Bain arrived on the scene together with the other Warriors of 8 Platoon and Callsign Zero Charlie under the command of Captain Bob Keating. As he approached in Zero Charlie, the driver, Fusilier John 'Grease' Grieve, engaged neutral and was out of his compartment and running towards the stricken Warrior before his vehicle had even stopped. In the rear of Callsign Zero Bravo, the company signaller, Corporal 'Bod' Harris, was trying manfully to give a 'situation report' and respond to the numerous frantic inquiries over the radio net.

Behind Two Two, half-blinded by flash burns, Private Meechan was trying to douse the burning uniform of Lance Corporal Fyfe with sand but, as section commander, the latter had moved round the side of the vehicle to try and help Private Lang. One glance at Lang's headless and limbless corpse was sufficient to indicate that he had been killed instantly. Corporal Phil Forsyth from Callsign Two One ran up and rolled Fyfe in the sand to extinguish the flames that were still consuming his uniform and flesh. With Meechan's help, Forsyth pulled the GPMG barrel out of Fyfe's thigh which began to bleed profusely. Screaming in agony, Fyfe kept crying 'Where's his f***ing head?'. Sergeant Tom Davison arrived and helped to carry him towards Zero Charlie. Fusiliers Jason King and Mick Toth from Two One now rushed over to help Meechan and Finnan. By now, the other vehicles of 8 Platoon had congregated around the devastated Warrior. Fusilier Simon Bakkor, the gunner from Two Zero, sprinted across to Sergeant Smith and demanded frantically - 'Where's Leechy?'. Smith pointed towards the burning Warrior. Bakkor climbed onto the turret of Two Two in a vain attempt to help his best friend, Kevin Leech, who had also died instantly as the missile exploded.

Fusilier David Halliwell drove his vehicle Two Three in a zig-zag course for fear of direct fire weapons, coming to a halt some ten metres in front of Two Two. Grabbing a bag of field dressings, he leapt out of the driver's compartment and ran across to help Fusilier Hunt who was screaming in terror as he desperately tried to prise open his hatch. The section commander and 2IC of Two Three, Corporal Mick Crozier and Fusilier 'Titch' Welsh, dismounted to consult with their platoon commander, Lieutenant Duxbury. Secondary explosions from the stowed ammunition in Two Two then blew Fusilier Bakkor off the vehicle wounding him in the thigh. Seemingly oblivious to the pain and exploding ordnance, Fusilier Bakkor again climbed onto Two Two to try once more and rescue his friend. Despite his efforts to help the trapped Hunt, Fusilier Halliwell was forced away - 'The driver of Two Two was in his hatch screaming. I went to give him assistance. I was trying to get him out but secondary explosions were starting and I was ordered to move back'. Major Kiddie in Two Two Bravo was observing the scene and recalls - 'At first we thought we'd missed a tank, a T-72. Everyone was back in their turrets, scouting about. Where's the tank? Was it a minefield? The prisoners were adamant there was no minefield. What had been a relatively straightforward clearance operation was suddenly very threatening.' Fusilier 'Titch' Welsh returned to the back of Two Three to tell the rest of the section to remain in the vehicle as the whole area was strewn with MLRS bomblets and scatterable mines. With the arrival of Major Bain, Lieutenant Duxbury decided to return to his vehicle. As the secondary detonations happened, he glanced back towards the burning Warrior and Two Three to its front.

At 1506 hours, a second A-10 launched a Maverick missile which penetrated the roof of Call Sign Two Three behind the turret. Everyone inside the troop compartment was killed outright by the blast, while Fusilier Welsh, who was standing at the rear door with one foot inside the vehicle, was blown clear with fragment wounds to his back, left buttock, arms and head. The bodies of two of those in the vehicle were blown onto the ground outside. The explosion wounded several Fusiliers rendering aid to those hurt in the initial attack and some of the latter were injured once more; Corporal Forsyth recalls - 'Everyone took a flying lesson. The missiles exploded with an ear-splitting crack – and an extreme stunning effect from the noise, not the blast. It was an eerie moment and with it there was an odd smell, like damp compost burning. The atmosphere transfixed me and lots of the other guys, we'd never heard such an explosion or smelt anything like it, then we just snapped out of it and got on with the recovery.' Fusilier Halliwell at the front of the vehicle was blown off his feet. As he lay on the ground with blood pouring from his face, he saw an A-10 banking across the sky. Sergeant Davison relates - 'All the lads from Two Zero, which was the vehicle I was in, debussed and ran over to Two Two. At the same time Two Three came round to the front of Two Two. A couple of lads got out of there and started dealing with the casualties from Two Two. It was at that point that Two Three got hit as well. All the lads in the back of there had obviously been killed. The last thing I remember was carrying Corporal Fyfe away from his vehicle Two Two and getting hit. When myself and one of my section commanders, Corporal Crozier, regained consciousness, the two vehicles were totally in flames, exploding, with bodies all over the place and everybody else had gone, at which point we thought, hang on, there is something wrong here, somebody should be picking us up by now. As it happens it was just a case of getting a grip of ourselves, getting each other up and picking up the lads who were injured.' Among the newly-injured were Lieutenant Duxbury with fragments in the face and burst eardrums; Corporal Crozier with a large fragment in the buttocks and Fusilier Toth with damaged eardrums and leg wounds. The gallant Fusilier Bakkor was injured once more when he was again blown off the top of Warrior Two Two.

As he struggled away from Two Two, Sergeant Smith was approached by Lieutenant Duxbury who asked - 'Are you alright?' Smith replied - 'I'm OK. Go and look after the lads first'. He was soon picked up by Fusilier Dave Halliley, the platoon runner. Smith continues - 'I had my arm round his shoulder. I happened to glance round and saw the other vehicle about to go.

It was going in and out like a pressurised can. I said to Dave, "Get down!" and I pulled him down onto the ground and fell down myself. Basically I just fell on the guy. There was no courage on my part to say "I shall save this man". I just fell on him. There was nothing heroic about that'. After the explosion, Fusilier Halliley wriggled out from underneath and manhandled Smith to Two Zero. Fusilier Hunt had been through a terrifying ordeal as he was trapped inside his driving compartment beneath his half open hatch after Two Two had been hit, only to see Two Three stop in front of him and it too explode. Eventually, he forced open his hatch and laboriously heaved himself out to slump on the engine decks before falling off his Warrior onto the ground and being rescued at last.

By now, the FV432 ambulance One Four Bravo had set up the company aid post some 100 metres from the burning Warriors. At the scene, the seriously injured were loaded onto Warriors for direct transfer to the RAP. Still smouldering and screaming in pain, Fyfe was placed in the rear of Zero Charlie together with Privates Finnan and Meechan, while Welsh was placed face down inside Two Zero because of the severe wound in his backside. As he fell unconscious, Welsh remembers the blood streaming down his arms and forming a puddle under his face. Several of the casualties were walked to the CAP by other Fusiliers. The crew of One Four Bravo frantically attended to the wounded but as Corporal 'Ed the Med' Crossland recalls - 'We tried to treat the casualties as best we could, but there were so many of them that Captain Keating and his blokes came over in their wagon as well as Two Zero and helped to treat the blokes. Me and Phil Forsyth went forward to try and get any more blokes back from the vehicles but they were exploding so much that we had to give up and go back to the ambulance.'

Within moments of the attack, a radio message had been sent to the regimental aid post stating - 'There has been an incident. Several dead and injured. Get here fast!'. After closing the distance and forming its defensive wedge, the RAP despatched a pair of FV432 ambulances to help One Four Bravo. The CO had been about a mile away with the No 2 Company on Objective Steel when he heard of the incident. To Lieutenant Colonel Larpent, such a situation was not unexpected - 'We had trained ourselves for such an eventuality; we conditioned ourselves to this and when we took casualties it was the battle shaping up as everyone had expected it to. The real worry was to check that the system was working properly; that the casevac was happening; that the bandsmen were doing their job; that the BCRs [Battle Casualty Replacements] were coming up. I looked at the people to make sure they were alright because we were carrying on come what may. This was not a surprise. This was what we expected. It was grim but it happened.' The CO stayed at the scene for approximately 15 minutes and, after assessing the situation and giving a brief O group to the vehicle commanders, he moved off to organise the forthcoming attack on Objective Tungsten.

Following their initial treatment at the scene of the airstrike, the wounded were transferred to the RAP which had been set up to receive them. As they arrived, the regimental medical officer, Lieutenant Colonel Stewart Kempster, conducted a thorough triage of the casualties and began to treat the most seriously injured himself. This was Corporal Fyfe. As the RMO, Lieutenant Colonel Kempster and the regimental chaplain, Captain Adrian Pollard, had devised a coded phrase in case a casualty was going to die. He summoned Captain Pollard and said - 'Padre, Corporal Fyfe would be really glad of a chat'. The padre sat on the ground and cradled Fyfe's head as they talked about the latter's sons for almost 20 minutes. Fyfe's last recollection before slipping into unconsciousness was having his head tilted back as Lieutenant Colonel Kempster performed a tracheotomy to help his breathing. His windpipe and lungs were badly scorched by smoke and flame inhalation. Fortunately, Corporal Peter Fyfe survived.

After dropping off the injured Highlanders, Callsign Zero Charlie returned to the burning Warriors to evacuate the last casualty, which was Lieutenant Duxbury with a suspected broken jaw and fragment wounds to the face. Some of the injured had suffered flash burns to the eyes which were bandaged with field dressings, rendering them sightless. They sat quietly and patiently in rows against the road wheels of the FV432 ambulances; a large M and the time inscribed on their foreheads if they had been administered with morphine. Lance Corporal Eddie Dean, the padre's driver, moved between them passing out lighted cigarettes as he swore profusely, threatening to kill any Iraqi on sight. Nevertheless, he was the first to offer water and succour to injured Iraqi prisoners when they were brought to the RAP. Sergeant Trevor Smith sat in the rear doorway of an FV432 ambulance with a field dressing over his eyes and a drip hanging from the door; smoking constantly and teasing the wound on his neck where his NBC suit had melted to his flesh in the explosion. Despite his injuries, he refused any morphine so that he could monitor the condition of his men. Corporal Forsyth recalls - 'One of my main memories is of how unselfish our Warrior Sergeant, Trevor Smith, was. True to form with a bandage around his eyes and a cigarette in his mouth, he kept on cracking a stream of awful jokes, unconcerned for himself, to keep the spirits up of everyone around him – he was fantastic.' After treatment, the 11 injured, with the most seriously wounded in Bhofar splints on stretchers, waited to be moved further back. Lying on one of the stretchers, Fusilier Welsh was desperately looking at the other casualties for his companions from Two Three and kept asking - 'Where's the blokes in the wagon?'. There was no answer. It was the same when a roll-call was held. Corporal Forsyth recalls - 'It was just like the one at the end of the film *Zulu*. We were in bits – a name called, no answer; another name, no answer and so on'.

Despite an earlier radio message that helicopters were on their way to evacuate the wounded, none arrived within the hour. Eventually, it was decided to move the wounded by FV432 ambulances to a rendezvous point where they would be transferred to hospital by wheeled ambulances. Unfortunately, they failed to find the 'ambulance exchange point' and returned to the RAP still carrying the wounded. As dusk fell, two helicopters finally landed and conveyed the wounded to field dressing stations. Most of them were now mercifully drugged with morphine but its unfortunate side effects soon became apparent when, despite his awful wounds, Fusilier Welsh was embarrassed to vomit AB biscuits over a flight crewman. With their eyes covered with field dressings, Sergeant Smith and Private Finnan sat holding hands for comfort; Smith fuming silently because he was not allowed to smoke and he had lost his cigarette lighter. On arrival, the badly burnt Corporal Fyfe was carried in on a stretcher. The doctor took one look at his blackened uniform and said - 'Put him over there with the other Iraqis'. From the depths of unconsciousness, Fyfe stirred and was heard to protest - 'I'm no f***ing Iraqi, I'm a f***ing Jock!'.

Nine soldiers died in this tragic incident. It soon became apparent that a flight of United States Air Force A-10 ground attack aircraft had been the cause. Fratricidal fire, or 'blue on blue' in the jargon of the British armed forces, has occurred in every war and remains extremely difficult to avoid but, in the context of the Gulf War, it appeared even more dreadful because of the few overall casualties in the conflict. However, such a small total was due for the most part to the overwhelming air campaign conducted by the coalition air forces and the US Air Force in particular. During Operation 'Desert Storm', it flew 114,000 sorties or an average of 100 an hour. This rose to 160 an hour during the land campaign when a further 16,000 sorties were flown. Half of the latter were as close air support to advancing ground troops. Mistakes are inevitable in the chaos of war. The US Air Force made remarkably few

The aftermath of the missile strike gives an indication of the devastation caused to Callsign Two Two. The Maverick hit the other side of the vehicle, blowing external stowage items across the desert. On the day after the war ended, Capt Keating returned to Objective Steel to reclaim the personal effects of the dead and injured. Before he left, he laid out the crew's helmets as a simple memorial.

The Fusiliers Battlegroup suffered the heaviest casualties within the 1st (UK) Armoured Division with nine of the 11 killed in action during the land war. A total of 47 British soldiers died during the course of Operation 'Granby'. The rifle section of Callsign Two Three of C Company is shown during training before the land war with (from L to R) Fus Thompson, Welsh, Atkinson, Cole, Satchell and Gillespie. All were killed instantly when their vehicle was hit by a Maverick missile, except for Fus Welsh who was badly wounded.

of them. In the 28 fratricidal fire incidents suffered by US forces in the Gulf War, 35 troops were killed and 72 were wounded. This represents 23 per cent of their 615 battle casualties in all. Of the armoured fighting vehicles destroyed, the proportion was 77 per cent with all seven Abrams MBTs and 20 out of 25 Bradley IFVs, the US equivalent of the Warrior. The first fratricidal fire incident of the war occurred on 30 January during the battle for the town of Khafji when a US Air Force A-10 fired a Maverick missile at a US Marine Corps armoured personnel carrier, killing seven Marines on board. In the British Army, there were four blue on blue incidents resulting in nine dead and 16 injured, with one due to air attack and the remainder to tank fire. Each one was a tragedy but the war continued and within the hour the Fusilier Battlegroup was on the move towards its next objective.

Postscript: Lieutenant Brett Duxbury and Sergeant Tom Davison were subsequently Mentioned in Despatches. The Queen's Gallantry Medal was awarded to three soldiers for their actions on that day but as one Fusilier has said to the present author - 'We didn't do it for the medals. We did it for our mates. We would have done anything to save them'.

THE BATTLE OF THE PIPELINE

The battlegroup advanced some five kilometres eastwards where it halted to reorganise. In the troop compartments of the Warriors, some of the younger Fusiliers needed reassurances after the losses on Objective Steel but there soon emerged a firm resolve to close with the enemy and continue the offensive. As the vehicles were being replenished, Lieutenant Colonel Andrew Larpent called Major Bain aside and inquired whether he wished for C Company to remain in the line. Reminiscent of Colonel Kingsley and the XX at the Battle of Minden after its fearful casualties, Major Bain immediately affirmed that he did and, indeed, C Company was to act as one of the lead infantry companies against Objective Tungsten. As dusk was approaching, Major Bain and Captain Keating conferred and decided to ask the attached Royal Engineers to return to Objective Steel and lay the remains of those killed on sheets of CARM for later collection. This they duly did which was greatly appreciated by the Fusiliers as it would have been an impossibly painful task for the men of C Company.

Later, with darkness falling, the padre, together with the two doctors from the RAP and two FV432 ambulances, approached the destroyed Warriors to recover the dead. Carefully following in each other's footsteps and treading in vehicle tracks wherever possible, the small group halted briefly as the padre led them in prayer, before they set about their grisly task. The Sapper team had collected the bodies of those killed outside the vehicles and placed them under a tarpaulin. The interior of the Warriors was still baking hot and much of the work had to be done by torch light. In time, the remains were collected and the nine body bags were placed in the rear compartment of the FV432 ambulance Callsign One Four Hotel. There they stayed until collected the next morning by the graves registration unit shortly before a church service held in their memory.

Orders for the night attack against Objective Tungsten were given during the early evening of 26 February. Once again, the Reconnaissance Group led the battlegroup on the approach march of some 30 kilometres towards a formidable obstacle, the Trans-Arabian Pipeline, that ran approximately north to south across the brigade's line of advance. Captain Paul Nanson, the reconnaissance platoon commander, recalls - 'My orders to the platoon took place at last light. The men were tired and somewhat subdued. Many had lost friends that afternoon and the realities of war were starting to sink in. They were all angry and ready for a fight and extremely glad to be given an opportunity for more action. The plan was to advance in the platoon's normal advance to contact formation. Two One (myself) and Two Two (Sergeant Oliver) Sections on the right with Two Three (Colour Sergeant McCarthy) and Two Four (Corporal Holloway) on the left. Colour Sergeant Budge's Mobile Milan Section moved a bound behind with Sergeant's Rudsdale's Engineer Section. The OC's command Group, with Captain Guy Briselden's Warrior Milan Section, were a bound behind them.

'As we began the advance the MLRS began to fire over our heads onto Tungsten some kilometres in front. It was a clear night and the visibility was good, a welcome change from the previous evening's advance towards Brass. My gunner, Lance Corporal Bruton, kept the platoon on course with the GPS whilst I observed the desert with the OTIS mounted on the top of the Scimitar. About an hour into the advance, Sergeant Oliver's section, which had pushed forward some distance, reported a sighting of vehicles to their front. I brought the platoon to a halt and the Milan section moved forward to observe the target with MIRA. From a distance the target did indeed look like a gathering of vehicles. The skyline was broken by what appeared to be large antennas. Conscious of the risk of fratricide, I broke radio silence on the command net and asked the CO to confirm that there were no friendly forces in front of us. He confirmed that there was only the Royal Scots on our left flank and they were some distance behind. I tasked Sergeant Oliver to move forward and investigate. From the map, the contact appeared to be on or about the pipeline. I allowed Sergeant Oliver to continue as I manoeuvred the remainder of the group around the area of the crossing. Sergeant Rudsdale had a good idea of the location of the crossing and was keen to get on with the marking before the rest of the battlegroup arrived. It was as we moved that Sergeant Oliver's section reported a contact and commenced engaging with HE and machine gun. The full report described a bunker complex around a series of buildings overlooking the pipeline. There was nothing on the map and so I assumed it must be some sort of pumping station, located at the crossing site. This was the only crossing for miles and so it seemed as though we would have no option but to fight. As contact reports started coming in from the other sections I sent my own contact report to BG HQ. Movement of men, vehicles and a report of a large-barrelled weapon of some sort prompted me to engage using the whole platoon.'

The padre, Capt Pollard, conducts a service in the field with the Duke of Kent's Band providing the musical accompaniment in the background; the latter also fulfilled their role as medical orderlies during the land war. The padre undertook his duties from a Land Rover called the HALO PATROL: HALO standing for Higher Authority Liaison Officer.

With considerable skill in the complete darkness, Colour Sergeant McCarthy's section escorted the Royal Engineer reconnaissance vehicles forward. A couple of suitable crossing points for the battlegroup were found over the pipeline which was some three metres off the desert floor. These were improved and strengthened by Lieutenant Mike Lobb's Sappers of 3 Troop, to provide a sand rampart capable of bearing the 70 tonnes of a Challenger MBT. Once across, the battlegroup had to turn northwards to the start line before Objective Tungsten but it took a significant time for all of its vehicles to negotiate the two crossing sites. Meanwhile, the reconnaissance platoon had observed some buildings beside the pipeline with numerous Iraqi soldiers moving about, so their vehicles formed up in line abreast and engaged the area with coaxial machine gun and cannon fire. The enemy returned fire and tried to manoeuvre an artillery piece into position near to the gate of the oil installation. This movement was observed by Corporal Dave Weaver in Four One Bravo which immediately destroyed it with a Milan missile. Similarly, Callsign Four One Delta acquired a heat source of a large body of men congregating inside the doorway of a building. Each time the door opened, the heat signature became clearer as the people inside were exposed to the MIRA sight. Corporal Geoff Green ordered his gunner, Fusilier Dale Tranter, to engage and, at a range of only 500 metres, the building disintegrated under the impact of the Milan missile from the MCTS which the crew had christened 'Appetite for Destruction'.

Captain Nanson continues - 'On the command net, the CO ordered the tanks forward in support and the mortar platoon reported that they were in position to provide indirect support. There was by now limited small arms fire coming from the enemy and a further two Milan missiles had reduced the activity around the bunkers. Sergeant Oliver's section was now only 200 metres from the complex and so, much to the disappointment of the mortars, I decided that I was too close for a fire mission. The engineers continued to mark the crossing and very soon Corporal [Eric] Haley in Callsign Two Four Alpha reported white flags in the vicinity of the bunker complex. Colour Sergeant McCarthy and Two Three crossed and covered the remainder of the platoon across. Prisoners were left for the RSM and the Reconnaissance Group continued onto the FUP. There were still a number of heat sources to our front and it was a relief to hear the tanks of B Squadron moving up to take over the engagement.' The firefight lasted for over half an hour and towards the end the tanks of B Squadron arrived and its squadron leader, Major Richard Shirreff, inquired of TAC HQ - 'Now that we are in contact do you want us to take over or for your less well protected callsigns to continue?'. The battle of the pipeline was over.

THE ATTACK ON OBJECTIVE TUNGSTEN

By now, most of the battlegroup was across the pipeline and the Iraqis in the oil pumping station were surrendering in large numbers so the Reconnaissance Group moved off to resume the advance. As it did so Callsign Two Two Alpha drove nose first into a tank scrape, badly winding the crew. Sergeant 'Ollie' Oliver ran across from Two Two and turned off the master switch before climbing onto the turret to help the crew only to find the commander, Corporal 'Spud' Taylor, gasping for breath. Believing himself to be badly injured, Corporal Taylor implored of Oliver - 'Ollie, don't let the bastards nick my pistol', referring to a weapon that he had acquired off an Iraqi the day before. 'Do you want an aspirin or what?' was the solicitous response. 'Don't make me laugh - it hurts'. Ensuring that its red tail lights were in view to the passing battlegroup, Sergeant Oliver tied a Cylume to the top of the radio antenna to attract the Samson recovery vehicle, which soon arrived and began winching operations. At this moment, a large number of Iraqis emerged out of the darkness much to the consternation of the REME mechanics but, in a surreal episode, they simply sat down cross-legged and began to chant - 'Down with Saddam! Down with Saddam!' After Two Two Alpha had been recovered, the Iraqis were ushered into the tank scrape and the CVR(T)s went on their way with the chanting diminishing in the distance.

Behind a massive artillery bombardment with the direction vividly marked by MLRS rockets 'spewing bright incandescent smoke trails into the sky and filling the horizon with fire', the brigade attack on Objective Tungsten began in earnest at 2230 hours, with the reconnaissance platoon forward with the tank squadrons as they engaged the enemy emplacements and vehicles. Interspersed amongst the Challenger MBTs, the CVR(T)s rocked under the concussion of the 120mm main armament guns but added their own firepower to destroy specific targets such as trucks and vehicles although AFVs were engaged as well. Corporal 'Jugs' Allen in Callsign Four One Charlie destroyed a tank identified as a T-62 with a single missile, while Corporal 'Wobbly Gob' Weaver came on the air stating - 'I have a possible heat source to my front'. The Reconnaissance Group commander asked - 'Can you identify heat source?' 'Not yet'. 'Are you sure it has a positive heat source?'. To which Weaver replied as he fired a Milan missile - 'Well it's going to very shortly', followed by - 'Yes it's got a good heat source now!', as the missile struck the rear doors of an MTLB and exploded inside.

Major Richard Shirreff, B Squadron Leader of 14th/20th King's Hussars, describes the part played by the tanks - 'Our new orders were simple. We were to regroup under command of 3RRF who were right forward battlegroup in the attack on Objective "Tungsten". We moved immediately and RV'd by 2100 when I was quickly given orders for the operation by the Fusiliers Ops Officer John Whitwam, while my signals sergeant was given CEIs and the relevant BATCO. Our task was to advance as left forward squadron ahead of C Company. 1RS Battlegroup was on our left. The approach march started at 2230 and, after a brief halt while the recce group to our front took on some enemy dug in around an oil installation, B Squadron crossed the pipeline at the southern crossing. We went firm in a bridgehead about 3000 metres plus of the crossing while D Squadron crossed and shook out on our right. While this was happening, we contacted a tank company to our front and destroyed at least five T55s using TOGS. We could see and hear D Squadron on our right doing the same. Having destroyed the enemy to our front, we moved on in troop line up to the limit of exploitation in what was almost a classic squadron advance to contact. We moved, made contact, formed line and engaged targets to our front. Once they were destroyed, we moved on again until more enemy were engaged, whereupon the same process was repeated. Once at the limit of exploitation, we received orders to form a hasty counter penetration line as left forward squadron. This was completed by 0500 on 27 February.'

Major Wicks of D Squadron recalls - 'At 2330 we moved off again. This time it was to the east, towards the southern half of Objective Tungsten. The Fusilier Battlegroup now consisted of ourselves, the two infantry companies and B Squadron who had joined us during the night [plus an engineer squadron]. The move east was in two columns, led by 3RRF's recce platoon. We came up against some resistance from a group of enemy who were defending an oil refinery but these were quickly bypassed. After crossing an oil pipeline obstacle, the squadron promptly ran into more enemy positions. These consisted of transport vehicles supported by well dug in tanks showing only their turrets. The whole area had a patchwork of anti-tank ditches defending it which took some careful navigating to get around.' Behind the tanks were the Warriors with C Company on the left behind B Squadron and A Company behind D Squadron on the right. Each of the battlegroups was on a narrow frontage of less than 1,500 metres and advancing slightly out of phase.

Major Alec Bain recounts - 'It was now pitch black and the target was a series of emplacements and fortifications over some 20 kilometres. For some peculiar reason the brigade commander had released the Fusiliers before the Royal Scots were ready to move so we ended up about two kilometres forward of them. As this is the distance that artillery normally fires in front of an advancing formation, their shells were exploding in line with C Company. Twice during the night their artillery encroached on our line of advance and each time I had to give the order 'Right form', at which everyone had to manoeuvre their vehicle to the right in unison and after some 100 or 200 metres of lateral movement swing back onto the original axis; a difficult manoeuvre at the best of times but at night and under fire - somewhat hazardous. Again, because they were two kilometres behind, they were often firing small arms and, on at least one occasion main armament, through and over us. Many of our wagons had bullet strikes on the back. My problems were compounded by the tank squadron to my front which insisted on attacking with its echelon in tow, so we were unable to use our 30mm Rardens for fear of hitting his ammunition trucks and fuel bowsers. We spent the whole night restricted to using the chaingun.'

A Company was moving parallel to C Company but with an open flank to the south. Accordingly, many pairs of eyes were observing to the right as the battlegroup advanced eastwards. In Callsign Two One, its commander, Corporal Phil 'Scouse' Jones, was having serious problems in the darkness - 'My Warrior [Delville Wood] had an electrical fault that had

During the attack on Objective Tungsten, Iraqi resistance was minimal. Once the objective was taken, the Iraqis surrendered in droves. Here, hundreds of Iraqis trudge towards the Warriors of 3 Section of A Company during the last hours of the war. After weeks of aerial bombing and disrupted supply lines, the Iraqi units in the frontlines were in a pitiful condition. Following the intense and ferocious bombardment of tube artillery and MLRS rockets that preceded all the allied attacks, few Iraqis were capable or willing to resist the coalition forces.

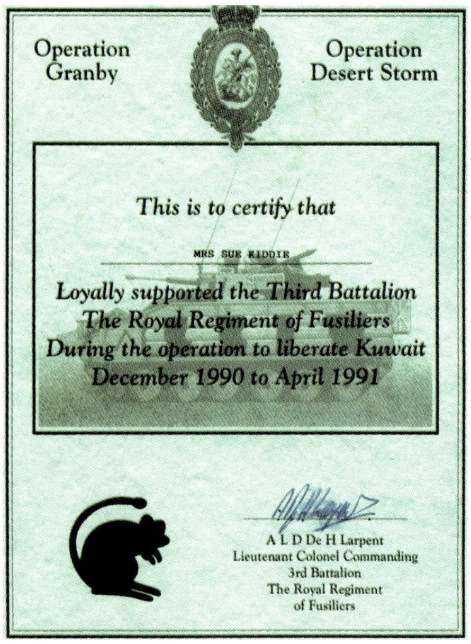
Operation Granby

Operation Desert Storm

This is to certify that

MRS SUE KIDDIE

Loyally supported the Third Battalion
The Royal Regiment of Fusiliers
During the operation to liberate Kuwait
December 1990 to April 1991

A L D De H Larpent
Lieutenant Colonel Commanding
3rd Battalion
The Royal Regiment
of Fusiliers

'They also serve who only stand and wait...' - there is no doubt, as in all times of conflict, that service families suffer greatly in their constant fear of loved ones becoming casualties and their desperate desire for accurate information.

'Iserlohn was a small relatively quiet backwater of Germany where I had hoped to while away our two-year posting. Little did I suspect that momentous events would occur which would have far reaching effects on all our lives, notably the fall of the Berlin War and of course the Gulf War. The battalion was very busy, exercising with their new Warriors and firing on the ranges. We became used to the men being away, albeit for short periods. However, despite the international news of Saddam Hussein's invasion of Kuwait and the Western nations' response, no one really believed it would come to war. So, it came as somewhat of a shock when it became apparent that the battalion would deploy to the Gulf with 4 Armoured Brigade in December 1990. This departure was somewhat different from the (Ulster) norm, in that there was no set end date; it was a case of 'I'll see you when I see you'.

'The initial reaction amongst the wives was almost of relief, because the run-up period to the actual deployment had been long and very disruptive on family life. After a very quiet Xmas on the patch, everyone had been lulled into a false sense of security as to whether anything would actually happen.

'In situations such as this 'The Wives Club' thrives and all the dependants tried to be supportive of each other, many of the younger wives being away from their extended families for the first time, and in a foreign country. A 'Gulf newsroom' had been established, but with few thoughts of what was required when 'real' military action occurred. The general feeling was that Saddam would back down at the last minute. So, when the air war started in January, the wives became visibly more upset, and some left for the UK to be with more immediate family. Iserlohn town centre became the focus for all the anti-war groups and we were confronted daily with small groups chanting anti-war slogans, mock-up Exocet missiles and leaflets. We all received leaflets urging our husband to defect and giving a safe house address in town, typically, it was six weeks too late!

'Despite all the build up and media coverage, when the ground war actually started there was a peculiar feeling of fear in the air especially after the previous RAF losses. On the second day of the ground war, I had been listening to the 10 o'clock news which had just announced that the 4 Armoured Brigade were ▶

plagued it since before deployment to the Gulf. I had no communications and my turret was live. It sparked furiously if anything metal touched the inside. Carrying the amount of ammo that we did was a stress forming factor that we had to live with. During the final attack onto Objective Tungsten, my night sight failed so I was forced to sit head-up and view with a CWS hand held night viewing device. As the column advanced I noticed on my right flank two moving vehicles that were shadowing our movement. They were moving through an Iraqi position and getting closer to our advancing column. I shouted to my driver Fusilier Pete Dunn to stop. As he slammed on his brakes the sharp jolt caused his night sight to black out too. From then on he drove blind. I then ordered my gunner Fusilier 'Jack' Hawkins to lay onto the first moving vehicle which I had identified as a ZIL-131 troop transporter. I shouted my fire control order to my gunner who sighted up the target in his night sight and pressed his electrically operated foot firing pedal. The gun failed to fire. In what seemed like minutes but in reality was only two to three seconds, both my gunner and I flew into our instinctive drills. I had to fire the 30mm manually while the gunner kept his sights on the first target. As I pressed the firing button thankfully the gun fired and we achieved a first round hit with an HE shell quickly followed by a second and the target exploded in a ball of flame. As it went up I quickly laid the gunner onto the second target which was a Soviet made Iraqi MTLB APC. We fired one HE round which ripped into the vehicle and exploded. We followed up with two sabot rounds. The vehicle wobbled as it was hit. A vehicle of 3 Platoon also took up the engagement on the MTLB even though it was destroyed by me and my crew.'

The other Warrior was Callsign Three Two commanded by Sergeant Stevie Hills who came up on the company net and stated he was tracking a target to the south. He sought permission to engage. Mindful of the recent fratricidal fire incident, company headquarters inquired of TAC HQ whether there were any friendly forces to the south. After some three minutes, Sergeant Hills was given clearance to fire and he engaged the MTLB with three rounds of 30mm sabot of which at least two hit the target. The vehicle was destroyed. He also engaged a ZIL truck that he had identified as a water bowser which was destroyed as well. On a separate occasion, Sergeant Hills identified and engaged a T-54/55 tank with six rounds of sabot at a range of over a kilometre. The outcome of this action is unknown but in the fog of war and at night, it remains difficult to determine the sequence and consequence of any engagement.

One of the reasons for the success of Operation 'Desert Sabre' was the excellent performance of the Warrior which, when employed with Challenger, proved to be a formidable combination of firepower and mobility. To their crews and rifle sections, the Warriors were their home and in battle their protection against the enemy. It was also an extraordinary way to prosecute warfare as this account from Sergeant Paddy Baines of 3 Platoon illustrates - 'To be perfectly honest all I can remember is being in the back of a Warrior and going from A to B. From going in until the oil refinery night, except for the time when the Warriors were hit, most of it was a blur of being in the back of the wagon, movement, getting out for a piss. There was very little that was specific. With red light on as opposed to white, it can be totally unreal in the back of the Warrior with music playing on the boogie box, having a brew or eating MREs, as it was easier on the move to take a boil-in-the-bag, put it in the BV and pass the bag to the driver or turret crew who might say "Hang on I'm engaging a target". When you're sat in the back of a Warrior, the effect of the chaingun or 30mm is minimal. Most guys are half asleep - you doze even in combat. The noise of the tracks behind your head is a constant so the most startling sound is when you stop - you'd be clanking along with the engine noise - but when it was idling, that was when you came to your senses. You couldn't see out because it was dark or the wagon was kicking up the dust. You couldn't hear anything except the clanking of the tracks unless you wore a headset which gave you a headache after a while - so you just go into yourself until someone shouts "Standby to debus", when you would wake up and get ready. What was required was to push on and to get as far into Iraq as possible. It was armoured warfare. If it was light resistance, you bypassed it. If they were surrendering, you bypassed them. The whole point of armoured warfare is moving at speed and punching into the enemy. That's what we were doing. There wasn't any time for getting out and clearing positions. There was no need to anyway.'

Fortunately, there were few occasions on Objective Tungsten when the Warriors had to engage the shattered and demoralised Iraqis and fewer still when the infantry sections had to dismount. It was after one such occasion however that there occurred an incident which exemplifies the fortitude and commitment of the Fusiliers in battle. Having dismounted to check out an Iraqi position, the rifle section of Callsign One One of 7 Platoon climbed back into their Warrior and when the section commander, Corporal John Mulheran, sat down at his position over the door ram he dropped his special integrated earpiece and microphone for the 349 radio out of the back of the vehicle. As he leant down to retrieve it, Fusilier Emmet pressed the door closure button without permission, whereupon the hydraulic ram forced Mulheran's left hand into the hinges of the door as it shut, trapping three fingers. With the characteristic noise when something is fouling its closure, Emmet tried to shut the door again with the same result.

Mulheran relates - 'There was no pain initially. I just broke out in a muck sweat. I knew my hand was in the door and I knew it was badly damaged. I shouted "Stop" because he was repeatedly trying to close the door and told him to open it again. Pulling my hand out I remember thinking "That's not the shape it should be", and I just slapped it on the leg of Alan Ward [his 2IC] saying "Put a field dressing on that bastard". He put one on either side of the hand. By this time it started to hurt like hell but I was concerned in case we had to debus so I couldn't allow them to give me morphine. Although they kept saying "Take some morphine!" I wanted to be *compos mentis* in case we had to mount an assault. At the end of the day, I was still the section commander and I was ultimately responsible, so I wouldn't let them give me any. The vehicle commander [Corporal Andy Fletcher] was getting all excited and he started going on the company net, and the OC said "Give him morphine!", but I wouldn't take it just in case something happened.'

Major Bain remembers - 'Corporal Fletcher came on the air and told me he had a problem in the back with this guy who had effectively lost three fingers of his hand. I got stroppy as they should be able to deal with something like this and told him to give him morphine. He came back a few minutes later, at which point I got more stroppy and said more morphine.' In the back of One One, Corporal Mulheran was in agony - 'It got worse and worse. I sat there trying to squeeze the pain away but I found with a bit of jiggling about I could still hold the rifle and support it properly. As it wasn't my right hand that was injured I could still operate the trigger and safety catch so I could still fight to a degree. I wasn't happy with that but it would do.' Major Bain continues - 'The next time we stopped I ordered the ambulance to evacuate the casualty but it overshot One One in the dark and, after this happened two or three times, I lost my temper completely.'

In the ambulance One Four Bravo, Corporal Eddy Crossland heard that Callsign One One had suffered a casualty at 0200 hours and continues - 'We went up the column to collect him but

involved in "heavy fighting" what did that actually mean? The imagination was running wild. It was just after the news had finished, when I heard from the CO's wife that we had sustained our first casualties and that ten were dead. It was a very frightening time as we had little other information to work on. We had, of course, no idea that it was a "blue on blue" incident and by the time the morning came we had few indications of what other casualties there might have been.

'The memory that will always stay with me is the look of total horror and desperation as we informed over 150 wives that 3rd morning of the known casualties. It was a very sad occasion. We were a family regiment and although all the casualties were single men, it was as if we had lost one of our own and many tears were shed. Senior officers and padres who were present helped reassure some of the girls who had been badly shaken by the news, but most sought comfort from their immediate friends.

'The rest of the war passed uneventfully for us although we were obviously in a highly anxious state. There was a natural feeling of intense relief when the cease-fire was announced. Unfortunately the battalion was to lose a further Fusilier in an accident before going into Kuwait City. This merely reinforced the fact that the war might have been over, but there was always an element of risk in soldering.'

The Warrior Captain of C Company, Capt Keating, stands atop of Callsign Zero Bravo on the last day of the war when virtually every vehicle in the Fusiliers Battlegroup flew a flag, both in celebration and as a mutual recognition device between the coalition forces. Behind Zero Bravo is Callsign One Four Bravo - the FV432 armoured ambulance of C Company. For want of a Union Flag, it is flying its red rallying flag to mark its position as a first aid post. Both of these vehicles and their crews were closely involved with the blue on blue incident on the afternoon of 26 February 1991. As an experienced soldier, Capt Keating carried a certain modicum of creature comforts on his Warrior including his own privy, complete with screening, which is visible on the engine decks.

To the victor the spoils, the CO and 2IC, Lt Col Larpent and Maj Kiddie, sit atop an Iraqi T-55/59 MBT at the Equipment Collection Point soon after the war. Despite suffering the highest casualties within the 1st (UK) Armoured Division, the Fusiliers never lost their humanity towards their enemy. Indeed, Fusiliers put themselves at risk in order to capture Iraqis rather than kill them as, for the most part, their will to resist had been broken.

went too far and landed up among the tanks. After a few attempts the OC told us to wait where we were and Callsign One One would come to us.' Unfortunately it took sometime before the two vehicles met by which time the assault was over and morphine had been administered to Corporal Mulheran. The medical log recorded a time of 0541 hours when the ambulance arrived and Corporal Crossland continues - 'We finally got to Callsign One One and Corporal Mulheran had been given morphine by his crew as he was in severe pain. He was very drowsy when we got to him. We put him in our panzer and gave him a brew but he jumped out of the wagon a few minutes later and vomited everywhere.' Corporal Mulheran recalls the arrival of the ambulance - 'The first thing I did was ask for a brew but I vomited all over the place including Eddy. I remember saying "Sorry Eddy", and he said "That's alright, it's one of the side effects of morphine".' After assessing the severity of the injury, Corporal Crossland immediately took Mulheran in One Four Bravo to the RAP, from where he moved down the casualty evacuation chain until he eventually arrived at the Royal Victoria Infirmary Newcastle, where his fingers were saved after reconstructive surgery. Despite agonising pain and a crippling injury, Corporal John Mulheran was unwilling to forgo his responsibilities as a section commander and the welfare of his men remained uppermost in his mind throughout his ordeal, until the end of the assault. Only then did he seek medical assistance. By his exemplary devotion to duty, his actions reflected great credit on himself and the Fusiliers.

Major Shirreff concludes the account of the action on Objective Tungsten - 'Although we contacted, engaged and destroyed a considerable number of enemy on Tungsten, we received almost no opposition. Enemy encountered were a tank company which we destroyed together with D Squadron; a D30 battery; another tank company; a mechanised infantry company equipped with MTLB and a logistic installation. Several vehicles were engaged while withdrawing but the bulk of the AFVs engaged were empty with their crews hiding until the storm of fire had passed and they could find someone to accept their surrender. At 0800 we received orders to regroup under command of the 14th/20th Battlegroup.'

THE AFTERMATH

The Fusilier Battlegroup moved into close leaguer at 0600 hours and most people were able to snatch some much-needed sleep, although the battlegroup was on immediate notice to move for a possible counter-penetration task astride the Wadi Al Batin to prevent any movement southwards or to move northwards, and continue the destruction of Iraqi materiel. Shortly after dawn, No 2 Company regrouped to the Fusiliers having spent the last night as brigade reserve for the assault on Objective Tungsten. After 90 minutes sleep, Major Alec Bain was woken to meet the battle casualty replacements for C Company comprising two pristine Warriors of 1st Battalion Scots Guards under the command of 2nd Lieutenant Lincoln Jopp who arrived as the battlegroup stirred back into life. He recalls - 'The only thing I can liken that morning to was perhaps seeing the remains of a very good, heavy party. One by one people were coming alive. Firstly into the hazy limbo between sleeping and consciousness only to be laid low by the steady realisation and remembering of what had happened the day and night before. Everything was softly spoken. It wasn't difficult to see the pain and the enormity of the shock in everyone around us.' It was to their eternal credit that, notwithstanding the understandable reservations of the Fusiliers, Lieutenant Jopp and his Scots Guards showed acute sensitivity to the situation, especially when the callsigns of the destroyed Warriors were applied to their vehicles with black masking tape.

At 0930 hours, Major Bain called his company together and appraised them of the situation as well as informing them of the events of the day before. Shortly thereafter a church parade was held to honour the dead of C Company. As the padre, Captain Adrian Pollard, began his address torrential rain fell on the assembled congregation. Picking up a packet of discarded tissues, he held them aloft and declared - 'The heavens weep for our dear departed'. Rain continued throughout the service until the final blessing when a shaft of bright sunshine burst through the clouds to illuminate the assembled men of the Fusilier Battlegroup. The CO recalls - 'The weather was foul - absolutely ghastly. The wind was howling and it was a really diabolic scene with gunfire in the distance. In this desolation, we held a short service before we cracked on. We were all affected at that time because there was a confusion of emotions. We were relieved we hadn't been bombarded with chemical weapons. It hadn't turned out to be a huge bloodbath. It was a great relief to be alive but there was the awful realisation that we had lost some of our own men.' The only consolation following the service was the decision to dispense with NBC suits which after 72 hours or so came as a huge relief.

In the early afternoon, the battlegroup was inundated with prisoners of war including the commander of the Iraqi 27th Infantry Division and his staff, who appeared in immaculate uniforms as compared to the bedraggled condition of the ordinary Iraqi soldiers. Similarly, their concern for the welfare of their men was non-existent and they thought nothing of taking any item from their soldiers if they so wished. They were rapidly taught some lessons in humility by the RSM and the regimental police who dealt with all prisoner handling. WO1 Bob Broadbent recounts his dealings with prisoners - 'For the first couple of occasions with prisoners, we formed them up and disarmed them, putting their weapons on the ground and destroying them by a few neutral turns in the Spartan. That was OK for groups up to a dozen but I quickly realised that because of the pace of the advance and the numbers of prisoners we were taking that they were becoming a complete hindrance. So after a while I simply showed them the direction to go, having disarmed them. If I had followed the instructions to the letter, I would have been away from the battlegroup for 12 hours or more, as I did not have the time or the resources to deal with that quantity of PWs. After 'Tungsten', I ended up with 1,400 prisoners with only my driver and Spartan and one of the provosts, Lance Corporal Paul Davis, whose countenance and size terrified the Iraqis. Many of the prisoners were sitting on pieces of cardboard and the officers would just take them so I made them give them back. I obtained some transport from echelon but the aides of this brigadier were trying to put him on a vehicle so I pulled him off and made him walk with his men. Any more trouble and they got 50 rounds of 7.62 over their heads. With my Spartan 'Archangel' leading, I drove them past brigade HQ where I met Brigadier Hammerbeck who asked - "What are you doing with all of them? It reminds me of scenes from the Western Desert".' As the quantity of prisoners grew, divisional headquarters kept pestering the battlegroup for an accurate estimate of the numbers of PWs. Time and again it demanded a precise figure until the 2IC, Major Keith Kiddie, in the turret of Two Two Bravo called down in exasperation to Captain Phillip Macey - 'Tell them we've got about three acres!'.

Meanwhile, the battlegroup was tasked to move north and destroy any enemy vehicles they encountered. Both A and C Companies had a satisfying time shooting numerous abandoned Iraqi vehicles until a blue on blue incident in a neighbouring battlegroup prompted a temporary ceasefire. During the course of the war, the Fusiliers Battlegroup had an attached US Army 'Psyops' unit in Humvees mounting massive loudspeakers and carrying Arabic linguists to induce the Iraqis to surrender. For four days, it had trailed the battlegroup without informing headquarters of its presence so it was much too late to employ it for its intended purpose. Accordingly, Lieutenant Colonel Larpent gave instructions for the vehicles to play 'Land of Hope and Glory' at high volume as the battlegroup moved into its final close leaguer of the war that night. At 0630 hours on G+4, Thursday 28 February, the battlegroup moved

The crew of One One Bravo pose for a celebratory photograph soon after the ceasefire with Lt Col Larpent standing between the operations officer, Capt Whitwam and CSgt Mickleson, the battalion gunnery sergeant. Besides the Union Flag, the CO's FV511 is flying a rose and primrose Regimental pennant.

eastwards across the Wadi Al Batin into Kuwait as part of the advance of 4 Armoured Brigade. Virtually every vehicle flew a flag as a battle ensign during the headlong pursuit across the desert. The ceasefire was declared at 0800 hours when the Fusiliers Battlegroup halted on Phase Line Sword to await further orders. At the same hour, the BBC World Service announced that US Air Force A-10 aircraft had been the cause of the C Company casualties.

The war was over. 4 Armoured Brigade had advanced 350 kilometres in 97 hours of which 54 had been in contact with the enemy. It had destroyed some 66 tanks, 90 APCs and 37 artillery pieces. Three divisional commanders, four brigadiers and their staffs together with 5,000 officers and men were captured. It was a consummate victory but many Fusiliers felt mixed emotions as Captain James Denny of A Company indicated in a letter home - 'It is difficult to express one's feelings. Strange really but the whole thing was an anti-climax plus a mixture of relief. Well, what did I do in those 100 hours? Not a lot really - just drive, advance forward and mop up any Iraqis who surrendered in their thousands, as you well know, plus destroyed a lot of kit. Obviously the most tragic event was when C Company lost two vehicles to the US Air Force. I could see the two explosions in the distance and listened to the horror unfold on the radio, such a waste; the pilot realised his error as soon as he fired. Back to the Iraqis, they were a pathetic bunch of people, no fight thank goodness, no belief in their cause and only too eager to give up and point out their officers and Baath party members. A poorly-trained conscript army. They had plenty of ammunition and although mechanically their equipment was in poor order, it still worked. Thank goodness for airpower. During the advance great groups of them would appear and try and give up. Eventually numbers overwhelmed us and we had to drive on and leave them to the follow on units. It is the way to fight a war - just clear up the mess and pick up the PWs. Rather that than fight. Although a great victory I think we all felt rather empty. I know I did.'

DARKNESS AT NOON

There was little time for reflection however as the Fusiliers took the opportunity to clean both themselves and their equipment and catch up on some much needed sleep. On Friday 1 March, the reconnaissance elements of all the brigade units began a wide ranging clearance operation. Its object was to gather up any remaining Iraqi PWs and identify enemy areas and weapons that might require clearing or destroying by the Sappers. During the early morning, Fusilier Chris Stacey of the Milan Platoon was shot in the arm following a negligent discharge. In a further accident, two Warriors collided and three Fusiliers suffered whiplash injuries. Meanwhile, the CO travelled to Al Jubayl to visit the injured of the blue on blue in 33 Field Hospital. On the following day, Captain Bob Keating returned to the destroyed Warriors to retrieve the personal belongings of the dead and injured. Before touching anything, he sat in quiet contemplation inside each vehicle for almost half an hour. With due reverence, he carefully collected any scrap of human tissue. All the remains were buried beneath a cross fashioned from a camp bed. The helmets of the fallen were arranged in lines as if on parade. Their surviving possessions of letters, photographs and even chocolate bars that had escaped the intense heat were collected in individual bivi-bags for despatch to the families. Before he left, Captain Keating laid a hackle beside each line of helmets.

As he sat some distance away waiting for a helicopter, a Toyota Land Cruiser approached. Such vehicles had been provided by the Saudi government for the commanders of many coalition units so Captain Keating was unperturbed until 12 Iraqis climbed out. Some were carrying white shirts as a mark of surrender. They were in fact an Iraqi army football team that had spent the war wandering around the desert. Captain Keating quickly summoned a helicopter and they were flown off to captivity leaving him with the Toyota as war booty. Mindful that enemy equipment had to be destroyed, he tried to torch the vehicle but the diesel fuel would not ignite. In exasperation, he vented his feelings by shooting at the engine block with his pistol.

Sunday the 3rd of March was a quiet day with the Fusiliers conducting a kite making competition. At 1930 hours, it was announced that Iraq had accepted every UN condition for the ceasefire. A spontaneous celebration followed marked by the discharge of numerous flares in white, red and green much to the annoyance of battlegroup headquarters. In the following days, a wide range of Iraqi military equipment was gathered at a collection point close to brigade HQ. Many Fusiliers took the opportunity to inspect the hardware and try out some of the weapons on improvised ranges. Organised games began to feature highly in the daily routine; one of the first was an inter-platoon tug of war competition which was won by 7 Platoon. The weather turned foul on Tuesday 5 March as storm clouds gathered and the rain fell in biblical quantities. By 1500 hours, the sky was so dark that vehicles needed to use headlights. Conversely, it was sometimes possible to read a newspaper at night by the light of the distant burning oil wells that had been sabotaged by the retreating Iraqis. That evening, the RSM took a number of soldiers back to Al Jubayl to begin rehearsals for the repatriation ceremony of the dead.

On the following day, the battlegroup was visited by the Prime Minister, John Major. A Company, under the command of Captain James Denny, was tasked to assist RAF crash investigators in their search for the Tornado aircraft which had been lost during the air war. The purpose was to retrieve any of their classified equipment which had not fallen into enemy hands and to determine how they had been shot down. The company departed on its two day mission on the morning of 7 March in two Chinooks escorted by three Army Air Corps Lynx helicopters armed with TOW anti-tank missiles. On the same day, the repatriation of the dead took place, with The Duke of Kent's Band providing the musical accompaniment as the nine coffins were carried to the C-130 for the flight to the UK. The knowledge of their departure affected those Fusiliers left in the desert deeply. Captain John Whitwam noted on that day - 'Life is now a drudgery. We live in the same trenches and vehicles as ever before, but without an enemy, a threat and any kind of clear direction and timescale, morale is dwindling. It rains heavily and the raging oil fires around Kuwait sometimes give the whole sky an eerie orange glow. With a constant wind whipping up the sand one can get miserable.'

On 8 March, A Company returned having flown deep into Iraq and becoming the most northerly of any British Army unit during the campaign, except for Special Forces. Captain Denny wrote in a letter home - 'We flew in a couple of Chinooks and found the two downed Tornadoes. One of the crash sites was on the outskirts of Basra and the other on Talil airfield, about 10km from the Euphrates. On our return we flew into Kuwait airport and saw the destroyed BA 747 [The British Airways Boeing 747 was bombed by the US Air Force just days before the end of the conflict] and then flew over Kuwait. Not too much damage but the defile where the Iraqis were caught on the Basra Highway was a real mess. Masses of twisted wreckage - cars, buses, military equipment - quite a sight.' During the trip, the Chinook had landed at a US Army facility to refuel. The Fusiliers took the opportunity to swap some combat rations for the American equivalent of MREs. The exchange rate for the Fusiliers was highly favourable as they returned with scores of boxes as well as some booty from Kuwait airport.

Life continued in the desert with a routine of basic training, sport and visits to other units to break up the monotony. On 10 March, the first batch of the 3rd Battalion personnel returned to Germany including Major Alec Bain to see his new-born twins. He was succeeded as OC C Company by Captain Philip Macey. Thereafter, the battlegroup was visited by scores of sundry personnel from the armed forces, MOD and the press. The weather continued to be fickle with one day fine and the next dank and dark with the smoke from the burning oil wells blotting out the sun. This gave rise to the use of the fluorescent green fluid from Cylumes to make frisbees visible in the dark but this was soon banned as a health hazard. On Saturday 16 March, 4 Armoured Brigade congregated for a group photograph following a visit by the GOC, Major General Rupert Smith. After the photograph, the battlegroup moved to a new location and an 'ideal home competition' was declared, with prizes for the vehicle crew that created the most comfortable and imaginative desert dwelling. This activity was to consume many hours for some Fusiliers over the coming days. Late on the next day, the Commander British Forces Middle East, General Peter de la Billière, came to stay overnight and visit the various elements of the battlegroup. Other visitors during this period who stayed with the battalion included the military artist, David Rowlands, who painted battle scenes for both the officers' and sergeants' messes.

Such was the fierce rivalry among the Fusiliers in the desert 'ideal home competition' that Corporal Eddy Crossland recalls stepping out of his vehicle at 0300 hours on the morning of 19 March - 'I had just got up for a pee and I saw all the blokes at Sergeant Briscoe's wagon

AL DIBDIBAH

In August 1990
Old Saddam had a plan
To use his planes and tanks and guns
To take a peaceful land
But little did he realise
For Fusiliers across the sea
His plans would come to nought
His plans would come to thwart
So then we did our training
In Hohne in the snow
Despite the awful threat of war
Fusiliers said let's go
They packed their Warriors and their kit
In boats that sailed the sea
With one thought clearly in their minds
To set Kuwait quite free.

We're Fusiliers, all Fusiliers
Yes we're Fusiliers with some Grenadiers
Rolling on to free Kuwait
From Saddam's mighty army.

Now Saddam's mighty army
Had dug in all quite well
With wire and mines and burning oil
He said he'd give us hell
But still he had no notion
Of just how much we cared
To free Kuwait's most peaceful land
And Fusiliers ain't scared.
We set up in the desert
And trained the whole day long
We learnt the way of the desert rat
Discovering right from wrong.
The sand it got quite everywhere
But still our kit could rust
We planned our thoughts on maintenance
And routines we could trust

Chorus

By now once we were halted
In desert, North Kuwait
The politicians talking
The Iraqi nation's fate
The ground war it had lasted
Only 100 hours
But we had seen 9 comrades
Cut down like summer flowers.
The war then it was finished
And we had done our bit
And shown our colours do not run.
Now here we are to tell the tale
And counter Saddam's boast.
Next time he wants some soldiers,
He should stick to using toast.

Chorus

Music by WO1 Peter Clark
Words by Major Keith Kiddie

At St George's Lines in Kuwait City, Fusiliers refurbish their vehicles as they prepare the Warriors for the handover to the 2nd Battalion Royal Anglian Regiment in April 1991

still working on his ideal home'. During the late afternoon of that hot day, the battlegroup held a Sods Opera, with the highlights being Fusilier Dale Tranter's interpretation of Stevie Wonder and No.2 Company's performance of *Brecon Billy*; both of which kept everyone in fits of laughter. The entertainment had been preceded by the judging of the 'ideal home competition' which featured many ingenious gadgets including working showers, gardens, animated door knockers and an aquarium stocked with combat ration pilchards; to many minds the best use for them. Finally, the CO awarded the first prize jointly to the crews of Sergeants Alan Briscoe and Tony Hay, both of C Company.

Over the next couple of days, there were visits by Brigadier Christopher Hammerbeck and General Fred Franks, the commander of US VIIth Corps, under whom 1st (UK) Armoured Division had served. Some lucky personnel were called forward for flights back to the UK and Germany, including The Duke of Kent's Band which had fulfilled their wartime role as medical orderlies. Saturday March 23 dawned with fog and rain that persisted through the day. Tragedy struck at 1115 hours when, during a field firing exercise, a CLAW rifle grenade exploded prematurely killing Fusilier Alexander Bunney and wounding four Highlanders. It was a desperate blow to the battalion so late in the campaign. In a moment of poignancy, Sergeant Willie Brown placed a hackle in the body bag with Fusilier Bunney as a helicopter approached to take him away. The four injured Highlanders were Lance Corporal McKinnon and Privates Bell, Turner and Mackenzie 35. The latter was injured again some days later when he was burned by white phosphorous from a smoke discharger grenade.

The sense of depression was compounded when it was rumoured that a battlegroup was to remain in the desert and, if so, it would be the Fusiliers. This was reinforced when the advance party for the return to Germany was stopped from departing on 24 March. Two days later it was confirmed during a visit by the British Ambassador to Saudi Arabia, Sir Alan Munroe, who had the unenviable task of telling the Fusiliers that their battlegroup was to remain as 'some teeth were needed in the desert'. Captain John Whitwam observed '...he was a sweaty toad of a man and was visibly shaken at the reception he received from the boys. He was so far out of touch with what we thought that he appeared surprised when he was told that we did mind sitting out in the desert doing nothing. Actually it was rather good fun baiting him and fun watching the Brigadier who was escorting him go redder and redder'. The response the ambassador received was hardly as he might have expected when Sergeant Tony Hay announced - 'If its teeth you want in the desert, you can have these f***ers!', throwing his dentures onto the sand.
(See Sidebar)

Fortunately, the ambassador's recollection is somewhat different. In his account of the Gulf War – 'An Arabian Affair', Sir Alan Munro recalls:

'Those who had drawn this short straw comprised a company of the 3rd Royal Regiment of Fusiliers, a squadron of the 14/20th Hussars, and a Royal Artillery battery. They gathered with their officers in a semi-circle in the sand. Chris Hammerbeck introduced me, saying I had been involved in the decision to keep a battle group in Kuwait and could explain the background to them. There was a disconsolate tone to their mood – understandable enough, I felt, in the light of their having been given to believe they were on their way home...

'I told those gathered around how it would be a grave mistake if, after all they and their fellows had achieved so magnificently in helping to drive the Iraqis out of Kuwait, Britain was to leave the field before the job was complete...But it would be wrong to throw away all the trust and goodwill we had gained with the Kuwaitis and our partners by leaving them to carry on at this stage, and after those present had achieved so much and above all sacrificed so much. For it was the 3rd Fusiliers who had lost nine men in the tragic air strike by supporting US aircraft during the heat of battle. I finished by saying that we therefore had to leave some teeth in the desert. That important role fell to them.

'There was a silence as the men pondered what I had said. Then a diminutive fusilier, sitting in the sand all encumbered with his battle kit, climbed to his feet. "Sir," he said in a broad Geordie voice, "you tell us we've got to leave some teeth behind. Well," putting his hand to his mouth and drawing out a set of false teeth which he threw down on the sand, "there's my teeth and I'll stay with them." The spell was broken and everyone rocked with laughter. I could have embraced that fusilier.'

The only consolation following this decision was the lottery for Fusiliers to visit HMS *Manchester* in the Gulf and the Royal Fleet Auxiliary *Sir Galahad* at the docks in Kuwait City for 'booze cruises'. Several Fusiliers subsequently returned to the battalion in a happy state of inebriation, including one nameless Fusilier, who was dropped off by naval helicopter, totally intoxicated and wearing a sailor's uniform. 27 March was a day full of incident with a fire at the main cookhouse. At 1730 hours, there was a CO's parade where it was announced that the battlegroup would be moving to Kuwait City in the near future. Another accident occurred in the evening during an O group near the CO's command vehicle. Lance Corporal Pete Spencer was checking the batteries inside One One Bravo when acid splashed his face, causing him to fall backwards and press the smoke discharger switch. White phosphorous grenades were launched into the air landing just beyond the assembled officers and senior NCOs, who scattered in all directions with only minor injuries being incurred. The RSM subsequently presented Lance Corporal Spencer with a charge sheet for the negligent discharge of a Warrior.

On 30 March, the battalion welcomed two auspicious visitors with Air Vice Marshal Ian Macfadyen, the newly appointed Commander British Forces Middle East, in the morning and General Norman Schwarzkopf, the overall commander of the coalition forces in the Kuwait theatre of operations, in the afternoon. Afterwards the battlegroup moved to an assembly area prior to its departure from the desert on the following day. The battlegroup arrived at the Adoha warehouse complex in Kuwait City in the morning. After a thorough cleansing, it was named St George's Lines which became the headquarters of the British forces in Kuwait. The day was notable to many Fusiliers as the first time that they had worn a beret and hackle for three months. To others, the most remarkable thing was getting used to walking on concrete after weeks on shifting sand; a sensation akin to acquiring sea legs. Over the next few days, parties of Fusiliers helped with the repair and refurbishment tasks in the city itself which had been comprehensively vandalised by the Iraqis, while others prepared the battlegroup's equipment for handover to the 2nd Battalion Royal Anglian Regiment. This was achieved on 5 April and one week later the battalion flew back to Germany in two flights, to a rapturous reception from families and friends.

On Minden Day 1992, the 3rd Battalion The Royal Regiment of Fusiliers was withdrawn from the Order of Battle of the British Army. On that day, the 1st and 3rd Battalions were merged to form a new 1st Battalion - the First Fusiliers. To mark the occasion, the Tower of London Guard, mounted by the 1st Battalion Grenadier Guards, was relieved by Fusiliers drawn from all battalions of The Royal Regiment of Fusiliers for 24 hours, each with Minden Roses in their berets. *SOLDIER Magazine*

The Regimental Sergeant Major, WO1 Broadbent, receives a welcoming glass of champagne from Fus Wickendon at Dusseldorf Airport on the return of 3RRF to Germany on 12 April 1991. Behind the RSM is the CO, Lt Col Larpent. Together, they displayed exemplary leadership of The Fusiliers Battlegroup throughout the Gulf War. This was recognised by the award of the OBE and MBE to the CO and RSM respectively.

FIRST
FUSILIERS
UNITED NATIONS
NATIONS UNIES
UNITED NATIONS
PROTECTION FORCE (UNPROFOR)
DRIVER'S PERMIT NO.
NAME
RANK
ID NO
is qualified and authorized to operate the following type(s) of
vehicle(s) belonging to the United Nations.
Chief Transport Officer
UNPROFOR.2 (3-92)
MINES/UXO AIDE
MEMOIRE
IFOR
BE AWARE
WHERE?
- Confrontation lines
- Routes: gravel roads
- Vacated buildings
- Woods and orchards
- Military establishments
- Strategic areas
- Road-blocks/Checkpoints
- Private property
INDICATORS?
- Mine signs
- Mine craters
AVOIDANCE?
- Stay on known safe areas
- Stick to approved routes
- Don't drive onto road shoulders
- Don't give in to curiosity
- Observe local behaviour
- Attend Mine Awareness Training.
- Obtain mine information
DO NOT TOUCH!

Working for Peace

'The Balkans are not worth the healthy bones of a single Pomeranian grenadier' Prince Otto von Bismarck

THE BALKAN TRAGEDY

The strategic shift created by the end of the Cold War, whilst bringing welcome relief from the years of confrontation across the Iron Curtain, presented the NATO nations with a greater and more varied number of challenges than anyone had imagined possible during the previous four decades. One recurring characteristic of this strategic change has been the resurgence of nationalism, particularly in eastern and southern Europe and in the Islamic countries. The Gulf War of 1990-1991 represented the higher end of the operational intensity spectrum while the peace support operations in the Balkans since 1992 have reflected lesser military risks but have all the same presented the British Army and the Regiment with their own particular set of arduous demands.

The Balkans have been a strategic fault line in Europe for over a thousand years. Influenced by the geographic boundary between Europe and Asia Minor, its principal source of conflict has rested upon the religious divide. For eight hundred years, the Balkans have provided the arena for a clash between Christianity and Islam. This has been compounded by the division between the Orthodox Christian Church and Roman Catholicism. It has been further complicated by the demographic friction between Slavonic and Latin civilisations. With tragic results, South-East Europe has provided the cockpit for interference from external powers and occupation for eight centuries. This has bred an acceptance and tradition of subjugation. Furthermore, conflicts have mirrored the culture, laws and attitudes of the resident populations in the Balkans. As a result, violence, feuds, corruption and cruelty have characterised life and war throughout the various states now known as the Former Republic of Yugoslavia.

The British Army's experience in the Balkans since 1992 has spanned the gamut of peace support operations. In the early days, the problems and challenges facing the soldiers of the United Nations Protection Force (UNPROFOR) in their thankless pursuit of peace keeping was compounded by the indecisive direction of a distant and idealistic United Nations in New York. With little understanding of the obstacles and complications facing the UN Commander and his forces on the ground, the Security Council enfeebled UNPROFOR through a lack of resources and commitment. As a case in point, when the UN declared the safe areas of Gorazde, Srebrenica and Zepa, military planners identified a need for 36,000 troops to implement the UN resolution. In the event, only the UK, the Netherlands and the Ukraine responded to the UN requirement but fewer than 3,500 troops were committed. Accordingly, the stratagem was deeply flawed from the outset yet it was those soldiers on the ground who suffered the consequences when the havens fell; notwithstanding the thousands of Muslims that were slaughtered in the ensuing Serb pogrom. In contrast, the operational imperative for decisive military action backed by firm political judgement was clearly demonstrated by the deployment of IFOR, the NATO peace Implementation Force, to fulfil the terms of the Dayton Accord in December 1995.

Fortuitously, the 1st Battalion The Royal Regiment of Fusiliers was centrally placed to participate in this critical transition from peace keeping to peace enforcement. The longer term challenges of peace support that demanded flexibility and subtlety, yet shadowed by the risk of ever expanding conflict, were then experienced by the 2nd Battalion during its later SFOR and KFOR deployments to Bosnia and Kosovo. These protracted, intensive and heavily scrutinised peace support operations have provided the British soldier with a greater and more subtle series of operational challenges in recent years than ever before. However, the strength of regimental character honed over three centuries and tempered by three decades of operations in Northern Ireland has made the British Army, and the Regiment's role in it, pre-eminent in the success of this novel and increasingly prevalent style of soldiering in the 21st Century.

YUGOSLAVIA
Tito once remarked that he was the leader of one Country with two Alphabets, three Languages, four Religions, five Nationalities and six Republics surrounded by seven Neighbours.

'Anyone who think's they know what's going on in Bosnia hasn't been paying attention' British Army briefing of journalists Vitez 1993

MING THE MERCILESS

On the 7 June 1993, the 1st Battalion The Royal Regiment of Fusiliers was assembled in the gymnasium at the Infantry Training Centre in Warminster to meet their new Commanding Officer. At the appointed hour, he strode into the auditorium and mounted the podium, adopting his characteristic pose of legs splayed and thumbs hooked into his equipment belt. An expectant hush fell that lengthened into complete silence as the CO's gaze moved backwards and forwards over the ranks of Fusiliers for a full minute. Finally, Lieutenant Colonel Trevor Minter spoke - 'Just thought I'd give you the chance to have a look and see if I really am the mean and nasty son of a bitch that everyone's told you I am'. The Fusiliers dissolved into nervous laughter. His nickname of 'Ming the Merciless' had preceded him and it was soon reflected in the reduction in numbers of Fusiliers charged for minor misdemeanours as few were inclined to face CO's Orders.

Hitherto, the task of Demonstration Battalion at Warminster was none too popular because of the number of repetitive exercises on Salisbury Plain but, with the introduction of the Combined Arms Training Centre Battle Group in its place, the First Fusiliers were party to the important changes in doctrine being introduced into the British Army following the Gulf War. The 1st Battalion was the first formation at Warminster to be equipped with Warrior and TES (Tactical Engagement Simulation). In their role of OPFOR (Opposing Forces), the Fusiliers tested the rest of the UK Field Army in battlefield tactics, drills and procedures as well as the accuracy of their fire, thanks to the enhanced realism to exercises provided by DFWES (Direct Fire Weapons Effect Simulation) through its use of lasers to inflict casualties on enemy personnel and their vehicles. In a configuration devised by the Demonstration Officer, Major Peter Cross, the Warriors and 432s of the First Fusiliers' Battlegroup were painted in a distinctive colour scheme of green and yellow stripes similar to that used at BATUS. As the OPFOR element of the battlegroup, those of Y Company were given a differentiating livery of red, green and grey, derived from a camouflage scheme used by German Panzers on the Eastern Front in World War 2, as they took on all comers in Exercises 'Red Shank', 'Phantom Bugler', 'Globe Trot' et al.

In August 1994, the battalion moved from Warminster to Somme Barracks in Catterick and converted to the mechanised infantry role equipped with Saxon wheeled APCs. Once more training as a complete unit, the battalion conducted Exercise 'Fighting Fusilier' at Stanford in Norfolk during October and in November, Exercise 'Panther's Fire' on Salisbury Plain as part of its workup programme before acceptance within 19th Mechanised Brigade of the 3rd (UK) Division. Warned off for an operational tour of peace keeping duties in Bosnia during 1995, training acquired a new urgency but deployment was deferred when the 1st Battalion The Royal Welch Fusiliers (1RWF) assumed the task instead. Although affiliated regiments, the First Fusiliers were bitterly disappointed. Morale did not improve with the announcement that

In August 1992, 1RRF moved to Warminster as the Demonstration Battalion at the School of Infantry. This evolved into the Combined Arms Training Centre Battlegroup comprising almost 900 men and 230 vehicles including an armoured squadron (A Squadron The Royal Scots Dragoon Guards), an expanded Royal Electrical and Mechanical Engineers (REME) LAD (Light Aid Detachment), an armoured reconnaissance troop and attached Royal Engineers under command. 1RRF was structured with a Headquarters Company, Y and Z as rifle companies with X Company as a technical company containing the FV432 APC, Warrior, reconnaissance and Signals platoons. W Company was the fire support company with the Mortar and Milan Platoons. This formidable force acted as the principal manoeuvre element for field training exercises conducted by the Combined Arms School, JDSC and the School of Infantry on Salisbury Plain.

Andy Cole was to move from Newcastle to Manchester United. However, they soon formed a Training Support Group to play the Balkan 'civpop' to various other units destined for Bosnia, with Corporal 'Flash' Wilson relishing his role as a Croat general and declaring to the CO of 19 Regiment Royal Artillery that - 'Lieutenant Colonels and Majors are two a penny. I will only talk to your senior commander'.

When the battalion undertook their own Bosnia training, a range of new skills had to be learned including knowledge of Serbo-Croat, negotiation techniques, rules of engagement, as well as Saxon driving and recovery and weapon systems such as the 0.50 inch calibre Browning heavy machine gun and the L37 turret mounted on Saxon. The Reconnaissance Platoon was the first unit to be equipped with the Combat Vehicle Reconnaissance (Tracked) Sabre - an amalgamation of a CVR(T) Scorpion hull and a Fox armoured car turret, but of a vintage older than many of the crewmen. This light tracked AFV was being introduced into service with the Reconnaissance Platoons of mechanised and armoured infantry battalions. However, during gunnery training at Lulworth, its coaxial chaingun proved to be unreliable because of the feed mechanism and it suffered from unacceptable stoppage levels. Accordingly, it was condemned as unfit for operational service by Major Peter Cross RRF which caused considerable consternation up the chain of command. Nevertheless, the Fusilier crews and REME artificers at the Armoured Trials and Development Unit devised suitable modifications that were incorporated into kits that were waiting for the Reconnaissance Platoon when it unloaded at Split. Within the framework of the battalion training programme, each company deployed on exercise to Otterburn training area, culminating in the CO's test exercise at Catterick. The final training exercise involved a battalion move by Saxon from Salisbury Plain to Sennybridge in a simulation of an opposed extraction from Gorazde to Belgrade. During July, the battalion was declared as fit for deployment on Operation 'Grapple 7' by the United Nations Training and Advisory Team. However, as the 1st Battalion went on pre-deployment leave, uncertainty remained as to whether it would actually go or in what strength and to where as events unfolding in Bosnia had thrown all plans into turmoil.

In the meantime, the situation in Bosnia had deteriorated markedly and, although there was a cease-fire between the Bosnian Croats and Muslims and a further trilateral cease-fire around Sarajevo, the United Nations declared safe havens of Gorazde, Srebrenica and Zepa were being invested by the Bosnian Serb Army (BSA), with UNPROFOR troops being virtual hostages inside these enclaves. While the principal role of UNPROFOR remained the escort and delivery of humanitarian aid under the auspices of the UNHCR (United Nations High Commission for Refugees) to all parties irrespective of race or religion, its authority was being continually undermined by the warring factions as their numerous vehicle checkpoints effectively denied freedom of movement to the UN; on occasions convoys had been delayed by up to 14 days.

OPERATION DELIBERATE FORCE

The failure of UNPROFOR to maintain the Muslim enclaves as safe havens and the subsequent massacre of 7,000 people at Srebrenica was a turning point of the war. In addition, the indiscriminate mortar attack on a Sarajevo marketplace on 30 August which killed 37 people was a further horrifying reminder to the world of this appalling war that had already claimed almost 170,000 civilian lives with a further 80,000 among the combatants. In essence, the United Nations suspended the peacekeeping mission and withdrew all of its personnel from Serbian occupied areas to preclude further hostage taking, so that a NATO air campaign could be mounted against the Bosnian Serbs. During August and September in Operation 'Deliberate Force', 3,500 air sorties were flown and 13 cruise missiles were fired against almost 400 targets, as well as the concerted bombardment of Bosnian Serb heavy weapons sites around Sarajevo by the artillery and mortars of the newly formed UN Rapid Reaction Force. Into this Balkan maelstrom of deceit and duplicity, the First Fusiliers had deployed to Bosnia as BRITBAT 2 between 21 and 22 August on a decrepit Tupolev 154 chartered by the UN. They congregated at 'DJ' - Camp Divulje - near the port of Split where they met up with their equipment which had come by sea.

After spending a night at the Palace Hotel in Split, 56 Fusiliers of X Company moved to Belgrade on 22 August in an even more decrepit Ilyushin 76 to assist with the withdrawal of

1RWF who were still stranded in Gorazde. The plan, codenamed Operation 'Balkan Extraction', was to take over the Saxons as they arrived at Belgrade so that 1RWF could fly home directly and then move the vehicles by road to Split where they would be refurbished for use by the Fusiliers Battlegroup. On the next day, Z Company and Battalion Headquarters moved by coach to Bugojno to relieve D Company, 1RWF, in place but outside the town they were halted by a Muslim road-block, of which more later.

As they arrived at Belgrade airport, X Company and their OC, Major Christopher Claridge, had their first encounter with the mindless bureaucratic officialdom that had stifled the erstwhile communist Former Republic of Yugoslavia for years. He was cradling an ammunition box containing almost 100,000 DM (£36,000) in cash to pay the various extortionate road tolls in Serbia and Croatia during 'Balkan Extraction'. Major Christopher Claridge recalls - 'At first we were held on the plane whilst officials debated on how we should be processed into the country. Initially we were to enter via the normal arrivals area but when it became apparent that we were armed, the officials became very agitated. After some friendly negotiations I reluctantly agreed we would centralise our weapons and, with a Fusilier escort, would travel separately. There was no other way to get out of the airport and, amid an atmosphere of uncertainty and suspicion, I had to take the risk in order not to jeopardise the mission at the first hurdle.

'Our destination was a light industrial compound at Dobanovici some 15 miles outside Belgrade which was in use by the UNHCR as a stopover point for convoys. The first problem was that the RWF liaison detachment were only able to provide us with one four-tonner and one Land Rover. This meant that we had to split the force and move in relays to Dobanovici. We crammed in as many men and equipment as we could into the four tonner (breaking all peacetime regulations) so as to limit the operation to two trips. I was feeling vulnerable - a tactically unsound decision but no viable alternatives. The first group to arrive at Dobanovici, commanded by myself, was readily allowed to enter and we set about unloading weapons and equipment to allow the truck to return. Whilst the second group were being transported the compound manager became aware of our weapons and there ensued a great hiatus which lasted long into the night. The manager wanted us out - "weapons were not in the contract and in any case the UN had not paid the rent for use of the compound for the last three months" - the police who had now arrived said if we left we would be arrested and our weapons confiscated. Half my force in and half out - welcome to the Balkans! Several hours of negotiations followed - some heated, some comical but most circular. By being persistent I avoided having to part with any cash to pay UN rent and I was not interested in bribery. I also held back on the slivo until a deal was concluded at about 1 am. We were to move to the Hotel Yugoslavia in central Belgrade (a 5-star hotel) and base ourselves there, coming back to Dobanovici only when required to meet RWF convoys. By this time we had another four tonner so we could move in one convoy to Hotel Yugoslavia only to be met by more police who remonstrated very strongly about our presence, particularly the weapons, which had to stay outside in a vehicle. Thinking they might be vulnerable, despite a guard force, we later smuggled them into the hotel inside our bergans. It was a bizarre experience for this small and isolated group - thrust into a very uncertain situation, in a strange and somewhat hostile capital city. Within 48 hours of leaving the UK, the X Company contingent found themselves enjoying silver service meals, rooms with en-suite bathrooms and all the trappings of a 5-star hotel.'

There the party waited for 1RWF to exfiltrate Gorazde which they successfully achieved without casualties. The first convoy of DROPS vehicles and low loaders carrying ISO containers arrived on Friday 25 August. The final contingent of Saxon APCs arrived in Belgrade on 29 August by which most of the Fusiliers had spent all their money and were confined to the hotel for lack of funds. After Gorazde Force had enjoyed an alcoholic interlude on the banks of the Danube, they flew back to UK leaving the First Fusiliers with the Saxons that were in a sorry state of disrepair with loose ammunition and weapons in the backs of some. Divided into two parties under Captain Paul Nanson and Lieutenant Adrian Newell, the Saxons left Belgrade for Split as soon as possible on the circuitous route via Zagreb so as to avoid numerous border crossings and their inevitable roadblocks. During the 5-day 1,700 kilometre journey, the Saxons broke down repeatedly, mainly due to contaminated fuel, and some had to be towed causing the weary drivers even more

Among the many distressing experiences that the Fusiliers endured in Bosnia was the exchange of refugees when often infirm and dying people were used as pitiful pawns in the power games of the warring factions. Here, overseen by a Saxon APC, an exchange is being conducted at Black Dog in November.

problems; one Saxon broke down near the Serb-Croat border alongside a column of Bosnian Serb T-55 tanks at the time that NATO had just renewed its airstrikes. Similarly the last convoy of containers and low loaders was subjected to showers of stones and petrol bombs as it left but not before the liaison officer in Zagreb, Captain Jules Irens, had received an agitated telephone call from the Ministry of Defence at 0200 hours inquiring whether there were any British soldiers left in Belgrade and if so to get them out immediately.

Eventually, all the vehicles made it to the Jadrantrans Factory in Split where they were reconstituted by 16 September thanks to the herculean efforts of the QM staff and REME, some two weeks ahead of the schedule set by HQ BRITFOR. Major Steve Ramsey, Captain Boris Spence and the QM staff were to remain the unsung heroes throughout the tour, ensuring support to the widespread and constantly moving battlegroup. While Operation 'Balkan Extraction' was underway, the remainder of X Company was billeted at Camp Doli, a UN tented transit camp whose principal occupants at the time were Pakistani and Malaysian troops as well as an Indonesian engineer contingent. Most of them strolled around all day in T-shirts and shorts which Company Sergeant Major Jock Stacey found quite unacceptable, as was the state of cleanliness. He approached the Bangladeshi RSM and, pointing to his own insignia of a Crown on his chest, introduced himself as the senior sergeant major in UNPROFOR. Thereafter, he instructed his counterpart to have his men tidy the camp which was in a sorry state. Feeding procedures in the mess tent were altered so that there were specific mealtimes for different nationalities with the British and French Foreign Legion being fed first.

Meanwhile, Z Company had found itself stuck at a roadblock outside Bugojno. For a while, consideration was given to flying the Fusiliers into the town by Mil 26 Hook helicopters but this was deemed to be too risky. The OC, Major Philip Stack, realised that the Muslims were allowing single vehicles to pass but not military convoys or indeed the buses carrying the First Fusiliers. At this time, a convoy constituted anything more than four vehicles. Accordingly, he withdrew the coaches some distance to the well-known landmark of brutalist communist sculpture called Tito's Fist. There he reorganised the company and, by using any type of vehicle travelling on its own, including the ISO containers on the backs of Royal Logistic Corps trucks, smuggled his platoons into Bugojno one by one. Much to the anger of the ABiH (Bosnian Muslim Army) liaison officer, the First Fusiliers relieved the Royal Welch Fusiliers in place without further incident and assumed responsibility for the Vrbas Valley on 28 August.

Within days, Z Company and the CVR(T) Sabres of the Reconnaissance Platoon were patrolling their area of operations to make their presence felt to the various factions. Battalion Headquarters and A2 Echelon were also established at Bugojno. The mission of the 1st Battalion was essentially to contribute to a stable security environment within the boundaries of their Area of Operations (AO) and to assist in the development of a durable peace within Bosnia-Herzegovina. This included helping in the reconstruction of the region's infrastructure through various non-governmental agencies and through their own efforts that were termed G5 tasks. These were executed by small dedicated teams working very much on their own initiative under the direction of WO2 Pete Richardson. Equally important was the escort and delivery of humanitarian aid which required freedom of movement throughout the road network

One of the first tasks for the Reconnaissance Platoon was to secure Route Diamond against a band of criminals known as The Fish Head Gang which was staging ambushes of vulnerable UN vehicles. These were either robbed of their contents or stolen entirely. So named because the gang operated near to a ruined fish farm above Gornji Vakuf, they were not so stupid as to tackle a pair of fully armed Sabres, so the Reconnaissance Platoon amused themselves when not escorting vehicles by staging time trials along Route Diamond, achieving speeds well in excess of 70 miles per hour. A further mission for the Fusiliers was the escort of resupply convoys to the British units in Sarajevo which, because the direct route was blocked by Serbian checkpoints, necessitated negotiating a circuitous and hazardous mountain track over Mount Igman along the only lifeline into the devastated city. Captain Bob Broadbent, WO2 Terry Crowe and Colour Sergeant Haley remained on this task in the midst of the ongoing hostilities.

On 13 September, the Serb held town of Donji Vakuf fell to 7 Corps of the ABiH as Operation 'Storm', the major autumn offensive of the Croat/Muslim Federation forces, drove northeastward towards Banja Luka, the largest Serb town in Bosnia. Before leaving Donji Vakuf, the Serbs looted the town and, as soon as they arrived, the Muslims continued the process. That night from 2300 hours, the sky was filled with tracer fire from all manner of weapons as the Muslims celebrated their victory. They expended more ammunition in the next two hours than they had in fighting for the town. Z Company established Observation Post BM8 overlooking the town to monitor the situation, but all attempts to dispatch UN personnel into the town to prevent further excesses were denied by the Muslims despite the requests of the local authorities for the battalion to restore order. Indeed one foray on the morning of 13 September by the battalion liaison officers, Major Ian Kippen and Captain Mark Lapping, was forced back by a hostile mob of Muslim military policemen firing their weapons in the air. All the while houses were being torched and systematically looted; much of it being witnessed by President Alija Izetbegovic, the Muslim leader of the Federation, who was visiting his new found territorial gains.

Mounting repeated sorties to expand their sphere of influence and enforce the UN mandate as widely as possible, the First Fusiliers were frustrated by the innumerable checkpoints of all

Three CVR(T) Sabres of the Recce Pl rest by the roadside just south of the Kupres Tunnel during a routine patrol. The recce platoon undertook considerable distances on its patrols; it commonly covered similar mileages every month in Bosnia to those it would do in a year in Germany.

In the distressing circumstances of Bosnia, much time and effort was spent in support of the civilian population and in the reconstruction of the country's ravaged infrastructure. Such work was undertaken against a background of mutual suspicion between the various ethnic groupings and it required Fusiliers of considerable patience and diplomacy to effect any improvements. Designated as G5 activities, one such Fusilier was WO2 Richardson, ably supported by his driver L/Cpl Parker despite driving in the wrong direction according to the road sign. His G5 team was responsible for civic support in the Bugojno area.

the warring factions on the main routes. In the words of Brigadier Richard Dannatt, Commander Sector South West, and subsequently of 4th Armoured Brigade - 'It was every Bosnian's dream to own his own checkpoint'. Often these were manned by only a few bored and truculent soldiers or militiamen but, when fuelled by drugs or alcohol and armed with the omnipresent Kalashnikov, they were always unpredictable and therefore dangerous. As they were no match for a Sabre or a Saxon, it was all the more galling for the Fusiliers as the following encounter affirms, which was typical of the situation prevailing in the months of September and October when the reputation of the UN was at its nadir.

FREEDOM OF MOVEMENT

In another attempt to gain access to Donji Vakuf during the morning of 14 September, a patrol of two CVR(T) Sabres, Callsigns 23 and 23 Alpha, ventured northwards from Bugojno along Route Opal but it was soon stopped at a checkpoint. After a period of negotiation in which it became obvious that the ABiH soldiers would not let the patrol proceed without further orders from above, the Sabres withdrew but the crews noticed a track leading off the road towards the north. Ordinarily, unpaved tracks were avoided for fear of mines but they offered some youths nearby a lift on the Sabres in the belief they would refuse if any anti-tank mines had been laid. When they agreed, the patrol set off and travelled several kilometres northwards before the track returned to the main road which was now teeming with drunken soldiers moving southwards, discharging weapons into the air and loaded down with their plunder from Donji Vakuf. Realising the dangers of the drunken mob, the patrol moved southwards as quickly as possible until it reached the checkpoint from behind and passed through much to the anger of soldiers manning the position. The two Sabres then stopped close by so that they could monitor the traffic, both military and civilian, passing in both directions.

Further attempts by the OC of Z Company, Major Philip Stack, to achieve access through the local police and the normal military contacts failed after they indicated that nothing could be done without the permission of the commander of 77 'Vrbas' Division ABiH, Colonel Senad Dautovic, or his staff who were in Donji Vakuf to which access was denied - a classic Catch-22 and all too typical in Bosnia. As UN concerns grew as to the events unfolding in Donji Vakuf so the ABiH prevaricated through the next day, until a final attempt to gain access was made by the 2IC of the First Fusiliers, Major Andrew Marriott, during the evening of Friday 15 September. At approximately 1800 hours, he approached the police checkpoint north of Bugojno in his Land Rover accompanied by two Sabres, Callsigns Two Three and Two Two, which took up positions behind and to either side of the vehicle which contained his female interpreter Brancka; the driver, Lance Corporal Mike McKee, and his signaller, Corporal Johnny Costello. Once more it was explained that the mayor of Donji Vakuf had requested an immediate and unlimited UN presence in the town. Again it was refused and again higher authority was sought. At 1850, two Bosnian officers, Captains Nermin and Sead, arrived in a battered VW Golf and declared that they were liaison officers of 77 Division. An acrimonious and abusive exchange then took place with all the legal and humanitarian arguments put forward by Major Marriott being met with derision. This encounter broke up around 1905 hours with the ABiH officers leaving but not before giving specific orders to the checkpoint commander that the UN were not allowed to proceed further.

Undaunted, Major Marriott continued negotiations with the civil police there, attempting to establish whether or not they were prepared to use lethal force to prevent the patrol's progress. As a precaution against unnecessary casualties, he instructed Colour Sergeant Dave Griffiths, the commander of Callsign Two Three, that if he was shot, the Sabres were to withdraw without retaliating. Colour Sergeant Griffiths demurred at such an order and recalls that - 'we would have trashed the place if a single round was fired'. With neither a mandate nor precise rules of engagement to force the checkpoint, Major Marriott offered a compromise whereby in ten minutes he would step past the barrier. If only the British commander was shot, no further action would be taken. Otherwise, it would be assumed that the patrol could proceed. After ten minutes had passed, the ultimatum was presented but this caused further consternation. The Muslims appealed for the Bugojno police commander to be summoned so that a decision could be taken by higher authority.

At this stage, the CO, Lieutenant Colonel Trevor Minter, who was monitoring the situation on the radio, counselled caution and to remember the nature of the mission as such a situation did not warrant the loss of British lives; paraphrasing the words of Otto von Bismarck that the Balkans were not worth the bones of a Pomeranian Grenadier let alone a British Fusilier. Even so, he dispatched a further two Sabres with the Reconnaissance Platoon commander, Lieutenant Guy Cartwright, in Callsign Two One and Corporal John Duthie in Two One Alpha to reinforce the Fusilier presence at the checkpoint but from a distance of 400 metres. There they did not exacerbate the situation but their firepower was readily to hand. Following the arrival of a senior police officer, a modicum of calm was restored with an apparent willingness for arrangements to be made for a meeting with Colonel Dautovic in the morning. However,

Throughout the 1RRF tour of Bosnia, the Fusiliers were constantly plagued by roadblocks set up by all of the warring factions for their own selfish ends. Often manned by soldiers or militiamen fuelled on alcohol and drugs, their behaviour was erratic and frequently irrational that posed a significant threat to the wellbeing of UNPROFOR troops. Here, Maj Marriott, the 2IC of 1RRF, listens patiently to the demands of local militiamen at a roadblock in the Vrbas Valley: a situation not dissimilar to that of 15 September 1995 during the major Federation autumn offensive which almost ended in a firefight between the Fusiliers' Recce Pl and Muslim troops with Maj Marriott in the middle

this required the recall of the ABiH liaison officers. Furthermore, darkness now dictated that any advance be postponed until the next day.

The checkpoint was now only dimly lit by a roadside bonfire and, when Captains Nermin and Sead returned at around 2300 hours, they informed Major Marriott that a commander would arrive shortly to explain the difficulties as to freedom of movement for UNPROFOR patrols. Major Marriott asked them to stay until he arrived but they refused and sped off without getting out of their motor car. Within moments the checkpoint was overrun by ABiH military policeman after a truck swerved around the roadblock and stopped behind Callsign Two Two, blocking its withdrawal while covering all three Fusilier vehicles with a machine gun that was revealed when its canvas tilt was pulled back. A situation, Major Marriott recalls, reminiscent of the scene in the film 'The Great Escape' when the British escapees were massacred, which was a sobering omen at the time. A yellow mini-bus followed and halted close behind Two Three. The 17 Muslims were heavily armed with Kalashnikovs and anti-armour weapons with at least one RPG-7 (Rocket Propelled Grenade) being trained on each Sabre from a range of a few metres; too close for them to be armed if fired but much too close for comfort. Major Marriott had three rifles pressed to his head as their leader, his rancid breath reeking of slivovitz, delivered an ultimatum demanding that the UN patrol leave within two minutes or otherwise it would be destroyed. With remarkable aplomb, Major Marriott replied that, as its local representative, the United Nations would not be intimidated by such blatant behaviour and the patrol would not depart under such circumstances. A short and heated argument followed with neither party willing to back down, while the interpreter became ever more nervous and agitated.

The principal vehicle of the Recce Pl of 1RRF in Bosnia was the CVR(T) Sabre; the marriage of a Fox armoured car turret with the hull of a Scorpion. Although recently introduced into service, the age of these vehicles was older than most of the Fusiliers serving in them. Callsign Two Two under the command of Sgt Gilling with Cpl Pender and the driver Fus Rose, was involved in the checkpoint incident of 14 September 1995.

As Major Marriott had been negotiating on the ground, Colour Sergeant Griffiths in Callsign Two Three and Sergeant Dave Gilling in Callsign Two Two, together with Captain Cartwright to the rear, had concocted a contingency plan whereby the latter and his companion vehicle Two One Alpha would fire their chaingun weapons down the roadside to either side of the two forward Sabres to eliminate the Muslims troops covering the Fusiliers. At the same time, both Sabres would switch on their highlights to dazzle the troops manning the roadblock. Two Three would then speed forward and crush the soldier with the RPG pointing directly at the CVR(T), while Two Two would reverse at speed into the truck mounting the machine gun. At the same time, both Sabres would rake the position with Rarden and chaingun rounds; Two Three from the centre outwards to the left and Two Two in the other direction. The gunner of Two Two, Corporal John Pender, advised Corporal Costello and Lance Corporal McKee in the 2IC's Land Rover - 'If it kicks off you had better duck as six rounds of sabot are coming straight through your back door'. Similarly, Captain Cartwright in Callsign Two One cheerfully radioed from his position to the rear - 'Don't worry. One shot and we'll hose the place with chainguns'. The drivers and gunners of both Sabres had been ordered to batten down but in Two Three, the driver's seat was jammed and could not be lowered. To his dismay, Fusilier Pete Bell found himself fearfully exposed facing an RPG some three metres to his front, a Kalashnikov pointing directly at him from his left and the muzzle of the Sabre's chaingun only inches above his head. In the turret, Colour Sergeant Griffiths prepared a couple of L2A2 hand grenades which he kept close at hand by the commander's periscope for instant use. As he did so, the Muslim to his left pointed to his Kalashnikov and then at Griffiths who responded by pointing to the Sabre's 30mm Rarden cannon and then back at the man.

By now several of the Sabre crewmen were convinced they were going to die. In Two Two, the driver, Fusilier Ray Rose, recalls - 'having never been so scared in my life including when I nearly drowned', but he engaged reverse gear in preparation for ramming the truck behind him. For several tense minutes, Major Marriott reiterated his demand for a meeting with the divisional commander, Colonel Dautovic. After that had been confirmed as understood, it was agreed that the UN patrol would withdraw but a single Land Rover would return later at 0100 hours to discuss the issue further; hopefully in calmer circumstances. Major Marriott with a crew of volunteers duly revisited at 0100 hours but once more no satisfactory answers for the denial of freedom of movement to UNPROFOR were forthcoming. After reaffirming the requirements for the meeting between Colonel Dautovic and the CO of the First Fusiliers at 0700 hours, the UN vehicle departed at 0120 hours. The Sabre crews had endured long hours of boredom interspersed with minutes of terror when their lives were undoubtedly in jeopardy, yet they prevailed in the execution of their duty. Throughout, they were at the mercy and whim of drunken looters, deceitful petty officials and ruthless local warlords. In the words of Colour Sergeant Dave Griffiths - 'Unlike the movies, the guys in white backed down every time'. It was a typical day for UNPROFOR in Bosnia.

Lieutenant Colonel Trevor Minter arrived at the checkpoint punctually at 0700 hours on Saturday 16 September 1995. Predictably, the ABiH failed to appear so the CO deployed a new weapon in his armoury in the form of the world's press. In a series of interviews with the BBC and other journalists, he exposed the looting and general indiscipline of the Bosnian Muslim Army (ABiH). Having found the UNPROFOR Public Information Teams to be largely ineffective and always too slow, Lieutenant Colonel Minter's proactive approach suited the daily deadlines of the journalists and there ensued a fruitful association with the media that was beneficial to all parties. In particular, the BBC News team headed by Martin Bell formed a lasting relationship with the First Fusiliers over the coming months.

In the meantime, on 17 September tension remained high around Donji Vakuf. During the evening, BM8 the main observation post, overlooking the town came under fire from a nearby hamlet. The section occupying the position was under orders to respond to any attack but as the firing points could not be identified with certainty, the Fusiliers held their fire. At 1900 hours, the section 2IC, Lance Corporal 'Rads' Radford, left the forward location to move back to the administrative area when he was engaged by a lone gunman with two rounds passing close over his head. Lance Corporal Radford identified the firing point and responded with five rounds that were aimed to pass just by the gunman as he withdrew. By his robust but measured reaction as befits a peace keeper, Lance Corporal Radford displayed sufficient force to deter further attacks against the OP. After several days, the battalion were eventually allowed access to Donji Vakuf but unconfirmed reports of atrocities in the area left a feeling of frustration in the face of the intransigence of the warring factions and confirmed the impotence of UNPROFOR to affect events to any marked degree.

THE EXPANDING AREA OF OPERATIONS

Shortly afterwards, the battalion's area of operations increased to encompass the Lasva Valley, including Vitez, Travnik and Turbe, where members of 1st Battalion The Royal New Zealand Regiment were operating. The Kiwi Company (or K Company) now came under the operational command of the 1st Battalion and the occasion was marked by a Maori Hakka for the Commanding Officer. With the Saxon APCs now refurbished, the first section of four vehicles was issued to 4 Platoon of X Company under the command of Lieutenant Andy Higgs. Reinforced by a section from Z Company, it was dispatched to Santici to assist the New Zealand armoured infantry company for ten days as the Kiwis exchanged personnel. The working relationship with the New Zealanders became so effective that Lance Corporal 'Tubby' Miller was offered on a free transfer as he seemingly went native with the Kiwis. On 4 October, the area of operations of the First Fusiliers expanded further when X Company under the command of Major Christopher Claridge assumed responsibility over an area known as the Maglaj Finger from the BRITCAVBAT, the 9th/12th Royal Lancers (Prince of

Men of the Kiwi Company perform the Hakka, a traditional Maori dance, to welcome Lt Col Minter as their new CO for UN operations in Bosnia. The Staff Sergeant wielding the machete gives the final challenge and dares the recipient of this honour to break eye contact in which case he is permitted to strike.

Wales's). An area devastated by the war, the Maglaj Finger was a Federation salient that was subject to concerted artillery attack as it was surrounded on three sides by Serbian territory.

Company Headquarters was based in the EKO Factory in Zepce. A platoon was ensconced in the school at Maglaj, close to the frontline with other detachments deployed to five outposts that served as checkpoints, observation posts and rebro sites. One of them was the curiously named 'Spotty Dog' checkpoint, so called on account of the numerous bullet holes in its walls which had been painted in a kaleidoscope of bright colours by previous units. In X Company's most northerly outpost, Captain Paul Nanson and his small team were installed in a house in Tesanj with the task of liaising with the 37 Division ABiH. As the Maglaj liaison officer, Captain Phil Hannah operated from the Maglaj school. There they observed Bosnian Serb military activity and endured sporadic artillery and small arms fire which was directed into the town of Maglaj.

With X Company was half of the Reconnaissance Platoon under Colour Sergeant Dave Griffiths who were conducting a drivers' and commanders' course on CVR(T) for company personnel, whereupon the latter used the Spartans of the departing cavalry regiment as well as their own Saxons for patrolling and checkpoints across the disputed area. By these means, X Company were able to have more men on the ground at any one time than the cavalry had been able to achieve as a regiment. X Company also had a platoon from W Company in support. The primary roles at this time were to expand the battlegroup's freedom of movement and continue to deliver humanitarian aid. The area of operations of the First Fusiliers now stretched from Prozor in the south to Jelah at the top of the Maglaj Finger in the north.

An agreement between the Federation of Bosnia-Herzegovina and the Republika Srpska (Serbia) was signed on 5 October 1995 that implemented a cease-fire throughout Bosnia-Herzegovina. It became effective from the 12th of the month. Despite the fact that this was the 37th cease-fire that had been negotiated between the warring factions, there was some room for optimism as this heralded the start of the Peace Process brokered by the United States of America. However, on the same day there occurred an incident that would have ramifications throughout the battalion's tour when a Mujahedeen was shot dead by a Fusilier. During the morning, a Saxon APC containing ten Fusiliers of 8 Platoon arrived at the village of Rudina near Donji Vakuf. Lieutenant Chris Griffin, the patrol commander, and six Fusiliers moved off on foot to conduct a survey of the area leaving Fusiliers Cowper, 'H' Harwood and 'Hewy' Hewitt to guard the APC. At 1100 hours, Fusilier Cowper saw a man approaching along a path and greeted him in Serbo-Croat. By his dress, it was apparent that he was a Mujahedeen and he became extremely agitated at the presence of the Fusiliers.

He then warned Fusilier Cowper to leave the village immediately or else he would be killed. While trying to calm the man, Fusilier Cowper motioned to Fusilier Hewitt for assistance. When the latter attempted to reason with the man, the Mujahedeen repeated his threat and drew a pistol which he pointed at Fusilier Hewitt's head. Believing that there was a direct and immediate threat to Fusilier Hewitt's life, Fusilier Cowper issued a challenge as he cocked his rifle and brought it to the aim. The Mujahedeen continued ranting with the pistol to Fusilier Hewitt's head, so Fusilier Cowper fired one round that knocked the assailant to the ground. When the Mujahedeen brought his weapon to bear again on Fusilier Hewitt, Fusilier Cowper fired two more aimed rounds that killed the man. The three Fusiliers then mounted their Saxon and drove off to inform the patrol commander of the situation.

This event precipitated a longstanding feud against the First Fusiliers by the Mujahedeen. 'One death for one death' became their clarion call and the battalion went onto a high state of alert for several weeks which increased from time to time as the Mujahedeen reiterated their threats of revenge. The Mujahedeen were a disparate band of Islamic fundamentalists including Bosniacs (Bosnian Muslims), Arabs, Iranians, Afghans and some Europeans. With their fatalistic attitude to death as the passage to paradise, they had been useful to the ABiH during the war as shock troops in the offence but with the coming of the cease-fire they had become an embarrassment. The closest the Mujahedeen came to retaliation was the ambush of an UNMO (United Nations Military Observer) Land Rover on 10 October on Route Emerald in mistake for one belonging to the First Fusiliers. In a ringing endorsement of Land Rover products, the CAV 100 armoured vehicle survived a direct hit from an RPG anti-tank rocket and 33 small arms strikes. Fortunately, the Mujahedeen immediately fled which allowed the occupants (two of whom were Muslims) to escape on foot, miraculously unhurt.

On 15 October, a patrol of K Company stumbled on a Mujahedeen camp and was stopped by the Mujahedeen leader. Speaking good English, he inquired what they were doing there. The Kiwi commander replied that they had freedom of movement in the area. Accompanied by threats and gestures of throat-cutting by his men, the Mujahedeen leader ordered the Kiwis to leave, at which some shots were fired over the top of the departing vehicle. Although this was a singular opportunity for the Mujahedeen to exact revenge, the patrol returned unharmed. In a further encounter in the Maglaj Finger on Friday 27 October, Major Christopher Claridge was faced with a dangerous confrontation when, in the company of the commander of 35 Division ABiH and accompanied by ABiH military policemen, his patrol was stopped by a Mujahedeen vehicle on the Blizna mountain. Despite the fact that they were travelling in the operational area of 35 Division, its commander deemed it appropriate to withdraw. As the three vehicles passed through the next village they were surrounded by almost 50 Mujahedeen* who adopted fire positions and demanded that all British personnel dismount with the implicit threat that they would be killed. All the Fusiliers kept completely silent while the commander of 35 Division tried to reason with the Mujahedeen. For some 15 minutes, the argument raged and despite their vehicles' windows being forced open and Kalashnikovs thrust inside, the Mujahedeen fortunately did not notice the Union Flag shoulder patches of the Fusiliers. Eventually, the the patrol was allowed to drive on but it had been a nerve-wracking experience.

On 23 October, the area of operations grew once more to include Kiseljak to the edges of Sarajevo when the Canadian Battalion departed and its duties were assumed by the Kiwi Company. CANBAT was followed by the Bangladeshis in early November. BANGBAT was based at Velica Kladusa to the north and was recognised in the jargon of UN operations at the time as a 'non-swimmer'. In reality, it was militarily ineffective and in the words of one Fusilier subaltern 'acted as 3rd Echelon to the Bosnian Army'. Indeed, the principal activity of its officers was the retail of UN aid and UNPROFOR fuel to civilian and ABiH clients at 60 per cent of local black market prices; the proceeds being stashed in Swiss bank accounts. On Friday 3 November, Task Force Talbot, or 10 Platoon under the command of Lieutenant James Fulford-Talbot, comprising four Saxon APCs plus support personnel such as chef, medics and an LAD Saxon deployed along Route Dog to Bihac; the normal two hour journey taking 12 because of the road conditions and the numerous checkpoints. There they supported the Regional Joint Commission process being set up in the area and provided cover for the departing Bangladeshis. At Coralici Camp, the platoon found the irrepressible Captain Bob Broadbent, the Mechanical Transport Officer, acting as the advance guard for the arrival of W Company Headquarters. They also found the Bangladeshi Officers Mess in a

*It is believed that these belonged to the particularly fanatical band of the Muslimski Odbrana Specijalizacija or Special Muslim Defence Group.

One of the first Regional Joint Council meetings involving the three former warring factions was held on the slopes of the Vlasic feature near Turbe. The representatives of the Croats, Muslims and Serbs were transported to the location in no man's land inside the back of an M-113 APC of the Kiwi Company in early November 1995. As the ground was frozen solid, it was impossible to pitch a tent. The meeting was chaired by the CO and decisions were quickly taken on account of the cold. It set a precedent for further meetings that forged the way for a lasting cessation of hostilities and the signing of the Dayton Agreement.

Corrimec container which was lined with wood panelling and sumptuously appointed. More importantly, it provided the best curry in theatre.

Soon thereafter, the BANGBAT base at Velica Kladusa was overrun by the ABiH which had decided to plunder the camp of all its valuable items before the Bangladeshis' withdrawal in a blatant contravention of the cease-fire. The Bangladeshis themselves had been incarcerated in a warehouse without firing a single shot even though they were only issued one weapon between five soldiers. 11 Platoon of Z Company under the command of 2nd Lieutenant Nick Wilcox was tasked by Headquarters Sector South West to restore the situation. This they duly did but not without difficulty. They were quickly replaced by 4 Platoon of X Company which were flown in by Sea Kings from Bugojno. On the first day after they arrived, a civilian petrol tanker drove into the camp and the driver, waving a wad of Deutsche Marks, demanded that it be filled up. He was soon disabused of the situation by the platoon commander, Lieutenant Andy Higgs. Thereafter, having lived on 10-man ration packs for almost a month, the first resupply run by Sea King helicopter from Split carried only a load of cabbages and out-of-date Black Forest chocolate gateaux; a typical example of what the CO termed as being - 'at the wrong end of the food chain'. Similarly, the first set of Combat 95 Pattern clothing to be seen in theatre was worn by an Adjutant General's Corps female captain educator attached to the battalion whose partner happened to be in the Royal Logistic Corps.

On 21 November, W Company TAC HQ under the command of Major John Whitehouse moved to Coralici Camp to assume command of forces in the Bihac area. The battalion's area of operations now covered 13,000 square kilometres and with only 484 Fusiliers, it represented one soldier for every half kilometre of confrontation line; in the words of the Commanding Officer - 'In size, infrastructure and attitudes our area of responsibility was equivalent to Northumberland - in about the 13th Century'. As of 23 November 1995, the 1st Fusiliers Battlegroup was responsible for an area that included two national contingents; three ethnic factions; six fully armed divisions; 72 brigade sized units; 257 kilometres of confrontation line; 72,000 armed troops and 425,000 civilians. At its largest extent, it took 12 hours for the CO in his 'Rover Group' to travel from one end of the AO to the other but the CO's driver, Lance Corporal 'Grommitt' Howitt, could talk the whole way.

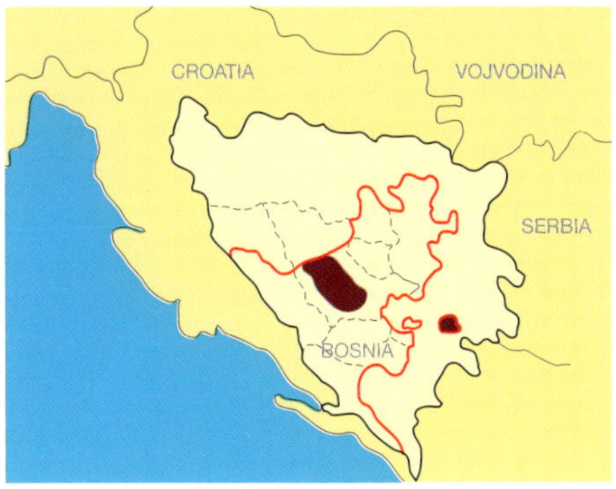

Intended deployment including Gorazde

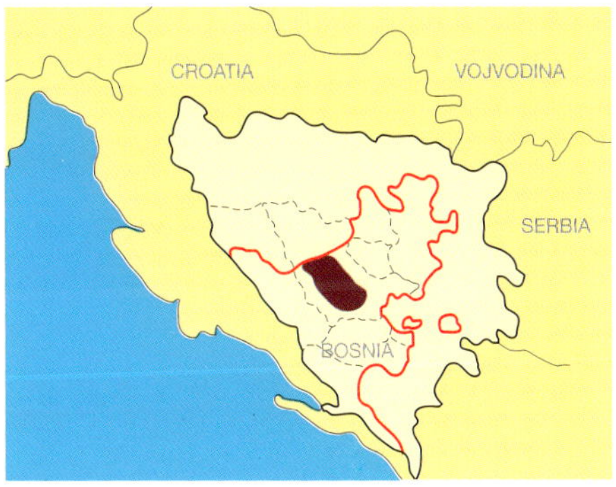

Initial deployment August 1995

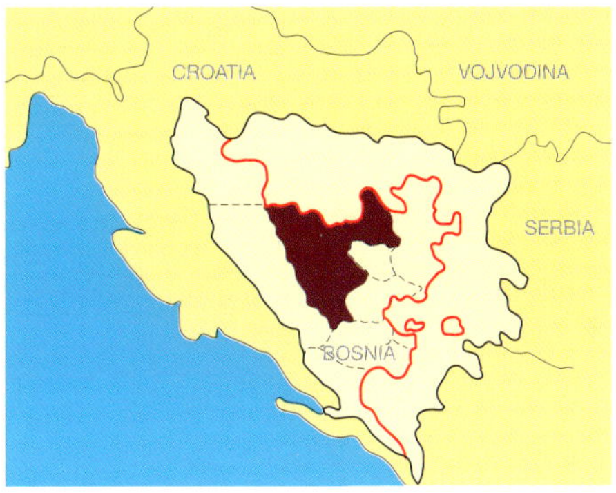

Early October 1995

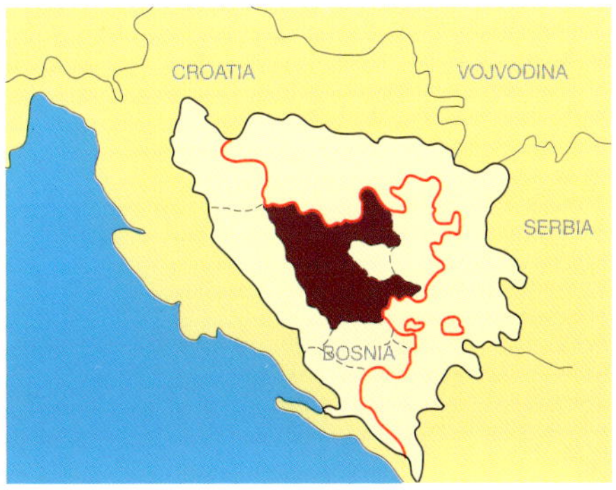

Late October 1995

At the height of 1RRF deployment

BLESSED ARE THE PEACEMAKERS

With the cease-fire in place, the First Fusiliers realised that an important part of the peace process was the development of trust and communication between all the parties. Regional Joint Commissions were established to create a means by which the various sides were brought together to discuss the implications of the peace agreement and resolve any local difficulties. As far as the Fusiliers were concerned, the major local difficulty remained the lack of freedom of movement because of the innumerable checkpoints that still existed. Armed with copies of the peace agreement in both English and Serbo-Croat, the Fusiliers visited every single checkpoint and military headquarters in their ever-expanding area of operations. Each location was given a copy of the agreement and a letter signed by the Commanding Officer with specific instructions on how to support the cease-fire. Typically, nothing happened immediately but with constant patrols maintaining the pressure and alternative routes being exploited, the checkpoints began to lose their stultifying grip on the countryside. The power of the press was harnessed again on 17 October when a UNHCR aid convoy, escorted by 11 Platoon and accompanied by Martin Bell and his BBC news team, managed to negotiate the Kupres tunnel and so open up one of the major routes through central Bosnia. The cameras were also on hand to record the Fusiliers shaming the ABiH into opening the checkpoint near Donji Vakuf that had been closed to them since the incident with the Mujahedeen.

The first Regional Joint Commission (RJC) meeting was arranged for Friday 20 October between the corps commanders of all three warring factions. It was chaired by the British sector commander, Brigadier Andrew Pringle at a site that had been secured by the First Fusiliers in a spectacular gorge some 25 kilometres south of Banja Luka. Although the Muslim commander failed to turn up, the Croat and Serbian representatives were willing to endorse the principles of the peace process and, after shaking hands, agreed to meet on the following day. Thereafter, the responsibility for chairing the RJCs fell to the First Fusiliers. Usually, these took place in no man's land between the frontlines at a site that had to be cleared of mines by Royal Engineer EOD teams. As winter was now blanketing the countryside under snow, tents and tables were often erected in incongruous places. The Fusiliers escorted each of the delegations from their respective side of the confrontation line and then provided security throughout the proceedings as the mutual mistrust between the parties was still palpable.

The Commanding Officer often chaired the first meetings in a specific area which was usually in no man's land. He soon realised, that beneath their bombastic bluster and their craven desire for status and respect, the local warlords remained petty communists at heart and were usually anxious to defer to a figure of authority. More often than not, all the delegates at a meeting, from the brigadier downwards, grasped dutifully for their notebooks when

The welfare and performance of any battalion is largely dependent on the strength of character of two men: the Commanding Officer and the Regimental Sergeant Major - Lt Col Trevor Minter and WO1 'Mac' Leyland. One of the great strengths of the British Army regimental system is that the two are rarely strangers and for 1RRF this was no exception as the two had known each other as 2/Lt and L/Cpl since 1973 with operational service together in South Armagh and Cyprus during the Turkish invasion of 1974 where the refugee problem was similar to that encountered in the Balkans.

Lieutenant Colonel Minter relayed his requirements and expectations.* It was only those commanders with no interest in ending the conflict that proved really problematical. However, the fundamental difficulty lay in the fact that any agreement made at one place or time was not necessarily relayed up and down the chain of command of that particular faction with the result that it was often not implemented on the ground.

Subjects for discussion ranged from recent cease-fire violations to the opening of roads across the confrontation lines to allow freedom of movement and the renewal of economic activity. This required considerable ground work by the battalion liaison officers who travelled many miles investigating each cease-fire violation and reporting these incidents up the chain of command. Their efforts however helped to build trust and confidence among the warring factions and the populace itself which was to pay dividends later in the tour once the battalion became part of IFOR. Other tasks that fell to the battalion following the RJC meetings were the laying of 'hotlines' across no man's land to enable the warring factions to talk to one another and to organise the exchange of displaced persons (DP) and dead bodies, as well as monitoring refugee movements between the various faction areas.

It was while undertaking a similar task that the battalion suffered its first casualties when, on Sunday 22 October, it was tasked with supervising the rescue of some HVO Croat soldiers who had fallen into the Ugar River gorge between the HVO and BSA frontlines in an area presumed to be mined. Neither side yet trusted each other sufficiently to allow a unilateral rescue. Accordingly, 12 Platoon, together with an UNMO team from Banja Luka, established a strong UN presence in the gorge and along the frontlines to either side. With HVO engineers in the lead, the Fusiliers accompanied a Royal Engineer EOD team assisting the operation. The patrol moved up the gorge behind the HVO soldiers followed by Captain Jones RE and Lieutenant Justin Henzie, the Fusiliers platoon commander. To the rear came the main body of the Fusiliers and a medical team under Sergeant 'Hawkeye' Hawkins.

Several groups of anti-personnel mines were discovered and cleared. The patrol stopped whilst another minefield was cleared, when an explosion occurred further up the track. Sergeant Hawkins and one of the section commanders moved forward to investigate and found that Lieutenant Justin Henzie had stepped on a mine injuring himself and Captain Jones. Realising that there was still a significant threat from mines, Sergeant Hawkins instructed the section commander to move his troops back onto a hard surfaced track and to radio for helicopter assistance. He then applied first aid to the casualties, both of whom were screaming in pain. Although the Croats had a stretcher readily to hand, they refused to move and Sergeant Hawkins had to call for a couple of volunteers to bring one forward. With the assistance of Sergeant 'Buzz' Bird and Corporal Pete Cockerill, he organised the evacuation of the casualties to a safe position where he treated their wounds and administered morphine. Because the helicopter refused to fly so close to the frontlines, Sergeant Hawkins accompanied the casualties in an ambulance on the hour's drive to a rendezvous point on a football field in Mrkonjic Grad, from where the helicopter evacuatedto hospital. Lieutenant Henzie made a full recovery but Captain Jones sadly lost an eye. Further tragedy occurred on 25 October when Fusilier Gary Riches was killed and Fusilier Lee Beddoes severely injured in a shooting mishap at the X Company base at Zepce. Riches' body was repatriated on 30 October, after which the company held a wake in his memory.

The purpose of the operation to extricate the HVO soldiers from the Ugar gorge had been in vain as they were all dead but the repercussions proved fruitful as the Croats and Serbs had been made to co-operate as never before and their respect for the UN grew significantly. The Muslims however remained difficult but they were persuaded to attend an RJC meeting on the Vlasic feature on 26 October, with the Kiwi Company providing security. Chaired by the 2IC, Major Andrew Marriott, the initial meeting was a decidedly frosty affair with no handshakes but only cursory nods of acknowledgement. However the process had begun and the talks continued over the coming weeks until the meetings were often concluded with a meal and the obligatory slivovitz. On 15 November, the first tripartite RJC meeting was

* As one senior staff officer from Headquarters Sector South West confided to the present author concerning the style of command of the CO of the First Fusiliers - 'Yea, though he walked through the valley of the shadow of death, he feared no evil because he was the meanest mother f***er in the Vrbas valley'.

In the midst of dismal winter weather, X Company withdraws from Zepce to Bugojno under the threat of Mujahedeen ambush in the early morning of 17 December. The company returned to Battalion Headquarters without incident in time to prepare its vehicles for D-Day and the incursion into Serb territory at the Black Dog checkpoint at the forefront of Operation 'Resolute Rat'; the first NATO ground operation ever.

held in the Maglaj Finger in X Company's area of operations. The preparation and planning of these meetings had to be meticulous to ensure that neither one side nor the other found an excuse not to attend or co-operate.

In this instance, Major Christopher Claridge conducted a detailed reconnaissance of the Muslim side at the north west tip of the Maglaj Finger. The entrenched positions, deep bunkers and communications trenches were reminiscent of the Great War. Such was the sensitivity of the area that none of the local forces were willing to expose themselves forward of their own lines. For the OC of X Company and a small team, it was a long, lonely walk into no man's land with only their blue berets for protection. Some anti-tank mines were hastily removed by the ABiH but others were just pointed out nonchalantly, so the team carefully stayed on the hard surfaces that were still intact. When the X Company team returned to the ABiH positions, they were jokingly offered a chance to take part in a shooting competition against live targets - the Serbs. Although it was an offer that was occasionally made to UN troops, Major Claridge politely refused.

On the day of the initial RJC meeting, the CO in was in the chair and the discussions highlighted the regular cease-fire violations even as firing could be heard around the meeting site. Most of these violations had been caused by the Muslims, resulting in several fatal sniper attacks. Just as importantly, the Proximity Talks held in Dayton, Ohio, for the Peace Agreement were making good progress during November. The most intractable problem remained the division of territory between the Federation and the Republic of Serbia. Many of the maps depicting the configuration of the Agreed Cease-Fire Line had been settled at RJC meetings chaired by the Fusiliers. Throughout November, the Reconnaissance Platoon patrolled the confrontation line and provided Global Positioning System readings to allow precise maps to be drawn and agreed by the FWF for submission to the negotiations in Dayton, Ohio.

On 30 November, just as the weather was getting into the grip of winter, Z Company began their return to UK with the prospect of an exercise in Kenya after Christmas. Y Company under the command of Major Philip Macey replaced them in Bosnia and deployed to the Shoe Factory in the desolated town of Mrkonjic Grad on 6 December. At the same time, the Reconnaissance Platoon was tasked with establishing a presence at Sipovo and left Bugojno with five days rations. After a ten-hour delay at one checkpoint, the platoon moved into a cardboard factory in the town in freezing weather; as the platoon commander observed - 'It soon looked like the underneath of Waterloo Bridge', but all the Fusiliers were grateful for the thermal insulating properties of cardboard. This coincided with the Peace Implementation Conference in London and the knowledge that the area known as the Anvil where Sipovo was situated was to be returned by the Croats to the Serbs. Accordingly, in time honoured fashion, the Croats began to loot and burn every town and village in the region. In Sipovo itself, there were no civilians remaining but about 1,500 HVO troops who indulged in widespread looting and destruction. On one night, almost 40 houses were torched by drunken HVO soldiers, followed by the warehouse adjoining the cardboard factory where the Fusiliers were based. The Reconnaissance Platoon remained there for three weeks on the basis that possession was the only law recognised in Bosnia and then only by force.

By day, the platoon patrolled in all directions to report on troop dispositions and the scale of destruction taking place. By now, their five day issue of rations had been exhausted and they were obliged to barter for chickens from the villages they passed for want of resupply from the battalion. Acting on the words of counsel from his father that ‘Looting is for profit while scavenging is for comfort’ (Colonel Ian Cartwright CBE, formerly SAS and CO of the 3rd Battalion), Captain Guy Cartwright obtained sufficient food to feed the platoon before the QM’s department was able to force their way through the numerous checkpoints to Sipovo. Indeed, the first supply convoy was only allowed through after the platoon’s LAD had repaired the car belonging to the chief of police in the town. In mid-December, the platoon moved to the Shoe Factory in Mrkonjic Grad to be co-located with Y Company and then to Zepce to cover the withdrawal of X Company. Thereafter, it returned to battalion headquarters at Bugojno for some much needed maintenance and preparations for a fundamental change in operating procedures.

UNPROFOR TO IFOR

On 14 December 1995, the General Framework Agreement for Peace endorsed at Dayton Ohio, was signed and ratified by all parties in Paris. NATO created a Peace Implementation Force which was known henceforth as IFOR. Its purpose was to ensure the compliance of all the combatants, now termed the Former Warring Factions (FWF), to the peace agreement. Fundamental to this coercion was the recognition that NATO was willing and able to employ weapon systems of overwhelming firepower as compared to the ageing Soviet designs of the FWF. Furthermore, with the deployment of American ground forces in the Balkans, the political will of the western powers was being vividly demonstrated, backed by three multi-national divisions drawn from most NATO countries. This was reflected in the new British codename for the Bosnian theatre of operations of Operation ‘Resolute’, although NATO called the overall enterprise Operation ‘Joint Endeavour’.

The 1st Fusiliers Battlegroup came under the command of the British led Multi-National Division South West based at Gornji Vakuf. The change to IFOR required another major reorganisation for the battalion with the companies moving to new locations across the area of operations. X Company was ordered to deploy to Bugojno but the withdrawal from the EKO Factory which was scheduled for 16 December was delayed following intelligence that the Mujahedeen were planning an ambush of the company. Three days earlier, five Mujahedeen had been shot dead near Checkpoint B7 by HVO military police and passions

DIARY OF LIEUTENANT COLONEL TREVOR MINTER
Tuesday 19 December 1995
Tomorrow we cross the line. It has been a long time coming in this scarred and troubled corner of Europe but the conditions now seem right for a more robust international intervention. I doubt whether it could have been done earlier because when people are determined to kill each other there is very little a third party can do to stop them. However since the Dayton Accord began to take shape people are starting to believe that this, the 37th cease-fire, might be the one that holds.

We have spent our last days in the UN Force paving the way for tomorrow through intense negotiations. The critical question on the lips of the warring factions is whether we will shoot them when we become IFOR! This clearly reflects a sense of guilt for the appalling way they have treated the international community over the last few years. But tomorrow the mandate changes, the rules change and our approach will change.

We do not know if this will be bloodless or whether we will have to fight our way through - but we will get through. With the full weight of NATO behind us we feel a mixture of outward confidence and private apprehension. One way or another a piece of history will be made tomorrow and we are privileged to have a lead role in it. I pray the fates are with us.

Members of the Recce Pl paint into history the white colour scheme of UNPROFOR, including Fus McClelland, L/Cpl Hornsby, Fus Cooper, Cpl Duffy, Cpl Duthie, Sgt Simpson, Fus Pate with Fus Bell on top of the turret painting the Sabre in tactical camouflage colours just prior to D-Day. The paint was still wet when Operation ‘Resolute Rat’ was launched on 20 December 1995.

WO2 Stacey and WO2 Hill mark the change from UNPROFOR to IFOR with the UN blue berets and flag being replaced by the beret and hackle and the Union Flag. This ceremony actually took place on 19 December 1995 for the benefit of the world's press to be broadcast on the actual day that NATO superceded the United Nations for military operations in Bosnia. MOD

were running high. Taking advantage of a thick blanket of fog, X Company, minus a small rear party, departed the Maglaj Finger in its Saxon APCs at 0730 hours on 17 December and returned to Bugojno without further incident, although there were a few scares on the way when unidentified vehicles nosed their way into the convoy. On the following day, 4 Platoon was given the disagreeable task of providing security for the exchange of bodies between Muslim and Serbian representatives. The latter turned up with the remains in individually tagged body bags. The Muslims, however, drove up in a truck loaded with putrefying corpses that had only recently been disinterred. Stacked like cordwood in the back and left out in the snow overnight, the cadaver on top of the pile was wrapped in Christmas paper.

By the terms of the Dayton Agreement, 20 December was chosen as the day for the transfer of authority for military operations in Bosnia from UNPROFOR to NATO. In the days leading up to it, there was frantic activity at Bugojno and in the other 1st Fusiliers Battlegroup locations as the vehicles were changed from their overall white colour scheme back to green and black tactical camouflage; as the CO observed - 'UNPROFOR was painted into history without regrets'. On 19 December, the First Fusiliers held a parade to mark the occasion in front of the world's press when the pale blue UN berets were discarded to be replaced by the familiar red and white hackle. Similarly, the new IFOR logo was painted on all their vehicles. With no inkling as to the possible reaction of the warring factions, the First Fusiliers prepared for war. The orders for the first NATO ground operation ever were given by 3rd Division via brigade headquarters in a document so comprehensive that it ran to 42 specific tasks and 26 annexes, as well as many appendices, whereas the operations order for the Iron Division on D-Day 1944 had run to just five pages. Unfortunately, there were several logistical problems with supplies being late to arrive from Split so that many vehicles deployed on operations with wet camouflage paint and without Union flags or air marker panels which understandably troubled many Fusiliers: two brothers of victims of the blue on blue in the Gulf were still serving with the battalion in Bosnia.

After the frustrations of UNPROFOR, NATO forces were now granted total freedom of movement and, by the new rules of engagement, were able to use lethal force if threatened or thwarted. Whereas previously the Fusiliers had jokingly learnt such useful Serbo-Croat phrases as - 'Please do not chain me to this bridge', they now added more seriously - 'NATO - nactjei stan ili pucan' (NATO - stop or I fire). However, there were tensions right to the end. In a preliminary deployment during the night before D-Day, X Company moved in convoy from Bugojno to Mrkonjic Grad, accompanied by Martin Bell of the BBC. As they passed through a Croat checkpoint where ordinarily they would have stopped, the HVO soldiers opened fire when they saw Martin Bell's civilian four-wheel drive vehicle (an incident he later stated as being one of the prime reasons he decided to retire as a war correspondent). Further down the road, X Company was obliged to stop and a furious argument ensued with the HVO. Conscious that the new rules of engagement were not yet in force, the OC of X Company was obliged to negotiate the safe passage of the convoy whereas, on the following day, such episodes could be met with force if necessary.

It was now time to put IFOR to the test. As Lieutenant Colonel Trevor Minter stated - 'Let no man stand in our way'. The 1st Fusiliers Battlegroup was the only infantry battalion in place across the whole of the country so it fell to them to assert NATO's authority on D-Day. At 1200 hours on 20 December, Operation 'Resolute Rat' was launched with X Company as NATO's lead unit on the ground. Led by the CVR(T) Sabre of Corporal Paul Goodwin in Callsign Two Four, the Fusiliers crossed the HVO front lines into Serbian territory at a place that was promptly named Black Dog after a stray that had been adopted at Headquarters Sector South West. With 4 Platoon leading, Company TAC HQ and 5 Platoon established Black Dog South at a cafe that had previously been used as an RJC site, while 6 Platoon set up Black Dog North astride the Serb lines. To general satisfaction, bunkers and checkpoints were bulldozed flat by Sapper plant equipment as a press contingent of over 50 and numerous general and staff officers looked on; all of whom expected to be fed by the battalion during the proceedings. Royal Engineer EOD (Explosive Ordnance Disposal) teams supervised the clearing of mines as the advance continued with B Squadron of the Light Dragoons passing through the Fusiliers on their way to Banja Luka in the Bosnian Serb heartland.

It was Martin Bell of the BBC who pointed out that the 'Rat' in Operation 'Resolute Rat' means 'War' in Serbo-Croat. Whether this influenced the exhausted Serbian forces remains uncertain but in the event none of the Former Warring Factions offered any resistance on D-Day and during the weeks that followed. Operation 'Resolute Rat' was a complete success but it had been a bluff. As the 1st Fusiliers Battlegroup was spread so thinly, several of the Saxon APCs that crossed the frontlines through Black Dog were manned by only their drivers and commanders with no troops in the back. The total battlegroup reserves on D-Day were six Fusiliers of the Milan Platoon in a single Saxon and the CVR(T) Sabre of the Reconnaissance Platoon commander. There is no doubt that much of this success was due to the weeks of patient work in the RJCs but as Sun Tzu observed - 'The best victories in war are those achieved without fighting'.

ENFORCING THE PEACE

As reinforcements including heavy armour and artillery were dispatched from the UK to augment IFOR, the Area of Operations of 1st Fusiliers Battlegroup was reduced to more manageable levels and it was given more resources to execute its tasks as the main effort of the 4th Armoured Brigade plan. At the same time, those contingents that were not part of NATO left Bosnia. Despite having been comprehensively beaten at rugby union, the Fusiliers were greatly disappointed to see the New Zealand company cease operations on D-Day as they had proved to be highly professional and dependable allies. After the traditional Hakka, the match had been played on a soccer pitch littered with empty small arms cases in Stari Vitez during December. Although of only company strength, the Kiwis accumulated a total of 15 tries against a modest scoreline to the Fusiliers.

However, other familiar faces arrived as Z Company did not, as expected, escape to the sunshine of Kenya for Exercise 'Grand Prix' but returned to a winter in Bosnia after a two week break in Catterick just before Christmas. They redeployed into theatre under the command of Major David Paterson on 23 December. Having just completed an SO2 position at the HQ ARRC (Allied Command Europe Rapid Reaction Corps) where the structure and objectives of IFOR had been devised, Major Paterson was given a simple set of orders. In a prime example of 'mission command', the CO told him - 'Take your company north of the confrontation line, find somewhere to live and implement the plan which you know all about'. On 21 December, they moved to an isolated base at Skender Vakuf in Serbian territory where they occupied the Knezevo Working Unit, a dilapidated flour mill and granary. From there, the CQMS, Colour Sergeant Dennis Kennedy, had to make a 320-kilometre round trip three or four times a week to keep the company supplied with provisions and stores; a typical example of the stalwart work undertaken by the quartermaster's department which served all elements of the battlegroup and the local populace. Z Company remained at Skender Vakuf monitoring Serb movements until 18 January. For the one month that Z Company was in the

On a school pitch in Vitez littered with empty cartridge cases, a 1st Battalion side under Capt Turner took on the Kiwi Company under Major Martin at rugby union and were comprehensively beaten - the final score 65-6. Andrew Martin subsequently became the coach of New Zealand's national team, the All Blacks.

Fus Dixon stands guard at the Black Dog check point during late December 1995 beside a Saxon APC of X Company fitted with snow chains for the bitter winter conditions. Despite its basic configuration and limited cross-country ability, the Saxon has proved to be well suited to peace support operations in Bosnia, being more economical to operate than Warrior and less overtly aggressive in appearance. MOD

PRESS COMMENT - MARTIN BELL

'We in the press, though we are hardly soldierly ourselves (we would never pass a sergeant major's inspection), have become connoisseurs of the infantry battalions passing through Bosnia. They come and they go, while we less fortunately seem to stay for ever. We note with interest and sometimes amusement the differences between them, in their style, their traditions and ways of doing things. (I must declare an interest here. I was once a corporal - even briefly an acting sergeant - in a now defunct infantry regiment, the Suffolk Regiment, long since amalgamated into something vaguely Anglian. So I know of whereof I speak, or at least pretend to.)

'We have developed instincts about these things. We took to the Royal Regiment of Fusiliers at once - or the First Fusiliers as they like to be called, to distinguish themselves from the other RRF, the Rapid Reaction Force, (and for that matter other Fusiliers, but we are in deep waters here). We liked their no-nonsense approach to Bosnia's complexities. And we loved the parade they held on 'D-Day' minus one, to exchange their UN blue beret for the familiar red and white hackle. This was when one of the Fusiliers remarked, 'Now I feel like a real soldier again.' It was also when the pipes and drums, in the snow of Bugojno, celebrated their release from the UN by playing the theme from 'The Great Escape'. And it was when the Commanding Officer, with arms akimbo somewhat in the manner of General Patton, stood in front of the massed ranks of X and Y Companies and sent a message to the bandit-commanders in Bosnia's hinterland, - 'Let no man stand in our way. Next I look forward to 'Colonel Minter - The Movie!'

'The First Fusiliers reminded me in some ways of the first British soldiers we dealt with in Bosnia, the Cheshire regiment more than three years earlier. The Fusiliers, like the Cheshires, were well led. And like the Cheshires they didn't seek publicity but attracted it especially when on the day of IFOR's deployment across front lines they were the spearhead of NATO's first ever ground operation. That was what I shall forever remember, as a humble ex-corporal, as the day when a corps commanded a battalion which commanded a company - X Company of the First Fusiliers. Its OC, Major Chris Claridge and its Sergeant Major, 'Jock' Stacey, became instant media stars, and deservedly so.

'We like the Fusiliers. Good luck to them. And may they - and not their wives - look forward to shining both their medals.'

Knezevo Working Unit, the factory manager tried to charge IFOR £13,330 for rent, damages and utilities, including £4,477 as the telephone bill. This was a typical example of Balkan rapacity in extracting monies from the peacekeeping forces. As no utilities were provided and there was nothing left to damage, it was little short of extortion; the fact that Fusiliers in the improvised guardroom were able to repair and reconnect the telephone to the international network is neither here nor there.

Whilst maintaining a strong, round the clock presence at Black Dog, X Company moved to the Bohac Dam on 23 December. This hydroelectric installation was vital to the region as it generated power both for the Federation and for the Serbs. It was supervised by Croats but lay in Serbian territory and its continued operation was essential for both political and humanitarian reasons. Accordingly, the Fusiliers were tasked with protecting the site and its personnel. As usual in such circumstances, any building that had survived the war and was suitable as a company base was invariably in an absolute disgusting state, with all its fixtures and fittings smashed and its floors inundated with human excrement, as none of the combatants appeared to have any notion of field latrines. Christmas Eve was spent cleaning sufficient of the building to create basic living and feeding areas for the company to hold a convivial Christmas lunch, thanks to the inventive powers of the battalion's chefs who improvised an oven out of a filing cabinet.

Operations did not stop at all over the Christmas period. On Christmas Eve, OC X Company held meetings on the confrontation line to agree access for Serbian engineers to the dam, as they were to take over control of the complex under the supervision of the Fusiliers. On Christmas Day, Captain Ian 'Guns' Harrison, the 2IC of X Company, led a patrol into no man's land to escort engineers that were repairing the power lines to Banja Luka. Y Company spent the days before Christmas locating Croat military positions along the cease-fire line, including weapons and minefields, to the north and west of their base in Mrkonjic Grad. They also celebrated a traditional Christmas with the Drums leading the officers and senior NCOs as they dispensed 'gunfire' at breakfast followed by a carol service - gunfire being a cup of tea liberally laced with rum or vice versa.

W Company remained at Coralici Camp but since D-Day, it had been attached to the Warrior mounted BRITBAT 1, 2nd Battalion The Light Infantry. As such, it was the most distant sub-unit within the battalion, which gave rise to the observation by Captain Bob Broadbent that - 'Nobody can hear you scream in Bihac'. As with all the companies, Christmas was almost ruined by the failure of the supply system to provide the traditional fare in time. It was only through the sterling efforts of the Quartermaster, Captain Boris Spence, and the SQMS, WO2 Steve Morgan, that turkeys and mince pies appeared on the Fusiliers' tables. Similarly, every unit was visited by Santa Claus dispensing largesse although he bore a startling resemblance to the RSM, WO1 'Mac' Leyland.

In a scene reminiscent of a James Bond film set, X Company set up base at the Bocac Dam on Christmas Eve 1995. Situated between Mrkonjic Grad and Banja Luka, the dam was a critical source of power to the Serbs while lying in Bosnian Croat held territory. As part of the Dayton Agreement, it was handed back to the Serbs with 1RRF ensuring it was not sabotaged first by the Croats. MOD

With the Regimental Crest resplendent above the letters 'IFOR', a Saxon APC overtakes an antiquated horse and cart in a land of antiquated attitudes during a patrol near Jajce. The Saxon APCs in Bosnia are fitted with an L37 7.62mm machine gun turret for self-defence. MOD

All the while, the battalion was preparing for the next phase in the peace accord which was the creation of a Zone of Separation (ZOS) between the FWF to a depth of two kilometres on each side of the Agreed Cease-fire Line. During the last days of December, W Company began operations in an area around the Vlasic Mountain north of Vitez while they established a base at Turbe. Once more the building was in a frightful state as it had previously been used as a munitions factory by the Croats and unexploded ordnance and asbestos lay around in abundance which had to be rendered safe by the Royal Engineers. On 29 December, C Company of 2nd Battalion The Light Infantry joined the battlegroup to augment its firepower for the forthcoming operation to create the zones of separation.

For the past month, Y Company had been busy in the Anvil conducting anti-looting patrols and liaising with the HVO about the provisions of the Dayton Accord. Looting was rife in all the company areas as the HVO prepared to depart. In one instance, the CO's 'R' Group chanced upon some HVO looters pillaging a house. Captain Jim Landon, the operations officer, got out and demanded that they stop. Since they outnumbered the Fusiliers considerably, the HVO soldiers ignored him and continued to load their spoils onto a truck. Fortuitously, a troop of Challengers of The Queen's Royal Hussars happened to be nearby and the CO summoned them to the scene. When one tank rolled to a stop with its 120mm main armament at a short distance from the windscreen of the truck, Lieutenant Colonel Minter took delight in informing them that the rules of the game had changed. The HVO soldiers decided to return the plunder to its rightful place. As Challengers were not always to hand, some company commanders threatened to implement a 'shoot to kill' policy for looters. A policy that was conveyed to the FWF with the result that looting diminished significantly.

As the principal town in the region to be returned to the Serbs, Mrkonjic Grad had been virtually destroyed since its capture by the HVO during Operation 'Storm' in the previous autumn. At the time, Y Company arrived, the area was virtually devoid of life with no sign of humans or livestock. Many had been driven out or slaughtered by the Croats whose preferred method of ethnic cleansing was to execute Serbs and then sodomise their bodies as the ultimate degradation. Others were decapitated with chainsaws. However no faction had a monopoly of evil and each was as loathsome as the others which exasperated the Fusiliers beyond measure and taxed their patience as peacekeepers to the full; a contemporary definition within the Fusiliers stated - 'Being impartial as a peacekeeper means being equally pissed off with all sides'.

On 7 January, Serb troops began withdrawing from the frontlines early so as to celebrate the Orthodox Christian Christmas although some still remained as a rearguard. One week later M-Day arrived and the FWF began their withdrawal from the zones of separation which had to be completed by 19 January. Thereafter any FWF military forces discovered inside the ZOS were subject to destruction by IFOR troops. All the while the Fusilier companies monitored the numbers of troops and equipment leaving and then verified that all the military positions had been vacated. Compliance was encouraged with the deployment of

B Squadron The Queen's Royal Hussars in its Challenger 1 MBTs and 26 Regiment Royal Artillery with its AS90 155mm self-propelled howitzers, as well as the Warriors of 2nd Battalion The Light Infantry and the Saxons all in the First Fusiliers Battlegroup. The operation went according to plan with all the FWF complying within the deadline and without trouble. No one was allowed to return to these areas in the interim so each of the companies deployed troops on the ground to create checkpoints so as to deny access to where it was not permitted. They usually comprised a Saxon APC parked across the road or track in such a manner that all traffic could be checked and regulated. The irony of now being the party manning all the checkpoints across central Bosnia-Herzegovina was not lost on the Fusiliers.

Despite the success of the IFOR plans so far, the dangers for the peacekeeping forces remained formidable as the next task was to verify the exact locations of the FWF within ten kilometres of the ZOS; often in areas close to the former frontlines incorporating extensive minefields most of which were not recorded on any map. This problem was particularly acute for Z Company which was operating across the cease-fire line in Skender Vakuf. As the only company in Serb held territory, they had no knowledge of the ground or the dispositions of the Serb forces who had to be advised of the requirements of the peace agreement. As part of the First Fusiliers Battlegroup, C Squadron The Light Dragoons suffered a tragedy on Sunday 28 January 1996 when a CVR(T) Spartan struck a mine and the crew of three were killed. Lieutenant Richard Madden and Troopers John Kelly and Andrew Ovington had made the ultimate sacrifice in the cause of peace.

At the beginning of February, the Anvil, also known as the Devil's Anvil, became the focus of the battalion's activities as D+45 approached when the area had to be cleared of Croats and returned to the Serbs. X Company remained at the Bohac Dam and the Black Dog crossing point while Y and W Companies continued to dominate the towns of Mrkonjic Grad and Sipovo respectively. Battalion HQ joined W Company in Sipovo. On D+31, Z Company handed over its base at Skender Vakuf to a battalion from the Netherlands but not before it had witnessed the installation of showers, a laundry, satellite phones and other creature comforts within days of the Dutch arrival. Despite the fact that the battalion had been based at Bugojno for months, the British Army only provided a shower facility a few days before it departed. In yet another move, Z Company deployed to Gornji Ribnik inside the Anvil where once again there was not even running water. When they arrived there were no civilians in the town and it had been systematically looted by the withdrawing HVO who had also killed virtually all of the livestock in the countryside. Only one 83-year old man could be found in the western part of the Anvil where formerly 58,000 people had lived. For months, he had sheltered in the woods living off the land and enduring what he believed to be the third world war in his lifetime. Two pigs were also found which were adopted by the company with the names of 'Lucky' and 'Blind Pugh' until they became bored with the Fusiliers and wandered away. Every other person and creature had been either driven out of the Anvil or killed by the Federation forces; often in unspeakable ways.

As the Anvil was bereft of electricity, running water, hospitals, schools or even housing fit for

Once the area known as the Anvil had been returned to the Serbs, its former inhabitants were desperate to return to their devastated homes despite the fact that the conditions were appalling without even the most basic amenities. The Fusiliers had to control the traffic as the returnees arrived by all forms of transport such as this tractor and trailer being searched by Fusiliers while Cpl Dear conducts a census at the Black Dog check point. MOD

human habitation, Serb returnees and DPREs (Displaced Persons and Refugees) were strongly encouraged not to come back until the more clement weather of the spring time. In the meantime, it was hoped that the devastated infrastructure could be repaired prior to their return. On Sunday 4 February 1996, the first day that they were allowed, over 4,000 Serbs crossed the checkpoint at Black Dog into the Anvil and at a rate of 1,000 a day thereafter. At this time, the primary role of the battlegroup was to provide security and reassurance to the returning population while ensuring no Serb military forces returned to the area as well; uniformed police officers equipped with pistols were the only civilians allowed to carry arms. The responsibility for supervising the return of the Serb refugees and displaced persons to the Anvil fell to X Company. Within days, the aid agencies were overwhelmed by the number of returnees. At the outset, the distribution of food was the responsibility of local officials but with their usual inefficiency and corrupt practices, the whole system soon broke down and the Fusiliers were obliged to take over. In the village of Bocac, where Serb refugees were now returning, there was aid to be had but the UNHCR had failed to organise and oversee distribution in the outlying ares. Seizing the initiative, Major Claridge set up a registration system for the village, created and issued the necessary identity cards and oversaw the distribution of the aid. The Fusiliers also cleaned and repaired the village clinic which was once more able to dispense medical care for the villagers.

In Mrkonjic Grad, the situation was particularly dire as the UNHCR aid warehouse had been looted and the local authorities had allowed the situation to descend into anarchy. When the Fusiliers found that the elderly and infirm were being robbed and abandoned, the OC of Y Company, Major Philip Macey, acted promptly and decisively. While the local bureaucrats wrung their hands and most returned to the comfort of Banja Luka, the Fusiliers effectively took over the town and instituted a benevolent autocracy. The first task was to replenish the UNHCR warehouse which was now under armed guard by the Fusiliers. Food distribution was coupled with a local census to gauge the scale of the new found population while at the same time being very careful not to create a dependency culture among the returnees.

Similarly, oil heaters were issued for want of electricity but only to those who registered at the local information and liaison centre set up by the Fusiliers. Their needs could then be co-ordinated with the various aid agencies and work allocated as each adult was obliged to assist in the repair of the town's infrastructure. A food kitchen was set up. The hospital was cleaned and a clinic was created with UN assistance. Other projects were undertaken such as the opening of another bakery. Hitherto, the only bakery in Mrkonjic Grad was owned by the local minister for food who forcibly discouraged any competitors to maintain his artificially high prices. By such means, the Fusiliers promoted basic economic activity and overcame the inertia of the communist mentality imbued in all the local officials. By the time, the battalion had completed its tour on 29 February some semblance of normality had returned although the ethnic communities remained as divided as ever.

During the final weeks of the 1RRF tour in February 1996, a pair of Fusiliers and their Saxon APC of Y Company guard the aid distribution warehouse in Mrkonjic Grad following the riots and looting that happened when it was under UNHCR supervision. At this time, Y Company was running the complete civic administration of the devastated town.

OPERATION LODESTAR - MAY TO NOVEMBER 1997

Lieutenant Colonel Gary Cass assumed command of the 2nd Battalion The Royal Regiment of Fusiliers at midday on 10 January 1997, as he passed through a check-in desk at Zagreb airport following his initial reconnaissance of Bosnia. The battalion was soon to embark on a deployment to Bosnia as part of NATO's Stabilisation Force or SFOR, the successor to IFOR whose mandate had expired after a year. During January and February, the battalion conducted Bosnia training, culminating in Exercise 'Green Star' at Sennelager which was held to determine its 'fitness for role' for the Bosnian theatre of operations. Having only recently converted to the armoured infantry role in Warrior, the battalion acquitted itself well and then took leave over the Easter period. On their return to Celle, the Warrior fleet was modified with the addition of Chobham armour panels for increased protection against crew served anti-armour weapons. St George's Day was celebrated early on April 12 because the advance party was flying to Banja Luka on the actual day.

The remainder of the battalion deployed to Bosnia during the last week of April. The Warriors disembarked from the Royal Fleet Auxiliary *Sea Crusader* at the port of Split on the Dalmatian coast and were conveyed inland by RLC tank transporters. With over 700 Fusiliers, the Second Fusiliers Battlegroup assumed command of the Vrbas Valley Area of Operations (AO) in central Bosnia-Herzegovina at midday on 28 April 1997 from 1st Battalion The Green Howards. The total included approximately 70 reservists and members of the TA from numerous cap badges with one from The Black Watch in C Company who would only wear his regimental red hackle in his Tam O'Shanter and not that of the Fusiliers. Battlegroup Headquarters was situated in the Tom Factory in Gornji Vakuf. B Company was in the same town at the Precision Factory with C Company at the Boiler Factory in Jajce and Echelon at Donji Vakuf. A Company was detached under the command of The Royal Scots Dragoon Guards Battle Group (later that of The King's Royal Hussars) and was located at the Shoe Factory at Mrkonjic Grad. Fire Support Company was split across the battlegroup with the company headquarters forming the nucleus of the G5 cell with the OC, Major Guy Moncur, acting as the senior G5 officer. The Mortar Platoon provided an MFC party in support of A Company. The remainder of the platoon reinforced C Company in Jajce as infantry mounted in Saxon and in their designated role in FV432s. The Anti-Tank Platoon retained its Warriors with a total of 20 firing posts. A section was deployed with A Company with the others reinforcing B Company in Gornji Vakuf as infantry and in the anti-tank role. The Reconnaissance Platoon in its eight CVR(T) Scimitars acted as the battlegroup reserve and was based in the Tom Factory at Gornji Vakuf. The battlegroup also had Artillery Tactical Groups from 4 Regiment RA and, from late June, 40 Regiment RA, under command as well as a Tactical Air Control Party.

The battlegroup AO extended over 4,594 square kilometres astride the Vrbas Valley in a strategically important region of central Bosnia, stretching from Banja Luka in Republika Srpska across the Inter Entity Boundary Line to the Neretva River south of Prozor: the town where the war between the Bosnian-Croats and Bosnian-Muslims began in 1992. In effect, it was a microcosm of the country as a whole with towns and villages containing all three ethnic groups. It was also a curious mixture of the medieval and the modern, with horse drawn ploughs juxtaposed Mercedes Benz motor cars and water wells with satellite dishes. For the most part, the region was both beautiful and fertile but everywhere it was blemished with the charred and gutted remains of buildings as evidence of the desperate war that had caused the deaths or expulsion of approximately half the population. Slowly but surely, life in Bosnia was returning to normality with rural communities producing basic foodstuffs while small scale industry re-emerged as the local infrastructure was repaired.

The mission of the Second Fusiliers was to maintain a secure environment in which democratic institutions and peace could grow and flourish. Such conditions were vital for the thousands of displaced persons and their families to return to whatever remained of their homes from which they had been 'ethnically cleansed'. The Former Warring Factions, now termed Entity Armed Forces, were confined to barracks and were only allowed out to train under the close scrutiny of SFOR. Any infringement was liable to be severely punished by the overwhelming firepower of NATO on the ground and from the air. In tandem with the military mission, the battalion undertook many tasks in support of civilian agencies helping to

The life and times of a modern infantry regiment are nothing if not full. On the following pages, various aspects of training and operations conducted by The Royal Regiment of Fusiliers between 1999 and 2000 are depicted in the sidebars and the main text in addition to the Bosnia tour of 2RRF. Here, dawn breaks on Day Six of Exercise 'Ulan Eagle 99' in Poland and the battalion has not slept for three days as the CO of 2RRF, Lt Col Murray-Playfair, with WO2 Millington as the gunner in the turret, prepares to lead his Warriors in a river crossing through the early morning mist. SD

rebuild the ravaged land. Nevertheless, an atmosphere of animosity prevailed among the different communities and civil strife was never far below the surface as events across the area of operations were to show. As the various elements of the battalion were so widely dispersed across the area of operations, the exploits of the three rifle companies are related separately with those of the Fusiliers Battlegroup first.

B COMPANY GROUP - HARNBY'S HEROES

Initially under the command of Major Bill Aldridge, B Company Group comprised some 177 personnel and 50 vehicles, including 25 Warriors, and 12 Milan firing posts from Fire Support Company. It assumed command of its area of operations and the base at the Precision Factory in Gornji Vakuf from B Company 1st Battalion The Green Howards on 1 May 1997. The Precision Factory was once a prosperous engineering complex; now leased to SFOR at an exorbitant rate by an absentee landlord residing in Switzerland. The camp was shared with a squadron of Sappers, a Signals detachment, a medical centre and a mobile laundry that doubled as a swimming pool. The Fusiliers lived in two or four man 'Corimec' cabins and whilst life was sparse it was comfortable.

With an area of 1,000 square kilometres encompassing 22 weapon cantonment sites and three major towns, the company inherited the largest AO. It was dominated by numerous mountains and forests in the centre of the Vrbas Valley with the Muslim town of Bugojno in the north and the staunchly Croat Prozor to the south. Day to day operations consisted of routine reassurance patrolling and the monitoring of the various Entity Armed Forces and the cantonment sites for their weapons. The majority of the company group operated from the Precision Factory while platoons rotated through the Prozor Platoon House for a month at a time in the south of the AO. This included the responsibility for manning the Tito's Fist Rebro Site on the Makljen Feature. It is worthy of note that just as the 1st Battalion had encountered their first checkpoint at Tito's Fist so did the 2nd Battalion. A patrol of B Company encountered an illegal checkpoint and immediately challenged the policemen manning the position. The patrol acted in a robust manner and forced them to move on; once they had confiscated their warrant cards and reported their activities to the International Police Task Force (IPTF) for censure.

At the end of May, Major Guy Harnby joined the Company as OC from Media Ops in Battalion Headquarters. Despite the geographical separation of the company groups, mutual support was given to each other as the need arose and various platoons of B Company deployed at several times during the summer in support of both A and C Companies. In particular, 7 Platoon under the command of 2nd Lieutenant Hamish McPherson reinforced C Company in Banja Luka in July during a tense time of political unrest. In August, 5 (Drums) Platoon under the command of Captain Stuart Nicholson assisted C Company as it strove to prevent ethnic tension directed towards Muslim returnees in the Jajce area. With their customary flexibility, the Drummers also carried out some ceremonial duties with several important engagements, including the Queen's Birthday Parades at the embassies in Sarajevo and Zagreb.

B Company supported the two firepower demonstrations staged by Multi National Division South West in the run up to the municipal elections in mid-September. These were held to convince the various factions that SFOR had such overwhelming firepower that any attempt to disrupt the elections would be met with severe retribution. The elections required much preparation and planning, with the creation of polling stations and their protection to forestall intimidation. In the event, the elections were held with few problems and any minor potential flash point was defused by the judicious deployment of a Warrior or two.

For the most part, the B Company area of operations remained quiet throughout the summer which allowed it to conduct some fruitful training on the Glamoc Ranges and at the large training area at Krupa where the Battlegroup Training Wing was based. Although the company did not have the opportunity to deploy on exercise as a whole, all of the platoons were able to conduct both mounted and dismounted live firing exercises at the Manjaca Ranges. Throughout its tour, the company group was very active in G5 projects in support of the local populace. In conjunction with 29 Squadron Royal Engineers, it undertook the complete refurbishment of a school gymnasium in Uskoplje. The gymnasium was dedicated

In a society that had been force fed state propaganda for years, the people of Bosnia Herzegovina were grateful for reliable information about events in their country. Cpl Payne of B Company 2RRF dispenses copies of the SFOR newspaper *'Mostovi'*, meaning Bridges, to the locals in the streets of Bugojno; one of many G5 activities. MOD

A local interpreter facilitates a reassurance patrol in the village of Duge where the resettlement of Muslims in a Croat dominated area was one of the major successes of 2RRF's tour in Bosnia in the summer of 1997. Due to their hard work, professionalism, compassion and humour, the Second Fusiliers achieved their principal mission of providing a secure environment in which the devastated country could be rebuilt and peace restored.

to the memory of Diana Princess of Wales and was opened by the British Ambassador to Bosnia, Mr Charles Crawford, on 17 September 1997.

There were many other projects in the area of operations that the company group accomplished to the benefit of the inhabitants. In particular, the company devoted considerable time and effort to fac the return and resettlement of Muslim refugees to the picturesque village of Duge, among a predominatly hostile Croat population who had threatened that the Muslims 'may plant seeds in the ground but they won't live to harvest the crops'. With regular patrolling of the village and the surrounding area, a secure and stable environment was provided which allowed some 30 displaced families to return to their ancestral homes. Duge was deemed to be a great success and a prime example of the achievements of SFOR and the international community.

The company was involved in wider activities such as the distribution of UNHCR aid to all the factions, many of whom lived in isolated villages and settlements in the mountainous terrain. The families back in Germany were also not forgotten. The company sergeant major, WO2 Tony 'Maggie' Margiotta, forged links back to the Fusiliers' home base at Celle via the British Forces Broadcasting Service and became a regular voice on the 'Calling the Balkans' show. This was particularly valuable after storms had caused serious damage to Trenchard Barracks during the night of 29 June.

Although the B Company Group area appeared quieter as compared to the others, it is a measure of its success that so much was achieved to enable DPREs to return and attempt to rebuild their lives. Just as importantly, it allowed them to hold the ring of the Fusilier Battle Group area whilst A and C Company Groups were deployed elsewhere.

C COMPANY GROUP - ZERO TOLERANCE

C Company took up residence in Richmond Camp, which was actually a disused boiler factory, in the town of Jajce in the middle of the battalion area of operations. The surrounding areas were mainly mountainous and wooded, dominated by a large plateau rising to some 1,200 metres called Pougarje. With its open fields and grazing sheep, this picturesque region became known to the Second Fusiliers as 'Heidi Country'. In the southern part of the AO was the bustling town of Donji Vakuf which had featured so highly in 1st Battalion's tour in 1995. C Company based one platoon in the town at Hollis House to provide a constant presence in the area. With such a diverse area of operations, the vital role of framework patrolling took many forms. In a typical week, a platoon might deploy in Warrior one day; by Blackhawk helicopter the next and then as a foot patrol in a town or on mountain bikes. Patrols lasted for anything up to three days and involved numerous tasks such as village surveys, police station searches, monitoring the activities of the various military factions and the dispersal of illegal road checkpoints, the vast majority of the population giving an unreserved welcome to the hackle.

C Company also acted as the Divisional Reserve force and in this capacity it was trained to deploy as either an armoured infantry company; as airmobile rapid reaction troops; as a mechanised infantry company or in an internal security role. The company had an additional 14 Saxons in their orbat to fulfil the mechanised infantry role for those occasions when the deployment of Warriors might be construed as too aggressive. For the duration of the tour, the company was on six hours 'notice to move' to deploy throughout the divisional area. To test this capability, the company took part in Exercise 'Joint Resolve' early in the tour when they deployed by Blackhawk helicopters to a preparation area and then met up with their Warriors at the Glamoc Ranges. There, reinforced by elements of A and B Companies, it conducted field firing as armoured infantry supported by Apache attack helicopters, AS90 self-propelled artillery and Milan ATGW. The exercise also acted a demonstration to the Entity Armed Forces of the overwhelming firepower available to SFOR.

In practice, C Company undertook several operational deployments as the divisional reserve; mainly to Banja Luka where it spent many hours in the Metal Factory waiting for the call. The first came early in July when part of the company was deployed to Prijador after the death of a PIFWC (Person Indicted For War Crimes) who had been killed by special forces after he opened fire on SFOR troops. The OC, Major James Denny, in his Land Rover and four Warriors rushed to the town over some decidedly rickety bridges in order to seal the site of the shooting to await the arrival of the Bosnian police. The latter, however, were not keen on SFOR troops being present and proved unco-operative. The local restaurant owner was also unhappy as she was losing trade so Major Denny felt constrained to buy large quantities of ice cream for his troops on the cordon in order to placate her. Subsequently, the company provided security for the funeral. As Major Denny had returned to England for the investiture of his MBE at Buckingham Palace, the latter part of this operation was commanded by the adjutant, Captain John Matthews. On 14 July, the company moved back to the Jajce and Donji Vakuf areas to assist in the return of Muslim DPREs into the Dnoluka Valley and elsewhere. Throughout the summer, this task continued with varying degrees of success as Croat opposition to any such resettlement grew.

On Minden Day, the main route to the Dnoluka Valley was blocked by vehicles and a crowd of some 300 people. Such activity presented a threat to IPTF and SFOR traffic and their freedom of movement. Despite the presence of C Company under the command of Major Guy Moncur in the absence of Major Denny on R and R, the intimidation of the Muslims continued as the Croats moved into the Dnoluka Valley itself. There, they threatened the inhabitants with firearms and iron bars to such a degree that the villages were abandoned over the next few days. SFOR's response to the incident was twofold with negotiations and mediation with the crowd organisers; village leaders and Croat authorities while at the same time maintaining a physical presence on the ground. During these disturbances, C Company deployed both static and mobile patrols of Warriors and Land Rovers, each with a fire team as the presence on the ground. The Scimitars of the Reconnaissance Platoon, as part of the battle group reserve, were also deployed as were elements of B Company to contain the rest of the area of operations. On occasions, the Fusiliers had to separate the two ethnic groups physically and act as a barrier between them. Yet again, the mandate did not allow for SFOR to become involved in civil disorder but the robust actions and professionalism of the Fusiliers undoubtedly saved many innocent lives. During this episode, the LAD Fitter Section was tasked with the removal of various roadblocks using its recovery vehicles. When this resulted in several cars, including that of the chief of police, being flattened, the REME Warriors were subsequently adorned with car silhouette kill markings in recognition of their participation in the operation.

The incidents in Jajce received much international media coverage. In the ensuing weeks, considerable interest was directed at the events and issues involved, both by the various agencies in Bosnia and the Office of the International Community's High Representative. Accordingly, it was decided that the DPREs would be given another more organised

As protection for Serbian property, the Quick Reaction Force, Callsign Zulu Two Four, deploys around the Orthodox Church at Pristina in Kosovo in April 2000 to prevent Albanian desecration, with L/Cpl Mason and Thompson as well as Fus Crossland, Moran and Ward standing guard. As part of 7 Armoured Brigade, 2RRF deployed to Kosovo in March 2000 to undertake Operation 'Agricola'. With a complement of 675, the battalion was tasked to control 150 Sq Kms of Kosovo including the capital, Pristina, with its burgeoning population of 500,000 people as against 260,000 in 1991. At the time, the city was a tinderbox with numerous criminal elements causing severe disruption and disorder, which the Fusiliers were able to contain through their constant presence on the streets. SD

opportunity to return, over the period of a week, in a phased operation arranged by the UNHCR and the Jajce municipality. Security for the operation was the responsibility of Croat and Muslim civilian police heavily monitored by the IPTF. The proceedings were underpinned by SFOR troops based on C Company Group with additional battlegroup, divisional and theatre assets. On one occasion, C Company, under the command of the 2IC Captain Jonny Laws, had elements from all four US services under tactical command including US Marines undertaking G-5 tasks, US Army Apache gunships on stand by, a US Navy combat camera crew and US Air Force P-3 Orion aircraft in overwatch. Despite this show of force, there were still several instances of intimidation including the sowing of anti-personnel mines in the gardens and grounds of the returnees' homes. Four Muslims lost feet or limbs to these dastardly devices. Corporal Paul Bland and Fusilier Lee Metcalfe performed admirably in carrying out life saving first aid after two of these tragic incidents. C Company then had to mount another operation to protect a UN demining team to clear the remainder. Such is the perversity of Bosnia-Herzegovina that the mine clearing team happened to be Serbs, protected by Fusiliers to operate in Muslim villages in a Croat dominated area whose Christian population were resisting the return of the original Bosniac residents. Nevertheless, this operation saw the largest return of DPREs in the country during 1997.

In such circumstances, the battalion was able to forestall much of the overt violence against minorities but could not repress centuries of tribal hatred and its appalling manifestation of ethnic cleansing. Throughout the tour of the Second Fusiliers, their Commanding Officer, Lieutenant Colonel Gary Cass, did his utmost to ease the plight of the returnees and refugees and achieved some significant successes, notably at Duge; but for every Duge there were still too many Dnolukas. As he recorded - 'The whole episode emphasised the complexities of Displaced Persons returns and it clearly demonstrated that at times the integrity and rigour of the civilian authorities were sadly lacking. Their weaknesses threatened the advance towards normality and that was frustrating. Conscious that the peace process would take a long time,

The commander of a Warrior of C Company, Cpl Jackson and his gunner Fus Clift, guide their driver, Fus Harvey, past a car belonging to some Displaced Persons rummaging in a rubbish tip on the road from Jajce to Kruscica. Although the military aspect of 2RRF's mission to maintain a secure environment was relatively simple to achieve, the plight of the Bosnian people and the thousands of refugees continued to be arduous throughout the battalion's tour in 1997. MOD

we set out on this tour with long-term objectives. Our presence was designed to influence the communities rather than dictate to them and we attempted to do that both directly and indirectly. Our conduct alone, as professional soldiers, was important...

'Despite the difficulties, we all felt that we had a worthwhile job to do and we were well received by the local people. On one occasion, the exiled mayor of Jajce cornered a Croatian official and demanded to know why a Croatian flag was hanging from a small school which had been turned into a DP reception centre. "This is not Croatia, this is Bosnia. That is not our flag." he said. He turned, exasperated, and looked down the hill to where a C Company Warrior was in overwatch and flying from its antenna was a small Union Jack. He pointed "That is the only flag that means something to us, without it we would not last a day".'
A symbol more potent than the powerful Warrior it adorned.

In the weeks leading up to the municipal elections, C Company Group was reinforced for their role as divisional reserve by B Company 1st Battalion The Royal Gurkha Rifles. The latter patrolled the area of operations in Saxon APCs when C Company was deployed to Banja Luka on 7 September for Operation 'Badger'. Over the night of 8/9 September, the company deployed in full riot gear to act as the final backstop to A Company in the Battle of the Buses. In the event, their IS skills were not used, much to the disappointment of company personnel as they were very keen to fire their riot guns in anger; particularly WOs Danny Massam and Mick McCarthy who wished to resolve an argument as to whether the 2nd or 3rd Battalion fired the most baton rounds during the 'Hunger Strike' Belfast tours of 1980 and 1981.

Some hours later, the company was tasked to mount an operation against the Radovce Bare MUP (Special Police of the Ministry of the Interior) barracks on the outskirts of Banja Luka which was the base of police unit loyal to the Karodic regime in Pale. Due to a narrow bridge on the approach road to the barracks, it was considered impassable to Warriors but, in the early hours of the morning, CSM Danny Massam walked the route and measured the bridge with his pace stick; he decided it was just possible to negotiate the structure in a Warrior. Accordingly, the operation was undertaken at 0600 hours with personnel of the Royal Military Police in support. At first, the MUP were reluctant to surrender but after the telephone lines had been cut and a Warrior arrived at their doorstep, they swiftly acquiesced. The company confiscated numerous weapons and uniforms, two VW police cars and seven tons of illegally held UNHCR humanitarian aid. In the best tradition of Robin Hood, the food was taken back to Jajce and distributed across the company area of operations to deserving Croats and Bosnians, the people for whom it was originally intended.

On the same day, the company redeployed into Banja Luka to assist in the evacuation of the pro-Karadic dissidents from the Bosna Hotel where they had been expecting the convoy of agitators from Pale and were now besieged by pro-Plasvic supporters. In the heat of the afternoon, C Company entered the city but four Warriors took a wrong turn and only just arrived at the RV point on time. Under the watchful electronic eye of the international media, some 70 sorry-looking Serbs were bundled into the C Company Warriors after they had been deprived of their sidearms and driven through a jeering, egg-throwing crowd to the Metal Factory for their own protection. On their return from Banja Luka, C Company was on hand to ensure the peaceful conduct of the municipal elections which passed without incident. Despite this onerous workload, the company was able to undertake some worthwhile military training whilst in theatre under the energetic guidance of the Training Wing based at Krupa. Much time was also devoted to G5 activities.

Accordingly, there were limited opportunities for sport although the most notable was a cricket match against the local International Police Task Force team in which the Fusiliers were comprehensively beaten on account of the number of Pakistani former international cricketers playing for the opposition (or so the story goes). Besides their two weeks of Rest and Recreation, the company and the rest of the battlegroup had the opportunity to enjoy four days adventure training at Povlja on the beautiful island of Brac off the Dalmatian coast. There they relaxed kayaking, dinghy sailing, sub-aqua diving, water skiing and windsurfing. During the final weeks of October, the battalion prepared for its return to Celle in Germany and for the handover to the King's Own Royal Border Regiment which became effective on 1 November.

Fus Ratcliffe of 12 Platoon Z Company scans the hedgerows through the SUIT sight of his SA80 rifle during a patrol in South Armagh. Like all soldiers on patrol in the hostile environment of Northern Ireland, he is equipped with electronic countermeasures to foil radio-controlled command detonated IEDs. He also wears a blackened capbadge to minimise aiming points for IRA snipers. SD

A COMPANY GROUP - TEDFOR

A Company Group deployed to the Shoe Factory in Mrkonjic Grad as the town was emerging from the grip of winter. It assumed responsibility for the surrounding AO from A Company 1st Battalion The Green Howards on Saturday 3 May 1997. On arrival, Major Ted Coates, the OC of A Company, was advised by his opposite number that - 'Nothing ever happens here' and that was the accepted view across the battalion. Having suffered the rigours of a Balkan winter, the Shoe Factory was in a poor state of repair. Within days, the company sergeant major, WO2 Eddy Aldred, had ensured that all signs of the XIXth Regiment of Foot were superseded by the Second Fusiliers. With snow still on the mountains but spring in the air, the Fusiliers built a patio and barbecue area overlooking the town itself. Meanwhile, their patrols began to venture across the area of operations.

In the jargon of the time the area of operations of A Company Group was a 'benign environment' and Major Ted Coates recalls - 'At the end of the first month we had sorted things out and had established a routine of patrols, guards, QRF (Quick Reaction Force), Krupa platoon and training. Sunday was organised as a day of rest or at least as a different regime with work down to a minimum. People could relax in sports kit all day unless they were on duty. Politically nothing was happening beyond the usual round of meetings with local officials which for the first couple of times were entertaining and established the necessary relationship but I was soon thinking - have I got another five months of drinking revolting slivovitz and being berated by hoods I don't respect? In a conversation with my 2IC [Captain Mike Butterwick] over a can of beer on the patio I remember saying - "That's it then, what are we going to do now? Is this it?".' Things were soon to change, not least of which was an invitation to the OC to be a judge in the 'Miss Mrkonjic Grad' beauty contest.

A Company Group came under the command of The Royal Scots Dragoon Guards (and later The King's Royal Hussars) to give their battlegroup a balance of Challenger MBTs, CVR(T) Scimitars and armoured infantry for greater flexibility. It was often inappropriate to deploy Challengers for operational reasons or because of the marginal road system. Acting independently from a platoon patrol base, a platoon from A Company Group was deployed in rotation to the village of Krupa some 30 kilometres north of Mrkonjic Grad. It operated in the

With their hackles prominently on display, the crew of a Warrior of C Company in SFOR markings pose for a photograph in the village of Kruscica. Many of the locals in the Vrbas Valley remembered the hackle from the previous tour of 1RRF and the unstinting assistance afforded to the people of Bosnia Herzegovina by the Royal Regiment of Fusiliers from both battalions. The Warrior is one of the most powerful tools in the force commander's armoury for operations on the ground in Bosnia. It has the presence of a tank to the uninitiated yet had far greater strategic mobility than a Main Battle Tank such as Challenger 1 or Leopard 2. MOD

northern part of the battlegroup area of operations conducting 'framework patrols' on the main supply routes which were intended to reassure the local inhabitants that they remained under the protection of SFOR. The Krupa platoon also monitored all VRS (Army of Republika Srpska) training on the nearby Manjaca Ranges. It was during this activity that a two-vehicle patrol suffered a serious traffic accident trapping Fusilier Paul Parker under his APV Land Rover. Thanks to the prompt action of Lance Corporal Craig Maxwell, his life was saved and he was flown by helicopter to Sipovo where he underwent a six and a half hour operation before being transferred to St George's Hospital Tooting in London for further medical treatment. Lance Corporal Maxwell received a GOC's Commendation for his deeds.

The company was configured as three rifle platoons; an anti-tank section of three Warriors carrying Milan and an attached troop of four CVR(T)s with three Scimitars and a Spartan from Nungshimum Squadron of the SCOTS DG. The latter and the three Milan Warriors were combined to form a fourth platoon; a term that caused untold grief to the cavalry, at least according to its commander, Sergeant 'Polo' Minto. At the outset, the platoons were busy accounting for all the military hardware of the EAF, from mines to MBTs, and ensuring they were stored in cantonment sites. In an early instance on Sunday 18 May, Captain Peter Stitt of 1 Platoon discovered the VRS were illegally firing a battery of 2S1 122mm self-propelled howitzers on Manjaca Ranges. The OC deployed to Manjaca with the QRF and sealed off the exits from the range with Warriors where he was joined by Lieutenant Colonel Austen Ramsden, the CO of the SCOTS DG. Together they were berated by the range commander, an obnoxious Serb by the name of Colonel Strabic, who stated that SFOR could take them if they could but there would be retribution as he had the best tanks in the world at his disposal. In laconic cavalry style, Lieutenant Colonel Ramsden casually replied - 'The last time I had a tank like yours in my sights was during the Gulf War. A few seconds later its turret came off.' After lengthy discussions into the night and much dialogue with SFOR HQ as to whether the correct paperwork existed, the Fusiliers finally confiscated them. At first light on the next day, after a brief driving lesson from the REME LAD, the three vehicles were driven back to Mrkonjic Grad by Sergeant Minto and two REME mechanics. Once back at base, the Company Sergeant Major, WO2 Eddie Aldred, summed up the situation - 'A Company 3 VRS 0'.

After a day on the ranges, a Warrior of Headquarters Company 2RRF with its crew and dismounts pauses in front of the Police Headquarters in Pristina which was the target for a cruise missile during Operation 'Joint Force' - the airwar against Serbia in 1999. Operation 'Agricola' has proved to be a considerable success as a peace support operation. The presence of NATO forces has largely maintained the peace in the province and the region while the pressure for democracy has grown inexorably in Serbia, leading to the overthrow of the communist dictator Slobodan Milosovic. Nevertheless, 2RRF was prepared for general warfare in its Warriors should the Serbians make an incursion into the Ground Security Zone between Serbia proper and Kosovo. SD

With a man down, Cpl Rutherford of X Company signals to his fire team to press on during a platoon attack against an enemy encampment in the jungles of Belize during Exercise 'Native Trail' in August 1999. Like street fighting, jungle warfare often incurs heavy casualties in personnel because of the short engagement ranges of many firefights. This is compounded by the problems of gathering clear intelligence of the enemy's dispositions as conventional reconnaissance methods, such as aerial surveillance, are often inadequate in such close terrain. The latter also makes logistical resupply and medical evacuation difficult. Accordingly, troops have to carry all their needs on their backs or belts. SD

IN THE LINE OF FIRE

Events in the Republika Srpska took a dramatic turn when the president, Madame Biljana Plasvic, suspended her interior minister Dragan Kijac, a crony of her predecessor, the indicted war criminal Radovan Karadzic. It was her intention to weed out the disruptive elements loyal to Karadzic in her government, in order to meet the conditions of the Dayton Agreement and so attract aid and investment to her country. However, many of the Special Police, known as 'muppets' to British troops, remained staunch supporters of the former regime as they were responsible for much of the ethnic cleansing during the war and realised they might be brought to account for their actions. Accordingly, they fomented a climate of insurrection to cause the downfall of the President. On the following Sunday afternoon, as A Company was enjoying a barbecue and their daily ration of two cans of beer, the operations officer of The King's Royal Hussars, Captain Nick Berchem, telephoned to inquire how quickly the company could get to Banja Luka where the Presidential Palace was situated. The OC gave a noncommittal answer based on travelling time and a generous allowance for unseen factors but was told to have two platoons ready for immediate deployment. In the evening, they were stood down but tasked to move to Banja Luka first thing in the morning.

Travelling via Krupa, the ten Warriors arrived at the outskirts at the height of the rush hour, to cause the maximum disruption, which was the intention of the GOC as they proceeded to his headquarters at the Metal Factory in the town. Despite being spat at and the butt of much gesticulation, the Warriors succeeded admirably as a show of force and this first deployment to Banja Luka set the scene for the rest of the tour. A recurring theme throughout the tour for both the Fusilier and KRH Battlegroups was operations working with or against the various police forces. In an attempt to control the unorthodox activities of the local police, the UN Mission IPTF was introduced under the terms of the Dayton Peace Accord with police monitors from far and wide across the world. Their role was essential to help create a legally accountable Federation Police Force and to allow the growth of a democratic society. Both battlegroups supported them throughout their area of operations in such tasks as 'checkpoint busting' where Bosnian Serb policemen set up illegal checkpoints to impede freedom of movement and extort money from the populace.

Shortly thereafter, Madame Plasvic contacted General Angus Ramsey, the GOC Multi National Division South West (MND SW), in the belief that she was about to be assassinated. Once more it was necessary for a show of force but at the same time it was essential for SFOR to be seen to be impartial. Major Coates was summoned to HQ MND SW to a meeting with the General, his Chief of Staff, the commander of 7th Armoured Brigade, Brigadier Andrew Stewart, Lieutenant Colonel Adrian Bradshaw, CO of The King's Royal

Hussars, a political adviser from the Foreign and Commonwealth Office and a representative from the UN Secretariat. In such exalted company he listened attentively 'on receive mode only', but the situation was deemed to be so serious that he was ordered to go to the Presidential Palace at once in order to guard it against attack. Major Coates immediately despatched 3 Platoon under the command of Colour Sergeant Lee Phillips before he gathered up some members of the QRF to travel with him in his Warrior Command Vehicle, Callsign Zero Bravo. Following in short order, he gave his driver free rein and the Warrior was soon travelling through the streets of Banja Luka at speeds in excess of 50 kph with cars careering out of its way until it pulled up outside the doors of the palace.

With no sign of 3 Platoon, Major Coates and his dismounts entered the building to guard the presidential quarters on the instructions of the armed plain clothes personnel inside. 3 Platoon soon arrived 'having taken the scenic route' and, together with some CVR(T) Scimitars of The Household Cavalry Regiment, formed an outer cordon around the palace. Within hours the troops were withdrawn but the presence of the Warriors that night undoubtedly prevented a major political crisis. However, the MUP police still posed a threat to stability and, in further show of force in early July, A Company deployed to Banja Luka to scotch another mutinous faction. With 14 Warriors and a Combat Engineer Tractor (CET), they were instructed to form up outside a police station in full combat kit and clear it by force if necessary. A few minutes before deployment, the operation was called off, much to the disappointment of the Sapper CET crew who had been tasked with demolishing the building.

A Company returned to Mrkonjic Grad where there was a power struggle developing between elements of the Bosnian Serb police. Coach loads of hard line police arrived in the town with the intention of ousting the local chief of police, a supporter of Madame Plasvic. The appearance of weapons on the streets prompted the intervention of A Company to calm the situation; a casual remark about - 'the red on the hackle being from French blood, but could just as easily be Serbian blood', caused consternation among the police and the civil population. It did however have the desired effect; the message was clear - 'Don't tackle the hackle'. With the return of normality, the company was able to undertake some basic military training before events in Jajce necessitated the deployment of 2 Platoon in support of C Company to help quell civil disturbances as Muslim refugees returned to the area. This, together with another stint in Banja Luka as the Quick Reaction Force for the city, stretched company assets to the limit. When Captain Mike Butterwick, acting as OC while Major Coates was on R and R, tasked a second QRF to an incident involving Muslim DPREs returning to a village in the Republika Srpska, he was informed that the only force remaining was Colour Sergeant 'Digger' Gardner and some chefs, and that the only transport available was some mountain bikes.

Warriors of C Company undertake a battle run during a firepower demonstration staged by the Multi National Division South West at the Glamoc ranges in Bosnia. Employing all arms of service at the disposal of the NATO commander, these firepower demonstrations were held before invited representatives of the former warring factions to convince them NATO had such overwhelming military assets that a return to fighting on their part would be futile in the face of such technological and tactical superiority. MOD

A Gazelle helicopter of 25th Flight Army Air Corps circles a jungle landing site as Maj Whitwam conducts OC's Orders in the field while the company clerk takes notes in the foreground at the conclusion of Exercise 'Native Trail' in Belize in September 1999. During jungle operations, the helicopter is vital for resupplying troops in the field and for casualty evacuation in case of injury or training accident. Helicopter Landing Sites (HLS) have to be hacked out of the secondary jungle by machete, chainsaw or explosives. An HLS such as this one will revert to dense jungle in a matter of months. SD

OPERATION 'SHIVA'

Meanwhile, the parliament of the Republika Srpska had begun impeachment proceedings against Madame Plasvic. Rumours were rife that she had been the victim of illegal surveillance and that the judiciary had been persuaded to find against her. The main police headquarters in Banja Luka, the Public Security Building, lay in the hands of police loyal to Karadzic. It was deemed to be the nerve centre of the plot against the President and the repository for weapons that would be used in any coup. On the evening of 19 August, she contacted General Ramsey, the GOC MND SW, and requested that SFOR eject the police inside the headquarters so that they could be replaced by policemen registered with the IPTF. This was to be undertaken as part of a wholesale reform of the police within the Republika Srpska and so strengthen her hold on the presidency. As this was the aim of NATO, General Ramsey ordered all SFOR assets in Banja Luka, together with A Company Group of the Second Fusiliers, to raid every police station in the city to this end.

Codenamed Operation 'Shiva', A Company was given the hardest task of seizing and searching the Public Security Building. As the police headquarters in Banja Luka, it symbolised the seat of power within the city and, by extension, in the Republika Srpska (RS) . At midnight on 19 August, orders were given for the operation to begin at 0600 hours. Through the long reaches of the night, Major Coates planned the assault and at 0300 hours called an O Group. A Company approached the three-storey building with the OC in his Land Rover, a troop of CVR(T) from The King's Royal Hussars under the command of 2nd Lieutenant Nick Perry and the Warriors of 2 Platoon under the command of Lieutenant Mark Canning carrying dismounts from 1, 3 and 4 Platoons, together with Zero Bravo commanded by the 2IC, with its chaingun loaded and a marksman, Fusilier 'Pie' Adam, in the back.

Major Ted Coates takes up the story: 'The plan was that 2 and 4 Platoons would provide the cordon at the front and rear of the building. 3 Platoon under Colour Sergeant Phillips would dismount and be the entry force. 1 Platoon under Sergeant Mornington would be the reserve. I was to arrive at the entrance to the building in a Land Rover and demand that it was handed over to SFOR or it would be taken by force. About a quarter of a mile short, I was informed by divisional headquarters that the police had got wind of our arrival and were intending to resist, by force if necessary. I then transferred to my Warrior. The intention was to arrive in force and attempt to bluff them. In the back was Fusilier Adam who was to fire a warning shot with his rifle as part of the escalation process. Colour Sergeant Phillips on foot positioned himself to enter on my order. On arrival we were shocked to see an IPTF policeman at the door. I checked with divisional HQ to find out if they were aware and if plans had changed. They had not. We were mandated to protect the IPTF, so clearly my plan was not appropriate under the changed circumstances. Having dismounted I was met by a German IPTF colonel who informed me that he had started negotiations and the RS police were being 'very' cooperative and that they intended to leave. I was a little suspicious. My Fusiliers had been placed in danger by a similar incident with the IPTF on the previous Sunday where the IPTF had believed all that they had been told by the police, leaving me holding the baby when they reneged.

'Having asked to be included in the negotiations it was apparent that the police were stalling for time and had absolutely no intention of leaving. Unbeknown to me my entry had been reported and interpreted as that I had secured the building. The consequence being that the pro-Plasvic police were being teed up to march from the Palace to the Security Building. At sometime after this the MUP reinforcements arrived. Plain clothed and unshaven, pockets bulging with pistols and machine pistols. They were lead by a man called Ecim who was later identified as one of the leading hoods and a former member of Arkan's Tigers. He quickly established himself as the real authority and that the RS police colonel was merely a figurehead. Ecim was not for shifting. He knew that once his side were out the evidence or wrong doing would be found and they would not get back in again.

'A period of tense negotiations started. My confidence was bolstered by the presence of Corporal Toon and Colour Sergeant Phillips - large men who could be relied on to cover my back. In a battle of brinkmanship I began to feel I was getting somewhere, lying through my teeth that SFOR wouldn't hand the station to Plasvic's men. Sadly it all came crashing down when I was informed that her men were enroute and due to arrive in a matter of minutes.

I hastened my negotiations, but to no avail, they turned up and my ruse was seen through. In an attempt to reduce the antagonistic effect of their presence and to provide for their protection, they were placed in the KRH Spartan. it was around this time that the warning came over the brigade net to Mike [Butterwick], who summoned me to the Land Rover to take the message to the effect that we were going to be attacked and take up a defensive posture. I quickly barked a few orders to the Fusiliers who saw the urgency and responded quickly and aggressively.'

Brigade headquarters had been informed that there was a pair of snipers in buildings overlooking the police station. One was armed with an RPG to engage the Spartan while the other was heard to say - 'I can do it! I can burn him now! I can do it!'. The Fusiliers immediately took up defensive positions and the Warrior turrets traversed backwards and forwards scanning for targets, whereupon the sniper was later reported to have said - 'They're on to me it's getting hot' before he departed. History does not relate who was the target of the sniper but it had come within seconds of a serious firefight which one observer surmised 'would have made Bloody Sunday look like an organised Bisley match'. By now, some of the Fusiliers of 3 Platoon had surreptitiously infiltrated the building from the rear. They were soon ushering out many of the younger policemen at gunpoint through the lobby while other Fusiliers took up positions on each floor of the building. After friutless negotiations lasting some 45 minutes, Major Coates nodded to Colour Sergeant Phillips and said - 'Colour, deploy the guys'. Mistaking the order, Colour Sergeant Phillips shouted above the hubbub - 'Clear!' and the Fusiliers on every floor began to break down doors and apprehend anyone who opposed them. The hard line Serb police capitulated. 1 and 3 Platoons then searched the building with gusto; the windows of each office were smashed and the curtains draped outside to indicate the room had been cleared. A vast array of weapons as well as all manner of surveillance equipment and tapes were found that indicated the President had indeed been compromised. Major Ted Coates and Colour Sergeant Lee Phillips were awarded US Army Commendation Medals, while Colour Sergeant Mick Barnett-Connolly received the US Army Achievement Medal for his adroit handling of the hostile crowd outside. Major Coates was subsequently Mentioned in Despatches for his outstanding leadership during Operation 'Shiva' and during the following incident.

During Operation 'Shiva', the occupation of the pro-Karadzic police stations in Banja Luka by NATO forces, the Public Security Building was raided by A Company 2RRF as part of the King's Royal Hussars Battlegroup on 19 August 1997. At the time, the police headquarters was authorised to hold less than a dozen shotguns or rifles. A Company removed over 2,000 weapons including heavy machine guns, assault rifles and even a Samurai sword. Here, C/Sgt Barnett-Connolly, the CQMS of A Company, loads up one of four four-tonne trucks needed to transport the illegal armoury away as Cpl Reid looks on with a hostile Serbian crowd in the background.

To the crew and the dismounts, a Warrior is their home during field training exercises and in times of war. It is sometimes said that the Fusilier of today is not as fit or resilient as his forebears. While it is true that advances in clothing and personal equipment have improved the lot of soldiers in the field their tasks, responsibilities and technical equipment have grown far more complex. The wearing of body armour and the issue of personal radios are just two changes that mark out the modern Fusilier from his predecessors for, with fewer soldiers available, more is demanded of the individual and more responsibility is devolved to the junior NCOs and Fusiliers. With the world's media often in close attendance, the young Fusiliers of today have to be confident in their ability to deal with a far greater range of potential problems than ever before. That they do it so well is a testament to their training and teamwork. As for fitness, this is subject to greater scrutiny than it was even 20 years ago. Comparisons with the past are thus inappropriate. Circumstances and evolution dictate that it is impossible to compare like with like except, possibly, in one area - that of the Fusilier's personal weapon. The Fusilier of 1914 carried an SMLE .303 rifle weighing 8lb 14 1/2oz unloaded. The introduction of the 7.62 SLR saw him carrying a weapon weighing 9lbs 8 oz unloaded while the 5.56 SA80 with SUSAT sight weighs 10lbs unloaded.* Although 5.56mm ammunition is lighter, the modern Fusilier carries more of it than ever before. When it comes to weight each generation of Fusiliers has had to shoulder a heavy burden but in terms of his rifle, the Fusilier of today carries a heavier one than he did a century ago and one that is less accurate at long ranges. Such is progress.

* Figures supplied by the Skill at Arms School Museum Warminster.

After a rural patrol in South Armagh, Callsign November Two Zero Alpha of 8 Platoon Y Company, with Lt Austin and Fus Bickket, Harbron and Marston, returns by helicopter to Golf Four Zero, otherwise known as 'The Rock' or the 'Crosslieve Hilton'. The Golf and Romeo towers dotted along the border with the Republic of Ireland act as observation posts to detect and identify suspicious activity and provide warning of terrorist intent within their fields of view as part of Operations 'Chesapeake' and 'Watson'. SD

OPERATION 'BADGER' - THE BATTLE OF THE BUSES

Between their various deployments, A Company helped in the continual task of rebuilding the infrastructure of the area. Captain Steve Vinall, on attachment from the Princess of Wales's Royal Regiment, was in charge of the G5 projects which included the refurbishment of the saw mill at Mrkonjic Grad, several village schools and the rebuilding of a destroyed village ready for the return of Muslim displaced persons. With the approach of the municipal elections, various polling stations were also established. The elections brought with them the renewed threat of a coup against Madame Plasvic. A Company was deployed once more to the north of Banja Luka, following reports that numerous armed Karadzic supporters were travelling from Pale in the American MND North area down Route Arkansas. After a brief skirmish in the Danish sector where an SFOR vehicle was set alight and a Danish officer was stabbed in the chest with a pitchfork, the coaches carrying the troublemakers arrived at Prinjavor in the afternoon of 8 September. Route Arkansas ran through a steep-sided valley with a stream meandering along its floor. Accordingly there were few areas to either side that a Warrior could deploy beyond the minor tracks, most of which led to small farmsteads or their outbuildings. The route of the convoy was being picketed by Bosnian Serb police but few in NATO had any faith in their ability or commitment to affect the proceedings. A Company was tasked with monitoring the situation and providing timely local intelligence as well as being a highly visible demonstration of NATO resolve should the need arise.

A Company were deployed along the road between Prinjavor and Banja Luka, a distance of some 35 kilometres. Furthest forward and closest to Prinjavor were the CVR(T) Scimitars of The King's Royal Hussars in their guise as 4 Platoon. The other three platoons were deployed along the route in descending numerical order at various points as pairs of Warriors. To their rear was the company RV where the 2IC, Captain Mike Butterwick, and his signallers were acting as the control station for the operation together with the CQMS and the REME LAD. Their position was situated at the final road junction before Fisherman's Bridge that led directly to Banja Luka with other roads allowing access to the city.

After a session quaffing slivovitz, the mob boarded the convoy, which was growing in size all the while, and proceeded slowly down the road past the CVR(T) screen. As it was passing the Warriors of 3 Platoon, divisional headquarters ordered the company to alter its mission from one of observation to containment, with the unequivocal instruction - ''These people are to be prevented under all circumstances from entering Banja Luka'. Reinforced by undesirables and malcontents hired for mischief, intelligence indicated that the mob would pose a serious threat to public order if it entered the city. With its Warriors spread along the length of the road, this presented a considerable problem as the company was deployed in a manner to monitor but not to interdict the coaches. Captain Butterwick informed Major

Devastated houses and buildings are a common feature across the length and breadth of Bosnia Herzegovina as shown here behind a Warrior of 3 Platoon A Company, with Cpl Toon and Fus Thorp in the turret and Fus Norton-Smith as driver, in the devastated village of Jezero in the Zone of Separation during an operation in support of C Company near Jajce during the summer of 1997. Callsign Three One was involved in the Battle of the Buses when Cpl Toon was called upon to delay the progress of a convoy of coaches carrying dissident policemen and other malcontents. One radio conversation was heard to go as follows:-

"Three One - this is One One. Be aware 2 kilometres to your front, two times civilian vehicles have been placed in the road to block your route."

"Three One - thirty tons say they don't."

"One One - Ha bloody ha - out." MOD

Coates of the new objective. He in turn discussed it with Lieutenant Colonel Adrian Bradshaw who was acting as the local commander on the ground.

Realising the urgency of the situation, Captain Butterwick ordered 3 Platoon to impede the convoy. At that precise moment the coaches were bypassing Sergeant Tony Gledhill, the acting platoon commander, and his two Warriors. It fell to 3 Platoon's Warrior Sergeant, Corporal Wayne Toon, to delay the convoy. In his Warrior, Callsign Three One Alpha, Corporal Toon recalls - 'I was tasked to delay three buses. The people on board were believed to be involved in a possible armed uprising. The three buses turned out to be 30! We dove two Warriors side by side down the road. This annoyed the occupants of the buses who decided to get off, run after the Warriors and brick us. We just battened down and continued. Quite a few optics were broken in the process. A few members of the rebel police force then drove a couple of four by fours after us with people sitting on the front cradling small arms and holding petrol bombs, so we picked up speed to avoid being set alight. Eventually, as we turned a corner I saw a police line and decided to split left with both Warriors jumping off the raised road and into a field. Both Warriors drove at speed down a goat track hitting trees to try and lose the two jeeps who were chasing us. We started to lose them and, on turning a sharp corner and seeing a cornfield, both Warriors left the track and jumped eight feet down onto the field. Both vehicles were then concealed, engines were cut and then the four by fours drove past. At this stage Corporal Urwin commanding my second Warrior reported his track had been ripped off.'

This delay, however, allowed time for sets of caltrops to be delivered to the other platoons by the CQMS, Colour Sergeant Mick Barnett-Connolly. Corporal Toon's action also bought enough time for the police to form a barricade across the road with a water cannon and several farm tractors. However, it had been established close to the cafe where the police had spent much of the day drinking coffee and did not extend across the forecourt of the abandoned service station opposite. Accordingly, the mob was able to bypass it with little trouble and, in the scuffle that ensued, the water cannon was captured and turned on the police who fled. Lieutenant Mark Canning in command of 2 Platoon remembers that it was pleasant sitting on his Warrior in the afternoon sunshine. On hearing the new orders, he immediately grouped his Warriors together and awaited the arrival of the coaches. Canning recalls 'The police were getting a hammering and the crowds were taking their kit - their batons, their tear gas and even their water cannon at which point I loaded the chaingun. There were a few charges at the police line. The press then flapped and started legging it down the road, falling over each other which was highly humorous.'

Fortified by slivovitz and brandishing stolen weapons, the convoy had grown to some 50 coaches and the crowd to about 2,000. By now, dusk was gathering and Major Coates ordered Lieutenant Canning to try and halt the convoy with caltrops so that another police line could be formed further down the road. Having thoroughly reconnoitred the area during daylight, he chose a particular spot at the top of an incline where the coaches would be travelling slowly in low gear and there were some bushes at the roadside to act as cover. He recalls - 'I had very few Fusilier dismounts at the time because of R and R and I had a section of Gurkhas so I put the other Fusiliers in the turret to take the wagon back to the company RV. I took Sergeant Hall who carried the caltrops, Fusilier West with a radio and five Gurkhas as a guard force. We tabbed about half a klick to the chosen spot where Sergeant Hall set up the caltrops but they were too short and did not extend across the road. As I recced a withdrawal route, Sergeant Hall attached the lazy tongs to a length of rope and strung it across the road.

'After the OC had checked the set-up and the police and the company Warriors had withdrawn, we hid in the bushes and waited. I was checking the road with the CWS and saw the convoy coming up the hill. They were hanging out of the coach windows with the water cannon leading and there were lots of people walking in front and along the sides. To me the rope was obvious on the road but the people were walking past about two metres away. We let the front wheels pass over the rope and then pulled the caltrops to puncture the rear tyres. We then turned and legged it into the dark. I knew there was a farmhouse nearby with a large dog so I had my rifle ready to shoot it if it barked. We heard angry voices and people coming down the track but not for long and we ran on till we fell into a barbed wire fence. It was then

Cpl Dodds of the Drums Platoon W Company relays a message prior to a patrol from an SF base in Northern Ireland. The beret and hackle is worn during periods of relative calm in the turbulent times of Northern Ireland. Over the years, it has given rise to various nicknames for the Fusiliers such as the 'Budgies'. On joining up, a Fusilier is provided with a single hackle; thereafter hackles have to be purchased at a cost of 70 pence each. A hackle lasts approximately one month before replacement is necessary. SD

A Warrior of A Company 2RRF thunders over the training ground at Drawsko-Pomorskie in Poland during Exercise 'Ulan Eagle' in October 1999. Unlike in Britain or Germany where environmental concerns do not allow AFVs to be camouflaged with natural vegetation, vehicles in Poland appear as they would do in general warfare. The Warrior is fitted with Direct Fire Weapons Effect Simulation equipment to enhance the realism of training for manoeuvre warfare.

that Fusilier West said - "F***ing hell. That was an adrenalin rush. Anymore of that and I'll stay in the army". We tabbed for miles bouncing off Route Arkansas if we saw the convoy and using tracks to progress towards the RV until I saw a Land Rover about 200 yards away. I ran like hell and chased after it. I banged on the side and rushed to the front window. It gave Steve [Vinall] a hell of a shock. We just dived in the back and away we went.'

Although 2 Platoon's caltrops slowed the convoy, the coaches pressed on regardless. It was then the turn of 1 Platoon to face the mob. The platoon commander, Captain Peter Stitt, recalls - 'The next thing I knew was the OC's Warrior came storming up and stopping in front of us. He then said words to the effect - just get off the road, make sure you're not boxed in but stay here as the rear link so that anyone caught on the wrong side of the crowd can come back with you. He then left with his rear doors open and interpreters running along behind trying to get on board. I got the two vehicles forward of me out of the way as we heard that the convoy was almost up to the last set of caltrops. By this time it was dark. It had kind of taken me by surprise that things had moved so fast. In the space of 30 minutes, we now had the brigadier on the net, people were talking of deploying snipers on roof tops around Fisherman's Bridge, an AS90 fire mission, a rapid cratering kit and all sorts. Having been aware that we were just monitoring the convoy, within half an hour the whole situation had radically changed and the crowd were almost up to me. The next vehicle we saw coming towards us was a Bosnian Serb police car which went straight over the caltrops taking out all four tyres but it wasn't stopping for anything and continued past us on its rims. We moved off the road and sat and waited.'

The crowd moved past with some of them firing tracer rounds into the air as they moved towards Banja Luka. Whenever any vehicles or the crowd approached, Captain Stitt moved his two remaining Warriors elsewhere to prevent them from being trapped in the marginal terrain. All the while he was monitoring the radio net in case friendly units were trapped behind the convoy. Eventually, a Land Rover turned up carrying Captain Steve Vinall, Lieutenant Mark Canning and Sergeant Tony Hall. After a quick check, they went on their way to the company RV. Captain Stitt in Callsign One Zero and Lance Corporal 'Bugsy' Malone in One One tried to find a route out but were repeatedly foiled by flimsy bridges that were unable to bear the weight of a Warrior. Each time they had to return to the main road. Captain Stitt decided to cross Route Arkansas. 'We booted it across the road between parts of the convoy and moved north. We tried to pick a route but those shown on the map actually led nowhere except small farms. By 0200 hours we were decidedly lost and doing neutral turns in chicken runs. Old ladies in nighties were screaming in the night and their

The Quick Reaction Force of B Company, Bravo One One Delta, deploys from a Land Rover APV as a show of strength at the YU Programme to deter Albanian retaliation against Serb families living in the adjacent block of flats in Pristina. The QRF includes L/Cpl Nelson, Dmrs Grice and Watkinson as well as Gdsm Melia on attachment from the Welch Guards. The principal task of the Fusiliers in Pristina was to support the 7,000 UN Police drawn from 39 nations in providing internal security for the city and the province of Kosovo until such time as an indigenous police force could be formed. SD

washing lines were entangled with our radio antennae. We eventually got back to the company RV at first light - totally knackered.' Meanwhile, the other Warriors that had been cut off by the convoy were making their way across country to the company RV. Sergeant Tony Gledhill of 3 Platoon travelled for miles by way of the Croatian border. Corporal Wayne Toon and his companion vehicle had the misfortune to shed, a track but the crews quickly erected a hide and effected repairs before returning safely.

Meanwhile, the irate mob had moved on with the water cannon running on its punctured tyres. It now approached the second police barricade which had been constructed thanks to the delaying tactics of the Warriors. It was far more formidable than before as it comprised heavy trucks blocking the road, backed up with a strong police line in riot gear. Unfortunately, this had been established without the knowledge of the Fusiliers and the OC's Warrior and Land Rover were now sandwiched between the barricade and the advancing convoy. As it arrived, the mob began to stone both the barricade and the SFOR vehicles. In the turret of Zero Bravo, Major Coates sent an urgent radio message to Lieutenant Colonel Bradshaw asking permission for his dismounts to use CS gas and baton guns to control the crowd. Such a request should have been relayed to the commander of SFOR himself but the matter was so urgent that Colonel Bradshaw readily gave permission. By now Major Coates had drawn his Browning pistol, causing the crowd to pull back, but he knew it would not be for long and visions of the unfortunate Royal Signals corporals caught in an IRA funeral procession in Belfast flashed through his mind.

Fortunately, Company Sergeant Major Eddy Aldred had climbed out of the OC's Land Rover and had forced his way through the barricade. He quickly found one of the truck drivers and in his words - 'I persuaded this driver very politely by putting my rifle to his head, dragging him to his vehicle and telling him "Move it!", and so he obliged'. He was able to move the truck far enough for the Land Rover and Warrior to squeeze through before the crowds surged forward and battle was joined once more with renewed fury. Wielding iron bars as well as rifles, the mob stoned and battered the police line. Occasionally the line faltered but each time it did, the policemen were reminded of their duty by Company Sergeant Major Aldred and they returned to the fray. It speaks volumes of the calibre of the senior NCOs in the British Army when their powers of persuasion are such that someone would rather face an armed mob than the wrath of a Warrant Officer. The stench of CS gas now filled the air followed by small arms fire as approximately 30 shots were fired in the direction of the police and the SFOR troops. Three policemen were hit, one in the head, one in the chest and one in the legs. Their comrades simply pulled them out of the line and dumped them at the

X Company of 1RRF congregates at the Guacamallo Bridge in the jungle of Belize at the end of a company attack during Exercise 'Native Trail' in September 1999. As part of British Army doctrine, its infantry must be able to operate in all operational theatres and environments from jungle warfare to the Arctic and from desert operations to peacekeeping duties. SD

The Tower of London formerly incorporated the Royal Menagerie until all the Royal animals were moved to Regents Park Zoo in 1831. The first antelope known to have been in the Royal Menagerie was an Albino Indian Antelope from Bombay which was presented to King George IV by Capt Dalrymple of the Vansittart. On 1 September 1999, the present Bobby moved from 6RRF in Coventry to take up residence in the moat of the Tower of London. In a ceremony to mark the occasion, a guard under the command of Capt R Coates was found by Y Company of the 1st Battalion.

roadside. WO2 Aldred and Colour Sergeant Barnett-Connolly applied field dressings before the wounded were evacuated in a Land Rover to the company aid post where they were tended by the KRH medical officer.

To the rear, Captain Mike Butterwick continued to act as the rear link to the battlegroup and brigade, ably assisted by his signaller, Fusilier Glenn Plaister, and the regimental signals detachment commander, Lance Corporal 'Geordie' Taylor. SFOR was determined that the mob would not enter Banja Luka. To this end it was vital that the junction short of Fisherman's Bridge was denied to the convoy, as once beyond it could take several routes into the city. Once inside Banja Luka, SFOR would no longer be able to constrain the reactionary Karadzic forces from toppling the regime of Madame Plasvic. If she and the moderate Serbs fell the whole of the Dayton Agreement would be in jeopardy. As this position was the last opportunity to halt the convoy before it reached the bridge, the ground to either side of the road was churned up by the tracks of the LAD Warriors to make it impassable to wheeled vehicles. The REME Warrior FV513 recovery vehicle also rooted up several trees to form another barrier across the road. In addition, C Company, as the divisional reserve, was tasked to block Fisherman's Bridge where its personnel stood by equipped with riot gear and baton guns, the first occasion that British troops had been deployed in the IS role in Bosnia-Herzegovina.

The assets assembled to forestall the convoy grew dramatically with Apache gunships in the air, Royal Engineers on the ground with a rapid cratering kit, and a Royal Artillery AS90 battery on standby for a fire mission of illuminating rounds. With the OC patrolling the road in his Warrior, the control of these forces devolved to the 2IC, Captain Mike Butterwick. As the operation unfolded, the brigade and divisional commanders flicked onto the company net to follow the proceedings. In consequence, the net was alive with radio traffic. Similarly, it fell to Captain Butterwick to know the whereabouts of every company vehicle at all times and ensure that the OC was kept fully informed, a major task of command and control from the turret of a Warrior.

The rapid cratering kit had never before been used in anger so no one fully realised its capabilities despite the reassurances of the Sapper sergeant who emplaced it. To the rear, the artillery were champing at the bit to conduct the first operational fire mission ever by an AS90 - a mission that had come about through a misunderstanding. At Fisherman's Bridge, Major James Denny, the OC of C Company, had informed Lieutenant Colonel Adrian Bradshaw that their only illumination capability in case of fighting at the bridge were some "one point five" inch flares. The battlegroup commander misheard this as a request for "one five five" millimetre illuminating rounds. The requirement was duly passed to the artillery who were more than willing to comply; a pallet of 155mm illuminating rounds had to be flown forward by Chinook helicopter especially. SFOR had also deployed some of its newest weapons technology. Above the incident, a P-3 Orion circled in the night sky transmitting live imagery to the office of the NATO Supreme Allied Commander Europe in Mons where General Wesley Clark was taking a keen interest in events on the ground: such was the importance of the Fusiliers' task. In the event TEDFOR was not found wanting.

Fortunately, the police line held. After some four hours, the battle subsided and the convoy returned whence it came. Next day, the company reoccupied the ground along the road to forestall any repetition. SFOR had once more saved the Plasvic administration but, to show its even handedness, C Company rescued some hard line Serb officials who were holed up in the Hotel Bosna in Banja Luka, from a hostile crowd of Plasvic supporters. The Battle of the Buses was the most serious incident faced by A Company. At its conclusion, many of the company had endured almost two days without sleep. WO2 Eddy Aldred received a GOC's Commendation for his part in the incident while Lieutenant Mark Canning was Mentioned in Despatches for his coolness in the face of the armed and belligerent mob.

Following the municipal elections on 13-14 September, things quietened down considerably for the last few weeks of the tour. Towards the end of September, the company deployed to Prinjavor to forestall another pro-Karadzic attempt to take over the police station. During October, the company was even able to conduct some live firing training on Glamoc Ranges. Far from being a quiet AO with nothing happening, A Company had been in the thick of the action throughout. As Major General Angus Ramsey remarked at the conclusion of their six month tour, - 'A Company has been directly responsible for the halting of three coup attempts over the last two and a half months and has prevented an assassination attempt against the President of Republika Srpska, Madame Biljana Plasvic'.

The Second Fusiliers had been involved in a complex and challenging tour of duty which demonstrated that the problems of the former Republic of Yugoslavia remain acute. However, much had been achieved and in the words of their Commanding Officer, Lieutenant Colonel Gary Cass, - 'There is no more worthwhile task for a soldier than to work for peace'. The SFOR mandate had been stretched creatively to assist its people but only they can find the solution. Subsequent events in Kosovo have shown this to be unlikely and NATO peacekeeping forces remain essential to any semblance of stability in the region. SFOR was created under UN Security Council Resolution 1088 on 12 December 1996. Its mandate was envisaged to last 18 months but it continues into the 21st Century. The key question is whether NATO and the European Union are willing to commit their troops indefinitely. It is probable that if the 'Pomeranian Grenadier' factor impinges and they are withdrawn, then the Balkans will be left to tear themselves apart once more. Whatever the outcome, The Royal Regiment of Fusiliers will continue to do their duty wherever and whenever they are deployed, be it Kosovo or South Armagh, steadfast in faith and valiant in battle.

A Fusilier of 1RRF manning an LSW Light Support Weapon gives covering fire as other Fusiliers of the Delta Fire Team move forward during an attack in the jungles of Belize. The British Army is capable of providing two battalions of infantry for jungle operations; one of Gurkhas and one composite battalion drawn from several regiments of companies that have most recently undertaken Exercise 'Native Trail' training in Belize. SD

Fusiliers of 5 Platoon B Company take a breather on top of their Warrior between serials during Exercise 'Ulan Eagle' in Poland. Despite all manner of high technology in modern warfare, the rifle section remains the basic component of the Army and its mission in the year 2000 remains the same as ever: 'To close with and engage the enemy, in concert with other arms in all operational theatres and environments, in order to bring about his defeat'. SD

Appendix 1

ALLIED HM SHIPS, REGIMENTS, THE RAF SQUADRON AND LIVERY COMPANIES

ALLIED HM SHIPS

The alliances between Her Majesty's Ships and the Regiment have been handed down from the four antecedent Regiments, although not all are officially recognised by the Ministry of Defence. There is no doubt that the affiliations between particular ships and the Regiment are much appreciated by both the ships' companies and the battalions who take every opportunity to maintain these special links. The Regiment has had affiliations with six ships which, in alphabetical order, are HMS *Antelope, Birmingham, Coventry, Euryalus, London* and *Northumberland.*

The sinking of HMS *Antelope* in San Carlos Waters on 24 May 1982 during the Falklands War brought to an untimely end the affiliation between successive HMS *Antelope's* with the Royal Warwickshire Regiment and the Regiment, which began in 1931. To mark the very close links between the Regiment and the ship, Commander Nicholas Tobin DSC RN, the last Commanding Officer, presented the port deck plate, which had been recovered from San Carlos Waters to the Regiment. It is now in the doorway of the Association Room at Regimental Headquarters in the Tower of London.

The Regiment has continued the former affiliation between the Royal Warwickshire Regiment and HMS *Birmingham*. The most recent HMS *Birmingham* was a Type 42 destroyer commissioned in 1974. After a major refit she was rededicated at Portsmouth in 1987 and hosted many Fusiliers onboard until she was decommissioned in January 2000.

HMS *Coventry* is one of only two allied ships remaining in service as this history is completed. She is a Type 22 Frigate and was commissioned at Portsmouth on 14 October 1988 when the Colonel of the Regiment was present. The association between the ship and the Regiment was thus established and confirms the long-standing links between the City of Coventry, the ship, the Royal Warwickshire Regiment and now the Regiment.

The links between HMS *Euryalus* and the Regiment are without doubt the most historic. Early links had been established between ship and Regiment in 1814 in North America but the association between ship and Regiment really dates from 25 April 1915 when the fourth ship to bear the name 'Euryalus' landed the 1st Battalion Lancashire Fusiliers at 'Lancashire Landing' on the first day of the Gallipoli Campaign, when six VCs were won. Since this time there have been many reunions and once, in July 1951, 42 men of the 1st Battalion Lancashire Fusiliers were on board in the Gulf for operational reasons. The sixth HMS *Euryalus* was decommissioned in Devonport on 31 March 1989 and the wardroom silver has been entrusted to the Regiment for safe keeping until a new HMS *Euryalus* is commissioned. The two deck plates were presented to the Regiment; the port one is at Regimental Headquarters and the starboard at the Lancashire Area Headquarters.

The sixth HMS *Euryalus* was commissioned in September 1964 as a Leander Class frigate. The photograph shows the 'Fighting Fifteen' in its final configuration with the 4.5 inch gun mounting replaced by the Ikara anti-submarine missile system in its role as Anti-Submarine Frigate during operational sea training off Portland. On 31 March 1989, the sixth and last HMS *Euryalus* was paid off in Devonport after nearly 25 years of service.

Meaning 'Wide Wanderer', the first HMS *Euryalus* was built in 1803 as a 36-gun frigate of 944 tons. During the blockade of the Franco-Spanish fleet in Cadiz, she lay off the harbour on constant guard for enemy movement for so long that she became known as 'Nelson's Watchdog'. Under the command of Captain Henry Blackwood, HMS *Euryalus* carried Nelson's famous signal 'England expects every man will do his duty' around the fleet for all to see at the outset of the battle of Trafalgar. Her Great War successor, the fourth to bear the name Euryalus, was a Cressy Class Large Cruiser of 12,000 tons built by Vickers at Barrow and launched on 20 May 1901. Of the 957 men of the 1st Battalion Lancashire Fusiliers who sailed with HMS *Euryalus* to the Lancashire Landings, 547 were killed or wounded while 63 of the 80 sailors who rowed them ashore were killed or wounded. Such a shared experience forged the closest alliance ever between a British Army regiment and a Royal Navy vessel. IWM Q13367

During the Falklands War of 1982, while acting as 'goalkeeper' in the air defence role to the Task Force landings in San Carlos Water, HMS *Antelope* was struck by two 1,000 pound bombs during an air raid by four Argentinian A-4 Skyhawk aircraft on 23 May 1982. Neither detonated but during subsequent bomb disposal operations, one exploded blowing the starboard side out of the ship. Shortly after first light on 24 May, the second bomb exploded causing HMS *Antelope* to break her back and sink. Two men were killed and two seriously injured. Thus, the association between HMS *Antelope* and the Regiment was lost but such alliances continue and will blossom once more, when and if another HMS *Antelope* is commissioned.

As a recognition of the longstanding alliance between the Regiment and HMS *Antelope*, a memorial service for the ship was held overlooking San Carlos Water on 29 January 1984. With the band of 2RRF providing the music, the service was conducted by Padre Alistair Heagerty and six sailors from the Naval Task Unit attended to represent the survivors of HMS *Antelope*.

The 1st Battalion Royal Regiment of Fusiliers holds the ship's bell of the last HMS *Euryalus*. HMS *London* was first associated with the Royal Fusiliers in 1931. The affiliation was formed in recognition of the fact that the ship and Regiment both bore the name of the City of London. The Mercers' Company who have had a traditional association with HMS *London* and The Royal Regiment of Fusiliers further cements the link. The huge and most substantial silver model of HM Tower of London, proudly displayed within the Association Room at RHQ, belongs to HMS *London* but is entailed to the Regiment for safe keeping. Whenever HMS *London* visited her home port, the Regiment was delighted to deliver it back to her, safe in the knowledge that it was far too bulky a piece of silver to be stowed onboard a modern ship. The most recent HMS *London* was the tenth ship to bear this name and was a County Class guided missile destroyer commissioned on 5 June 1987. As a consequence of the Strategic Defence Review, HMS *London* was decommissioned in June 1999.

HMS *Northumberland* is the second of two allied ships still in commission as this history concludes. Named after the Duke of Northumberland she was commissioned on the 29 September 1994 at Plymouth. The keel was laid by the Duke of Northumberland in April 1991 and she was launched a year later. She is a Duke Class Type 23 Frigate with the pennant number F238. The affiliation between HMS *Northumberland* and the Regiment was established after the commissioning of the Ship in 1994 and symbolises our mutual historical connections with Northumberland and the Percy family.

Resplendent in his bearskin cap, the Drum Major leads the Corps of Drums of the 2nd Battalion in a rendition of 'Those Magnificent Men in their Flying Machines' in front of a Tornado GR1A of 13 Squadron RAF, with which the Regiment formed an alliance on Minden Day 1991. Military bands remain an integral part of all three Services. The Regiment has inherited several particular pieces of music from the antecedent regiments including 'Blaydon Races'; 'Warwickshire Lads'; 'Fighting with the 7th Royal Fusiliers' and 'The Minden March'. The Regimental March is 'The British Grenadiers' and its Slow March 'Rule Britannia'. The latter is in recognition of the years of service as Marines aboard ships of the Royal Navy by three of the antecedent regiments: the 5th in 1778; the 7th in 1742-44 and the XX in 1702-03.

ALLIED SQUADRON ROYAL AIR FORCE

On Minden Day 1991, an affiliation between 13 Squadron RAF and the Regiment was established. 13 Squadron is currently a Tornado Reconnaissance Squadron and trains with all battalions. Regular exchange visits take place. The Squadron is based at RAF Marham in Norfolk. Once a year the Squadron is able to host an annual Ladies Dinner Night within the Association Room in Her Majesty's Tower of London, a privilege they much appreciate. Battalion Seconds-in-Command and Company Commanders are frequently able to 'wave their magic wand' and impress their Fusiliers by producing at short notice aerial photographs of their defensive positions or of their armoured vehicles on manoeuvres, courtesy of 13 Squadron.

ALLIED REGIMENTS

The following Regiments, which were allied to the former Regiments, are now allied to or have affiliations with the Royal Regiment of Fusiliers.
The Royal Welch Fusiliers
The Royal Victoria Regiment
31 Combat Engineer Regiment (The Elgins)
The Royal Canadian Regiment
The Lorne Scots (Peel, Dufferin and Halton Regiment).
The Royal Westminster Regiment
The Hauraki Regiment

ALLIED REGIMENT AUSTRALIAN ARMY

The Royal Victoria Regiment

The previous alliance with the Royal Fusiliers was formed in 1963 as a result of the Royal Melbourne Regiment being amalgamated with the Victorian Scottish Regiment and the City of Essendon Regiment to form the 1st Battalion the Royal Victoria Regiment. The Melbourne Regiment became allied to the Royal Fusiliers in 1930. It received the title 'Royal' in 1935. The Regiment is a militia visit for the Australian Army and it was formed in 1960. The Regimental HQ is at Melbourne.

Over the years, the Royal Regiment of Fusiliers has formed many friendships with the units of other armies. Some of these have been formalised into specific alliances although these are not officially recognised by the Ministry of Defence. The Regiment enjoys such an arrangement with seven Allied Regiments within the British Commonwealth, including the two shown here with the 6th Battalion (Hauraki) The Royal New Zealand Regiment and its Colour party leading a company of the 1st Battalion The Royal Victoria Regiment through the streets of Tauranga, the home town of the Hauraki, on 28 March 1981. The Australians were in New Zealand for annual training.

ALLIED REGIMENTS CANADIAN ARMY

As recently as March 2000 the Colonel of the Regiment, Brigadier D A K Biggart OBE, visited all four of our Allied Canadian Regiments. His visit was triggered by the Royal Canadian Regiment's invitation to attend their centenary anniversary ball commemorating their Paardeberg 2000 Centenary.

The Royal Canadian Regiment

The previous alliance with the Royal Fusiliers was formed in December 1961 as a result of the London and Oxford Fusiliers (formerly the Canadian Fusiliers (City of London Regiment)) having been renamed 3rd Battalion The Royal Canadian Regiment. The Canadian Fusiliers were first allied to the Royal Fusiliers in 1927. The Regiment is on the regular establishment of the Canadian Army and was formed in 1883. The Regimental HQ is at Petawawa, Ontario. There are three regular battalions of the Regiment and one militia battalion. It was customary for an officer of the Regiment, usually in the rank of captain, to exchange appointments for two to two-and-a-half years, with an officer of the Royal Regiment of Fusiliers.

31 Combat Engineer Regiment (The Elgins)

The previous alliance with the Royal Northumberland Fusiliers was formed in 1929 as a result of the connection between the Regiment and Col Talbot, who commanded the 2nd Battalion of the Fifth 1795-1803, and who was largely responsible for the settlement of Elgin County, Ontario. Until 1997 the Regiment was a militia regiment of the Royal Canadian Armoured Corps and it was formed in 1866. On 25th September 1997 the Regiment was re-roled as an Engineer Regiment and renamed 31 Combat Engineer Regiment (The Elgins). Notwithstanding this, both the Elgins and the Fusiliers are determined to maintain the alliance and this determination was much in evidence when the Colonel visited them in the Millennium year. The Regimental HQ is at St Thomas, Ontario.

The Lorne Scots (Peel, Dufferin and Halton Regiment)

The previous alliance with the Lancashire Fusiliers was formed in 1929 as a result of the Regiment's application to be allied to the 20th. A Major Crockett, an officer of the Regiment, which was then called the Peel and Dufferin Regiment, had served with the 20th in the 1914-18 war. The Regiment, now known as the Lorne Scots, is a militia regiment of the Canadian Army. It was formed by the amalgamation of the Peel and Dufferin Regiment with the Lorne Rifles in 1936. The Regimental HQ is at Brampton, Ontario. Our Colonel-in-Chief, Field Marshal HRH The Duke of Kent, KG, is also the Colonel-in-Chief of the Lorne Scots.

The Royal Westminster Regiment

The previous alliance with the Royal Warwickshire Fusiliers was formed in 1932 as a result of the Regiment's application to be allied to a British infantry regiment preferably to the Sixth as several Westminster Regiment officers had served in the Sixth. The Regiment is a militia Regiment of the Canadian Army and it was formed in 1924. The Regimental HQ is at New Westminster, British Columbia.

ALLIED REGIMENT NEW ZEALAND ARMY

The Hauraki Regiment

The previous alliance with the Royal Warwickshire Regiment was formed in 1925 as a result of close associations during the 1914-18 war, both Regiments having served in Gallipoli and fought together in at least one engagement. Also the Hauraki Regiment was previously designated '6th Hauraki Regiment' and there was thus a common titular association with the 6th. Until 1999, the battalion was a Territorial Force Battalion of the Royal New Zealand Infantry Regiment, titled 6th Battalion (Hauraki) The Royal New Zealand Infantry Regiment. It was formed in 1911, however in 1999 it suffered the same fate as so many militia units, and was reduced in size and restructured as one of six dimensionless regiments. Currently, combined with elements of an armoured regiment, they have a specialised role of armoured reconnaissance. They remain based at Tauranga.

There is also a long-standing relationship confirmed in a bond of friendship between the Royal Welch Fusiliers and the Regiment. This goes back to the early 1800s and is especially remembered for the events of the 'Fuzileer Brigade' at Albuhera on 16 May 1811. The account by Sir William Napier recalls: 'The Fuzileer battalions, struck by an iron tempest, reeled and staggered like sinking ships; but suddenly and sternly recovering they closed on their terrible enemies, and then was seen with what strength and majesty the British soldier fights'. As recently as 1999 the two Regiments were neighbours, this time in Northern Ireland with the Welch Fusiliers in Ballykelly and the 1st Battalion in Londonderry.

LIVERY COMPANIES

The Mercers' Company is the Senior Livery Company in The City of London and originally its members were merchants. Today they are extremely influential within the City and control and own much property within the City of London. Mercers' Hall was rebuilt on the site of the original Hall as recently as 1958. Many members of the Regiment have been fortunate to have visited the Hall and they have always been made most welcome. The Colonel-in-Chief himself became a member of the Mercers' Company in February 1972. The Association between the Regiment and the Company dates back to 1957 when the Company decided to form an Association with the 1st Battalion Royal Fusiliers (City of London Regiment). Since then it has continued to give its support to the Regiment. New Regimental and Queen's Colour belts were presented by the Company to the 1st Battalion in September 1967. In 1968, the association was continued with the 3rd Battalion Royal Regiment of Fusiliers but after 1992, on the merging of the 3rd Battalion with the 1st and 2nd Battalions, the Company kindly agreed to maintain its association equally between both of our two regular Battalions.

The Company generously gives an annual charitable grant to each of the Commanding Officers for the welfare of the Fusiliers in the Battalions. Ceremonial Guidon Poles, first presented to the 3rd Battalion and now housed in the Officers' Mess of the 1st Battalion are used to mark out the parade ground on all Battalion parades. The 2nd Battalion holds the gold Mercers' Cup. In 1960 a Regimental expedition conquered an unclimbed peak of 9,000 feet in the Canadian Rockies and named it Mercers' Peak. To commemorate the 1st Centenary of its association with the City of London in 1965, the Regiment presented the Company with a statuette in silver of an 18th Century Regimental Drummer. This is proudly displayed in Silver Vaults within Mercers' Hall. Over the years some long lasting friendships have been established between Mercers and members of the Regiment. These have often started when Mercers have visited Battalions, especially when those Battalions are overseas. Friendships are further strengthened by the annual Golf Matches between the Regiment and the Mercers' Company. Coinciding with the Millennium the Mercers' Company have recently commissioned two new silver cups, one for each Battalion, called the Mercers' Fitness Challenge Cups. On these will be recorded the names of those who achieve the highest individual scores in the obligatory bi-annual fitness tests. These will further cement the ties between the Company and the Regiment.

The Cordwainers' Company established in 1272 has since 1954 most generously supported the Fusilier TA Company in Balham and more recently two Fusilier badged ACF units, 212 and 22 Companies. They have provided mini-busses to these detachments. The Cordwainers' first contact with the TA was with 624 Light Ack-Ack Battalion (Royal Fusiliers). Each year the Cordwainers entertain all ranks of C (City of London) Company, now part of the London Regiment, their ACF Fusiliers and members of the Area Headquarters London to a sumptuous livery dinner in Chancery Lane. The Cordwainers' Company is unique in entertaining all ranks, rather than selected officers, to such livery dinners. Very close relationships have consequently developed over the years between the Company and the Fusiliers in London.

REGIMENTAL SILVER
With almost 1,200 years of accumulated history, The Royal Regiment of Fusiliers has acquired a fine array of Regimental Silver exemplified by this splendid centrepiece of St George killing the dragon that was once the property of the Fighting 5th - the Royal Northumberland Fusiliers. It is now held by the 1st Battalion. In the background are the Battalion's Colours with the Wilhelmstahl Colour in the middle. SD

Beneath the watch tower of ROMEO 16, Lt Craig Taylor pauses beside the memorial to Fus Andrew Grundy at the site of ROMEO 15 on a routine patrol in South Armagh during the 1RRF tour of 2000. SD

Appendix 2

THE ROLL OF HONOUR

THOSE WHO DIED DURING SERVICE WITH THE ROYAL REGIMENT OF FUSILIERS
FROM 23 APRIL 1968 TO 23 APRIL 2000

BLACKSTOCK J. LIEUTENANT COLONEL MBE Natural causes – Minehead Hospital	22 November 1968
RAYMENT A W. WARRANT OFFICER CLASS 1 Natural causes – Queen Alexandra's RMH, Millbank	22 January 1969
JEFFS A D. LANCE CORPORAL Natural causes – Royal Herbert Hospital, Woolwich	13 April 1970
HUDSON G E. MAJOR MC Natural causes – Queen Alexandra's RMH Millbank	27 November 1970
FORSDYKE A J. FUSILIER Natural causes – Radcliffe Infirmary Oxford	27 November 1970
HOPE D. FUSILIER Road Traffic accident – UK	4 July 1971
HOGG N. LANCE CORPORAL Natural causes – Naval Hospital, Gibraltar	18 October 1971
SNOW J J E. MAJOR Of wounds received in Northern Ireland	8 December 1972
SCRAGG R A. LIEUTENANT Natural causes – Queen Alexandra's RMH, Millbank	13 January 1972
KELLEHER M. FUSILIER Drowned on training near Colchester	6 July 1972
CANHAM K. FUSILIER Terrorist action in Northern Ireland	14 July 1972
TINGEY A B. FUSILIER Terrorist action in Northern Ireland	23 August 1972
DAVIS J. LANCE CORPORAL Of wounds received in Northern Ireland	15 September 1972
GREY A S. FUSILIER Accidentally drowned at sea – Essex coast	18 November 1972
NAPIER D. CORPORAL Traffic accident on mobile patrol – Northern Ireland	9 March 1973
MARCHANT C J. FUSILIER Of wounds received in Northern Ireland	9 April 1973
WENLOCK G H. FUSILIER Natural causes - Catterick	16 April 1973
HAUGHTON C. CORPORAL Terrorist action – Yorkshire	4 February 1974
McSHANE J. LANCE CORPORAL Terrorist action – Yorkshire	4 February 1974
HYNES J. FUSILIER Terrorist action – Yorkshire	4 February 1974
WHALLEY S. FUSILIER Terrorist action – Yorkshire	7 February 1974
HOLMES G. BANDSMAN Natural causes – Catterick	7 March 1974

SIMMONS A. FUSILIER Terrorist action – Northern Ireland	15 November 1974
HIND R. CAPTAIN Natural causes	14 October 1974
BERRY I. FUSILIER Natural causes	26 November 1974
LLEWELLYN D. CORPORAL Road accident	25 September 1975
GLEESON E. CORPORAL Terrorist action	9 October 1975
FRANCIS S J. SERGEANT Terrorist action	21 November 1975
SAMPSON M J F. FUSILIER Terrorist action	22 November 1975
DUNCAN J D. FUSILIER Terrorist action	22 November 1975
McDONALD P L. FUSILIER Terrorist action	22 November 1975
ROLLINS K J. FUSILIER Natural causes	25 November 1975
PRINGLE R. FUSILIER Road accident	19 December 1975
JAMIESON J. CORPORAL Homicide	22 September 1975
TRAYNOR D. CORPORAL Terrorist action	30 March 1976
LAVERTY B. FUSILIER Road accident	5 October 1976
HYAM J R. FUSILIER Road accident	19 November 1976
PETERSON A C. CORPORAL Range accident	22 April 1977
HALL N. FUSILIER Vehicle accident	25 June 1977
KEECH M. FUSILIER Road accident	18 August 1977
SHIELDS E E. FUSILIER Road Traffic Accident BAOR	1 January 1978
BURROWS A G. FUSILIER Death by Misadventure	7 July 1978
CLARKE E. BANDSMAN Road Traffic Accident	31 March 1979
LORD I. LANCE CORPORAL Road Traffic Accident BAOR	28 April 1979
HALL S J. FUSILIER Road Traffic Accident	30 August 1979
WHITEMAN J. FUSILIER Road Traffic Accident	30 August 1979

VAN DEN BERGH G A. FUSILIER Road Traffic Accident BAOR	4 November 1979
GIBSON W. FUSILIER Natural Causes	20 March 1980
SHIELDS D E. FUSILIER Road Traffic Accident BAOR	18 May 1980
FOXALL G W. FUSILIER Accidental Death – Northern Ireland	16 June 1980
FAULKNER R D. CAPTAIN Natural Causes BAOR	16 June 1978
FOXALL T. FUSILIER Road Traffic Accident, Northern Ireland	19 June 1980
BARKER P. CORPORAL Terrorist Action, Northern Ireland	25 January 1981
STAMP R. FUSILIER Natural Causes QEMH Woolwich	11 August 1981
LOCHHEAD G S. CAPTAIN Training Accident, Belize	11 October 1981
WALKER G D FUSILIER Accidental Death	12 April 1982
CLARKE A J. SERGEANT Road Traffic Accident, Berlin	10 October 1982
LIGHTFOOT S. FUSILIER Natural Causes, QEMH Woolwich	20 October 1982
MAKIN W T. LANCE-CORPORAL Accidental Death, Northern Ireland	3 January 1983
CALLENDER M O B. CORPORAL Road Traffic Accident, Berlin Corridor	6 April 1983
BRUNSKILL A E. FUSILIER Accidental Death, BAOR	28 April 1983
AGAR T H. CORPORAL Terrorist Action, Northern Ireland	18 May 1984
HUGGINS R V. LANCE-CORPORAL Terrorist Action, Northern Ireland	18 May 1984
WADE R G. CORPORAL Natural Causes, Catterick Camp	21 May, 1987
GALLIMORE P W. LANCE-CORPORAL Terrorist Action, Northern Ireland	18 October 1984
MOORE D W. COLOUR SERGEANT Training Accident, Warminster	7 March 1986
THORNTON P N. FUSILIER Road Traffic Accident, Wales	7 March 198
COOKMAN A J P. WARRANT OFFICER CLASS 2 Natural Causes, Catterick Camp	23 April 1987
BROWN N C. MAJOR Natural Causes, Bassingbourn	25 November 1988
DUFFIELD K. FUSILIER Accidental Death, Newcastle-upon-Tyne	24 December 1988
STREET R. SERGEANT Natural Causes, Catterick	14 April 1989

GRIFFITHS K C. WARRANT OFFICER CLASS 1 Natural Causes, Canterbury	3 August 1990
BROWN M. FUSILIER Accidental Death, Gibraltar	8 October 1990
ATKINSON P P. FUSILIER Killed in Action, Gulf	26 February 1991
COLE C P. FUSILIER Killed in action, Gulf	26 February 1991
GILLESPIE R A. FUSILIER Killed in Action, Gulf	26 February 1991
LEECH K. FUSILIER Killed in Action, Gulf	26 February 1991
THOMPSON L J. FUSILIER Killed in Action, Gulf	26 February 1991
SATCHELL S T. FUSILIER Killed in Action Gulf	26 February 1991
GOODES A L. WARRANT OFFICER CLASS 2 Natural Causes, Bassingbourn	4 March 1991
BUNNEY A. FUSILIER Training Accident – Gulf	23 March 1991
O'NEILL T CORPORAL Terrorist Action – Northern Ireland	25 May 1991
GRUNDY A J. FUSILIER Terrorist Action – Northern Ireland	1 May 1992
BESWICK M J. LANCE CORPORAL Terrorist Action – Northern Ireland	9 February 1993
DODDS R T F. CORPORAL Natural Causes – North Shields	19 November 1993
RICHES G. FUSILIER Accidental Death – Bosnia Herzegovina	25 October 1995
METCALFE P. FUSILIER Misadventure – Warwickshire	8 April 1996
MURRAY M J. FUSILIER Misadventure – Warcop Training Camp	25 June 1996
GILLAN P. WARRANT OFFICER CLASS 2 Misadventure – Celle German	9 November 1996
PARTRIDGE M. FUSILIER Burns Injury – Newcastle	9 September 1997
CASE M J B. FUSILIER Training Accident	22 April 1999
GIBSON D. FUSILIER Training Accident	18 August 1999
NESBITT T R. FUSILIER Misadventure	11 December 1999

In the grounds of Bessbrook Mill, WO2 Dave Satchell pauses in a quiet moment of contemplation on St George's Day 2000 beside the memorial stone to the Fusiliers killed in South Armagh between 1975 and 1992. Dave Satchell's brother, Stephen, was killed in the blue on blue incident during the Gulf War. SD

Appendix 3

THE REGIMENT'S FORGOTTEN ARMY

Assault Pioneers of 6RRF (V) with from L to R Cpl Henderson, WO2 Burn and Cpl Turner prepare a bridge for demolition during annual camp at Longmoor in 1993 in a practice task for the battalion's wartime NATO role of rear area security duties in Germany. *SOLDIER Magazine*

AT THE SHARP END

After 11 rain soaked days on the north German plains during Exercise 'Red Claymore', the men of the 5th (Volunteer) Battalion Royal Regiment of Fusiliers huddled in their muddy defensive positions around two strategic bridges over the Weser River. As the forward elements of the 3rd Armoured Division, they, together with a Royal Engineer detachment, were tasked with demolishing the bridges at the last possible moment once all the allied forces were across the river and through their positions. The last units were to be from the Bundesgrenschutze whose Leopard tanks would be showing yellow markers. As yet, they had not arrived. More ominously the sound of helicopter engines had been heard on both flanks, but no intelligence had been received as to whether or not they were hostile.

Battalion headquarters was concealed in a barn by the side of the road. As the rain streamed down, they became aware of the unequal battle between the rearmost sentries from C (Balham) Company and orange enemy forces, represented by 1st Battalion King's Own Scottish Borderers. The enemy had been landed by helicopter behind the battalion and now swept through the positions of 5RRF. Despite having sited Fusiliers to cover this eventuality, reduced visibility and sheer weight of numbers meant that the defenders were soon overwhelmed and one of the bridges was captured intact. This scenario happened during an actual field exercise in 1981 to test the volunteer regiments of the Territorial Army in one of their real wartime deployment tasks in the event of an offensive by the Warsaw Pact in northern Europe. Mercifully, no such battle occurred in reality but ever since 1945 one question repeatedly vexed the Regular Army, 'What do we do with the Territorials?'. The Fusiliers have felt the effects of this conundrum more than most.

The Regular Army has always had an ambivalent attitude towards its Territorial comrades; a sort of 'can't live with them, can't live without them' relationship. Ever since the Volunteers raised during the Napoleonic Wars had been effectively abolished in 1814 and the Local Militia shortly thereafter - voices were raised for and against the creation and maintenance of a Volunteer force designed to protect mainland Britain in the event of war. Matters came to a head in 1848 when the Duke of Wellington and Sir Charles Napier called on Parliament to provide for the defence of Britain. The new C-in-C of the Army, HRH The Duke of Cambridge, was not convinced of the value of volunteers and expressed his sentiments in a letter to Lord Panmure (the then Secretary of State for War) they were blunt, - 'If such a system were to be adopted, the spirit of the Regular Army would be destroyed and jealousies would at once be engendered'. However by 1859, sabre-rattling by France and general instability in Europe overcame these prejudices and, following much public pressure, a Volunteer force was authorised as an individual force separate from the Regular Army. Tasked with the defence of mainland Britain, there was no liability for service overseas. It was not until 1908 that the Volunteers became part of the Regular Army's structure following the adoption of the Haldane Reforms, with a new title, The Territorial Force. This force was itself demobilised in 1920 to be followed in 1922 by the creation of The Territorial Army whose members now had an obligation to serve overseas if required - the 'Territorials' had arrived.

During a field training exercise on the Gareloch Head Peninsula in Scotland, members of 6RRF (V) mount the final attack on an 'enemy' position during preparations for annual camp in 1996.

The forward elements of X Company 6RRF (V) clear the DZ as another RAF Puma comes into land during Exercise 'Merlin Lift' in 1986. With their light scales and good level of skills, TA infantry formations were well suited to airmobile operations, where their lack of full combat fitness was less significant. Unfortunately, the TA was not required to fulfil this role for long.

BIRTHING PAINS

Following WW2, the Territorial Army was reconstituted in 1947 as part of the Regular Army following the provisions of the National Service Act of 1939. In 1963, the last of Britain's conscripts was discharged, but under the terms of the National Service Act of 1950, they still had to serve a further 3 years and 6 months part time in the reserves. The Suez crisis of 1956 had shown that reservists had been deficient and not deployable on active service without further training. Furthermore, despite the attendance of National Servicemen, many units in the TA were woefully small and militarily ineffective. In its current form the TA was unsustainable. Accordingly, having rid itself of the burden of conscription, the Regular Army set about revising the TA while at the same time attempting to reduce costs and instil a greater level of professionalism and readiness into the Volunteers.

By 1966, there were six TA infantry battalions in the Fusilier Brigade - 4th/5th, 6th and 7th Battalions; Royal Northumberland Fusiliers; 7th Royal Warwickshire Fusiliers; the City of London Battalion Royal Fusiliers and the 5th Battalion Lancashire Fusiliers. At the time, all were thriving, well-recruited and motivated battalions but this cut little ice with the functionaries in Whitehall. Changes were instituted to the TA with a complete lack of sense or sensitivity. On 1 April 1967, the Territorial Army and Volunteer Reserve (T&AVR) was formed, comprising three separate organisations, each with a distinct role and different conditions of service. T&AVR I had an establishment of 1,600. It was tasked with providing logistical support for NATO operations and to combine with the 'Ever Ready' soldiers drawn from T&AVR II which had an establishment of 50,800. This Special Army Volunteer Reserve had a liability to serve for 6 months when mobilised. Its soldiers were paid an annual bounty and did a 15-day camp each year. Every third year, this was held abroad. Most bizarre of all was the creation of the 23,000 strong T&AVR III of mainly cadre units whose soldiers were not entitled to a bounty and were allowed only an eight-day camp per year.

The changes to the Fusilier battalions of the day were little short of cataclysmic. The effect of these cuts meant one battalion existed as T&AVR II and two as T&AVR III but the latter would exist as a cadre only, each with a nucleus of eight men from which a battalion was supposed to appear in time of mobilisation. In Warwickshire, the 7th Battalion The Royal Warwickshire Fusiliers was disbanded on 31 March 1967, having come into existence only four years previously when the Royal Warwickshire Regiment had joined the Fusilier Brigade. It reformed on 1 April as the Fusilier Volunteers consisting of Battalion Headquarters, Headquarter and B Companies in Coventry; A Company in Newcastle upon Tyne; C Company in Balham, London and D Company in Bury, Lancashire. The Fusiliers in Northumberland were to see three thriving battalions reduced first to two battalions, the 4th/5th/6th and the 7th, and then to one company and two cadres of about eight men each. Colonel Bill Etches realised that these TA reforms were handled very badly and, as in the struggle to secure the regular elements of the former regiments, little thought had been given to the effects of reorganisation on the TA as a whole or in part. Charged with explaining the proposed changes and not being one to flinch from a tough problem, he went to see the three battalions at Redesdale Camp in Northumberland and took Captain Patrick Robinson with him. The latter recalls, 'I think Colonel Bill took me along as a sort of hostage because I was from Northumberland. Before we faced the assembled officers we sat in the staff car in a lay-by outside Redesdale and worked out the changes there and then; almost a back of a fag packet job'. There is no doubt that this period gave rise to a general distrust of the Regular

At 84 years of age, Chelsea Pensioner T. Morris looks on as members of D Company 5RRF (V) march into the Parish Church Bury on Gallipoli Sunday on 15 April 1975.

Army in the TA, especially in the north-east, rather than the Whitehall functionaries who bore the true guilt. Regulars were viewed with suspicion and were well advised to tread carefully as not all were temperamentally suited to working with the TA. Indeed, some left a legacy of bitterness that lasted long after they had moved onto other appointments. Many in the TA saw the regulars as intruders with little understanding of them - especially if they found fault, pruned the slackers and rooted out perceived bad practice. Similarly, many regulars, from the MOD downward, let their 'arrogance and ignorance' prejudice their dealings with the TA. There is no doubt that, when given the right tools, resources and guidance the Territorial invariably surprised the outsider - but to those regulars who served with them this was no surprise at all!

On St George's Day 1968, the Fusilier Volunteers became the 5th Battalion Royal Regiment of Fusiliers and in the following year they gained an additional company, E (Northumberland) Company based on Ashington and Alnwick. Lieutenant Colonel 'Paddy' Baxter found himself in command of one of the largest and most disparate military tribes ever seen. Realising that the surgery had been too traumatic, the MOD authorised the limited expansion of the T&AVR. On 1 April 1971, The Northumbrian Volunteers were formed in the north east as a multi-badged battalion. With its headquarters in Bishop Auckland, the battalion was commanded by Lieutenant Colonel Charles Baker-Cresswell and saw the expansion of each of the two cadres to company strength. The 4th/5th/6th RNF Cadre became C Company and the 7th RNF Cadre became D Company in the new battalion.

The next few years were marked by a series of re-adjustments. At first everyone involved 'got on with making the new system work', but it was obvious from the outset that the new TA structure was impractical as far as the Fusiliers were concerned. The sheer distances involved between companies, the inadequacies of the road and rail system (not to mention the unreliability of staff cars) meant that it was impossible to maintain a realistic level of day to day control over such a broad church. Calls for the establishment of a second battalion based on the north-east where it was more than able to recruit enough soldiers proved irresistible. On 1 April 1975, A and E Companies of the 5th Battalion and C and D Companies of The Northumbrian Volunteers merged to form the 6th (Volunteer) Battalion The Royal Regiment of Fusiliers. The first commanding officer was Lieutenant Colonel Mike Kelly and the battalion headquarters was established in Alnwick. The companies were titled X, Y, Z and HQ Companies. X and Y Companies were based in Newcastle, with Z Company at Ashington and HQ Company at Alnwick and Berwick. X Company also had a detachment at Hexham. In April 1978, a fourth rifle company was formed which was designated W Company. It was based at Berwick and Alnwick.

GETTING THE BALANCE RIGHT

The main problem following the formation of the Royal Regiment of Fusiliers was finding a viable a role for the Territorials. Initially, the 5th Battalion and later the 6th were tasked with 'reinforcing NATO forces in Europe'. In keeping with all other TA units, this meant an annual camp in Germany every three years which was both a climax to the TA's three year training cycle and a chance to exercise in their intended theatre of operations. Unfortunately this indeterminate role meant that regular formations in Germany, often woefully ignorant of the

Fusiliers of Z Company 6RRF man a slit trench during Exercise 'Lionheart 84' during major manoeuvres in Germany during September 1984 with from L to R L/Cpl Oliver, Fus Marshall, and Cpl Rutherford. With many miners from Ashington, Z Company was renowned for the quality of its field emplacements. The TA Fusiliers were in the field for 11 days and nights

TA and its capabilities, frequently employed TA units for inappropriate tasks. On one recce the 3rd Battalion of this war role deployment in 1978, the astonished staffs were told that the vital ground to the rear of the brigade was to be held by the 1st Battalion The Yorkshire Volunteers (1 YORKS). When pressed as to the wisdom of this it was firmly stated that '1 YORKS will arrive on time'; and there was no obvious fallback plan.

The role problem was compounded by the TA's natural desire to 'do something interesting and worthwhile' both on exercise and for real. Initial attempts to satisfy both sides were, on occasions, fraught. Just how fraught can best be illustrated by the experiences of the 5th Battalion during Exercise 'Gryphons Galore' in Germany in 1978. This was an exercise conducted by 5 Field Force and a third of all the troops involved were from the T&AVR. *The Fusilier* Regimental Journal contains a full account of what took place but described in such a way that the casual reader would think it had been a wonderful high-octane experience. The battalion deployed into the field immediately on arrival in Germany which was, as the Journal records, 'a stimulating experience; like learning to drive a car on a deserted aircraft runway and, having mastered the basic rudiments, being invited to drive round Hyde Park Corner in the rush hour! Coupled with the problems of driving on the right, reading German maps, and not knowing even at section level who you've got in your team until you shake out on the ground, I like to think all this produces a situation which might make even a seasoned regular raise an eyebrow'. Invited to go on Exercise 'Crusader' two years later, only the Anti-Tank Platoon took part. The perceived wisdom was 'the battalion cannot afford another Gryphons Galore'.

Someone took the post exercise lessons to heart. Exercise 'Crusader' in 1980 saw the deployment of the 6th Battalion as part of the 20,000 strong TA contingent deployed on the exercise. TA because in 1979 the unpopular T&AVR title had finally been replaced by the evergreen and popular title, 'The Territorial Army'. Exercise 'Crusader' was a great success and proved that by giving TA units a few days to shake out, a central deployment task for them to practise (defence of a bridge/feature/village or major headquarters), and then a number of subsequent tasks to perform, they could more than hold their own. This is exactly what the 5th Battalion did a year later on Exercise 'Red Claymore' and both battalions repeated on Exercises 'Lionheart' in 1984 and 'Keystone' in 1987. On the latter exercise, the 6th Battalion's defensive position was judged so good that it attracted a stream of visitors, from MPs to foreign Arms Control observers. Even the exercise enemy was impressed. When the position was attacked by the Gordon Highlanders one company, during the ensuing battle, was told by their Sergeant Major, 'Now I hope you are looking carefully, because this is how to construct a slit-trench'.

SWINGS AND ROUNDABOUTS

By the mid-1980s, the TA was almost fully recruited and the MOD began to look once again at re-organising the TA or its 'Phased Enhancement'. In 1985, the 5th Battalion gained an extra company, A Company based in Sparkbrook, Birmingham, and the 6th Battalion became the proud owners of a Home Service Force (HSF) Company. Given the title St Lucia Company and dubbed (inevitably) as 'Dad's Army' by the Press, with two applicants for every place the company was fully recruited from scratch within ten weeks! Although only allowed 12 days training a year, a strong bond quickly developed, epitomised by their motto, 'Old Age and Treachery will defeat Youth and Skill'. Their role was to defend Key Points (KPs) in the event of war and they quickly set about preparing plans for the defence of such KPs as radio-relay sites, power stations and sewage works across the north-east.

On 1 April 1986, amid rumours that they too were to get a HSF Company, the 5th Battalion gained another company, C (Lancashire) Company based in Ashton-under Lyne. This company re-badged from the 4th Battalion The Queen's Lancashire Regiment (4 QLR) as a prelude to the formation in the Midlands and North West of a four rifle company battalion and a new TA Battalion in London. This latter event meant the eventual transfer of C (Balham) Company in 1988 to the newly-formed 8th Battalion The Queen's Fusiliers (City of London) under Lieutenant Colonel Nick Brunt RRF, the 5th Battalion's HSF Company having arrived in November 1987 and was subsequently based in Birmingham with the title G Company.

The 1980s closed with both battalions finding their static roles developing into more fluid and 'light' roles, with increasing use of helicopters as the TA infantry's numbers and training standards made them ideally suited to acting as a heliborne mobile reserve. However, in the wider world, events were unfolding that would once again throw the organisation of the TA into the melting pot.

THE END OF THE AFFAIR

The disintegration of the Warsaw Pact and the indecent haste with which the Army was forced to make savings, first through the introduction of the 'New Management Strategy' and then 'Options for Change' were all compounded by Saddam Hussein's incursion in the Gulf.

When the new TA Home Service Force Company was formed in Newcastle in 1985, the press inevitably christened it 'Dad's Army' but, like the World War 2 forebears, there were many volunteers for the role with 200 applicants for 95 places. The new unit was officially called St Lucia (Home Service Force) Company 6RRF (V) or 'St Lucia Company' for short after the island where the hackle was first acquired. Here, four new members of the company, with L to R Fus Riding, Lilley, Wright and Henry, are kitted out with uniforms and hackles.

Sixteen TA Fusiliers from the 5th and six from the 6th Battalion volunteered to serve in the Gulf while the trickle of TA soldiers on attachments with the Regular battalions that had begun in the mid- 80s now assumed a real significance; indeed the 1st Battalion had taken 18 TA Fusiliers to South Armagh in 1988.

'Options for Change' for the TA, announced in 1992 and reflecting the perceived military realities of the day, saw the 5th Battalion lose its North Western companies and MILAN Anti-Tank Platoon but it gained a company from the Worcestershire and Sherwood Foresters. D Company in Bury now became C Company in 4 QLR and C Company in Ashton-under Lyne re-roled after a year into a Field Ambulance unit. In the north-east things were not so bad as the 6th Battalion lost Y Company but were chosen as one of only eight TA Battalions assigned to the newly-formed ACE Rapid Reaction Corps (ARRC) and placed under operational command of 19 Mechanised Brigade at Catterick. 8th Queen's Fusiliers were now re-titled The London Regiment and was expanded to include London Scottish and London Irish companies. Sadly, with non-ARRC battalions now being given greater responsibility for Home Defence, the HSF was disbanded. One small change to the battalions' titles also came about at this time; henceforth they were to be known as the 5th (Warwickshire) and 6th (Northumberland) Battalions, a change that reflected their geographical deployment.

Within 12 months the rumour machine was in action again with the 'Home Defence' role being changed to one of 'General War' and more proposed changes in the pipeline under the heading of a 'TA Review'. In the meantime, more and more TA Fusiliers found themselves volunteering to serve with the Regular Army (where manpower gaps were appearing at an alarming rate following the 'Options' redundancy programme), and TA battalions were regularly being asked to justify why they should not lose their Commanding Officer, Training Major, Quartermaster or Adjutant for a six months tour to help fill a short term commitment somewhere – a phenomenon that continues to this day.

In 1995, the TA Review was announced. The 5th Battalion lost its 81mm Mortar Platoon and the 6th lost its MILAN Anti-Tank and 81mm Mortar Platoons to help create 'Fire Support Battalions' elsewhere in the TA. By the end of the year, the 6th's flirtation with the ARRC had ended as it, like the 5th, was re-designated a General Reserve Battalion. Both battalions remained well recruited, despite all this turbulence, and increasingly more and more Fusiliers were spending time with the Regulars; 16 from the 6th Battalion alone went with 1st Battalion to Bosnia and TA Fusiliers could regularly be found in Northern Ireland and elsewhere. C (City of London Fusiliers) Company of the London Regiment has had some TA Fusiliers, usually up to ten per cent of the company, away on operational service in Northern Ireland or the Balkans continuously since 1995. Despite this, following the change of Government in 1997, the MOD announced a further review of the TA as part of the Strategic Defence Review (SDR). By now the manpower needs of the Regular Army were growing acute. 'Overstretch' and general undermanning meant that operational manning levels could not be met without increased use of the TA. Some regiments were luckier than others; while

Fusiliers of the Army Cadet Force and the Combined Cadet Force represent an important part of the Regiment with some 2,958 cadets wearing the hackle. The various affiliated ACF and CCF contingents include the Northumbria ACF, the Warwickshire and West Midlands (South Sector) ACF, Bury Grammar School CCF, King Edwards School CCF, Solihull School CCF, Mill Hill School CCF, Rugby School CCF, Warwick School CCF and Trinity School CCF. Here, cadets of the Northumbrian County ACF are shown on Newcastle Central Station on their way to annual camp in the early 1970s.

the 2nd Battalion deployed to Bosnia in 1997 with a small, mainly Fusilier TA contingent, their successors brought with them over 120 TA soldiers from several cap-badges!

SDR's impact on the TA was reminiscent of the trials of 1967 – but worse. Despite having two of the best-recruited and most militarily effective TA battalions the Regiment found itself emasculated and all its previous achievements counted for nothing. The 5th Battalion was reduced to a company in Birmingham, part of a newly formed West Midlands Battalion while the 6th Battalion was reduced to two companies in Newcastle and Ashington as part of the newly formed Tyne-Tees Regiment. The Fusilier company in Bury was reduced to a platoon and only in London did the status quo remain as far as the Fusiliers were concerned. It was difficult for many to remain objective when it was evident that smaller less effective and more poorly recruited regiments' TA components were reprieved at the expense of the successful; especially at a time when the Regular Army was relying increasingly on TA reinforcements.

POSTSCRIPT - TWICE A CITIZEN

Anyone who has managed to read thus far may be suffering from a form of déjà vu, indeed if the TA experience teaches us anything it is that all things are cyclical and that quality will always win through in the end. In one area in particular the Regiment can feel particularly proud and that is in the number and quality of its affiliated Cadet units, whether CCF or ACF. As the Editor of the December 1999 edition of the journal wrote, '..after the recent cuts there are 50% more Cadets than adults who wear the hackle (3,000 Cadets and only 2,000 adult Fusiliers)'. Our Cadets have been involved in so many aspects of Regimental life, from taking part in parades, freezing on exercise with the TA and HSF, collecting for charity and all the other public occasions where their presence and bearing has drawn praise from all quarters. Field Marshal The Lord Slim described the Territorial as 'Twice a Citizen'. It is fitting that this history should end at the grass roots, from where our future grows and where it is our duty to provide the environment and nourishment needed to allow the Fusiliers of the future to flourish.

The future of the Royal Regiment of Fusiliers lies with the young, exemplified by Cpl Alison Dunn of the Northumbria ACF - a 4-Star cadet with a bronze Duke of Edinburgh Award and qualifications in .22 shooting.

'These are the stories our Colours have to tell, these the lessons the names upon them teach. Not merely gallantry in action - that is a small thing, and one inherent to our race.

'They teach of privations uncomplainingly borne, of difficulties nobly surmounted, of steadfast loyalty to the Crown, and of obedience to orders even when that obedience meant certain death.

'These are the honours which have found an abiding place on the Colours of the British Army'

Postscript

I recall an instructor of mine at the former Army Staff College saying to a visiting politician who had characterised the Army as being elitist and set apart from the 'ordinary man' – 'well - I've always regarded myself as a member of a nationalised working institution now more than 300 years old!' That instructor reached the Army Board in due course.

No one can read a history like this without being struck by the great strength and inspiration a Regiment derives from having served the Crown continuously, without a single break, for over three centuries. Of course there have been changes in designation, organisation, role and size over the years, much of it in the last three decades, but the essential structure remains. I believe it is now generally accepted that the Regimental family system is what gives the Army, its 'teeth arms' specifically, its value and effectiveness in both peace and especially in war. The best size for the family remains a matter for discussion - ideas for 'large' and 'single parent'. Regiments and even more radical concepts have been with us at least since the late 1950's and the end of National Service. Personally, I consider we were wise in our generation to form The Royal Regiment of Fusiliers the way we did: we were certainly fortunate in having at the crucial time the leadership to make it work successfully, supported by the knowledge, staff ability and sheer hard work it demanded from Regimental Headquarters. I believe it has been an exceptional achievement, keeping and merging all that gave the original four Regiments their quality and character into a unity that manifestly works brilliantly - witness the record since 1968 in Northern Ireland, Cyprus, the Gulf and latterly in the Balkans, as well as elsewhere in many less hazardous roles.

Our territorial links remain vital and need constant nurture: here I would wish we had retained more of our Territorial Army units than we did in the outcome of the last Defence Review. Perhaps there will be some restoration… meanwhile it is reassuring to note the continuing support we get from our Counties, Boroughs and Cities, the Mercers Company (an even more long-lived and distinguished family!), the Cordwainers Company and the other organisations and affiliations country-wide and indeed overseas.

For the future, one can only hope for stability: the so called 'Peace Dividend' seems illusory, at least to an old infantryman, and I guess to the young Fusilier who has already earned several campaign medals in former Yugoslavia. I can do no better than quote the tablet near Europa Point in Gibraltar from 1842, recording the Fusiliers' labours there:

"Thus has been	Sic fuit
Thus ever will be	Sic semper erit
The true British soldier	Milis Britannicus
In war brave	Bello fortis
In peace orderly and useful	Pace bonus et utilis"

Major General David Woodford CBE
Colonel of the Regiment 1982 -1986

Acknowledgements

In a book of this nature, many people have made contributions, both large and small. To them all, I extend my thanks for their time and trouble in relating their recollections of their service with The Royal Regiment of Fusiliers. I also wish to thank the officers and men of the regular battalions for their kind hospitality during repeated visits to the Fusiliers in the field, from Belize to Bessbrook Mill and from Poland to Pristina.

WO2 Eddie Aldred
2Lt Johnny Austin
Col Alec Bain
WO2 Paddy Baines
Cpl Mark Balkham R SIGS
WO2 Mick Barnett-Connolly
Cpl Pete Bell
Lt Col Nick Beswick
Brig David Biggart
Maj Charles Bishop
Cpl Steve Boyd
Capt Tony Boyd
Maj Colin Bowes-Crick
Capt Guy Briselden
Maj Bob Broadbent
Capt Mike Butterwick
Capt John Caiger
Maj Fred Calvert
Capt Mark Canning
Sgt Paul Carr
Maj Guy Cartwright
Col Ian Cartwright
Lt Col Gary Cass
Maj Christopher Claridge
Capt Richard Coates
Maj Ted Coates
Maj John Collicut
Lt Col Peter Cross
C/Sgt Eddie Crossland
Capt Dennis Currie
Capt John Davis
Sgt Eddie Dean
Lt Col James Denny
Maj Brett Duxbury RLC
Capt Bill Edmonds
Col Bill Etches
Maj Hugh Evans
Sgt 'Fish' Fisher
Cpl Steve Forrest
Lt Charles Frisby
Lt Col Andrew Ford W GDS
C/Sgt Phil Forsyth
Capt James Fulford-Talbot
Sgt Peter Fyfe QO HLDR
C/Sgt 'Digger' Gardiner
WO2 Dave Gilling
Col Brian Gorski
Sgt Geoff Green
Maj & Mrs Andrew Greenwood
Sgt John Grieve
C/Sgt David Griffiths
Maj Jack Hall
Maj John Hallam
Maj Iain Hallam
Capt David Harding RGR
Maj Guy Harnby
Sgt 'Bod' Harris
Capt Andy Harris
Capt Phil Harris
Sgt 'Hawkeye' Hawkins
WO2 Tony Hay
Sgt Tom Hewitson
Capt Andy Higgs
Capt Jim Hill
Lt Col Kevin Hill
WO2 Steve Hills
WO2 Harry Hinnell
C/Sgt 'Spike' Holloway
Cpl Steve Hornsby
Cpl George Jay
Lt Col and Mrs Alan Jones
Capt Gary Jones
C/Sgt Phil Jones
Capt Malcolm Johnston
Capt Bob Keating
Lt Col Stuart Kempster RAMC
WO1 Dennis Kennedy
Lt Col & Mrs Keith Kiddie
Maj Ian Kippen
WO2 Brian Lammond QO HLDR
Lt Col Andrew Larpent
Capt Jonny Laws
Capt 'Mac' Leyland
C/Sgt Tom Loan
WO2 Howard Lycett
Maj Philip Macey
Cpl Joe MacGregor
WO2 Tony Margiotta
Capt & Mrs Peter Marr
Maj Simon Marr
Lt Col Andrew Marriott
Sgt James Marshall
Capt Mick McCarthy
2Lt Simon McCulloch
Drum Maj Dave McKenna
Sgt Derek McManus QO HLDR
Capt Alfie Meades
Capt Chris Mears
WO2 John Mickleson
Maj & Mrs Richard Mills
WO2 'Scouse' Millington
Maj David Milo
Brig Trevor Minter
Lt Col George Molyneux-Carter
WO2 Paddy Mooney
C/Sgt 'Ginge' Mornington
Col Philip Mostyn
WO2 Mark Moulding
WO2 John Mulheran
Capt Tom Murphy
Lt Col James Murray-Playfair
Maj Paul Nanson
WO2 'Chinney' Needham
Maj Gen Cosmo Nevill
Sgt Paul Noble
Capt John O'Grady
WO2 'O.G.' O'Grady
WO2 Ian Oliver
Lt Col David Paterson
Lt Rob Pavey
Capt Simon Peacock
Maj Corin Pearce R ANGLIAN
Cpl Mark Pearson
Lt Col George Pettifar
Rev Adrian Pollard
Lt Col James Porter
Maj John Powell PWRR
Maj William Pringle
Lt Ed Pugh
WO2 Jimmy Raynard
Capt Tony Reddy
Lt Gen Sir Jeremy Reilly
Brig Jonathen Riley RWF
Maj Neil Richardson
C/Sgt Darren Robinson
Capt Jeremy Robinson
Col Patrick Robinson
Cpl Ray Rose
WO1 Dennis Samways
WO2 Dave Satchell
Maj James Sayer
Sgt Tom Sayers
Brig Richard Shirreff KRH
Brig Peter Sincock
Sgt Trevor Smith R ANGLIAN
Lt Col David Spackman
Lt Col Philip Stack
Capt Jock Stacey
Capt Peter Stitt
Sgt Nick Stubbs
Lt Craig Taylor
Maj Steve Thomas
Maj Ian Thompson
Capt Matt Thorp
Maj Angus Welch
Cpl Dave Welsh
WO1 Peter West
Maj Andy Whelan
Maj John Whitwam
Maj Alistair Wicks KRH
Brig Roy Wilde
Lt Col Jolyon Willans
Capt Justin Wilson
Maj Gen David Woodford
Lt Col Geoff Youll

Due to limitations of space, all awards and decorations have been omitted.
Unless otherwise noted everyone listed above is either a former or current member of The Royal Regiment of Fusiliers.

I am honoured and deeply indebted to His Royal Highness The Duke of Kent for kindly writing the Foreword to 'For England and St George'.

I also extend my thanks to those who have assisted in many ways by providing their advice, pictures, expertise or that most precious commodity – time.

André Balkham
William Carman
Mike Chappell
Randolf Cooper
David Filsell
Simon Forty
John Harding
Rod Joyce
Colin Pooley
Desmond Chan
David Cohen
David Fletcher
Vanessa Harber
Philip Haythornthwaite
Martin Pegler
Jenny Spencer-Smith
Martin Windrow
Ralph Lillford

Unless otherwise stated all the photographs are courtesy of The Royal Regiment of Fusiliers via Regimental Headquarters, the various Battalions or the Regimental Museums. Fusiliers have contributed many photographs to their Regimental scrapbooks, which cannot be attributed to particular individuals to whom I extend my thanks and apologies.
Those photographs credited to the MOD are courtesy of Media Operations Land Command Wilton and the Director Public Relations Army.

I am particularly indebted to the Royal Armouries and the Imperial War Museum. Both institutions have waived their reproduction charges to assist in the production of this non-profit making regimental history. The staff of each museum has been unfailingly helpful and has responded to my varied inquiries and requests with courtesy and professionalism.
It is regrettable that not all national museums can provide such an efficient service to the general public.
All the photographs credited to the Imperial War Museum have IWM and a reference number appended and these may be obtained from:-

Photograph Archive, Imperial War Museum, Lambeth Road, London SE1 6HZ
photos@iwm.org.uk

CD-Rom copies of 'For England and St George' have been deposited with the Royal Armouries and the Imperial War Museum for posterity and reference purposes. The weapons illustrated in this book were kindly provided by the Weapons Department of the Royal Armouries.
These and other examples from their fabulous collection can be seen in the galleries of the museum at:-

The Royal Armouries, Armouries Drive, Leeds, LS10 1LT

I wish to acknowledge the kindness of David Rowlands for permission to reproduce one of his paintings, which he created following his visit to The Royal Regiment of Fusiliers in Kuwait soon after the end of the Gulf War.

My thanks are extended to the curators and staff of the four Regimental Museums. They have provided much information and illustrative material for the book. Each is well worth a visit. CD-Rom copies of 'For England and St George' are available for reference in each museum.

As ever, SOLDIER Magazine has been a splendid source of information and photographs. SOLDIER Magazine's remarkable archive is an unrivalled record of the British Army from World War 2 up to the present. The managing editor, Chris Horrocks, has kindly waived reproduction fees and provided photographs free of charge in support of this regimental history; my thanks also to Graeme Main and Stuart Robinson for their time and attention. The archive may be consulted at:-

SOLDIER, Ordnance Road, Aldershot, Hants GU11
www.soldiermagazine.co.uk

Mention must be made of the unstinting assistance given by the staff at RHQ who have provided admirable hospitality and assistance throughout the project. They have been unfailingly helpful during my many visits and include LCpl 'Geordie' Allan, Maj Gerry Daykin, Miss Pam Feltham and Adrian Tindall.

In particular, I wish to record the considerable debt owed to the Regimental Adjutant, Major Andrew Greenwood RRF, who, among a myriad of other duties, has undertaken the roles of historian, travel agent, minder, editor, reference librarian and general factotum. His contribution has been considerable and invaluable. Without his unflagging and cheerful support, this history would never have seen the light of day.

Finally, my thanks to Kate Cabot - like the other contributions large or small, hers was vital for the book's progress and completion.

SIMON DUNSTAN LONDON 2000

Bibliography

HISTORICAL RECORD OF THE 20TH FOOT - Adjutant Generals Office 1847
A COMPANION TO THE BRITISH ARMY 1660-1983 - David Ascoli (Harrap) 1983
BRITAIN AND HER ARMY - Corelli Barnett (Allen Lane) 1970
DARK DESTROYER - Nigel Benn (Blake) 1999
FRIENDLY FIRE - Richard Townshend Bickers (Leo Cooper) 1994
TOMMY GOES TO WAR - Malcolm Brown (Dent) 1978
THE VANISHED ARMY - Tim Carew (Kimber) 1964
BIRMINGHAM PALS -Terry Carter (Leo Cooper) 1995
THE SEVEN AGES OF THE BRITISH ARMY - FM Lord Carver (Weidenfeld and Nicolson) 1984
HISTORY OF THE ROYAL WARWICKSHIRE REGIMENT 1919-1955 Marcus Cunliffe (William Clowes) 1956
THE BRITISH ARMY IN NORTHERN IRELAND - Lt.Col. Michael Dewar (A&AP) 1985
THE ROYAL FUSILIERS - MIchael Foss (Hamish Hamilton) 1967
1914 - VCs OF THE GREAT WAR - Gerald Gliddon (Alan Sutton) 1994
BANDIT COUNTRY -The IRA and South Armagh - Toby Harnden (Hodder & Stoughton) 1999
PIG IN THE MIDDLE - The Army in Northern Ireland 1969-1984 - Desmond Hamill (Methuen) 1985
OPERATION DESERT SABRE - THE LIBERATION OF KUWAIT 1990-91 - Inspector General Doctrine and Training (MoD) 1993
OPERATION GRANBY - Inspector General Doctrine and Training (MoD) 1991
A HISTORY OF WARFARE - John Keegan (Hutchinson) 1993
THE STORY OF THE ROYAL WARWICKSHIRE REGIMENT - Charles Kingsford
THE WORKS OF LYN MACDONALD:-
-1914-1918 VOICES AND IMAGES OF THE GREAT WAR (Michael Joseph) 1988
-1914 THE DAYS OF HOPE (MIchael Joseph) 1987
-1915 THE DEATH OF INNOCENCE (Michael Joseph) 1993
-SOMME (Michael Joseph) 1983
-1918 TO THE LAST MAN (Michael Joseph) 1998
FOR LOVE OF REGIMENT - 2 VOLUMES - Charles Messenger (Leo Cooper) 1994
THE BRITISH INFANTRY 1660-1945 - Frederick Myatt (Blandford) 1983
THE LONG WAR -The IRA & Sinn Fein - Brendan O'Brien (The O'Brien Press) 1999
A POCKET HISTORY OF THE IRA - Brendan O'Brien (The O'Brien Press) 1997
THE ROYAL FUSILIERS IN THE GREAT WAR - H.C. O'Neill (Heineman) 1922
1914 - GLORY DEPARTING - Edward Owen (Buchan & Enright) 1986
THE ROYAL NORTHUMBERLAND FUSILIERS - Basil Peacock (Leo Cooper) 1970
THE SHIELD AND THE SABRE - Nigel Pearce (HMSO) 1992
SUMMARY OF THE HISTORY AND TRADITIONS OF THE FIFTH - THE NORTHUMBERLAND FUSILIERS - Maj. R. Pratt (Private Publication)
THE LANCASHIRE FUSILIERS - Cyril Ray (Leo Cooper) 1971
BRITISH REDCOAT 1740-1793 - Stuart Reid (Osprey) 1996
BRITISH REDCOAT 1793-1815 - Stuart Reid (Osprey) 1997
KING GEORGE'S ARMY - 2 VOLUMES - Stuart Reid (Osprey) 1995
WEAPONS OF THE BRITISH SOLDIER - Col. H.C.B. Rogers (Seeley) 1960
THE RUC 1922-2000 - A Force under Fire - Chris Ryder (Arrow) 2000
TYNESIDE IRISH - John Sheen (Pen & Sword) 1998
SALFORD PALS - Michael Stedman (Leo Cooper) 1993
XX THE LANCASHIRE FUSILIERS - Maj Gen. G Surtees (Malcolm Page) 1952
PROVOS THE IRA & SINN FEIN - Peter Taylor (Bloomsbury) 1998
MONS - John Terraine (Batsford) 1960
THE BRITISH ARMY 1660-1704 - John Tincey (Osprey) 1994
A HISTORY OF THE ROYAL NORTHUMBERLAND FUSILIERS 1674-1902 - John Walker (Murray) 1919
INFANTRY UNIFORMS 1742-1855 - R & C Wilkinson-Latham (Blandford) 1969
INFANTRY UNIFORMS 1855-1939 - R & C Wilkinson-Latham (Blandford) 1970
THE GREAT WAR AND THE SHAPING OF THE 20TH CENTURY - Jay Winter and Blaine Baggett (Penguin Studio) 1996
HISTORY OF THE BRITISH ARMY - Peter Young and Lt-Col. J.P. Lawford (Arthur Barker) 1970
THE FUSILIER - The Journal of The Royal Regiment of Fusiliers
HISTORY AND TRADITIONS OF THE ROYAL NORTHUMBERLAND FUSILIERS (Gale & Polden) 1944
Journal of the 14th/20th King's Hussars - The Gulf Supplement
Journal The Queen's Own Highlander - Summer 1991
THE NORTHUMBERLAND FUSILIERS - THE FIGHTING FIFTH - (Private Publication) 1915
THE ROYAL FUSILIERS - (Pyramid Press) 1954
THE ROYAL FUSILIERS IN AN OUTLINE OF MILITARY HISTORY 1685-1926 - (Gale & Polden) 1926
THE ROYAL REGIMENT OF FUSILIERS - (Pitkin) 1979
A SHORT HISTORY OF THE ROYAL WARWICKSHIRE REGIMENT - (Private Publication) 1922
A SHORT NARRATIVE OF THE FIFTH REGIMENT OF FOOT - (Private Publication) 1873